GLOBAL POLITICAL STUDIES SERIES

NEPAL IN THE 21ST CENTURY

GLOBAL POLITICAL STUDIES SERIES

The Kim Jong Il Regime in North Korea
Charles W. Tarrington (Editor)
2009. ISBN: 978-1-60692-807-3

The Political Context Behind Successful Revolutionary Movements
Raymond Millen
2009. ISBN: 978-1-60692-809-7

Buffer States: Power Policies, Foreign Policies and Concepts
Tornike Turmanidze
2009. ISBN: 978-1-60692-901-8

The United Nations. Past, Present and Future: Proceedings of the 2007 Francis Marion University UN Symposium
Scott Kaufman and Alissa Warters (Editors)
2009. ISBN: 978-1-60741-450-6

The United Nations. Past, Present and Future: Proceedings of the 2007 Francis Marion University UN Symposium
Scott Kaufman and Alissa Warters (Editors)
2009. ISBN: 978-1-60876-687-1 (Online book)

Democracy – A Destiny of Humankind?
A Qualified, Contingent and Contextual Case for Democracy Promotion
Rein Müllerson
2009. ISBN: 978-1-60741-369-1

Nepal in the 21st Century
Surendra R. Devkota (Editor)
2010. ISBN: 978-1-60741-348-6

Foreign Policy in an Interconnected World
George T. Overton (Editor)
2010. ISBN: 978-1-60876-079-4

Political Facts and Perceptions
Jeffry L. Radel
2010. ISBN: 978-1-60876-636-9

United Nations Peacekeeping in the 21st Century
Efram R. Isely (Editor)
2010. ISBN: 978-1-60741-562-6

GLOBAL POLITICAL STUDIES SERIES

NEPAL IN THE 21ST CENTURY

SURENDRA R. DEVKOTA
EDITOR

Nova Science Publishers, Inc.
New York

For permission to use material from this book please contact us:
Telephone 631-231-7269; Fax 631-231-8175
Web Site: http://www.novapublishers.com

LIBRARY OF CONGRESS CATALOGING-IN-PUBLICATION DATA

Nepal in the 21st century / Keshav Bhattar ... [et al.].
p. cm.
Includes index.
ISBN 978-1-60741-348-6 (hardcover)
1. Nepal--Politics and government--21st century. 2. Nepal--Economic conditions--21st century. 3. Nepal--Social conditions--21st century. I. Bhattar, Keshav. II. Title: Nepal in the twenty-first century.
JQ628.A58N464 2009
954.96--dc22

2009011431

Published by Nova Science Publishers, Inc. ✢ New York

CONTENTS

PREFACE

In the 20th century Nepal was in isolation until 1950, and afterwards, the pace of socio-political and economic progresses faced lots of ups and downs. The 1950 revolution of people tried to established people's sovereignty, but hijacked by the then king in 1960 and imposed his party-less system. Multiparty polity was reintroduced in 1990 by another movement of people. Nearly after five years of multiparty polity, Communist party of Nepal- Maoists launched 'People's War' in 1996 which ended after it signed a comprehensive peace agreement with interim government in 2006, and as of now they are enjoying as a major political party and leader cum partner of a coalition government.

Initial years of 21st century in Nepal seemed dark due to a mysterious royal slaughter of 2001 that wiped out the then King Birendra and his entire family member – a sort of virtual end of the Shah dynasty of nearly 240 years. The formal end of monarchy happened only after the election of the Constitutional Assembly in 2008 which adopted a resolution of abolition of monarchy in Nepal. For further details of socio-political means and ends, chapters two and three are noteworthy. Chapter one is about demographic trends and contemporary social structure in Nepal. In chapter two, Professor Kramer explicitly discusses political evolution of modern Nepal. It vividly accounts the rise and fall of the Shah dynasty in Nepal. Chapter three focuses on how to consolidate democracy for better socioeconomic development.

Chapter four examines the structure of Nepal's economy, and argues to enriching human capital in order to break a never ending vicious circle of poverty in Nepal. Chapter five provides a comprehensive analysis of education polices and highlights future strategies including 'education for all'.

Chapters six, seven and eight are about energy sectors. Chapter six gives a visionary approach of energy sector. Seven is about the hydro-energy: its use and abuse. Chapter eight is about role of energy in socioeconomic development planning and policy making.

Chapters nine and ten discuss about irrigation sectors and farmers managed irrigation system in Nepal – one of the indigenous skills of Nepali farmers. Chapter eleven outlines how people of Nepal are reversing the tragedy of commons by managing local forests.

Chapters twelve is about population pressure and planning options in Kathmandu Valley. The chapter vividly elucidates how the valley has already exceeded its carry capacity. Chapter thirteen briefly outlines about creating and sustaining federalism in Nepal.

Nepal in 21st century has yet to address other sectors and will continue to embrace in future series.

In: Nepal in the 21st Century
Editor: Surendra R. Devkota, pp.1-42
ISBN 978-1-60741-348-6

Chapter 1

DEMOGRAPHY, ETHNICITY AND SOCIETY

***Keshav Bhattarai*[*,1] *and Dennis Conway*[2]**
[1]University of Central Missouri, Warrensburg, MO, USA
[2]Indiana University, Bloomington, IN, USA

INTRODUCTION

Nepal is a multi-ethnic and multi-lingual, culturally complex nation. This South Asian landlocked country has a diverse topography populated by over 62 different ethnic groups who speak different languages.

As a predominantly low-income agrarian rural society, with one major urbanized area in the Kathamandu Valley and 58 small towns, its demographic complexities are many, such as high birth rates, a contemporary surge of its young-age population into adolescent, reproductive stages, uncontrolled urbanization, urban overcrowding, low literacy rate, and, in particular, an unacceptably low female literacy rate (Agudelo, 2004a; BBC, 2008; CG, 2005; Josse and Rose, 1966; Leone *et al.*, 2003; Musoke, 2001; NMH, 2002; Thapa, 2001; Shrestha *et al.*, 1999; Shrestha and Bhattarai, 2006; Simkhada *et. al*, 2006; UNESCAP, 2008).

This chapter analyzes the demographic characteristics of ethnic communities living in various geographic locations and identifies the nature and extent of the long-term and proximate causes of the country's demographic problems.

This helps to identify ways to ameliorate demographic problems, while taking into account the cultural backgrounds and value systems of the numerous, regionally-diverse ethnic communities.

The basis of the argument is that such an understanding of location-specific demographic characteristics will be useful for planners and policy makers to enable them to develop long-term policies that will help alleviate population problems in the 21st century in the newly declared federal democratic republic (FDR) of Nepal.

The health and well-being of national populations are fundamental to humankind. A country's well-being is determined by how well it copes with the demographic forces of geography, fertility, mortality, demographic transition, migration, economic conditions, and

[*] e-mail: bhattarai@ucmo.edu

occupations (Thomlinson, 1967), land holding status and their upward mobility (Shrestha, 1989; Shrestha, 2003).

To paraphrase the saying of the third-century Christian priest Tertullian, 'the vast population of the earth becomes a burden as she scarcely can provide for human needs as demands grow greater, and complaints against nature's inadequacy are heard by all' (CG, 2005; Thomlinson, 1967). Population is necessarily limited by its means of subsistence, and it invariably increases where the means of subsistence increases, unless prevented by very powerful and obvious checks, as Malthus opined. Though scholars have long criticized Malthusian's ideas for failing to foresee the possible contributions that technological changes bring to the nexus of population-resource equations, recent day scholars and politicians alike have revived Malthusian views in various new guises: as neo-, pro-, anti-, semi-, or quasi-Malthusian points of view (CG, 2005; Thomlinson, 1967). Concerning the balancing act of population and resources, their relationships and interdependence, demographers directly or indirectly base one of their main arguments on how the growth of population is related to the availability of food and sustenance (water, land, etc). In Nepal's case, "availability of food" and living conditions become major concerns when attempting to solve demographic complexities in rural subsistence economic settings which are the majority of the country's territorial landscapes. While people living in developed countries, such as North America and Western Europe started to be concerned with obesity in the early 1960s because of the daily consumption of high calories (>3,000) food, the majority of the Nepalese struggled to get food for survival (Thomlinson, 1967) and many people are forced to live with less than 2000 calories daily food-intake. In terms of per capita income, Nepal's demographic conditions are not at all comparable with those of developed countries. For example, the people of Sweden, the USA, the Netherlands, and Israel enjoy high per capita income (> $35,000), 100% overall literacy rate, and a high life expectancy (>= 82 years), while the Nepalese life expectancy is barely close to 60 years with $350 per capita income, and <45% overall literacy rate (CG, 2005; NMDG, 2005; Thomlinson, 1967).

On a positive note, the population growth rate in Nepal has fallen dramatically from 4.5% in the 1960's to just over 2.25% at present. However, given the country's resource constraints, even this moderate growth rate has become a great concern for demographers, planners and policy makers (Dahal *et al.* 2008; Leone *et al.*, 2003; NDHS, 2006; Paudel, 2006; Thapa, 2001; Sazaki, 2007). In the early 1950s and 1960s, the overall population-to-land ratio was relatively low in Nepal, but accompanying this seemingly promising man-land relationship, land productivity was equally poor, so that the low density population was sustained by rudimentary technology. Currently, the population to land ratio is considerably higher after, and in response, land productivity in the southern part of Nepal- the Tarai plains - has increased, in part due to technological improvements, and in part due to increased labor inputs and irrigation. Though some modern farming systems have been introduced in the mid-hills, current and future scenarios for increase land productivity have resulted in or have the potential to create the environmental problems of landslides, deforestation, soil erosion, and loss of soil fertility. As a result, food production has become only one of many problems despite the fact that increases in food production is needed to support the growing rural population, even if only at an overall subsistence level. In addition, "standards of living" disparities have increased rapidly in recent decades, in large part due to unequal access to resources in urban versus rural environments. For example, a minority proportion of urban dwellers enjoy modern infrastructures and amenities, while a large number of rural dwellers still live in a very traditional manner, either eking out an existence from subsistence farming, or relying upon remittances from off-farm or overseas laboring or using a mixture of these survival strategies.

In such contrasting situations between the developed and developing countries and disparities within the country, demographers and planners need to work together to find out how the Nepalese people will live in the 21st century, as the national population doubles every third decade with the current average growth rate of >2.25%. Such rapid population growth in recent decades has forced more and more people into marginal and environmentally sensitive areas where as a result, people are forced to live in swamp, flood prone, steep slope, and unproductive areas (Karan and Ishii, 1994; TKP, 2004; UNFPA, 2005). In the health sector too, the overall well-being of Nepal's people still remains very poor. For example, despite implementing the second long-term Health Plan 1997-2017, which aims to reduce the maternal mortality rate to at most 250 per 100,000 live births (HMG, 2002), and despite prioritizing maternal health in the national health programs (UNDP, 2005) through the increase in the number of medical institutions at various levels, national, regional, and local levels, no significant progress has been made in either of these sectors.

This chapter portrays the contemporary demographic, development, and socioeconomic situations across the various geographic regions of Nepal in relation to culture, ethnicity, and caste identities. The analyses that follow utilize three ecological zones, five development regions, 75 districts, and 3919 Village Development Committees (VDCs) that also include 58 municipalities as the units of observation and explanation. First, it briefly presents the geography of the country with reference to the historic trends of population distribution in various geographic regions. Second, it reviews ethnicity, language and literacy, and social problems and analyzes demographic problems associated with these factors in various geographic settings. Third, it examines population planning and stages of demographic transitions. Fourth, it presents economic conditions, occupations, and problem areas concerning the standard of living. Finally, the conclusion presents some plausible suggestions for improvement.

GEOGRAPHY

Landlocked Nepal, with an area of 147,181 square kilometers (sq. km), has borders in the west, south and east with India: in the north, it borders with the Tibet region of China. Ecologically, the country is divided into three major regions, high mountains, mid-hills, and Tarai and these three ecological regions are divided into five regional development units and 75 administrative districts (Figure 1).

The sparsely populated northern mountainous region covers 26.85% of the total geographic area of the country. It includes the world's tallest peak-Mount Everest (29,035 ft) bordering with China in the north. The mountainous region also borders with India in the far west (Figure 2) with many lower Himalayas again serving as the border. As per the census of 2001, the mountainous region supports only 1.62 million (m), 6.97 % of the total population with an estimated annual growth rate of 1.5% (Gurung, 2002; UNFPA, 2002). This region supported 8.9% of the total population in 1952/54, 8.70% in 1971, 8.50% in 1981, 7.8% in 1991, 6.97% in 2000, and 5.50% in 2008. Many people left this region for other parts of the country after the 1956 Nepal-China treaty which recognized Chinese sovereignty over Tibet and officially terminated the centuries-old Tibetan tribute to Nepal in 1957 (Joshi and Rose, 1966).

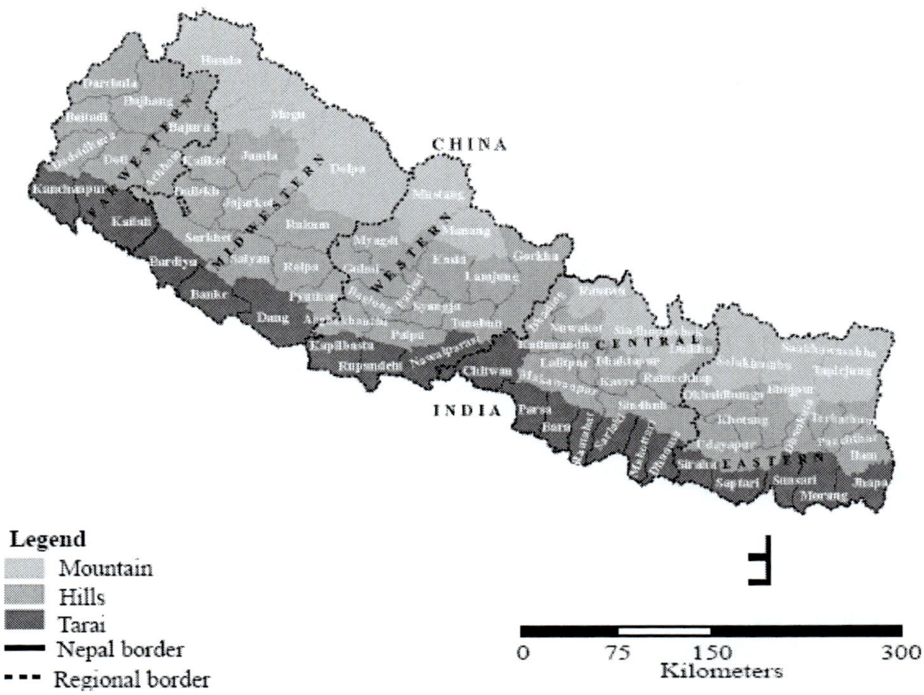

Figure 1. Nepal's three ecological regions, five regional development regions, and 75 administrative districts.

Additionally, after the Sino-Nepalese border treaty of 1961 defined Nepal's Himalayas as a frontier region, its population decreased further as out-migration continued. This region experiences perennial snow, which contributes melt-water to the watersheds of Nepal's major rivers, and all these rivers flow southward through deep Himalayan gorges. Due to such steep slopes, mountainous terrain, and perennial snow cover, rarely cultivable lands are found in higher elevation; only some scanty and tundra types of vegetation are found in the higher elevation regions. Only a few seasonally-cultivable lands are found along the foothills of the Himalayas, which form the transition zone between the mountains and mid-hills.

The mid-hills are the sections of the lower Himalayas that cover 50.56% of the total geographic area of Nepal. This region includes flat mountains, valleys, and fertile lands suitable for farming. As of the 2001 census, this region supports 10.2 m (43.97%) of the total population of Nepal with an annual growth rate of 2.55% (Gurung, 2002). This also includes the Kathmandu Valley, the country's most densely populated area and urban hub of administrative, economic, and cultural activities, centered on the nation's capital, Kathmandu. The current annual population growth rate of the highly-urbanized Greater Kathmandu Valley is greater than 5%, which includes both natural increase and in-migration into the valley. In addition, this urban conurbation also received a major population influx from nearby rural regions as soon as Nepal was opened to the outside world after the overthrow of autocratic Rana regime in the 1950s (MDM, 1971).

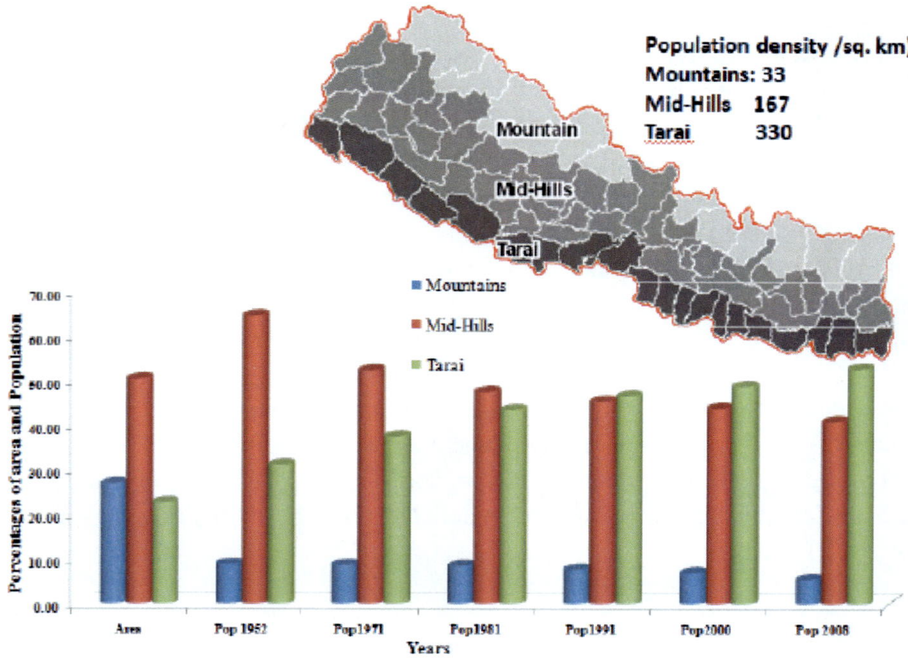

Figure 2. Physiographic regions and population distributions.

The hill region was one of Nepal's cultural hearths, where many Indo-Aryans, especially the Brahmins and Rajputs, migrated to avoid the religious crusades during the Mughals' (Muslims') invasions of India in the 10-11th centuries (Joshi and Rose, 1966). According to the 1952/54 census, this region supported 64.8% of the population, 47.7% in 1971, 46.60% in 1981, 43.70% in 1991, and 43% in 2001. Until the early 1980's, major developments were centered in those pocket areas of the mid-hills that were linked with India by Tribhuvan *Rajpath* (trans. highway) via Hetauda, and Prithivi *Rajmarg* (trans. highway) via Pokhara and to China by Arniko *Rajmarg* (Figure 3). Until the early 1980s, 80% of bureaucratic elites were from this region including the civil service, the army, and the police, with the dominance of Brahmans, Chhetris, and Newars. Of the 80% population in high-ranking bureaucracy, 13% were Newars from the Kathmandu Valley, whose share in the total country's population was a mere 3% (TRN, 2001).

The southern land adjacent to the Indian border is an extension of the Indo-Gangetic belt of India (Figure 1) that includes virtually all of the cultivable land at low elevations. It covers 22.59% of the total geographic area of Nepal. In 1952/54, this region had 31.1% of the country's total population, which increased to 37.60% in 1971, 43.60% in 1981, 46.70% in 1991, and 49% in 2001 (CBS, 2001, 2002, 2006; Gurung, 2002). Migration from other parts of the country to this forest-frontier region started after the late 1950's when malaria was eradicated from this region (Shrestha and Conway, 1981).

A wide variety of development interventions, including the availability of drugs to control malaria, made this region an internal migration "safety valve" for the people of the neighboring densely populated hills (Muller-Boker, 1999; Shrestha, 1990).

The opening of East-West Highway passing through this region connecting Mechi in the east to Mahakali (Figure 3) in the west also increased the rural-to-rural influx of population to this lowland region. Since then, there has been a massive and persistent inflow of people from the mountain and hill regions into this region, and another accompanying influx also originated from the neighboring state of India (Muller-Boker, 1999). Some leading national newspapers of Nepal put the current national proportion of this southern region's population at 53.9% (Spotlight, 2004; TKP, 2004; TRN, 2001).

Some specific population samples support these claims. For example, in the 1990's, Kohalpur VDC of Banke district (Figure 1) had a population of 11,090 with 1,857 families, while in 2001, the population had doubled to 20,138 with 3,875 families. Likewise, the population of Rajhena, another VDC of the same district, was 7,000 in 1991, and in 2001, it was 14,900 (Khadka, 2002) with the majority of the people migrating from the mountains and hills.

Also adding to the claim that mass in-migration has occurred relatively rapidly throughout the southern region of Nepal, there are other areas, such as Jhapa, Biratnagar, Janakpur, Birgunj, Butwal, Siddharthanagar, Krishnanagar, Dhangadhi, and Kanchanpur (Figure 3), where the population has almost doubled since the 1970's (Karan and Ishii, 1994; UNFPA, 2002).

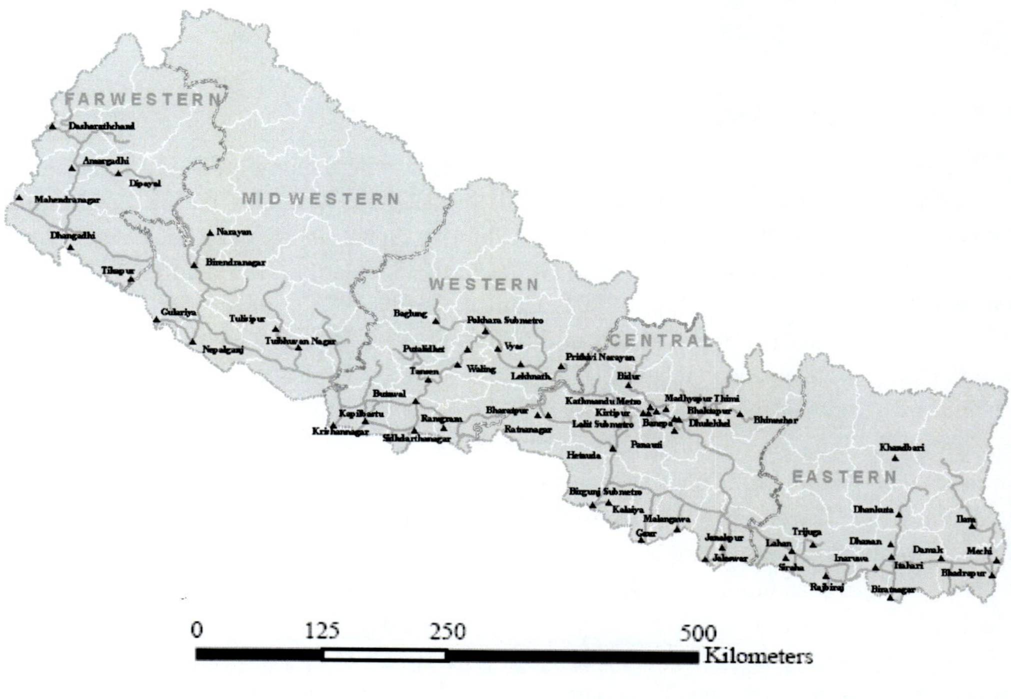

Figure 3. Location of urban centers and road network (only blacktopped roads).

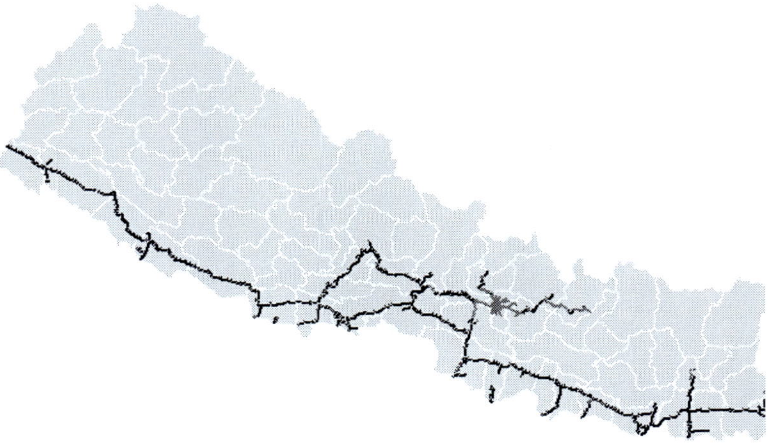

Figure 4a. Road network in 1975.

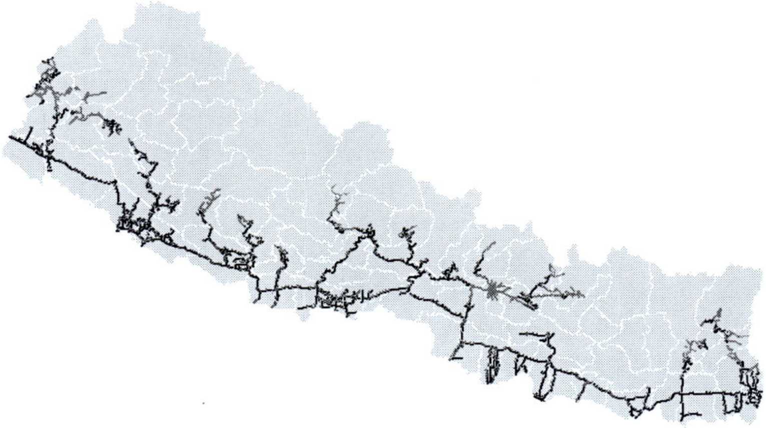

Figure 4b. Road network in 1990.

Figure 4c. Road network in 2000.

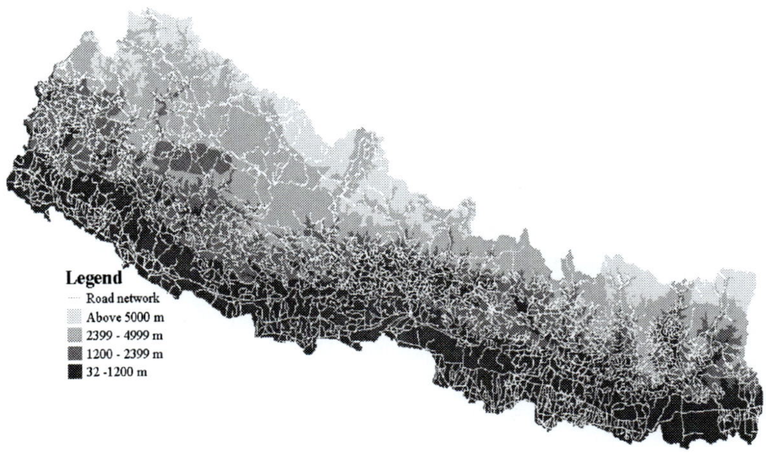

Figure 4d. Road network at various elevations.

Additionally, the region's proximity to the Indian markets for business and commerce, cultural affinities with India, and development of a region-wide road network over time attracted a large number of Indians from Bihar and other neighboring areas across the Indian border. More road networks were developed in these lower elevations than at higher elevations (Figures 4 a, b, c, c, and d), reflecting cost differentials brought about by topographic differences and the influence of border town-accessibilities at the Indian border, which stretched all along the southern border.

Many Indian in-migrants, who "crossed to border", settled in neighboring towns in Nepal, where they became engaged in semi-skilled laboring and merchandizing activities and also in farming and tree-felling (Shrestha, 2001).

Though the internal flows of Tarai in-migration which started from the 1950s as a safety valve for the mountain and mid hills of Nepal (Gurung, 2002; Shrestha, 2001) have continued virtually unabated, the recent ethnic and political problems, as well as the recent flood catastrophe occurring in the Tarai region, appear likely to bring about significant changes in the migration patterns into this region, reducing it, changing its dynamics, and/or perhaps reversing flows (NMH, 2002, TKP, 2008).

Additionally, many present Tarai dwellers of the original hill migrants are showing strong ethnic affiliations with certain geographic regions in the north and are making political demands for separate autonomous states.

These local political upheavals associated with the mid-hills and mountain regions, are following the pattern of the recent political turmoil in the Tarai regions, which appears to have won central government concessions for one aggrieved "minority ethnic" group of protesters-the Madeshi Janadhikar Forum (MJF), Tarai Madesh Democratic Party (TMDP), and Sadbhavana Party-who have been in conflict over local control of the Tarai region and have sought more equality in terms of their group's representation in the civil services and in the Nepal Army.

The above accounts describe the population distribution by ecological region, based on the administrative districts as the micro-units of estimation. However, if the population is distributed by elevation, the dependent population seems to be concentrated more in the lower elevation, indicating that the population at lower elevations is growing more rapidly than in the northern, higher elevations (Figures 5 a and b).

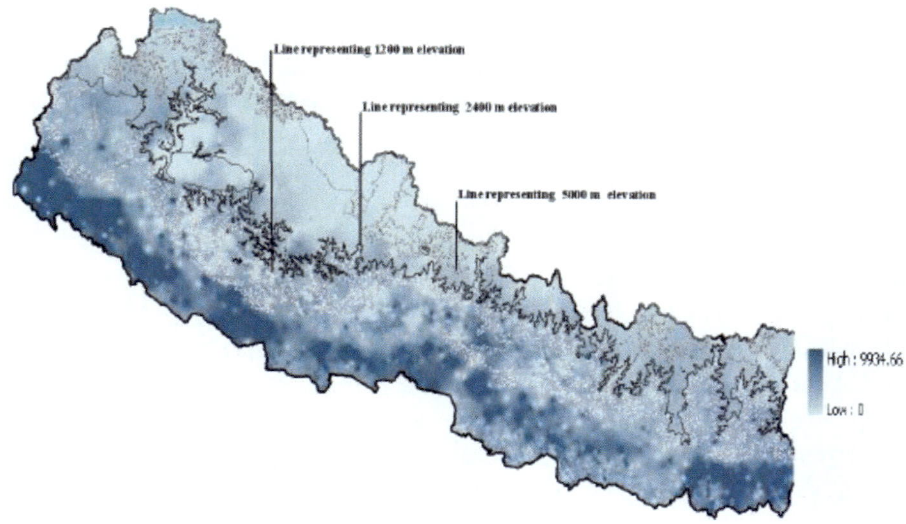

Figure 5a. Dependent population (<15 years) in 2001 by elevation.

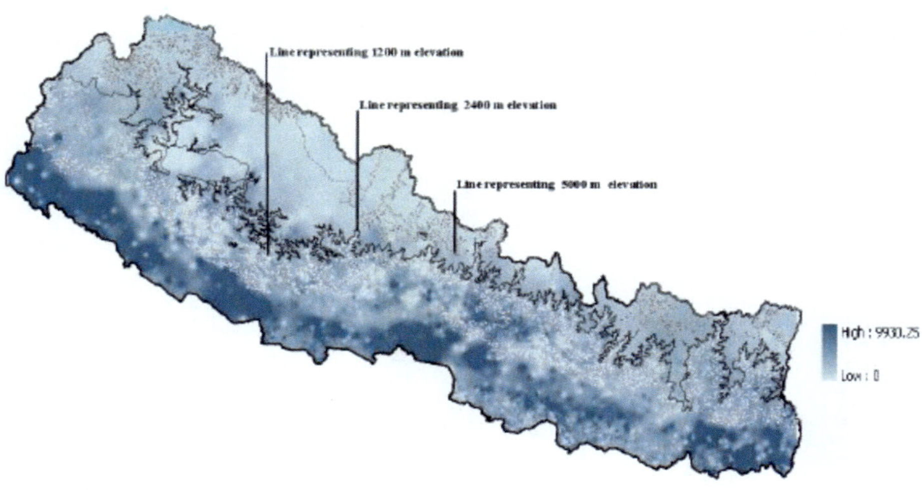

Figure 5b. Working age (>16 to 64 years) group in 2001 by elevation.

DEMOGRAPHY

Population Growth

Nepal has conducted a census every decade for nearly 100 years starting from 1911. According to the 1911 census taken by *Gosvara Adda* (trans. Public Revenue Office), the total population of Nepal was 5.5 million (m) (Maharjan, 2002). Except for 1911-1930, all census period enumerations showed a continuous growth of population. However, the 1961 census count suggested that the earlier censuses of 1911, 1920, and 1930 underestimated the nation's total population by about one-third. While adjusting for the undercounting, it was revealed that from 1911 to 1971, Nepal's population doubled from 5.5 m to 11.6 m (TRN,

2001). The 1980 census then recorded a growth rate of 2.66% with the average family size of 5.8 persons, and an average life expectancy of 50 years, and ten years later the 1990 census recorded 19.25 m people with an annual growth rate of 2.65% (CBS, 2006; DHS, 2006; TRN, 2001). A regional breakdown of the average population growth rate for that period revealed 4.2% for the Tarai region, 1.7% for the Hill, and 1.5% for the Mountain (Gurung, 2002). Gurung (2002) and Shah (2005) argued that the average population growth rate of Nepal, according to the 2001 Census, was greater than 2.27%, and 23 Tarai and inner Tarai districts had a higher population growth rates than the average, while 52 hill districts had a low growth rate. The projected population for 2005 was 27.1 m (UNFPA, 2005); in 2006, the population was estimated at 28 m with a growth rate of 2.25% (CBS, 2006; DHS, 2006). UNFPA (2005) projects that if the current population growth rate continues (Figure 6), Nepal will have over 51 m people by 2050. Despite some favorable demographic and social-economic indicators, Nepal's current population growth is considered very high when the country's overall economic growth rate is factored into the equation.

Though the Nepali government plans to reduce the total fertility rate to 2.1% by the end of the Twelfth Plan in 2017 and aims to find a balance between population growth and economic development, the population would double after 31 years if the present trend of population growth continues (Gyawali, 2008). Undoubtedly, Nepal's government needs to slow the nation's population growth rate down and only major economic and social reforms look to be the likely means for achieving this imperative.

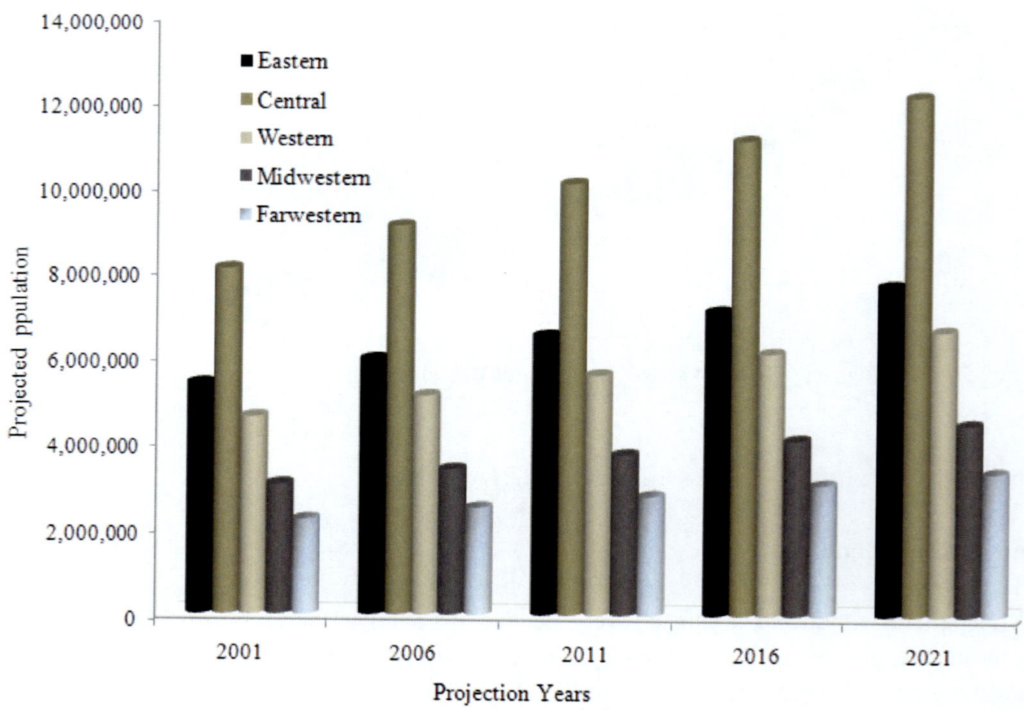

Figure 6. Population growth rate under the medium vibrant projection (2001-2021)
Data source: http://www.cbs.gov.np/population_projection_nepal_tables.php.

Though Nepal's average 2.25% population growth rate is relatively low when compared to 3.0% for Bhutan, 2.4% for Pakistan and 3.9% for Afghanistan (UNFPA, 2005), given the country's resource constraints, this current growth rate is still too high. The relatively low fertility rate of Nepal is probably due to Nepal's efforts to increase the contraceptive prevalence rate through increases in school enrollment, which as of 2001 records showed 50% for males and 39% for females (Dahal *et. al*, 2008; Stash, 1999; UN, 2005; USAID, 2003). However, the rapid increase in population size is a manifestation of rapidly declining mortality and slowly declining fertility, resulting in a high proportion of adolescents in the total population. Almost half of Nepal's population is estimated to be below the poverty line (NLSS, 2003-04; Daniel, 2008). Although the proportion living at or below this poverty level has remained almost stable during the last three decades, the absolute number of impoverished people has increased significantly. Frontier land in the south has already been brought into cultivation, which has further added to environmental deterioration due to rapid deforestation (Figure 7 a, b, and c).

Figure 7a. Land use and cover conditions in relation to road network in 1975.

Figure 7b. Land use and cover conditions in relation to road network in 1990.

Figure 7c. Land use and cover conditions in relation to road network in 2000.

According to UN Population Projections, Nepal's population is likely to double and reach 44 m by the year 2035 (Musoke, 2001) which will lead to further stresses on the environment as the large section of population is entering into the adolescent stage. For example, as per the 2000 census (Figure 8), 13% of the population comprised of 10-14 years, 15-19 years was 10.51%, 20-24 years was 8.87%, and 25-29 years was 7.59% (Agudelo, 2004b; CBS, 2006; Poudel, 2004; Sazaki, 2007). In Nepal, 100 of the working age population (15-60 years) are supporting 85 children; the population will grow rapidly as these children enter into reproductive ages. Without a reduction in the current total fertility rate, it will be almost impossible to check, or counter, overpopulation in Nepal.

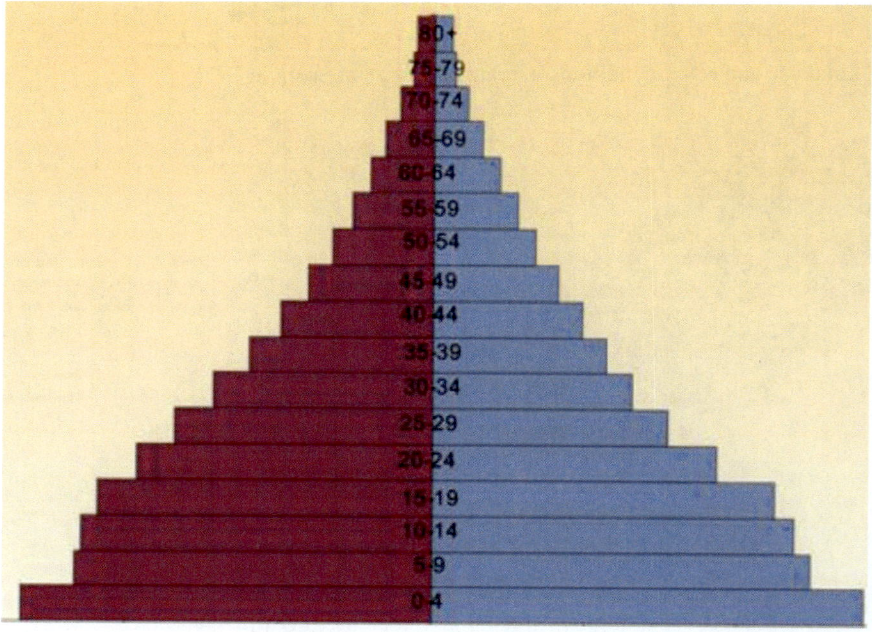

Figure 8. Population profile 2006 (Data source : http://www.cbs.gov.np/population_profile.php).

Fertility

Declines in the total fertility rate (TFR) - the average number of children a woman might bear during her active reproductive life - were not experienced in Nepal as much as in other South Asian countries, even after the wide acceptance of modern family planning methods. The 2000 records for South Asian countries showed that less than 48% of couples used contraceptives (UN, 2005). This below 50% contraceptive-use proportion was particularly the case in Nepal, where the total fertility rate is among the highest (Agudelo, 2004b; Sazaki, 2007). Some researchers claim that the low rate of contraceptive use in Nepal is due to son preferences and lack of better health care (Karki, 1988; Leone *et al.*, 2003; Schuler and Goldstein, 1986). Studies conducted by Leone *et al.* (2003) and Stash (1986) have shown that son preference is prevalent across some socio-cultural and ethnic groups, and thus the use of contraceptive varied across them (Figure 9). In 1971, Nepal's TFR was 6.1; it came down to 5.6 in 1981, 4.6 in 1991 4.1 in 2001, and was down to 3.1 in 2006 (Sazaki, 2007). Some attribute this gradual decline of TFR to the use of contraception and to women's education, while others attribute it to a relatively higher TFR among the Asian countries to son preferences and rural settings. Some researches attribute the relatively high TFR to geographic variations, and low female education, and ethnicity (Figures 9a and b). For example, women in Nepal's mountain region with low educational status still bear 4.1 children in their lifetime as compared to 3 children in the hills and 3.3 children in the Tarai. Both mid-western and far-western regions have higher TFRs (3.5) than central (3.0) and eastern and western regions (3.1) (Sazaki, 2007).

Again, these rates differ between rural and urban areas within the same region. For example, a 2005 study found a child difference between the urban (TFR = 2.1) and rural (TFR = 3.3) area. In 1997, the Nepalese government adopted a 20-year goal to achieve a national family norm of two children (Dahal *et al.* 2008), aiming to reduce the fertility rate at the replacement level (2.1) by 2017 (NMH, 2002).

It is hoped that with the increase in urbanization and educational status of women, the overall TFR will decline until it reaches replacement level, around 2.0-2.1. In the present context, if 1.8 children are reduced per decade per women, it is expected that the fertility rate will drop to the replacement level by 2056, by which time the total population might reach 77 m (Thapa, 2001). The current trend shows that the TFR and crude birthrate have remained high and fairly constant for the past several decades, whereas the crude death rate has been declining consistently, thereby contributing to rapid population growth. Attention is needed to improve a) quality of women education; b) change the reproductive life styles of adolescents; c) bring about improvements in health service delivery and increase utilization of primary health services; d) staff services with trained manpower, especially skilled birth attendants; and e) provide choices of family planning services throughout Nepal. However to decrease the TFR, it is essential to decrease the mortality rate to ensure survival rates of infants.

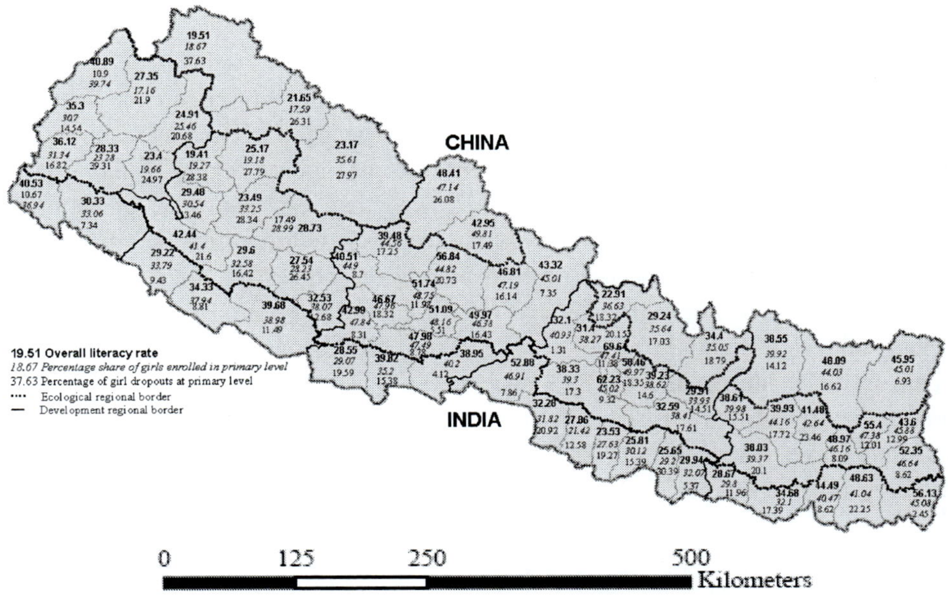

Figure 9a. Percentage of overall literacy, girls enrollments, and dropouts.

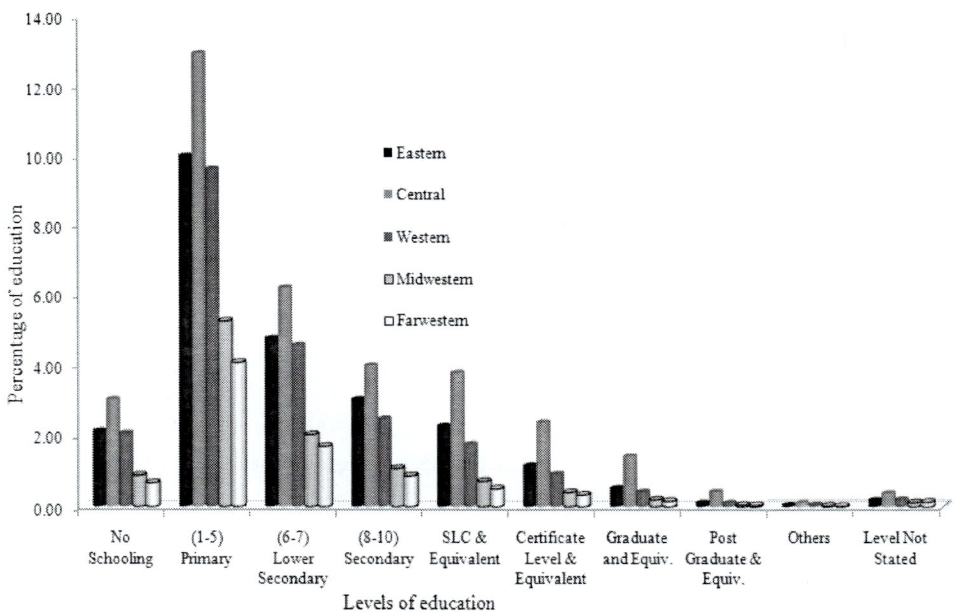

Figure 9b. Literacy percentages by various development regions.

Mortality

Mortality is defined as the number of deaths in a given time and/or place that varies with specific ages, such as high mortality among infants, elderly people, and first-time child-bearing women. The mortality rate also varies with geographic locations because of the limitation of medical facilities.

In Nepal, over two decades of public attention and policy enactment have helped to reduce the mortality rate since the early 1980s; for example, there have been decreases in infant mortality rate from 147 per 1,000 in 1985 to 101 per 1,000 in 1989, and to 79-85 per 1,000 in 2001. Successive governments of Nepal have claimed successes in reducing the infant mortality rate through the improvement in maternal health services. However, critics often complain that due to the lack of strong political commitment, proper laws, and enough resources, many mothers in rural areas are still deprived of essential health services. For example, Xinhaua (2008a) news and NDHS (2008) report that about 60 newborns and six mothers die every day in Nepal for lack of maternal and neonatal health services. Such deaths vary widely among the three geographic regions, greater death rates at higher elevations than in lower elevations. Additionally, infant mortality rate is almost twice as high in rural areas as compared to urban areas; for example, the mortality rate among rural children is 112 as opposed to 66 urban babies per 1,000 (WHO, 2006), a clear indication of the lack of health services in rural areas. Though the Nepal government claims to have reduced the infant mortality rate, the average mortality rate in Nepal is higher among many Asian countries due to the lack of proper health services, specially, due to the predominantly rural settings (Xinhua, 2008b), where 281 out of 100,000 mothers die during postnatal stages. The same Xinhua (2008b) news revealed that three infants died every hour and one mother died every four hours infants.

On the other hand, UNICEF has identified Nepal as one of the seven countries in Asia which has successfully cut infant mortality by 2/3 in the last one and a half decade (Zeenews, 2006). UNICEF attributes such decreases to a) proper management to reduce neo-natal tetanus infections; b) launching a national measles campaign and reaching out to millions of rural children in all the districts; c) the successful distribution of vitamin A supplement to rural women; d) vaccination, better treatment of pneumonia and diarrhea; and e) an extraordinary network of over 48,000 female community health volunteers. Nonetheless, UNICEF concedes that some 65,000 children under five still die each year in Nepal due to lack of proper treatment. NHDS (2007) revealed that in 2001, over 540 women died per 100,000 live births in Nepal, though the NHDS reports a reduction in such death rates to 280 in 2007 due to a) the combination of government and private initiatives as well as policy changes; b) reduction of pre- and post-delivery hemorrhage; c) regular immunization; d) availability of trained manpower in delivery services (Aryal, 2007); e) legalizing abortion since 2002; and f) providing comprehensive care training. However, during the period of the Maoist insurgency (1996-2006), routine services were often disrupted, many health workers were confined to headquarters, doctors were rarely available in rural areas, and health services were not upgraded. The majority of the people with low incomes were unable to afford treatment in India and in distant urban centers of Nepal.

The Nepalese economy is still mainly based on primary activities with low income (<$1.00/day), not enough to support adequate nutrition. Over 50,000 children die each year due to malnutrition. Additionally, over 50% of the children in Nepal are underweight and 3/4 of pregnant women are anemic (UNICEF, 2006). Further, a few cases of wild polio virus cases have been reported along the Nepal-India border. People are compelled to consume contaminated well water, often containing high arsenic (15% Nepal's wells are contaminated by arsenic) in Tarai. Many houses lack proper toilet facilities. Besides these medico-economic problems, political indoctrination of underage children and forcing children to participate in civil wars have increased the chances of casualties.

Though UNICEF identified 300,000 disadvantaged households in 237 villages and 8 municipalities in 2006 to help them improve rural living conditions and has involved over 60,000 young people in health care programs, still rural health services are very poor. UNICEF claims that it has strengthened the Decentralized Action for Children and Women (DACAW) program to reach rural communities in the national measles campaign and has helped to immunize nearly 10 million children. It also claims to have effectively dewormed children and provided vitamin A supplements to reduce malnutrition and anemic problems among 12,000 children. Additionally, WHO (2005) also confirmed the significant alleviation of neo-natal tetanus problems from Nepal. Likewise, the "Welcome to School" campaign initiated by UNICEF has greatly increased enrollment and literacy rates for girls and disadvantaged children. This approach has helped to increase birth registration rates to maintain appropriate records, which will help to find the actual causes of deaths. With an attempt to minimize infant mortality that might result due to conceptions before marriages, UNICEF has helped to establish over 300 community-based paralegal committees to respond to issues such as domestic violence and rape. These paralegal committees have been helpful to reduce the deaths of nearly 6,000 women and 30,000 infants annually (UNICEF, 2005). The sad story is that the "World Disasters Report 2006" equates Nepal with Afghanistan and Sub-Saharan African countries as the "the deadliest places in the world to give unsafe birth." Demographers attribute unsafe birth to the inadequacy of health workers with 1,300 doctors, 90,000 undertrained health workers, 87 hospitals, and fewer than 1,000 health centers, nationwide to serve over 26 million people. The report also claimed that many of the country's 4,000 villages have no health centers and that 90% of infants are delivered in homes without the help of trained nurses. Cultural barriers, such as forcing mothers and infants to stay in "unclean" conditions in cowsheds or isolated places for the first specifically 11 days after the delivery in some remote hilly districts of western Nepal, have negative impacts on the survival rate of babies and mothers (KDHSR, 2005).

Government documents claim that decades of efforts have resulted improvements trends in the Nepalese demography from 1960 to 2001. These achievements include a) a decrease in infant mortality from 200 to 70 per 1,000; b) an increase in life expectancy from 42 to 62 years (Musoke, 2001); c) a decrease in crude birth rate (CBR) from 74 to 31 per 1,000, d) a decrease in crude death rate (CDR) from 70 to 11 per 1,000; e) a decrease in infant mortality rate from 147 to 64 per 1,000; and f) a decrease in maternal mortality rate from 2,000 to 539 per 100,000 (Pradhan *et al.* 1997; Simkhada *et al.*, 2006). The 2008 record puts maternal mortality at 281 per 100,000 live births. Still the current maternal mortality rate in Nepal remains one of the highest in the world (Irrinnews, 2005). The Ministry of Health in Nepal has estimated that nearly 4,500 women die every year from pregnancy-related complications, mostly due to the lack of skilled birth attendants, the absence of emergency services, and poorly equipped rural health centers providing emergency services (Simkhada *et al.*, 2006).

Though some achievements have been made in the health sectors with the opening of new medical facilities and a new population policy to reduce total fertility rate (TFR), birth rate, and infant mortality rate, some records indicate that each day 2,128 babies are born and 617 persons die, with a net population rise of 1,511 persons (Anon, 2005; Sazaki, 2007). Gyawali (2008) points out that the maternal morbidity and mortality rates are higher among adolescent mothers than relatively older age groups. Despite the claim that significant improvement in expansion of health services have been made, only 13% of births are attended by skilled health personnel (Agudelo, 2004b). Among these service recipients, 61% are high school graduates while 39% are non-educated rural women. However, in urban areas 81% of women properly receive such antenatal care services. About 64 of 1,000 infants die before celebrating their 5th birthday, and the majority of these are girls (Musoke, 2001; NMH, 2002; USAID, 2003; Stash, 1999) with higher casualties in rural than in urban areas. These figures indicate sex discrimination, which is high in Nepal among South Asian countries. High mortality rate due to poor health services, cultural traditions, and sex discrimination, all of which have negative effects on the pace of demographic transition (DT).

Demographic Transition (DT)

Countries with rapid economic development have experienced shorter and swifter DTs, such as Taiwan, South Korea, Thailand, and the States of Kerala and Tamil Nadu in India. Even Bangladesh is exhibiting a faster DT than Nepal though both countries had the same levels of fertility in the 1970's (Musoke, 2001). The slow pace of DT in Nepal might be due to disorders related to infectious diseases, maternal and prenatal ailments, and nutritional deficiencies. However, improvements are seen in the urban areas, where among educated women, TFR is almost half of the national average, suggesting that improvements in socio-economic development, education, health and women's empowerment is pathway to the realization of a relatively fast DT.

The pace of socio-economic development has been comparatively slow in Nepal, and so has been the country's movement through the demographic transition (Musoke, 2001). The other problems Nepal faces at present is an over-concentration of population between the age of 0-4 years (30%) (Figure 8). This age cohort will enter into the reproductive ages within a decade and a half, at which time Nepal will experience rapid increases in population size due to this built-in demographic mechanism (Agudelo, 2004b). One set of population projections has estimated that in 2001 there were 4.6 m people between the ages of 15–24 years, which would grow to 6.5 m in 2021--an increase of 41% (Sazaki, 2007). However, no government policies address this scenario, which may further complicate the demographic problems of Nepal. Additionally, even though a decline in mortality and TFR is observed in every age group over the last 10 years, larger declines are seen in older women, but at various rates for different development regions and ecological zones (CBS, 2001) (Figure 1). Efforts are needed to ensure that Nepal achieves and completes its demographic transition as quickly as possible to be in sync with her South Asian counterparts.

Political instability remains a threat to health care delivery in Nepal. Unprecedented road closures, damage to health facilities, and physical threats to health workers during the Maoist insurgency period (1996-2006) resulted in the deaths of many women during childbirth because of the lack of obstetric emergency services (UNFPA, 2005). Although this insurgency was just for a decade, this incidents coupled with the lack of institutional commitments, negatively impacted population planning.

Population Planning

The Government of Nepal has implemented the National Population Program (NPP) to properly manage and improve life quality of the growing population since the Third

Development Plan (1965-70) with a focus on population planning. The subsequent development plans have embraced population, family planning, child, and mother health as inseparable components. The Fourth Development Plan (1970-1975) was targeted to provide family planning services to at least 15% of married couples. In the Fifth Development Plan (1975-1980), serious attempts were made to reduce the birth rate by direct and indirect means, including family planning. To coordinate the government's multi-sectoral activities in population and reproductive health, a population policy coordinating board was established in 1975 under the National Planning Commission (NPC). In 1978, this board was named as the National Commission on Population (NCP). In 1983, the Sixth Development Plan (1980-85) brought a long-term population strategy followed by institutional measures such as the reinforcement of erstwhile NCP through organizational restructuring and proper coordination among different line ministries, non-governmental organizations (NGOs), and relevant stakeholders (Karki, 2008). In the 1980's, Nepal was quick to adopt and initiate policy measures in population-related health and development sectors, including basic needs fulfillment programs to meet Asian standards, but no progress was made.

The Seventh Development Plan (1985-1990) not only emphasized family planning, but also focused on long-term concerns to encourage small family norms through education and employment programs aiming at raising women's status and decreasing infant mortality. This included programs in reproductive health, agriculture, forestry, urbanization, employment, education, and women's development, as well as community development programs. In 1990, the NCP was dissolved; in 1995, the NCP's role was given to the Population Division of the National Planning Commission and the Ministry of Population and Environment (MoPE) with the formulation of various population policies. The MoPE and its other sectors were assigned the responsibilities of implementing recommendations made by the International Conference on Population and Development (ICDP) to meet the living standard of the 21st Century. The goals include reduction of child mortality, improvement in maternal health, protection from HIV/AIDS, and malaria, universal primary education, poverty eradication, and gender equity. In view of these needs, in 1996, the government established a National Population Committee (NPC), comprised of various ministers and chaired by the Prime Minister, in order to provide strong political leadership and guidance to formulate and implement population policies. The Eighth Development Plan (1992-1997) continued with the integrated development approach taken in earlier plans. The Ninth Development Plan (1997-2002) was developed as a 20-year long-term plan to reduce population growth through social awareness, expansion of education, and family planning programs to reduce the population at the replacement level.

Investment in family planning is considered one of the most cost-effective policies for a low-income country, such as Nepal, where millions of young people reach active reproductive age each year. Through proper family planning methods, the Ninth Five-Year Plan (1997-2002) envisaged the total fertility rate (TFR) declining to 4.2 by the end of the plan period and aimed further to reduce total fertility rate at the replacement level of 2.1 by 2016 (DHS, 2006). The Tenth Development Plan (2002-2007) encouraged a small family norm, focused on the promotion of an educated and healthy population, and discouraged out-migration of skilled labor. In 2005, MoPE was dissolved and its Population Division was merged into the Ministry of Health with the formation of Ministry of Health and Population (MoHP). These planning efforts have helped to increase the use of family planning methods from 26% (1996)

to 44% (2006), a 70% increase over the decade. Such awareness was expected to alleviate problems associated with rapid population growth among various ethnic communities.

ETHNICITY

Ethnicity in the Nepali language is expressed by the term *jat* (group) or *jati* (subgroup), and these terms are used interchangeably to denote a certain ethnic group (Sharma, 2008: 3). Nepal's population is composed of diverse ethnic groups (Figure 10a) distributed in various geographic regions (Figure 1). The largest single ethnic group is Chhetri (16%) followed by Hill-Brahman (13%), Magar (7%), Tharu (7%), Tamang (6%), Newar (5%), Muslim (4%), Kami (4%), Yadav (4%) and 'others' (34%). The complex ethnicity of Nepal is the result of a long intermingling of Tibeto-Burmans migrants from the north, especially Tibet, and Indo-Aryans migrants from the south, especially, from the Indo-Gangetic plain (Sharma, 2008).

Nepal has a long migration history and this nation-state is considered as a land forged in immigration (Gellner, 2007). For example, some ancestors of the Brahmins and Chhetris came from Kumaon, Garwal, and Kashmir of India. These immigrants include Indo-Aryan and East Asian 'mixed' peoples, belonging to Brahmins, the high-ranking Thakuri and Chhetri, and an untouchable category.

Some untouchable categories are grouped under the *Pahari* or *Parbate*, which means people from the hills and mountains. These *Paharis* are the result of racial intermixture with various Mongoloid phenotypes and are known by their individual caste names (Gurung, 2003), but are grouped under Indo-Nepalese communities.

The in-migrants of Indo-Nepalese ancestry dominated the country not only numerically with over 50% of the total population, but also socially, politically, and economically. Subordinate to them were the native *Paharis* and Tibeto-Burmans in caste hierarchy. Their higher caste ranking was also due to their superior educational systems (Joshi and Rose, 1966). Consequently, their overall domination in languages, religions, and social organization has had tremendous significance in terms of the country's multi-ethnic power structure until late 1980s. The Brahmins and Chhetris spread throughout the whole of the mid-hills, but not in the immediate adjacent northern border as these areas are neither agriculturally suitable nor are they good for commercial trade with India. These areas were periphery in terms of administrative importance and peoples' representation. Some segments of this Chhetri population belonged to the former royal families, who ruled the country for 240 years, starting from 1769 BS (Bikram Sambat). Also, among the mid-hill dwellers were Newars, who originally inhabited the Katmandu Valley (Figure 10b). These Newars were mainly engaged in trades and businesses. Today, Newar communities are found virtually in all the market centers of the country, while the *Paharis* are scattered throughout Nepal, including the more fertile lower hills, river valleys, and Tarai plains in the south.

Other ethnic groups such as Gurung and Magar, trace their origins to North Burma and China (Yunnan), while Rai and Limbu living in the east and Sherpa (including Bohtia) living in the north all trace their ancestors to China-Tibet. Oppitz (1973) argued that Sherpa could be the indigenous group of Nepal's Khumbu region. A large number of Bhotias live in the central section of the Mountain Region, while many of these ethnic groups-including Tamangs, Sherpas, and Mananges-with high income derived from mountaineering or British

Army (Gurkha Regiment)-have moved to various urban centers (Figure 3), such as the Kathmandu Valley, Pokhara, and Butwal (TRN, 2001).

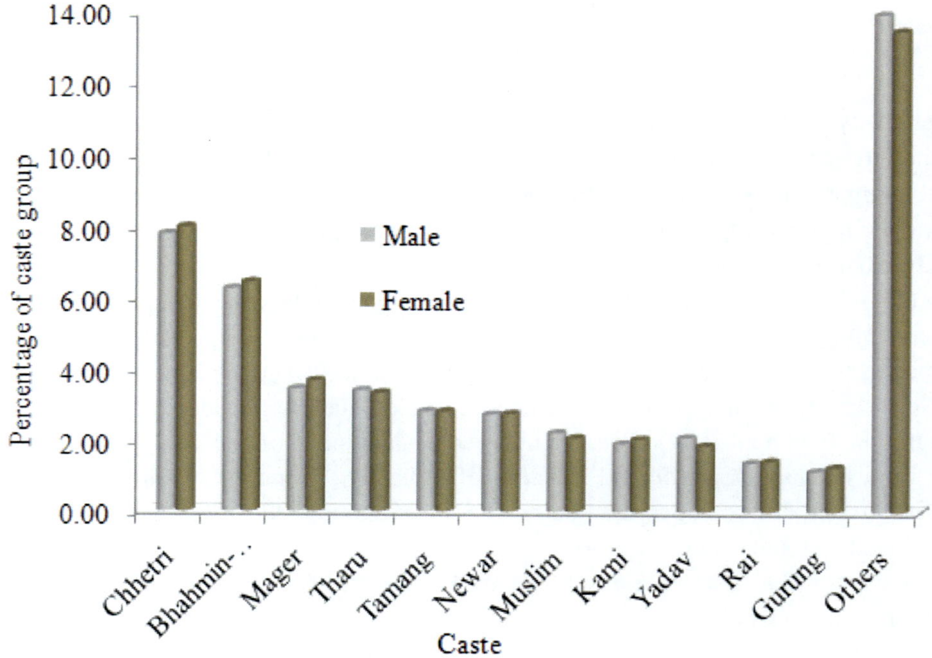

Figure 10a. **Percentages of ethnic/caste groups by gender** (2001) (Note: **'Others' languages include** ethnic groups not accounted for the specified caste/ethnic groups).

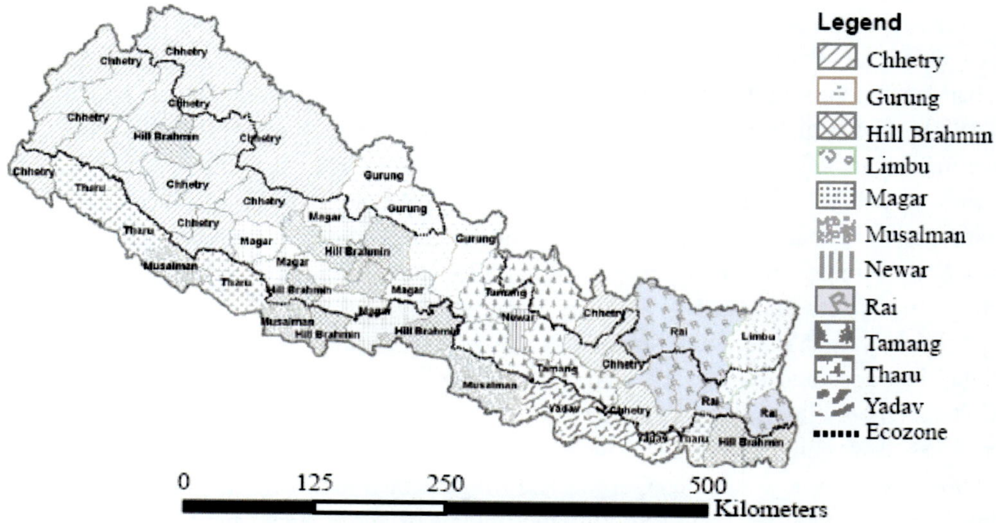

Figure 10b. Distributions of ethnic/caste groups and castes in various ecological regions.

The Tibeto-Nepalese (Mongols) still live in the deeply cut valleys and high ridges of the remote mountainous region. These varied geographic features further divide ethnic groups into many small, relatively isolated, and more or less self-contained communities. For example, the Sherpa, a subgroup within the Bhote, are concentrated in the northeast, around the Mount Everest area, and make their living from mountaineering, herding, and pastoral activities rather than from crop farming. The Gurung, Magar, Tamang, Rai, and Limbu inhabit the medium and low hills south of the high mountains and depend more on agriculture. Likewise, Kirats, the earliest inhabitants of the eastern mid-region also depend upon agriculture. These Tibeto-Nepalese ethnic communities are less educated than the Indo-Nepalese communities and have relatively larger family size, where large families become engines for farming.

Tharu and Yadav are aboriginal tribes of the southern Tarai region, who mainly depend on farming and herding. Other indigenous, but smaller groups comprising a number of tribal communities, such as the Dhimals and Mushar, also live in Tarai. They are thought to be the remnants of original/indigenous communities, with their inhabitation predating the advent of Indo-Nepalese and Tibeto-Mongol communities. In the Tarai, the resident, native population is physically and culturally similar to the Indo-Aryans of northern India. In addition, there are Indian migrants, who were encouraged by the government of Nepal to move into the Tarai to settle during the nineteenth and early twentieth centuries. Additionally, many Indo-Nepalese and Tibeto-Nepalese communities have migrated to the Tarai region for business and farming.

Peoples of Indian origin who settled in the Tarai were in the periphery of the political power structure (Josse and Rosh, 1966) until the 1990s, but have recently emerged as a very powerful 'activist-party' under the umbrella of *Madhesi* communities. Political analysts argue that the failure to address the grievances of the *Madhesi* people by successive governments, as well as by treating them as second-grade citizens, has resulted in the recent ethnic tensions and the political movement they have fomented. Ethnicity has emerged as a major issue in the contemporary demographic, development and political discourse, and it has been thought that this issue cannot be ignored further. The Constituent Assembly (CA) in Kathmandu has created the State Restructure Commission to address the federalist and local autonomy demands of the ethnic communities. Since this 'ethnic' basis for federalism has been given center-stage in the interim constitution 2007, political pundits argue that such restructuring would address the call for autonomy not only of the *Madhesi* communities but also of other ethnic communities without the disintegration.

However, such restructuring might result in many problems and rupture at the cost of the social harmony that has had a long history since the birth of Nepal as a nation state in 1769. Considerable, albeit conflicting evidence has already appeared on this point. For example, in July 2008, several ethnic-based organizations self-declared autonomy in three eastern Tarai districts-Morang, Jhapa, and Sunsari (Irinnews, 2008). The Federal Limbuwan State Council (FLSC) declared some parts of the eastern districts as a "Limbuwan State," while the Dhimal named some portions of the eastern districts as "Kochila State," yet, an alliance of nine groups known as the Tarai Indigenous Janjati Organization (TIJO) named it the "Morang Autonomous State." Likewise, the Kirant Janbadi Workers Party (KJWP)—*janjatis*—declared the area of the Bhojpur and Khotang districts as an autonomous state. Ethnic fundamentalism is naturally giving birth to communalism, leading to mistrust and hatred among various ethnic communities. Over the past few years, pro-*Madhesi* armed groups have been demanding the establishment of a single Madhesi province and have attacked the *Pahari* people of hill origin (Irinnews, 2008), forcing many to leave the Tarai region, which they had settled earlier.

Though small in number both in population size and representation to the Constituent Assembly, this *Madhesi* group has been successful in playing a significant role in the country's fragile politics since the 1990's. Indeed, and reflecting this shift in regional power away from the Kathmandu Valley's elites, Nepal's first elected president and vice-president from the 2008 Constituent Assembly, who took over the ceremonial roles of the ex-king, are both from the Tarai region.

The current set of political parties in Nepal--ranging from the Maoists on the left to the Congress party on the right – appear to be in considerable agreement that after the abolition of the feudal monarchial system, which has just recently occurred, the social bases of this age-old feudalist hierarchy of central power and absolute authority would disappear from Nepal along with the caste-based elites' controlling influences.

The caste system has been 'legally outlawed' in Nepal as a rigid, hierarchical, 'social class' system; however, the political and social dilemma exist. Despite all parties agreeing to eliminate the caste systems, they emphasize much on ethnicity as the source of their political bases because these ethnic groups are agglomerated in many places (Table 1) and can influence the election outcomes from different geographic pockets (Table 2; Figure 11) of various administrative units (Table 3).

Table 1. Number of ethnic/caste groups by population size category, 2001

Population size	No. of ethnic/caste groups	Population	Percent	Cumulative percent
>1,000,000	6	12,173,809	53.5	53.5
500,000-999,999	5	3,941,155	17.3	70.9
100,000 – 499,999	20	4,206,632	18.5	89.4
50,000 - 99,999	16	1,231,779	5.4	94.8
25,000 – 49,999	10	406,055	1.8	96.6
10,000 – 24,999	15	258,045	1.1	97.7
5,000 – 9,999	9	69,090	0.3	98.0
<5,000	19	40,068	0.2	98.2
Total identified ethnic/caste groups	100	22,326,633	98.2	
All total (including unidentified)	103	22,736,934	100	100

Ethnic groups and total population belonging to different ethnic/caste groups indicate how much influences a group of ethnic group could have on the political outcomes (Source: Adopted from Sharma, 2008:10).

Table 2. Social and spatial dimensions of the ethnic/caste population, 2001

Spatial/altitudinal dimension							
Dimensions			Mountain (Himal/ Bhot)	Hills (Pahad, including Bhitri Madesh)	Tarai (Madhesh)	Other	Total population
Sociostructural dimension	Non-Hindu, Non-hierarchic	Ethnic	Bhote, Byansi, Serpa, Thakali, Walung = 5 groups Total population: 190,107 (0.84%)	Baramu, Bhujel, Bhote, Chepang, Chhantel, Danuwar, Darai, Dura, Gurung, Hyolmo, Jirel, Kusunda, Lepcha, Limbu, Magar, Newar*, Pahari, Rai, Sunuwar, Tamang, thami, Yakkha, Kumal, Majhi, raji, Raute = 27 groups	Dhimal, Gangai, Jhangad, Kisan, Koche, Kushwadia, Meche, Munda, Rajbansi, Satar/Santhal, Tajpuria, Tharu** Total population: 1,787, 538 (7.86%)	Uniden-tified adivasi-janjati Popu-lation: 5259 (0.02%)	8,272,551 (36.38%) 45 groups
	Hierarchic Hindu caste groups	Other castes		Bahun, Chhetri, Sanyasi, thakuri = 4 groups Total population: 7,023,220 (30.89%)	Badahi, Baniya, Barai, Bhediyar, bin, Tarai Brahman, Dhanuk, Dhauniya, Hajam, halwai, Jaine, Kahar, Kalwar, Kamar, Kanu, Kayastha, Kewat, Koiri, Kumhar, Kurmi, Lodha, Mali, Mallah, Marwari, Nuniya, Nurang, Rajbhar, Rajput, Sundi, Teli, Yadav = 31 groups Total population: 3,317,752 (14.59%)		10,340,972 (45.48%) 35 groups
		Dalit		Badi, Damai, Gaine, Kami, Sarki = 5 groups Total population: 1,615,577 (7.11%)	Bantar, Chamar, Chidimar, Dhobi, Dom, Dusadh, Halkhor, Khatwe, Lohar, Musahar, Sonar, Tatma = 12 groups ; Total population: 1,113,929 (4.9%)	Uniden-tified Dalit popu-lation: 173,401 (0.76%)	2,902,907 (12.77%) 18 groups
	Other				Bengali (9860; 0.04%), Churaute (4893, 0.02%), Punjabi (3054; 0.01%), Muslim (97,1056; 4.27%) Total population: 988,863 (4.35%)	Unidentified caste/ethnic. Popu-lation: 231,641 (1.02%)	1,220,504 (5.37%) 5 groups
Total popu-lation			190,107 (0.84%)5 groups	14,928,444 (65.66%) 36 groups	7,208,082 (31.7%) 59 groups	410,301 (1.8%) 3 groups	22,736,934 (100%) 103 groups

* Newar are an exception in that 84%, which includes all Hindus; **. Tharus also inhabit inner Tarai districts (Source: Sharma 2008: 11).

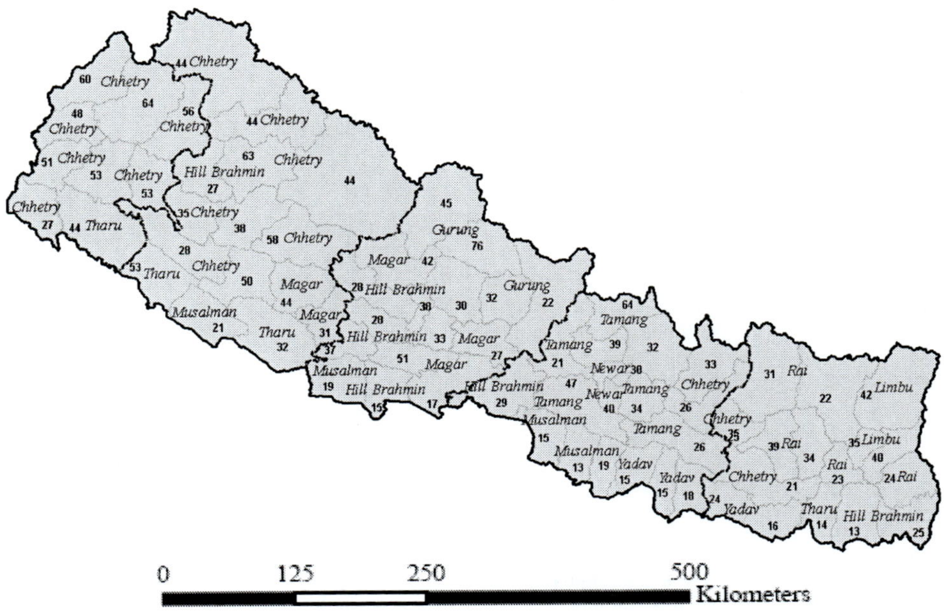

Figure 11. Distribution of major ethnic/caste groups by district as proportion of district population, 2001. (Note: if a caste/ethnic group is dominant in more than one contiguous district, only one label is placed on the map at the border of contiguous districts).

Table 3. Distribution of ethnic/caste groups in absolute majority by VDC/municipality, 2001

Number of VDCs/ municipalities	Ethnic/caste groups (number)
200	Chhetri (1)
100-199	Magar, Tamang, Tharu, Bahun (4)
50-99	Gurung, Rai (2)
25-49	Limbu, Yadav, Muslim, Newar (4)
10-24	Sherpa (1)
5-9	Thakuri (1)
1-4	Chepang, Kami, Bhote, Thami, Koiri, Sunuwar, Chhantel, Dhanuk, Gangai, Bantar, Byansi, Dura, Kurmi, Lepcha, Pahari (15)

Source: Sharma (2008:18).

The caste system has been one of Nepal's continuing societal paradoxes that political parties are willing to firmly oppose the power and authority of a feudal caste system while continuing to nourish the ethnic system for popularity's sake. Ethnic identity and allegiances and feudal caste systems, are very much intertwining and isolating them from each other, continue to be extremely difficult.

Caste System

The feudal caste hierarchy, modeled after the ancient and orthodox Brahmanic system, arrived with the influx of Indo-Aryans in the hills of Nepal, divided the society into four classes: Brahmin (priests and scholars), Kshatriya or Chhetri (rulers and warriors), Vaisya (merchants and traders), and Sudra (farmers, artisans, and laborers). Still a fifth class, the untouchables-outcastes and the socially polluted group, called *harijan* (trans. children of God after Mahatma Gandhi in India) is also identified. The fourth and fifth ethnic/caste categories were created for menial work. The Pahari caste divisions based on the Hindu system are not strictly upheld by the Newars; however, they claim to have their own caste hierarchy, which, they argue, is parallel to the Pahari Hindu caste divisions (Josse and Rose, 1966).

No single, widely acceptable definition of caste system exists in all societies. In each system, caste (*jati*) is ideally an endogamous group in which membership is both hereditary and permanent.

Caste is functionally significant only when viewed in a regional or local context and at a particular time (Josse and Rose, 1966). This system is rapidly eroding in urban areas with the democratization of the country.

The assumed correlation between the caste hierarchy and the socioeconomic class hierarchy, which many scholars have documented, does not always hold true. Because of numerous institutional changes over the years and increased expansion of the caste hierarchy stemming from inter-caste marriages, many high-castes are demoted while many low-castes are promoted to the higher status.

Democratization on the one hand and simplification of the *Sanskritization* and inter-caste marriages on the other have contributed to the weakening of the feudal caste bases. Though inter-caste marriage often carries a social stigma when a union takes place between two extreme castes, such as Brahmin and Sudras, it is occurring at a faster pace in all communities with the advancement of education and understanding of the very basis of the caste system that was founded on the division of work and economic status of the ancient society. Since various castes are living together in many geographic and administrative regions (Table 4), it is obvious to have inter-caste marriages despite social stigmas.

There is no single administrative unit that has purely one caste; however, dominance of one caste is common in many areas. Nonetheless, since her formation as nation state in 1769, Nepal has been a Hindu State, and the majority (86%) of the population still practices the Hindu religion, and the caste system prevails in the rural areas. Many ethnic communities and castes use different languages to link with their cultures.

Languages

Nepal is rich in the diverse linguistic heritage evolved from four major language groups: Indo-Aryan, Tibeto-Burman, Mongolian, and various indigenous languages. According to the 2001 national census, 92 different living languages are spoken in Nepal, and many ethnic groups coincide with the language they speak (Karan and Ishii, 1994). The major languages of Nepal are Nepali (49%), Maithili (12%), Bhojpuri (8%), Tharu (6%), Tamang (5%), Newari/Nepal Bhasa (4%), Magar (3%), Awadhi (2%), Rai (2.79%), Limbu (1%), and Bajjika (1%) (Figure 12, Table 5). People living in different parts of the country speak other 77 languages (Figure 12) as their mother tongues; however, Nepali serves as a lingua franca and is the official, national language of different ethnolinguistic groups. Hindi is also widely spoken, especially in the southern Tarai region (BBC, 2008). Additionally, many government offices and businesses use and speak the English language while dealing with international institutions.

Table 4. Presence of major ethnic/caste groups by VDCs/municipalities, 2001

Ethnic/caste group	Number of VDCs/municipalities with				Degree of Concentration ([b] as a % of [c])
	Majority population share (a)	Largest population share (b)	Total (c)	Percent of total VDCs/ municipalities	
Chhetry	387	541	928	22.9	41.7
Bahun	102	389	491	12.1	20.8
Magar	175	187	362	8.9	48.3
Tharu	106	204	310	7.7	34.2
Yadav	38	270	308	7.6	12.3
Tamang	159	142	301	7.4	52.8
Muslim	36	242	278	6.9	12.9
Rai	76	104	180	4.4	42.2
Gurung	77	53	130	3.2	59.2
Limbu	44	77	121	3.0	36.4
Newar	29	55	84	2.1	34.5
Koiri	3	48	51	1.3	5.9
Sherpa	22	20	42	1.0	52.4
Kurmi	1	38	39	1.0	2.6
Dhanuk	2	34	36	0.9	5.6
Thakuri	8	27	35	0.9	22.9
Kewat	0	24	24	0.6	0.0
Rajbansi	0	18	18	0.4	0.0
Kami	4	13	17	0.4	23.5
Tarai Brahman	0	14	14	0.3	0.0
Teli	0	14	14	0.3	0.0
Sunuwar	2	9	11	0.3	18.2
Other ethnic/caste groups with largest population share in <10 VDCs*	20	142	162	4.0	12.3
	1291	2665	3956	97.7	32.6

* Includes ethnic/caste groups that are dominant in 10 or more VDCs from a total of 45 ethnic/caste groups. Source: Sharma (2008:19).

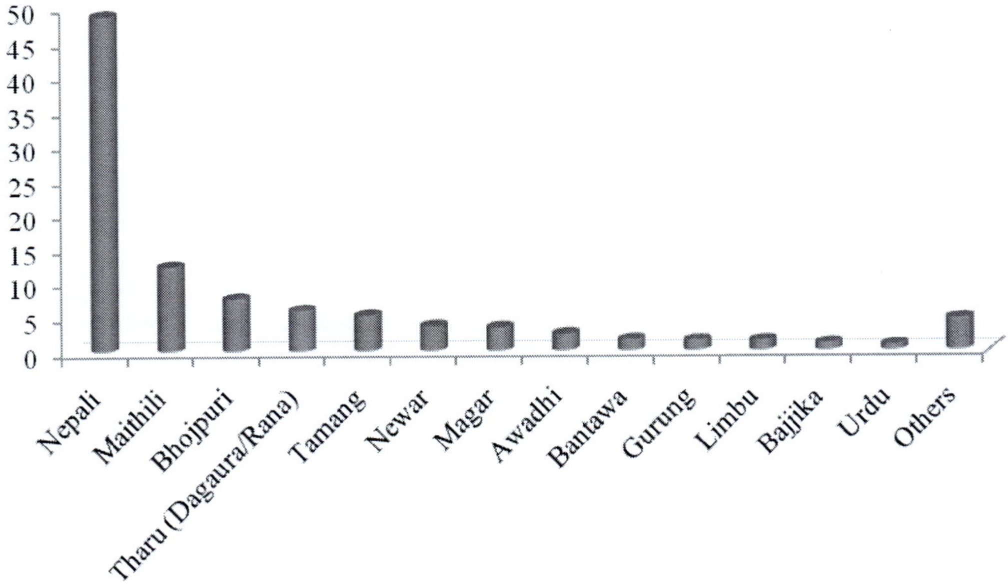

Figure 12. Major languages spoken in Nepal. Others include Rajbansi, Sherpa, Hindi, Chamling, Santhali, Chepang, Danuwar, Jhangar/Dhangar, Sunuwar, Bangla, Marwari (Rajsthani), Manjhi, Thami, Kulung, Dhimal, Angika, Yakkha, Thulung, Sangpang, Bhujel/ Khawas, Darai, Khaling, Kumal, Thakali, Chhantyal/Chhantel, Nepali Sign Language, Tibbetan, Dumi, Jirel, Wambule/ Umbule, Puma, Yholmo, Nachhiring, Dura, Meche, Pahari, Lepcha/Lapche, Bote, Bahing, Koi/ Koyu, Raji, Hayu, Byangshi, Yamphu/Yamphe, Ghale, Khariya, Chhiling, Lohorung, Punjabi, Chinese, English, Mewahang, Sanskrit, Kaike, Raute, Kisan, Churauti, Baram/ Maramu, Tilung, Jero/Jerung, Dungmali, Oriya, Lingkhim, Kusunda, Sindhi, Koche, Hariyanwi, Magahi, Sam, Kurmali, Kagate, Dzonkha, Kuki, Chhintang, and Mizo.

Table 5. Distribution of major languages in districts and VDCs/municipalities, 2001

Major mother tongue	Percentage of major mother tongue speakers in total population	Number of districts		Number of VDCs/municipalities	
		with highest % of mother tongue speakers	with majority mother-tongue speakers	with highest % of mother tongue speakers	with majority mother-tongue speakers
Nepali	48.6	56	49	2076	1853
Maithili	12.3	6	5	505	476
Bhojpuri	7.5	3	3	324	312
Tharu	5.9	1	1	128	96
Tamang	5.2	2	1	197	161
Newar	3.6	1	1	32	29
Magar	3.4	0	0	115	101
Awadhi	2.5	2	1	99	91
Bantawa Rai	1.6	0	0	55	31
Gurung	1.5	1	1	69	54
Limbu	1.5	2	0	76	39
Bajjika	1.1	1	0	51	50
Sherpa	0.6	0	0	41	32

Source: Sharma (2001:64).

Nepali language is a branch of the Indo-European language family, which was derived from Sanskrit and is written in *Devanagari*, like Hindi. Though Nepali script is similar to Hindi, Maithili, and Bhojpuri and all belong to the Indo-European family, , by no means is Nepali identical with them.

Another language Newari, mostly spoken in urban areas, belongs to the Tibeto-Burman language family. Other languages, such as Tamang, Limbu, Rai, Gurung, Thakali, and Magar, belong to this family and are used in ethnic names (Karan and Ishii, 1994) mostly in the northern parts of the country (Figure 13).

These ethnic groups tend to use their caste names to express their identities (Figures 13 and 14, Table 5). Karan and Ishii (1994) argue that Nepal is a place where Indo-European and Tibeto-Burman--speaking people meet (Figure 13).

Though Nepali is used as the official language and a medium to teach in educational institutions, recent political changes in Nepal have radicalized the use of ethnic languages. The FM radios and regional newspapers have promoted various ethnic languages. Local languages are more frequently used in rural than in urban areas; however, the use of non-Nepali languages in official businesses by representatives of some ethnic communities often sparks conflict (BBC, 2008). Nonetheless, in urban areas various language speakers maintain close harmony and use Nepali as a lingua franca.

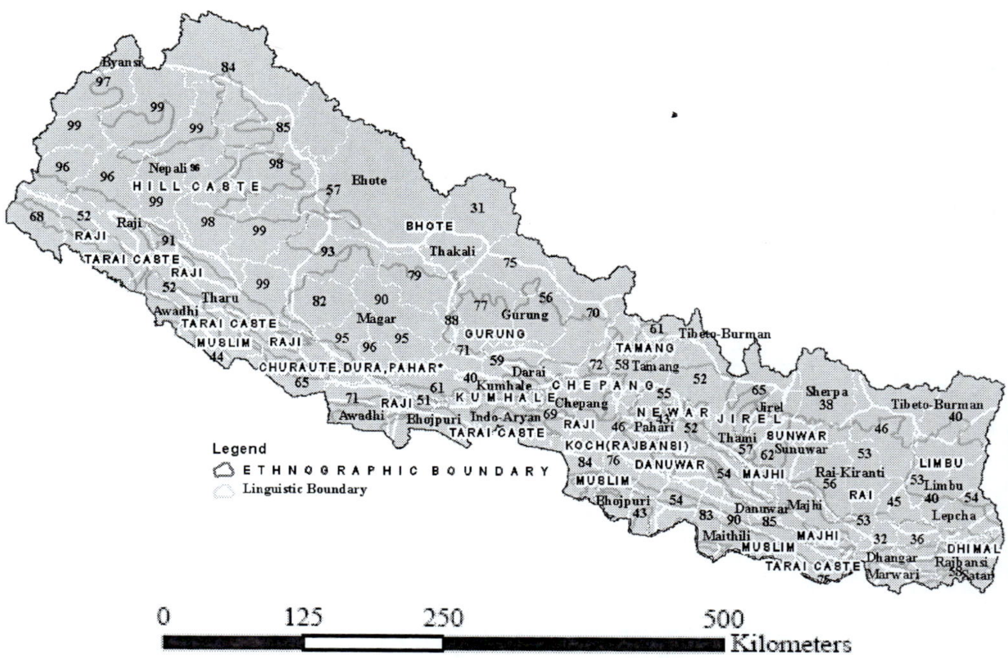

Figure 13. Relationships among castes, ethnicities, and their languages by geographic regions, Numbers in each districts represent percentage distribution of major languages in each district. On the map, thin white lines represent the boundaries of 75 districts and thick white lines represent the linguistic boundaries.

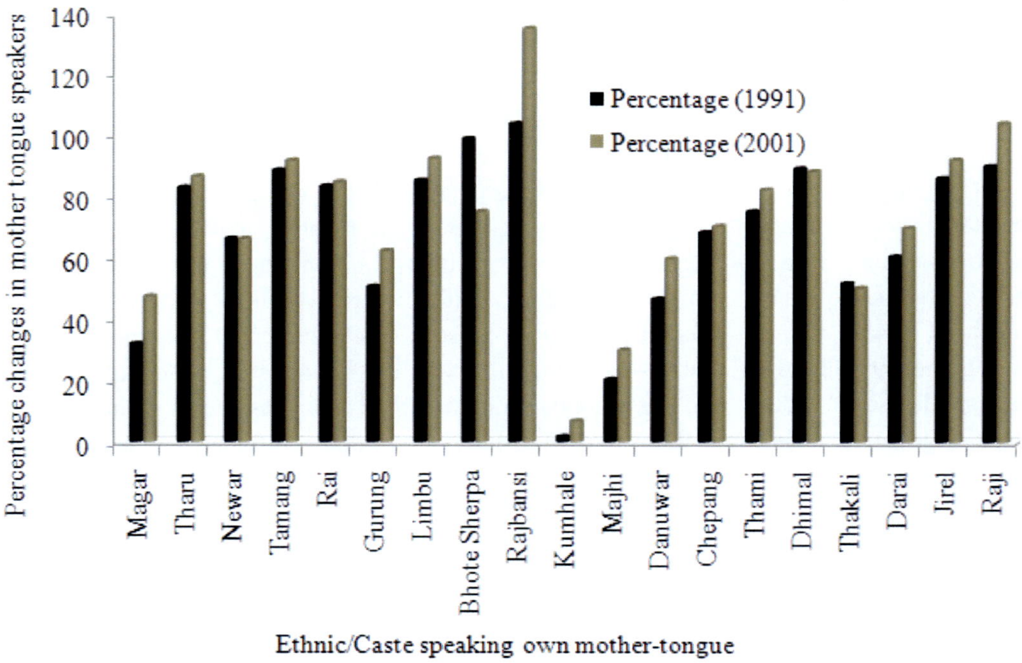

Figure 14. Percentages changes in mother tongues (1990-2001). This figure is an indicative of how the smaller minority groups have begun asserting their own separate identities with the rise in ethnic consciousness.

SOCIETY

Urbanization

Urban population/urbanization is defined as the percentage of total population living in a designated urban area. In Asia, about 160,000 people move from rural to urban areas each day, however, as of 2008, only 16% of the urban populations live in 58 urban centers in Nepal (Figure 3). The dominance of subsistence agriculture in the economy and topographic barriers have produced a loosely integrated urban network, making the flow of goods and services more seasonal and directed towards the Indian markets than within Nepal (Karan and Ishii, 1994). If the historically--based correlation between urbanization and economic development experienced by many industrialized nations is accepted, then Nepal has a long way to go before it becomes economically advanced. In 1952-54 censuses, there were only ten urban centers, and only 2.8% of the total population lived in urban areas, of which 50% of the urban centers with over 75% of urban population were located in the Kathmandu Valley (Karan and Ishii, 1994). In 1961, six more urban centers were added, and urban population increased 41% of the 1952-54 urban population. In 1971, however, the urban population increased only by 37% of the 1952-54 census because some of the previous urban centers were dropped from the urban list between 1961 and 1971. In 1976 some new urban centers were added, and by 1981, the urban population doubled (108% with more than 8% annual growth) to the 1971 urban population. In 1981, 6.4% of Nepal's total population was living in 33 urban areas. In

1987, the number of urban centers grew to 33. In the 1990s, the urbanization rate was 8% with 9.2% of the total population living in the urban areas. As per the 2001 census, only 14.2% of the total population lives in urban areas though annual urban population growth rate is 5% as compared to 2.25% of the rural area. Of the 14.2%, over 60% population lives in the Kathmandu urban areas (CBS, 2002).

The population in almost all the urban areas (Figure 3) is swelling rapidly (Figure 15) due to internal and international migration. Demographers and planners attribute such a swell in urban population to a well developed transportation and communication networks and the strong presence of the government machineries. The internal rural-to-urban migration has increased rapidly after the internally displaced persons (IDPs) swarmed into the urban areas during the 1996-2006 of Maoist--led civil unrest in the countryside. A concentration of young, adolescent, elderly, and IDP population in the urban areas has been a great concern of Nepal's government because this situation is likely to be the root cause of conflict due to increasing deprivation and social exclusion of a large number of growing populations in resource--limited urban areas (Poudel, 2004; TKP, 2004). Early signs of overcrowding have been visible in Biratnagar, Birgunj, Hetauda, Janakpur, Kathmandu Valley, Kanchanpur, Nepalgunj, Pokhara, and other urban centers (Figure 3).

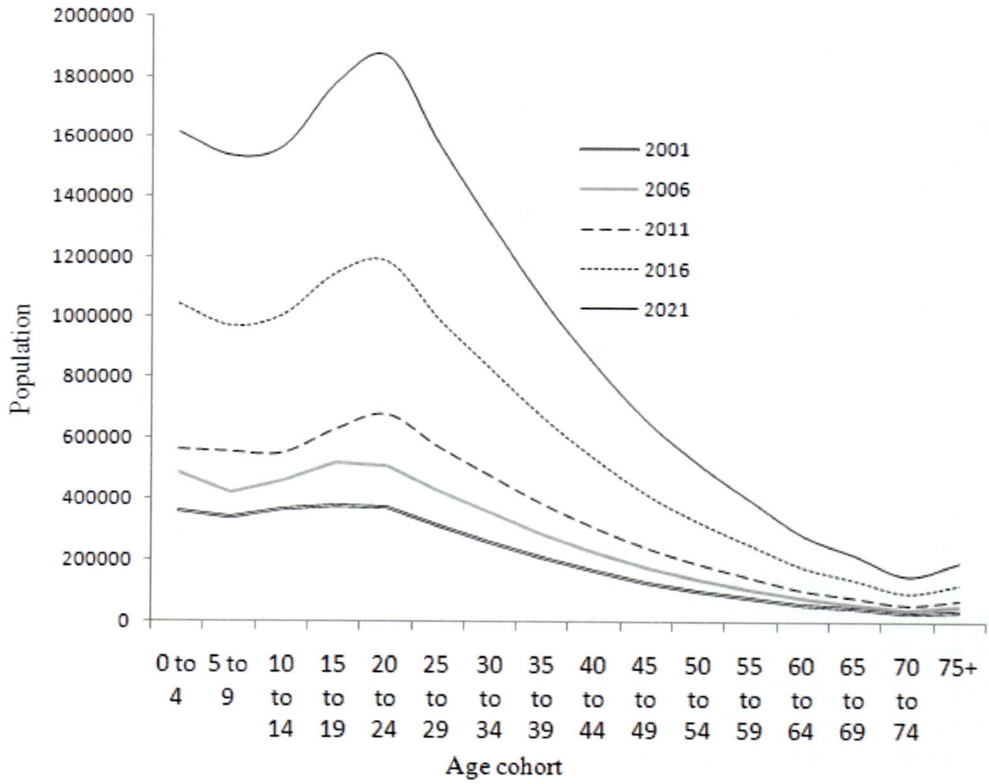

Data source: http://www.cbs.gov.np/Population/Projection/Table%208.htm.

Figure 15. Urban population growth (2001-2021) under medium vibrant assumption by age-cohort.

The distribution of urban centers has not been uniform across Nepal. Between 1950 and 1971, the central mid-hill region had the highest number of urban centers, whereas in 1991, distribution of urban population was skewed in favor of the eastern Tarai region, with fourteen of the twenty-three big urban settlements found in the Tarai, and the majority of the urban centers located in eastern and central Tarai (Figure 3) followed by the central mid-hills (Karan and Ishii, 1994). The Mountain Region had no urban settlements except for the Dolkha district (Figures 1 and 3). This situation clearly demonstrates that many parts of Nepal not only remained predominantly rural, but also that the existing urban areas were neither well developed nor well connected in terms of their spatial distribution. A large body of literature suggests that rapid urbanization is necessary to alleviate poverty, deprivation, and social exclusion because targeted programs can be implemented with lower transition costs in urban areas than in serving sparsely populated rural areas. Many industrial and modernization activities are concentrated in urban areas. These activities make some areas most affluent, and uneven development becomes a common phenomenon due to the skewed distribution of resources among geographic areas and social groups. If properly planned, urban centers can ease the process of service delivery at a reasonable cost giving economy of scale, and even help in proper demographic planning. For example, women in urban areas are relatively better educated and with a TFR of 1.5-2, which is almost close to the TFR of the developed world; while their rural counterparts have 4.5 kids (Agudelo, 2004 a and b; Sazaki, 2007; Spotlight, 2004). Urban centers also have better educational facilities, for example, Nepal's adult literacy rate increased from 23.3% in 1981 to 39.6% in 1991 and 57.6% in 2001 with most increases in urban areas.

On average, the literacy rate of women increased from 25% in 1981, 26% in 1991, and 45% in 2001, but the urban literacy rate has been consistently higher than these figures though it is still low as compared to other Asian countries (UNFPA, 2005). However, girls' education is far behind boys' schooling (Agudelo, 2004b) despite so many promises made in various plans. Literacy is very important to plan population, and it is only through the education, women would be able to shape their reproductive life styles. Notable differences have been observed between the rural and urban lives, where educated urban dwellers have smaller families than their rural counterparts. Due to better service delivery, population planning in urban areas becomes much easier than in rural areas as urban areas have better accesses to all kinds of modern forms of communication including radio, newspapers, television, and the Internet. Thus, urban centers are considered engines for economic development.

Economy

Almost 2/3 of the Nepal's economy is based on primary activities, and approximately 91% of the economically active population is engaged in agriculture and allied activities. The details of the rural and urban household characteristics and their overall features compiled from the 2008 household survey by Nepal Rastra Bank (Nepal National Bank) are presented in Table 6. These features clearly indicate better quality of life in urban than in rural settings.

One of the major challenges facing those who live in rural areas is the lack of farmland who are often living in landless or nearlandless situations (Shrestha, 2003). Critics blame the Nepal government for expanding conservation areas, despite such landless or nearlandless situation. For example, from 1995 to 2004, protected land in Nepal increased (Figure 16) by three-fold for wildlife conservation purposes (Upreti, 2006), while the number of landless is increasing rapidly.

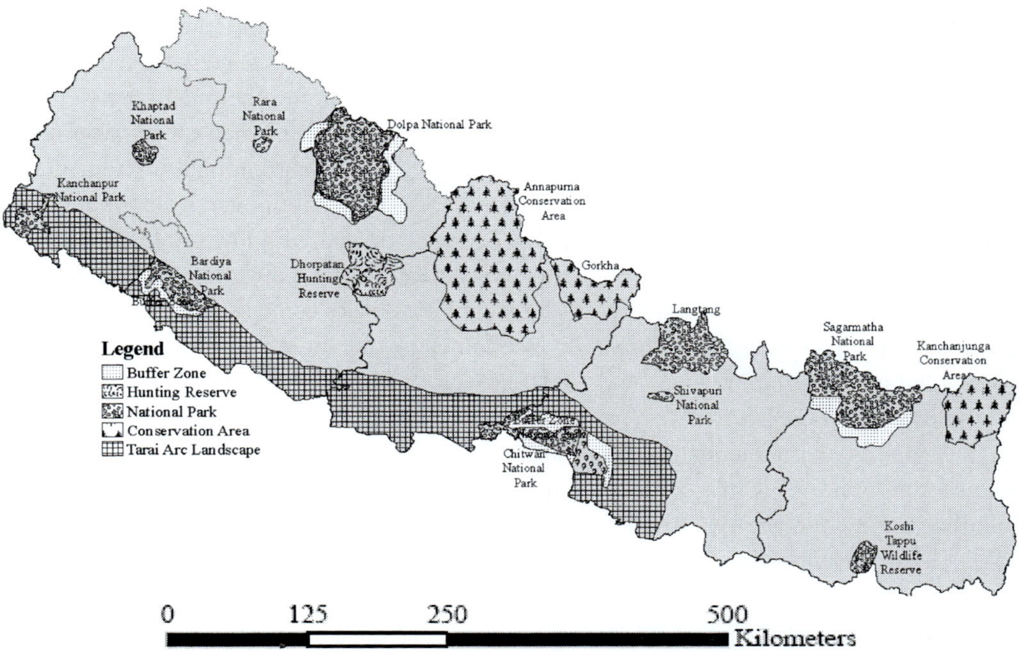

Figure 16. Conservation areas of Nepal (2001).

Existing farmland is not enough to support the growing population. As a result, once a net exporter of food grains, today Nepal imports grains. Of the 75 districts in the country, 45 hill and mountain districts face food deficits. The absolute number of people living under poverty is increasing (Thapa, 2001) mainly due to unemployment. Nepal's labor force is increasing at a much faster rate than economic growth; for example, labor force increased from 8.8 m in 1990 to 11.7 m in 2003, while the average annual growth rate for the period increased by only 2.2%. Statistical Yearbook (2003) and NLSS (2003/04) revealed a 5.1% annual unemployment rate. According to a recent study conducted by the National Planning Commission (NPC), over 300,000 to 400,000 youths enter into the job market annually, but Nepal's domestic market is too small to accommodate all of them. The 24.1% of the population earns < US $1/day, and 31% of the population is living below the abject poverty line (NMDG, 2005). In 1980, the GNP per head was reported $220, and since then the GNP increased only by US $16 a decade and barely reached US $250 in 2000, but it declined to US $249 in 2002 due to socio-political instability and insecurity in the country. It increased to US$300 in 2004/05 (NMDG, 2005). Such a meager increase in per capita GNP has little impact on the overall economy of the country, and many people are forced to live under poor hygienic conditions. Over 80% of the households are without proper toilet facilities (Figure 17a), and >30% of the total population lacks drinking facilities (Figure 17b). Despite these poor living conditions, the share of annual health expenditure as percentage of the national budget was 5.1 in 2001-2003, and the UNDP ranks Nepal 138 of 177 countries in its human development index (HDI). Though the HDI index increased from 0.291 in 1975 to 0.527 in

2004 (Nepal Annual Report DOHS, 2002-03, HDR, 2006), it is still low among South Asian countries (World Development Indicators, 2005).

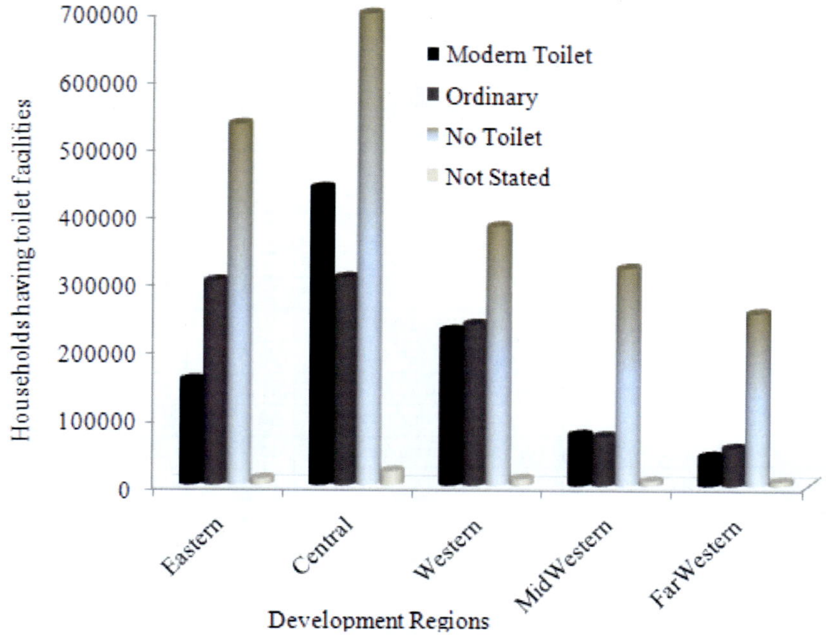

Figure 17a. Toilet facilities to various households (2001) by development regions.

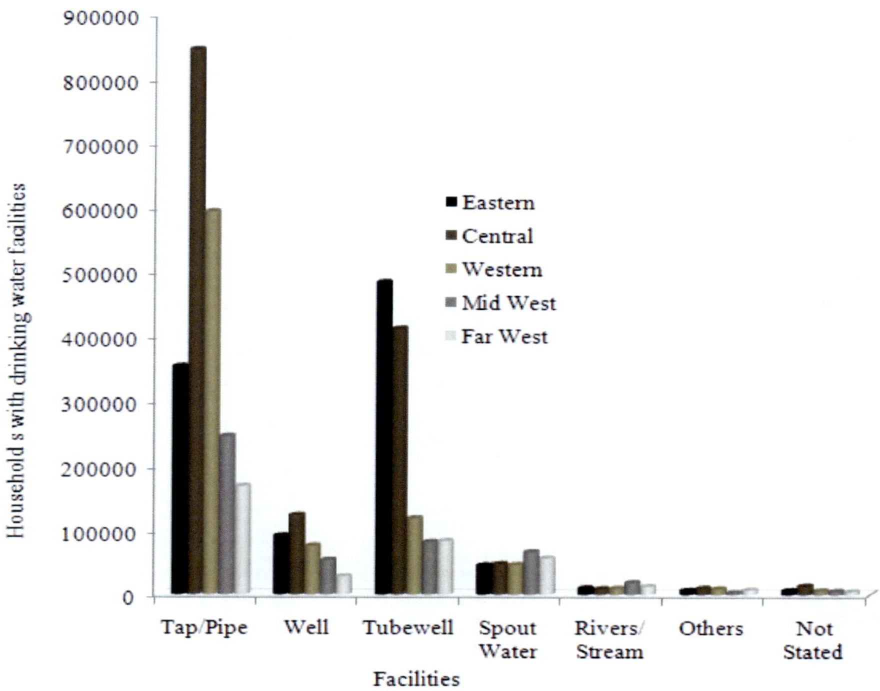

Figure 17b. Drinking water facilities by various development regions (2001).

Table 6. Rural and urban household economic characteristics, 2008

Particulars	Units	Household family characteristics	Rural	Urban	Overall
Family size)	Member	Average family number	5.21	5.49	5.36
Sex ratio	Ratio	Percentage of males	93.8	97.5	95.8
Children	Ratio	Child dependency ratio	54.2	38.4	45.2
Women	Ratio	Child woman ratio	0.28	0.22	0.24
Household	Head (person)	Male (%)	86.1	78.9	82.5
		Female (%)	13.9	21.1	17.7
	Ages (years)	15-24 (%)	2	1.4	1.4
		25-59 (%)	78.2	65.6	71.6
		> 60 (%)	19.6	33.7	27.1
Household heads	Literacy status (%)	Illiterate	19.2	21.7	20.5
		Read/write	23.5	21.0	22.2
		Primary education	10.8	6.7	8.6
		Secondary education	34.8	27.8	31.1
		Tertiary education	11.7	22.8	17.6
Economic activities	Household involvement in percentages	Agriculture	27	11.4	18.7
		Business/industry	17.9	21.7	23.7
		Service/teaching	17.9	21.4	19.8
		House wives	5.6	9.7	7.7
		Students	0.2	0.1	0.1
		Wage earners	8.2	6.7	0.1
		Others	15.2	29.1	22.6
Marital	Status (household %)	10 years and older	56.4	56.5	56.45
		Widow/widower	4.4	4.9	4.7
Dwelling units	Ownership patterns (%)	Own dwelling unit	86.6	88.5	87.6
		Rented house	11.1	10.0	10.5
		Free rent	2.4	1.5	1.9
House types	Types (%)	Super *pakki* (cement-rod concrete)	28.0	60.0	45.0
		Semi-*pakki* (cement, bricks, wood)	29.3	23.4	26.2
		Kacchi (mud-mortar)	41.6	16.4	28.2
		Other types	1.1	0.2	0.6
Water source	Types of water sources (household %)	Tap water (%)	67.7	72.5	70.3
		Wells	5.2	9.2	7.3
		Tube wells	31.6	31.6	31.6
Toilets	Household users (%)	Within household compounds	42.5	74.7	59.6
		Outside housing compounds	29.7	13.6	21.2
		Collective toilets	3.7	1.7	2.6
		Public toilets	1.7	0.9	1.3
		Nearby toilets	22.4	9.2	15.3
Electricity /telephone	Household (%)	Access to electricity	88.4	94.9	91.9
		Access to telephone	20.7	61.8	42.6

Particulars	Units	Household family characteristics	Rural	Urban	Overall
Households' Occupations	Household (%)	Agriculture	12	4.7	7.9
		Business/industry	13.3	12.3	12.8
		Service/technology	8.4	12.9	10.9
		Housewives	19.5	22.3	21.1
		Study	29.9	27.4	28.5
		Wage earner	4.3	3.6	3.9
		Domestic workers	1.2	1.7	1.5
		Others	11.3	15.2	13.5
Employment	Household (%)	Self-employed	13.7	11.8	12.6
		Service	8.5	12.9	11.0
		Unpaid family workers	12.8	6.3	9.1
		Wage earners	4.3	3.6	3.9
		Others	61.8	65.4	63.4
Distribution of income	US $	Average income per household	296	425	361
	Household (%)	Per capita income (US $)	56.85	77.56	67.20
		Agriculture	10.8	5.1	7.3
		Salary	22.7	31.4	28.1
		Business/service	29.4	29.4	29.4
		Remittance	20.6	13.3	16.1
		Imputed rent	7.5	11.9	10.2
		Miscellaneous	9.0	8.7	8.8
Household	US $	Annual expenditure patterns	159.8	238.67	201.8
	Income share (%) used in	Income share (%) spent on food	44.1	35.83	39
		Income share (%) spent on non-food	55.89	64.17	61

Source: Nepal National Bank (2008). http://red.nrb.org.np/publica.php?tp=study_reportsandandvw=15.

CONCLUSIONS

The Government of Nepal and its thoughtful citizens have been aware of the problems posed by the rapid population growth and possible problems it would pose in the 21st century. Reproducing couple must take a more active role in practicing contraception if family planning is to be successful and must change the psychology of the son preferences at any demographic cost. Recent demographic data indicates that a fertility decline started in the 1970's, but has not yet declined at the required level as in other South Asian countries.

Given the skewed distribution of population in the 0-15 year cohorts, no conceivable fertility decline can prevent Nepal's population from doubling every 28 years. Population growth has already exacerbated poverty and stresses on the environment (UNFPA, 2004). The major cause of this rapid population growth is attributed to both high TFR and improvement in Nepal's health and medical services.

For instance, major communicable diseases like cholera, malaria, and smallpox, which were some of the causes for the deaths of hundreds of people each year until the 1970's, have been brought under control.

However, per capita income has not been increased to meet the South Asian standard. Given the development status of Nepal, Malthus' pessimistic outlook and his theory is still relevant for this country.

With a current total of over 26 m people doubling every 28 years, Nepal still lacks a comprehensive population policy to address demographic problems. These problems are compounded due to the lack of proper health services at various geographic locations, education and job opportunities for adolescents and youth, proper settlement of internally displaced populations, and proper planning in urban areas (Musoke, 2001). Nepal often quickly endorses any new programs and plans, hoping to garner foreign support. For example, while participating in the first International Conference on Population and Development (ICPD), held in Cairo, Egypt, in 1994, Nepal was quick to promise to improve the quality of life and provide access to health services, education, and a clean environment to all the citizens to meet goals set by the UN (Agudelo, 2004).

Despite promises made, many demographic problems are exasperated by other factors. For example, many mothers die due to childbirth complications of pregnancy, which is preventable (Obaid, 2004). Nepal has one of the highest maternal mortality rates in South Asia with 905 per 100,000 in 2003 (UNFPA, 2005) mainly attributed to early marriages and lack of maternal care to young women.

Generally, Nepali couples marry early. These young and poorly educated mothers are likely to suffer from early pregnancies as they often had three or four children at an early age in many rural settings having only a fewer skilled health professionals. Signs of decline in the birth rate have been visible in certain areas with trained doctors and paramedical personnel, reliable administrative machinery, and satisfactory public relations. However, such facilities are only concentrated in urban areas, while the rural agrarian society still suffers.

The rural communities living in primary activities are suffering due to the progressive deterioration of the ratio of people to land. Though the average population density is just 102 persons/km^2, the high agricultural population density (> 6.1 persons/hectare) with a rudimentary agricultural technology has placed greater stress on the country's environmental conditions. Nepal's ability to reclaim more land in order to accommodate a rapidly growing population has already reached a maximum threshold. At such a juncture, Nepal faces multiple demographic challenges including brain drains.

Unstable political conditions have added many woes among rural folks, and rural-to-urban migration has been unchecked as urban development is considered an engine for economic progress and employment opportunities. However, urban planning is generally poor.

Today, the majority of the urban dwellers are composed of unemployed young cohorts. The unemployed young population is used as a force for political instability in the country that often creates civil unrest, and economic activities are badly affected by frequent closures of industries. These unemployed adolescents will be mobilized by political parties to create social turmoil once minor disagreements are seen in the governance. Until and unless specific programs are introduced to employ adolescents and address their concerns, such political instability will continue to occur in the future.

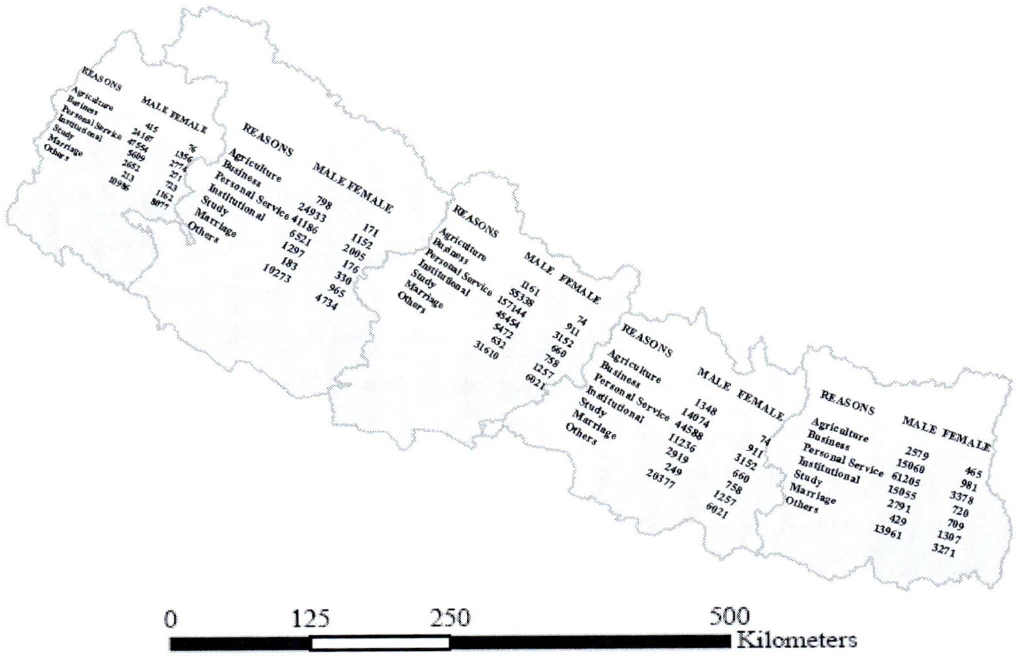

Figure 18. Migrations from five development regions for various purposes.

The civil unrest from 1996-2006 created a large pool of under-educated and under-employed youth. With ongoing political conflict and increasing unemployed young manpower, violence is likely to continue in Nepal. As a result of such difficulties, many working age people leave home for various reasons—a trend of brain drain (Figure 18, Appendix 1).

Although the ceasefire and peace accord of 2006 are major accomplishments, post-conflict Nepal remains fragile. There are many challenges ahead. First, there is the question of how to reach the rural population, the majority of which are illiterate and do not have access to education. Second, there is a need for integrating population activities into a program of a wider network of sectoral agencies, local bodies, and people's organizations for constructive works. Third, the psychological barriers of son preference and over emphasis on ethnic divisions for political benefits must be handled carefully.

The 21st century Nepal expects that no citizen will have to beg for the next meal, become homeless, sleep on the city streets, lives the life of an illiterate, suffer from a curable or preventable disease, and lead a demoralized life of enforced idleness. The future citizens of this recently declared federal democratic state must have pride in their cultural heritage, feel dignity as valued members of the community, and hope for an ever-better future of peace and prosperity for succeeding generations.

Though the Maoist revolution brought rapid awareness in the rural areas to alleviate problems associated with caste and feudal systems, in a fledgling democracy, there is much need to utilize accumulated human and social capital by government agencies, universities, policy makers, professionals, and commentators. Unless these resources are fully harnessed, improving living conditions equivalent to the South Asian standard will become a pipedream in the 21st century.

APPENDIX 1. MIGRATION FOR REMITTANCE PURPOSE (2001)

Countries	Gender	Eastern	Central	Western	Midwestern	Farwestern	Total
India	Male	60099	55881	233071	80718	90731	520500
	Female	7239	7627	30109	9288	14287	68550
Pakistan	Male	93	191	120	30	32	466
	Female	14	41	18	6	13	92
Bangladesh	Male	116	316	214	61	77	784
	Female	17	94	25	8	24	168
Bhutan	Male	256	182	42	12	18	511
	Female	56	34	2	5	2	99
Sri Lanka	Male	40	72	54	6	4	176
	Female	4	10	8	2	1	25
Maldives	Male	128	68	122	12	1	334
	Female	2	18	7	5	4	36
China	Male	166	534	230	49	39	1018
	Female	59	172	75	9	21	336
Korea	Male	447	501	1403	63	19	2433
	Female	37	66	138	4	1	246
Russia	Male	108	304	156	33	32	633
	Female	18	54	27	8	7	246
Japan	Male	299	1209	1439	38	21	3087
	Female	59	279	286	9	6	639
H-Kong	Male	2743	1268	4032	72	28	8143
	Female	1368	553	1920	15	2	3858
Singapore	Male	1034	510	961	163	11	2679
	Female	254	118	260	50	2	684
Malaysia	Male	2540	1019	2944	180	59	6742
	Female	22	7	39	3	0	71
Australia	Male	291	1149	470	47	34	1991
	Female	74	327	86	6	7	500
Saudi Arab	Male	22907	13687	27432	2452	151	66629
	Female	272	186	343	23	7	831
Qatar	Male	9186	4503	10092	374	53	24208
	Female	70	44	72	2	1	189
Kuwait	Male	1165	516	1278	68	17	3044
	Female	292	176	172	1	3	644
UAE	Male	4094	2501	5319	316	68	12298
	Female	63	89	89	5	0	246
Bahrain	Male	1432	261	890	30	3	2616
	Female	79	11	28	3	3	121
Others (Asian)	Male	758	1098	1142	111	21	3130
	Female	163	236	298	16	6	719
UK	Male	1386	2097	2329	143	42	5997
	Female	260	505	482	17	10	1274
Germany	Male	238	562	579	30	11	1420
	Female	32	109	74	3	0	218
France	Male	33	119	42	3	0	197
	Female	7	37	8	1	0	53
Others (Europe)	Male	174	743	689	20	14	1640
	Female	36	188	129	2	3	358
North America	Male	882	4912	1287	91	55	7227
	Female	265	1749	279	25	12	2330
Others (South America)	Male	465	507	473	69	52	1566
	Female	69	110	95	17	20	311
Grand total		122832	108965	333320	94851	106062	766030

REFERENCES

Agudelo, H. (2004a). Poverty, illiteracy exacerbating high population growth: Dr. Hernando Agudelo, the Country Acting Representative of the United Nations Population Fund (UNFPA) for Nepal. http://www.kantipuronline.com, Posted on: 2004-07-13 05:37:37 (Server Time).

Agudelo, H. (2004b). Nepal is experiencing the demographic transition, *Spotlight*, Vol. 23 (45), May 28 - June 03, 2004 (Jestha 15, 2061 BS.).

Anonymous (2008). State of world population report 2005: Call for Gender Equity; *Spotlight*, October 28, 2005.

Aryal, Mallika (2007). Staying alive Maternal mortality rates are falling but there is room for improvement; Nepal Demographic Health Survey, *Nepali Times*, http://www.nepalitimes.com.np/issue/378/Nation/14273 ISSUE #378 , December 14-20).

BBC(2008). Nepal language protests intensify, http://news.bbc.co.uk/2/hi/south_asia/7528454.stm, retrieved on July 28, 2008

Bhattarai, K. (2001). *Household landownership and the use of forests in the Bara district of Central Tarai Region of Nepal.* Unpublished Ph.D. Dissertation, Indiana University, Bloomington, Indiana.

Bhattarai, K., Conway, D., and Shrestha, N. R. (2002). The vacillating evolution of forestry policy in Nepal: Historically manipulated, internally mismanaged. *International Development Planning Review,* 24(3), pp. 315-38.

CBS (2007) Central Bureau of Statistics, Government of Nepal, Katmandu.

CBS (2002). Central Bureau of Statistics, Government of Nepal.

CG (2003). Nepal. The Columbia Gazetteer of the World Online. New York: Columbia University Press, 2005. http://www.columbiagazetteer.org. Accessed: July 19, 2008.

Dahal, Govinda P., Sabu S. Padmadas and P. R. Andrew (2008). Hinder fertility-limiting behavior and contraceptive choice among men in Nepal, *International Family Planning Perspectives*, 2008, 34(1):6–14

Daneil, Ugochi (2008). United Nations Population Fund (UNFPA) country representative in e-Kantipur online.com.

Gellner, D. N. (2007). Caste, Ethnicity and Inequality in Nepal, *Economic and Political Weekly*, May 19, pp. 1823-28.

Gurung, H. B. (2002). Nepal's population trend towards lowlands', www.nepalnews.com, *The Katmandu Post*, Kathmandu Tuesday, December 25, 2001 (Paush 10, 2058).

Gurung, H. B. (2003). *Social Demography of Nepal: Census 2001*. Lalitpur: Himal Books. Published by New Era, Kathmandu, Nepal.

Gyawali, B. (2008). Unchecked, Nepal's population to double in 31 years, www.chinaview.cn 2008-07-12 12:21:06, retrieved on July 19, 2008.

HDR(2006). Human Development Report, 2006.

HMGN (2002). The Tenth Plan 2002-2007. National Planning Commission, His Majesty's Government of Nepal, Kathmandu. Available at http://www.npc.gov.np/tenthplan/docs_in_english.htm.

Irinnews (2008). Nepal: Analysts warn of rising ethnic tensions. Find more IRIN news and analysis at http://www.irinnews.org; http://www.reliefweb.int/rw/rwb.nsf/db900SID/PANA-7HHGGW?OpenDocument, Retrieved on August 14, 2008 at 8.04 am.

Irinnews (2005). The conflict's dangerous impact on health services. Available at http://www.irinnews.org/webspecial/nepal/50549.asp the UN Office for the Coordination of Humanitarian Affairs. Accessed on August 17, 2008.

Josse, B. L. and L. Rose (1966). *Democratic Innovations in Nepal: A Case Study of Political* Acculturation. Berkeley: University of California Press.

Karki, N. B. (2008). Population in development plans, http://www.nepalresearch.org/society/population.htm, retrieved on July 19, 2008.

Karki Y. B (1988). Sex preference and the value of sons and daughters in Nepal, *Studies in Family Planning,* 1988, 19(3):169–178.

KDHPR (2005). Kaiser Daily Health Policy Report. Advisory Board Company and Kaiser Family Foundation. http://www.kaisernetwork.org/dailyreports/ healthpolicy. http://www.medicalnewstoday.com/ articles/59553.php.

Khadka, Rudra (2002). Mass exodus, *The Kathmandu Post*, Kathmandu, Saturday Dec. 21, 2002 (Paush 06, 2059) http://www.nepalnews.com.np/contents/ englishdaily/ktmpost/2002/dec/dec21/features.htm#5.

Leone T, Matthews, Z and Zuanna, G. D (2003). Impact and determinants of sex preference in Nepal, *International Family Planning Perspectives,* 29(2):69–75.

Maharjan, Uttam (2002). Population growth: A challenge to development, *The Rising Nepal*, Kathmandu Monday May 06, 2002 (Baishakh 23, 2059).http://www.nepalnews.com.np/contents/englishdaily/trn/2002/may/may06/features.htm#1.

Medicalnews (2006). Nepalese Maternal Mortality Rate Among Highest Worldwide, IFRC Report Says 22 Dec 2006 - 15:00 PDT http://www.medicalnewstoday.com/articles/59553.php.

Muller-Boker, Ulrike (1999). *The Chitwan Tharus in Southern Nepal: An Ethnological Approach*. Frnaz Stener Verlag Stuttgart.

Musoke, J. Bill (2001). Nepalis must take the initiative for their development Vol. 21 (20). *The National Newsmagazine*, Nov 30 - Dec 06, 2001.

NDHS (2006). *Nepal Demographic and Health Survey.*

Nepalnews. Com (2006). Nepal's population crosses 26 million mark, http://www.nepalnews.com, July 12 06.

Nepal Research (2008). Website on Nepal and Himalayan Studies: http://www.nepalresearch.org/society/population.htm.

NLSS(2003/04). Nepal Living Standard Survey 2003/04.

NMH (2002). Nepal Ministry of Health, New ERA and ORC Macro, *Nepal Demographic and Health Survey, 2001,* Calverton, MD, USA: Nepal Ministry of Health, New ERA and ORC Macro, 2002.

NMDG (2005). Nepal Millennium Development Goals: Progress Report.

NPPC (2002). Nepal National Planning Commission, *Tenth Plan (2002–2007),* Singh Durbar, Nepal: Department of Printing, 2002.

Obaid, Thoraya Ahmed (2004). Thoraya Ahmed Obaid, Executive director statement posted on the UNFPA web-site on the occasion of World Population Day.

Oppitz, M. (1973). Myths and Facts: Reconsidering some data concerning the clan history of the Sherpa. In *Contributions to the Anthropology of Nepal*, Christophvon Furer-Haimendorf. Warminster (eds): Arts and Philips Ltd.

Poudel, Keshab (2006). Young population: Changing dynamism, *Spotlight*, June 30, 2006.

Pradhan A, R. Aryal, G. Regmi, B. Ban and P. Govindasamy (1997). *Nepal Family Health Survey 1996*. His Majesty's Government, Nepal. Ministry of Health, New ERA; Macro International Inc, Calverton, Maryland and Kathmandu.

UNDP (2005). *Nepal Millennium Development Goals: Progress Report*. Available at http://www.undp.org.np/publication/html/md g2005/mdg2005.php. Accessed on 06-01-06.

UNFPA (2005). Nepal's population hits 27 million mark, UNFPA, October 22, 2005.

Sazaki, Junko (2007). If Nepal is to benefit from demographic bonus, utilize the window of opportunity, *Spotlight*, July 20, 2007.

Schuler, S. R. and Goldstein, M. C (1986). Family planning in Nepal from the user's and non-user's perspectives, *Studies in Family Planning,* 17(2): 66–77.

Sharma, Pitamber (2008). *Unravelling the mosaic: Spatial aspects of ethnicity in Nepal.*

Shah, R. K. (2008). Population explosion, http://www.kantipuronline.com/kolnews.php?andnid=17744, Posted on: 2004-09-25 04:22:54 (Server Time), retrieved on July 19, 2008

Shrestha, N. R. and K. Bhattarai (2004). *Historical Dictionary of Nepal*. Vision Books Pvt. Ltd.ISBN: 8170945763, 464p.

Shrestha, N. R. (2001). *The political economy of land, landlessness and migration in Nepal,* Nirala Series: p311.

Simkhada, B., E. R. van Teijlingen, M. Porter, and P. Simkhada (2006). *Kathmandu University Medical Journal*, Vol. 4 (2), Issue 14, 258-263.

Spotlight(2004). State of the World Population 2004: Hopeful Signs Despite intensification of insurgency, Nepal has made progress in population sector, *Spotlight*, Vol. 25 (11), Sept 24 - Sept.30, 2004 (Ashwin 08, 2061 BS).

Stash S (1999). Explanations of unmet need for contraception in Chitwan, Nepal, *Studies in Family Planning,* 30(4):267–287.

Stash S (1996). Ideal-family-size and sex composition preferences among wives and husbands in Nepal, *Studies in Family Planning,* 27(2):107–118.

Thapa, S.(2001). Population growth in Nepal: The challenges ahead, *The National Newmagazine*, Vol. 21(16): Oct 12 - Oct 18 , 2001.

Thomlinson, R. (1967). *Demographic Problems: Controversy over population control.* Dickenson Publishing Company, Inc., Belmont, California; California State College at Los Angeles, www.questia.com, Publisher: Dickenson Publishing. Place of Publication: Belmont, CA. Publication Year. http://www.questia.com/PM.qst?a=oandd=9152189.

TKP (2004). Population explosion worsening poverty, *The Kathmandu Post*, www.kantipuronline.com, Posted on: 2004-09-15 19:27:10 (Server Time).

TRN (2001). Lack of education cited for rising population, *The Rising Nepal*, Kathmandu Thursday November 08, 2001 Kartik 23, 2058.

UNESCAP (2008). Population and Social Integration Section (PSIS), http://www.unescap.org/esid/psis/population/popin/profiles/nep.asp, retrieved on July 19, 2008.

UNFPA (2005). Nepal Conflict Aggravates Women's Reproductive Health Risks. Press release, 30 November, Available at http://www.unfpa.org/news/news.cfm?ID=7 *21,* United Nations Population Fund.

UN (2005). UN, World contraceptive use 2005 wall chart, New York: Department of Economic and Social Affairs, Population Division.

UNICEF (2006). Issues facing children in Nepal. http://www.unicef.org/infobycountry/nepal_nepal_background.html.

Upreti, B. R. (2006). Civil War in Nepal, Environmental Stress and Demographic Change: Underlying Conditions and Nepal's Instability, November 01 2006, 12:00 p.m. - 2:00 p.m. http://www.wilsoncenter.org/index.cfm?fuseaction=events.event_summaryandevent_id=205735; Paper presented in Woodrow Wilson Center for International Scholars; retrieved on August 20, 2008.

USAID (2003). U.S. Agency for International Development Interagency Gender Working Group, *Reaching men to improve reproductive health for all: Resource Guide,* Washington, DC: Population Reference Bureau, 2003.

WB (2005). The World Bank, *World Development Indicators*, 2005.

Xinhua (2008a). Issues facing children in Nepal. http://www.thaindian.com/newsportal/world-news/60-newborns-six-mothers-die-in-nepal-every-day-survey_10025656.html.

Xinhua (2008b). Nepal stands highest in maternal death rate in South Asia www.chinaview.cn 2008-03-15 21:11:11 http://news.xinhuanet.com/english/2008-03/15/content_7797296.htm.

Zeenews (2006). Nepal successful in cutting infant mortality rate: http://www.zeenews.com/South-Asia/2006-09-19/ 323689news.html.

In: Nepal in the 21st Century
Editor: Surendra R. Devkota, pp. 43-83
ISBN 978-1-60741-348-6

Chapter 2

POLITICAL EVOLUTION OF MODERN NEPAL

Karl-Heinz Krämer
Department of Political Science at the South Asia Institute,
University of Heidelberg (Germany)
InWEnt - Internationale Weiterbildung und Entwicklung
(Capacity Building International), Germany

ABSTRACT

After 10 years of a bloody Maoist insurgency and a gradual royal putsch, the people's movement of April 2006 has laid the foundations for a new political beginning. Nepal's numerous problems must be understood against the background of historical and social developments of the modern state. The multiethnic, multicultural, multireligious and multilingual modern state of Nepal came into existence in the second half of the 18th century when the Shah monarchy of the principality of Gorkha unified about 50 small states by military force. The Shah kings organized the new unitary state along the rules of traditional Hindu law with all its aspects of a stratified hierarchical social system. A small coterie of male members of so-called high Hindu castes became dominating in all public spheres while the other groups and the women became excluded, a situation that is still prevalent today and that gives reason to growing unrest.

This article is going to analyse the reasons why Nepal has problems with the process of democratization that showed its beginnings in the 1950s before the country was again thrown back by the royal coup of King Mahendra in 1960. A second process of democratization has been initiated with the people's movement of 1990 but it again ended up in political chaos, unrest and another royal putsch. Now, the country undertakes its third attempt to introduce democracy and there is good reason to assume that it will be its last chance. The more is it necessary to understand what went wrong in the past and to try to avoid such mistakes in the process of reconstruction.

Important questions that have to be answered are: What has been the reason for the failure of the political parties, especially after 1990? Why could the restoration of monarchy get the upper hand over the process of democratization in the 1950s and why could the king even stage a coup once again in the 21st century? What role did the state of education and the extent of traditional thinking play in this context? How could the Maoist insurgency arise and what have been its intentions? What have been the circumstances of the peace agreement of 2006 and the inclusion of the Maoists into the government, and can the latter be trusted? Can the interim constitution of February 2007 be a good basis for reconstructing the country and its political system? Can the elections for a constituent assembly of April 2008 provide the foundation for a new and inclusive Nepal against the growing tensions along ethnic, regional and gender lines? Is there a special role for civil society and how can it be involved? What could be future political scenarios, unified leftists and their roles and responsibility, Nepali Congress's political characters and its leadership crisis, role of international community including India, etc.?

INTRODUCTION: BETWEEN MONARCHY AND DEMOCRACY

In the course of millennia, numerous population groups have immigrated into the territory that today constitutes the country of Nepal. Most of the ethnic groups (about 40% of the population) obviously have come from regions north of the country according to their anthropological, linguistic and cultural characteristics. Of about the same strength is the group of Hindu castes of the hills (Pahad) that goes back to the former Khas population of Western Nepal, with a share of less than 30% for the so-called high Hindu castes and more than 10% Dalits.[1] Finally, in the Tarai flatlands along the southern border to India live some ethnic groups and numerous Hindu castes that have immigrated from the south. The immigration of Hindu castes from neighbouring Indian regions only started after 1850 when the then ruling Rana family invited them to exploit the fertile Tarai strip economically.

There were more than 50 small principalities on the territory of what is now Nepal when the Shah monarchy of Gorkha started to unify the country by military force in the mid 18th century. Some of these small states, like Gorkha herself, had politically and socially already been organized on the basis of Hindu law. But there were numerous other states with customary law that was strongly influenced by local ethnic traditions and cultures.

The expansionist tendencies of Gorkha were put to an end by the Anglo-Gorkha War of 1814-16. The central elite that almost exclusively consisted of Chhetri and Bahun families from Gorkha which had been helpful to the Shah monarchy during the expansion phase then tried to standardize the judicial and social order on the basis of the Hindu law as it had been practiced in Gorkha. The process was concluded with the publication of the *muluki ain*, the first Nepali law codex, in January 1854.[2] This law with its stratified social order directly reflected the thinking and value system of the so-called high caste male elite of the state. On top of this order were the *Tagadhari*, the wearers of the holy thread, i.e. Bahun (Brahmans of the Pahad region), Chhetri (Nepali for Kshatriya) as well as some corresponding 'upper' castes of the Newar, the ethnic group that has traditionally settled in the Kathmandu valley.

The numerous ethnic groups, all of whom with the exception of the Newar are socially organized in clans, were included into this social system as castes below the Tagadhari.

---

[1] The figures are based on the census of 2001 [http://www.cbs.gov.np/national_report_2001.php]. Before 1990, the surveys had been manipulated in the interest of the centralized state under the leadership of the Hindu monarchy. [See Dahal, Dilli Ram. Social Composition of the Population: Caste/Ethnicity and Religion in nepal. In: Central Bureau of Statistics (ed.). Population Monograph of Nepal, vol. 1, Kathmandu 2003, pp. 87-135] This manipulation is reflected by the continuous and considerable changes in the censuses of 1991 and 2001. Further changes may arise in the future when the about one million people are included that have been awarded Nepali citizenship for the first time as part of the preparations of the elections to a constituent assembly in early 2007.

[2] Höfer, András. The Caste Hierarchy and the State in Nepal: A Study of the Muluki Ain of 1853. Innsbruck: Universitätsverlag Wagner, 1979.

Below castes declared ethnic groups, the state elite included the then numerically still small number of Muslims and Europeans followed by the Dalits, the so-called untouchable Hindu castes. Rights, duties and forms of punishment were different for each of these groups. A real participation in the tasks of the state and in the administration was only given for the male members of the Tagadhari circles.

The system also had economic effects since the process of unification contributed to an enormous shift in landownership. In many ethnic areas, for example, most of the land had not been owned by individuals but by the clans. After the conquest of these territories, the Shah monarch declared all this land as his own and partly distributed it to persons from the Tagadhari circles who had been helpful to the Shah rulers during the phase of expansion. This had the side effect that the original settlement areas became more and more disintegrated, because the Hindu castes that had before mainly settled in the western part of the country now spread across the whole territory. Administrative structuring during the next one and a half centuries, like the repeated change of district boundaries, further promoted this process. The good one hundred years of Rana rule (1846-1951) only brought changes at the top of the state but it did not change the non-inclusive social system in general.

The cooperation between the Rana rulers and the British colonial power in India had ensured that Nepal became hermetically secluded from the outside world. It was only after the abolition of Rana rule (1950/51) that Nepal opened up to the world and thus came in touch with foreign social and political thinking. At that time, the people in Nepal almost exclusively lived from subsistence agriculture. The education system was extremely poor; there were hardly any schools outside of Kathmandu. Only few people had come in contact to foreigners before, e.g. Gurkha soldiers who had fought for the British in two world wars as well as a relatively small group of Nepalis living in Indian exile. The latter were mainly members of small economic and social upper and middle classes who had left the country to evade Rana despotism. Others were sons of such families who had been sent by their parents to Indian schools for good education. In the 1940s, this group was joined in exile by an ever growing number of dissatisfied Ranas who had been excluded from the Rana ranking system after Prime Minister Juddha Shamsher reformed the latter in 1934.[3]

These groups of exiled middle and upper class male Nepalis developed a political consciousness in India that was oriented along world political ideologies and outlooks. Many of them actively participated in the Indian independence movement and joined Indian political parties, especially the Indian National Congress and the Communist Party of India.

After 1946, some of them formed independent Nepali parties in Indian exile, among them the two till today most important parties of Nepal, the Nepali Congress (NC)[4] and the Communist Party of Nepal (CPN).[5]

---

[3] Since the early days of Rana oligarchy, the sons of the Ranas were included into the Rana ranking system at the moment of their birth. With growing age they climbed up the ladder of this hierarchical system entering more and more responsible positions. Because of the great number of Ranas in the early 1930s, Juddha Shamsher arranged the offspring of the Ranas in three groups – A,B and C – depending on the caste status of their mothers. The C-Ranas, whose mothers came from ethnic groups, became totally excluded from the ranking system. This drove them to join the growing opposition circles in Indian exile. In the 1940s, they were further joined by B-Ranas who then also became excluded from leading positions in the Rana administration.

[4] In January 1947, a party under the name Nepali Rastriya Congress (Nepali National Congress) was formed under the leadership of B.P. Koirala. In April 1950, it was joined by the Nepali Prajatantrik Congress (Nepali Democratic Congress), a party dominated by Rana dissidents, and further on called itself Nepali Congress.

Five features are characteristic for Nepal's long and eventful way towards democratization and rule of law after 1950. There is first the Shah monarchy which was freed from its golden cage with the abolition of Rana oligarchy. Its main goal was the restoration of its traditional power position. It was supported by those circles of society that had gained economic and social advantages through the politics of early Shah and Rana times.

Ostensible rivals of this monarchy were the young political parties and their inexperienced leaders. As given by the formation history of the parties, their leaders for the most part were male members of the so-called higher Hindu castes.[6] A distinctive feature of these party political leaders was and is till today that they distinguish themselves by a high degree of division and personal striving for power. This became further reinforced by the typical Nepali mentality, that the own people (*aphno manche*) on the other side await personal advantages and privileges from 'their' leaders. This special attitude of Nepali party politicians has been the main reason for the numerous formal or at least internal fissions that have affected all parties time and again. Ideological differences were in this context only of minor importance. As a fatal consequence did this help to pave the way for monarchy to regain its absolute power position within only ten years after the abolition of the Rana system. The putsch of King Mahendra, the father of the now former King Gyanendra, on 15 December 1960 marked the end of all efforts for democratization for about thirty years and prevented every kind of social and economic development of the country.

The second characteristic feature is the only hesitant development of civil society. The general backwardness of the country and the great lack of education left the common people unaware of their fundamental rights and of international standards and values for the whole decade of the 1950s. After 1960, the development of civil society was suppressed by the authoritarian and restrictive politics of the monarchy. The democratization of the political system in 1990 for the first time provided the necessary preconditions for civil society organizations. The then fundamentally improving education, the development of free and independent media and the work of numerous NGOs have contributed that civil society became a powerful and influential instrument within only fifteen years.

The third characteristic factor are the external influences. Conditional upon Nepal's geographical location and historical developments, India has to be mentioned in the first place here. Even today, Indian politicians find it hard to accept that Nepal has always been an independent state. In the early 1950s, the weakness and inexperience of the party politicians allowed massive Indian intervention into Nepali politics. This changed in 1955 when King Mahendra ascended the throne. He saw the danger potential of intensive Indian influence, but at the same time he also regarded the democratic Indian state as a potential threat to his endeavour for absolutist power. So, a special distance to India became one of the characteristic features of the new national identity which Mahendra provided to the country. Since then has more democracy always been equalled with surrender to India by the monarchy and the feudal circles. As a consequence has Nepal's relationship to India two faces till today. On the one side is India the most important partner for development aid and has

[5] Originally, this party called itself Nepal Communist Party (NCP), a term that is still used in the Nepali form of the party name (Nepal Kamyunist Parti). From 1990 onwards, the English term Communist Party of Nepal prevailed. To avoid confusion, I only use this latter spelling here.

[6] In the hierarchical system of Hindu society, they are called Tagadhari (wearers of the holy thread). I use this term further on to avoid the complicated paraphrase 'so-called higher Hindu castes'.

supported Nepal's democratic forces in very critical phases.[7] On the other side has India often made Nepal feel its dependency, so during negotiations on trade and transit rights, in Nepal's efforts to cooperate with China, or time and again in context with the use of Himalayan water resources. Also in 2006 was India active when the institution of monarchy was to put in its place or when the peace process with the Maoists was to get moving. On the other hand failed India after Gyanendra stepped down from his powers, when it was necessary to participate the Maoists in power to safeguard the peace process. Then India repeatedly turned out to be an impediment by closely cooperating with the US government.

The fourth feature of modern Nepali history after 1950 have been the numerous compromises for which the democratic forces, i. e. mainly the political parties, have let themselves in with the traditionalist circles whose outstanding symbol is the Hindu monarchy. Until today, Nepal has not been able to draw a line under a single epoch of the past. Rather it has always retained inherited problems, what by turns has frustrated every new beginning. For example, the end of the Rana system in 1950/1 has been termed as 'revolution' (*kranti*) in Nepali history books though the most decisive agreement, the so-called Delhi compromize that was mediated by Indian Prime Minister Nehru, only intended a quick end of the militant conflict between Rana and Nepali Congress troops. The Ranas, for the time being, were further participated in the government; the Rana prime minister remained in office; there were no claims on the Rana's privileges and properties, that had been amounted by them on the people's expense; and there was no reviewing of the injustices, discriminations and crimes of the Rana times. Even democratic India backed more the traditionalist force of monarchy than the young political parties. The consequences are well-known: After only ten years of cautious democratic experiences King Mahendra reinstalled absolute monarchy by a coup d'état and set back democratization for decades.

When Mahendra's son, King Birendra, announced a national referendum on the future system of government on 24 May 1979, the democratic forces got a second chance to get even with the traditionalists. But once again, the leaders of the different political parties were not able or willing to cooperate. Even internationally recognized personalities like B.P. Koirala, the chairman of the Nepali Congress, preferred to speculate on his chances of becoming the prime minister of an interim government that would possibly be formed after the referendum instead of trying to coordinate the efforts of the democratic forces. Even after the lost referendum, did this outstanding leader, who was already suffering from poor health, not distance himself from the royal regime but, instead, initiated the so-called politics of national reconciliation, a slogan that buzzes around in the minds of the leading Congress politicians till today and prevents the understanding of necessary dissociations and changes.

The events of early 1990 introduced by far greater changes than the 'revolution' of 1950/1 had done which had only been the work of some elitist circles. Nevertheless is the movement of 1990 simply called a 'people's movement' (*jana andolan*) what, on the other side, reflects the important role that the general people had played. For the first time had the two main democratic forces, the Nepali Congress and an alliance of communist splinter groups, the United Left Front, been able to join for a common movement. In fact, this movement was

[7] For example in 1950/1 when Rana rule was abolished, in the early 1960s after the putsch of King Mahendra when India supported the oppositional activities of the Nepali Congress, in the phase of the national referendum on the future of the Panchayat system in 1979/80, or in 1990 during the first Jana Andolan (people's movement).

able to make King Birendra give up his claim to absolutist power and to accept the role of a constitutional monarch.

Both party camps agreed to institutionalize a democratic system of state but they already disagreed in how far the changes should go. It turned out that the party elites that were overwhelmingly dominated by male Tagadharis were deeply rooted in their own system of values and world view. As a consequence, the party leaders once again made great compromises with the traditionalists and the necessary reviewing of the Panchayat era was avoided. So, persons who had been chief responsible for the politics of suppression by the non-party royal regime could smoothly run on to become "democratic" leaders of the new system. This happened either within the newly founded conservative National Democratic Party (Rastriya Prajatantra Party or RPP) or within the Nepali Congress that welcomed former Panchas with open arms. The monarchy, as well, retained a powerful position that went far beyond that of a merely constitutional monarch. Instead of making Nepal a modern democratic state, the party leaders clung to defining Nepal as a Hindu state, i. e. the foundations of the state remained linked to the culture and thinking of the ruling elite.[8] This prevented the establishment of an inclusive state with which all social groups of the country could identify. A number of discriminations were already written into the constitution of 1990. So were on the first view well defined fundamental rights limited by principles of the Hindu state. A system of reservations for disadvantaged groups, as it is practiced in India, was rejected by the male Tagadhari elite. There was only a small concession towards female candidates in parliamentary elections but the grotesque number of 5% female candidates was never exceeded by any of the political parties in the three parliamentary elections after 1990.[9] All parties failed to adopt internal democratic structures. So, the leadership of the parties remained firmly under the control of the traditional male elites. Women, ethnic groups, Dalits and Madhesis (the Tarai population of Indian origin), i. e. more than 80% of the total population, remained excluded as before. At the same time missed the persons in power to fulfil the directive principles and policies of the state as they were prescribed by the constitution to guarantee an integrative and just system of state. All this was a fertile soil for revolutionary ideas.

Parties and Politicians: The Failure of the System of 1990

The constitution of 1990 has laid sovereignty into the hands of the people. The people got the chance to take influence upon the political, economic and social state formation and development by general and free elections, and they could control the elected representatives of the parties. After 1990 the people could make use of this right three times in parliamentary and twice in local elections. The participation in the elections by over 60% may be proof enough that the people were willing to play their political part. With the exception of the local elections of 1997 all elections can be called peaceful. Disturbances did not arise from the

---

[8] I must underline that this is understood here as a mere political term. Hindu nationalist and conservative groups tend to equate critics in the Hindu state with an attack on Hindu religion. Hinduism has never been defined as state religion in Nepal. Only the foundations of state and society became bounded up with the responding thinking of the Tagadhari state elite.

[9] Parliamentary elections under the 1990 system took place in May 1991, November 1994 and May 1999.

people but mainly from representatives of the political parties, and no party can acquit itself of guilt.

But even more impressive was the way the people have voted. Let us have a look at the parliamentary elections. In 1991 the people clearly voted in favour of the old traditional party of the Nepali Congress. It seems that the reason for this was not only the important role the party had played during the democracy movement of 1990 but also the memory of the glorious past of the NC: The people gave their vote for the same party that had been expelled from power by King Mahendra's coup d'état in 1960. In this context, it may be characteristic that irrespective of the many undemocratic features of the constitution of 1959 the NC of the 1990s always spoke of the restoration of democracy and not of its introduction. So in the eyes of many people the restoration of democracy was identical with the restoration of the political power of the Nepali Congress.

But the elections of 1991 had also some other aspects of fundamental importance. The developments of 1990 had produced great a number of parties, 20 of which took part in the first parliamentary elections. Contrary to expectations, the people with their clear vote avoided a stalemate in parliament. With the exception of very few parties, all the minor ones were totally ignored. The latter trend continued in the 1994 elections, when only five parties were able to win seats in parliament.

Another important feature of the 1991 elections was the crushing defeat of those forces that had "represented" the people under the Panchayat system. This defeat of the then two Rastriya Prajatantra Parties, which together only won four out of 205 seats, led to their unification in the aftermath of the elections.[10] In 1994 this conservative party obviously had recovered winning 20 seats and becoming the third strongest party-political force. This improvement of the RPP was not only caused by its formal unity but also by the peoples dissatisfaction with three and a half years of NC government.

And finally we have to mention the election of the CPN (UML) as main opposition party in 1991 and then as strongest party (according to seats) in 1994. Abroad, there had been lack of understanding for this election behaviour of the people at a time of world-wide decline of communist systems. Parts of the western press even wrote about political immaturity of the Nepali people. But there were several reasons why the people thought it necessary to vote for this party. First, the CPN (UML) had deviated from the traditional ideology of communist parties since its foundation in January 1991[11]. The party declared its support to constitutional monarchy, the multiparty system, parliamentarianism and even a free market economy on the basis of the constitution of 1990. Compared to other parties world-wide, the CPN (UML) had become more a social-democratic than a communist party, but it stuck to its name because of its historical development. Thus the party fulfilled a function, which at the times of B. P. Koirala had been that of the NC, while the NC of the 1990s in many aspects had become a liberal party, partly even right of the centre.

In a society characterized by poverty and socio-religious inequalities the people were looking for a kind of political representation that opened up perspectives and hopes for changing their fate. The masses in general had been deeply disappointed by the NC, and so

---

[10] Before their had been two separate parties under the same name led by Surya Bahadur Thapa or by Lokendra Bahadur Chand respectively.

[11] The two strongest parties of the United Left Front of 1990, CPN (Marxist) and CPN (Marxist-Leninist) united under the name CPN (Unified Marxist-Leninist) to have a better chance against the NC in the elections of May 1991.

they elected the party out of government in 1994. The NC was not only suffering from a distinct turn to the right, but it was also shaken by deep rooted interior problems. The few remaining personalities of the first hour – Girija Prasad Koirala, Krishna Prasad Bhattarai as well as Ganesh Man Singh who died in 1997 – had been fighting each other publicly punching below the belt since the elections of 1991, when the then interim Prime Minister Bhattarai was not elected and had to give way for Girija Prasad Koirala. Singh finally even left the party, Bhattarai handed over the NC presidency to Koirala and the latter facing a possible split of the party laid the leading role in parliament into the hands of a younger generation. But also the experiment to make Sher Bahadur Deuba the party leader for the years to come poorly failed. The one and a half years of his coalition government based on a majority of only one vote, overshadowed by corruption, nepotism and abuse of authority, led to the absolute low of the young Nepali democracy.

All political parties were facing problems with implementing intra-party democracy. Confining our view to the three leading parties we see that NC and RPP elected their presidents in a democratic manor, but then endowed them with enormous power. The persons responsible for the ideological line of the party, like the members of the central working committees, were not elected but nominated by the party president on his own decision. Krishna Prasad Bhattarai even delayed these nominations for many months at a time of greatest conflict within the party. Only within the CPN (UML) the central committee was directly elected by the national congress, towards which it was responsible. The undemocratic structure of the leading parties made the introduction of a broad based and equal participation of all strata of society even more difficult. Only the established party elites, which in all parties mainly belonged to the Bahuns and Chhetris, decided, if other groups of society were allowed to participate or not, for example when election candidates had to be nominated. This was for the disadvantage of those groups that already had been disadvantaged before the advent of democracy: the ethnic groups, the Dalits (the so-called untouchables), the women in general and the Tarai population.

With greater parts of the people still having no positive perspectives, the leading parties steadily lost control. One of the best symbols was the fate of the NC. Being the strongest party in parliament in 1991 with an absolute majority of seats and winning the local elections of 1992 with about 60% of the seats, the party had been falling into an abyss. In November 1994 the NC lost its majority of seats in parliament and in May 1997 it was swept out of the local bodies securing only 30% of the seats.[12] The split of the CPN (UML) in March 1998 again made the NC the strongest party in parliament. Girija Prasad Koirala became prime minister for a second time, first as head of a NC minority government, then as leader of a coalition with the CPN-ML, the splinter group of the CPN (UML), and finally as prime minister of a coalition of NC, CPN (UML) and Nepal Sadbhavana Party (NSP). As the 1999 general elections approached, Koirala even presented his party rival Krishna Prasad Bhattarai, who so far had lost three elections, as the coming prime minister of Nepal.

The conservative forces represented by the RPP had been in an upward trend since the local elections of 1992, irrespective of their participation in the Deuba government, for whose failure the RPP had been especially responsible. But like the NC, the RPP, too, was split into two camps headed by Lokendra Bahadur Chand and Surya Bahadur Thapa respectively. Both of them led coalition governments in 1997/98. First Chand was prime minister of the absurd

[12] The local elections of 1997 were won by the CPN (UML) with about 52%. The RPP slightly improved to 10%.

coalition government of RPP and CPN (UML) that had been forced by the CPN (UML) rebel Bam Dev Gautam. After half a year, this coalition was brought down on the intention of Chand's party colleague and president, Surya Bahadur Thapa, who then headed a coalition government of RPP, NC and NSP. This government was again brought down, when Chand split his party forming the so-called New RPP in early 1998.

The main beneficiary of the negative trend of the NC was the CPN (UML). Several reasons could be mentioned in this context. Nepal's masses were living in great poverty. It was under the first government of Girija Prasad Koirala that the people recognised, that the NC was no longer a party representing the interests of the poverty stricken and backward strata of society. This position became more and more filled by the CPN (UML) whose verbal ideology was concentrated on the hardships of the poor. This had already been decisive for the party's success in the parliamentary elections of 1994. The minority government of Man Mohan Adhikari, which lasted for only nine months, initiated such great a number of populist measures in interest of the rural masses, that the NC saw no other chance but to overthrow the government, if it did not want to loose possible mid-term elections that were speculated on. Even the later coalition of the CPN (UML) with the rightist RPP did not bring any harm to the party in the eyes of the people, as the great success in the local elections of 1997 has shown.

But the politics of the CPN (UML), too, became more and more guided by power ambitions. One prove may have been the already mentioned coalition with the RPP accepting a former *pancha* as prime minister. Another evidence was the intra-party struggle and later split of the party initiated by Bam Dev Gautam. For sure, the party still had internal problems with the integration of radical communist forces into a more and more social-democratic party conception. So, similar to the NC and the RPP the CPN (UML) was suffering from internal tensions, conflicts and power struggles. Such insufficiencies of the leading parties were increasingly provoking activities of radical extra-parliamentary forces.

Four and half years als chaotic coalition politics with unclear majorities were ended by the parliamentary elections of May 1999. The NC won an absolute majority with 111 MPs out of a total of 205. Krishna Prasad Bhattarai could win parliamentary elections for the first time and became the new Prime Minister. Another fact of the results was that the CPN (UML) became a strong opposition party with 71 MPs. One could ask if Nepal was on her way to a two-party system. The RPP of Surya Bahadur Thapa faced a strong set-back winning only 11 seats.

Unmistakable was the popular vote against both the great splinter groups CPN-ML and RPP (Chand). In spite of their huge number of candidates, both parties were strongly neglected by the voters compared to their respective mother parties. Both did not win a single seat. It appeared as some kind of punishment for the splitting of their parties. This was especially true for the CPN-ML, where prominent candidates like Sahana Pradhan, Padma Ratna Tuladhar, Chandra Prakash Mainali, Bam Dev Gautam and Radha Krishna Mainali lost their traditional strongholds far behind other candidates.

So, the overwhelming victory of the NC was simply the expression of the clear political will of the voters, if one believed in the statements of NC leaders or some press comments. But the careful analysis of the results provided another picture. According to the number of mandates, the CPN (UML) for the first time had become the strongest party in the House of Representatives in 1994. This depended upon the Nepali plurality system with single-member constituencies. According to the number of votes, the NC had still been the strongest party in

1994. And this was even true in 1999, if you compared it to the votes of the CPN (UML) only. But a comparison to 1994 was only realistic if one included the votes for the CPN-ML. Then it became clear that the UML, in case it had not split, for the first time would have won clearly more votes than the NC.

And if you went even further and compared the figures of each and every constituency, then it became clear that the split of the CPN (UML) had influenced the outcome of the 1999 elections in a most decisive manor. In not less than 42 constituencies, the NC could only win because the candidates of CPN (UML) and CPN-ML rivalled each other. Without splitting, the CPN (UML) would have won another 3 seats from the RPP respectively NSP. In other words: If Bam Dev Gautam and his followers had not split the party in 1998, the CPN (UML) would have been the clear winner of the elections according to votes as well as mandates. Thus, the trend towards the left that was visible from the two earlier elections was continued in the 1999 elections.

Table 1. Parliamentary elections 1991-99

Party	absolute figures						percentage					
	votes			seats			votes			seats		
	1991	1994	1999	1991	1994	1999	1991	1994	1999	1991	1994	1999
NC	2752452	2545287	3214786	110	83	111	39.5	34.5	37.2	53.7	40.5	54.1
CPN (UML)	2040102	2352601	2734568	69	88	71	29.3	31.9	31.6	33.7	42.9	34.6
CPN (ML)			567760			0			6.6			
CPN (UML+ML)			3302328			71	0.0	0.0	38.2	0.0	0.0	34.6
RPP		1367148			20			18.5				
RPP (Thapa)	392499		902328	1		11	5.6	•	10.4			
RPP (Chand)	478604		295812	3		0	6.9		3.4			
RPP (Thapa + Chand)	871103		1198140	4		11	12.5	0.0	13.9	2.0	0.0	5.4
SJMN	351904	100285	74669	9	0	1	5.0	1.4	0.9	4.4	0.0	0.5
NSP	298610	265847	278435	6	3	5	4.3	3.6	3.2	2.9	1.5	2.4
NMKP	91335	75072	48685	2	4	1	1.3	1.0	0.6	1.0	2.0	0.5
RJMN			121426			5	0.0	0.0	1.4	0.0	0.0	2.4
RJMM/RJMP	34509	79996	94860	0	0	0	0.5	1.1	1.1	0.0	0.0	0.0
Other parties	225323	126717		2	0	0	3.2	1.7	0.0	1.0	0.0	0.0
Independents	303723	471324	251930	3	7	0	4.4	6.4	2.9	1.5	3.4	0.0
entitled to vote	11191777	12327329	13518839				100.0	100.0	100.0			
votes cast	7291084	7625348	8894566				65.1	61.9	65.8			
invalid votes	322023	241071	244902				4.4	3.2	2.8			
valid votes	6969061	7384277	8649664				95.6	96.8	97.2			

Source: Krämer, Karl-Heinz. Elections in Nepal: 1999 and before. In: Human Rights Yearbook 2000, pp. 29-47, Kathmandu: INSEC 2000.

The Maoist Insurgency

Influenced by the Naxalite Movement led by Charu Majumdar and Kanu Sanyal in neighbouring Darjeeling District of India and inspired by Mao's Cultural Revolution, radical ideas had entered Southeast Nepal in the late 1960s. Jhapali Samuha (Jhapali group), one of the far extremist communist groups, beheaded some landlords in Jhapa District in 1972 and attempted to seize power by force. This group started a single-stage revolution adopting a militant line to finish their class enemies, especially the landlords. In sharp contrast to the past they were successful in capturing national and international attention by changing the focus of

Nepali communism, which was sporadic but effectual. The movement was led by Mohan Chandra Adhikari, a former disciple of Pushpa Lal Shrestha, the founder of the CPN. It was the first real peasant revolt in Nepal based on Marxists' line.

This was followed by a period of gradual unification among the extremists working under different names but for the same purpose. Some of these groups came closer and formed the All Nepal Communist Revolutionary Coordination Committee in June 1975, a forerunner organization of the CPN (Marxist-Leninist or CPN-ML), which was founded on 26 December 1978. At that time, there was a growing conviction that national liberation could be reached close to the Chinese model. So, the radical leaders took the option of violent action to solve the political, social and economic problems of the country.

While the initially radical CPN-ML later transformed into a democratic force[13], other left groups remained true to their radical principles. A so-called Central Nucleus had been formed in December 1971 to reunite the different communist splinter groups. The Nucleus was not successful and later split itself when Mohan Bikram Singh organized his own fourth party congress in India in September 1974. He named this new group as CPN (Fourth Congress). This party comprised of radical revolutionaries who more and more distanced themselves from other communist groups.

Mohan Bikram Singh had become a member of the CC of the CPN in 1957. After the dissolution of parliament in 1960 he was imprisoned until 1971. After that he worked in underground or from India. By the time, he identified more with the ideas of the Revolutionary International Movement (RIM). The latter called the post-Mao Chinese politics as reactionary and counter-revolutionary.

Another split of this left extremist party occurred in 1986 when a small group under the leadership of Nirmal Lama retained the name CPN (Fourth Congress) while the bigger group around Mohan Bikram Singh formed CPN (Masal). This partition was caused by different opinions about the question of participation in the second direct elections for the Rastriya Panchayat (National Legislature). While Lama saw the participation as a means to fight the Panchayat system and to destroy the feudal forces, for Singh, on the other hand, India was the main enemy – all democratic developments in Nepal after 1950 would be part of the reactionary spread of Indian hegemony. He called for "total revolution" and rejected all kinds of cooperation with other forces to bring down the Panchayat system. CPN (Masal) split again in 1987 when a group under the leadership of Mohan Vaidya called itself CPN (Mashal).

After the successful multiparty movement of early 1990 Vaidya's CPN (Mashal), Lama's CPN (Fourth Congress) and another splinter group of CPN (Masal) run by Sital Kumar joined loosely under the name CPN (Unity Centre). The political wing of the Maoist centre was the United People's Front Nepal (UPFN) or Samyukta Jana Morcha Nepal. It won nine seats with about five percent popular votes in the parliamentary elections of 1991 and became the third strongest force in the Pratiniddhi Sabha, Nepal's House of Representatives.

The break-up of the Unity Centre in 1993, however, ended its fortune to become an effective political force. Not only that, in following days it split into two groups led by Babu Ram Bhattarai and Niranjan Govinda Vaidya respectively. The Election Commission (EC)

---

[13] The CPN (ML) was one of the main groups of the United Left Front during the people's movement of 1990. In January 1991, it united with the CPN (Marxist) to form the CPN (UML, which together with the NC became the most important party of the political system of 1990.

recognized Vaidya as the official successor organization of the original UPFN and allowed it to take part in the elctions of November 1994. Similarly, the group led by Bhattarai changed its name into Revolutionary Joint People's Front or Krantikari Samyukta Jana Morcha in July 1995.

The group around Lama retook its old name CPN (Fourth Congress) after the break-up of the Unity Centre. Similarly, another splinter group of CPN (Masal) led by Pushpa Kamal Dahal, better known as Comrade Prachanda, called itself CPN (Maoist) in February 1995. It was later merged with Baburam Bhattarai's front.

In late 1995, the CPN (Maoist) tried to built up its organization in the districts of Rukum and Rolpa in mid-western Nepal. A police operation under the name 'Operation Romeo' was launched by the government of Sher Bahadur Deuba to prevent this. It was supported by the local NC leaders. On 4 February 1996, the CPN (Maoist) approached the government with a catalogue of 40 demands.[14] When the Prime Minister Deuba totally disregarded these demands, the Maoists initiated their so-called *jana yuddha* (people's war).

During the next years the conflict remained restricted to the local level of a few regions of the country. So-called 'people's actions' as parts of cultural events served more for the information of the people than for militant activities. But when the Maoists established 'guerilla zones', the 'elimination of enemies' became an integral part of their politics.[15] Part of the third plan (June 1997 - June 1998) was the boycott of the local elections and the dissolution of Village Development Committees (VDC). This made the governance of rural areas more and more ineffective. The violent police operation 'Kilo Sierra II' was the reaction of the state in May 1998 which brought the conflict to a new level of brutality. The Maoists, on their side, felt the necessity to build up their People's Liberation Army (PLA) to meet the police activities. From February 1999 onwards, the PLA began to operate in the 20 districts that were under the control of the Maoists then. It served to force bandhs and to attack and raid police posts.

The Maoists now controlled administration, judiciary and education system in many rural areas. They intimidated local officials or forced them to leave their villages. The police forces proved unable to stop the extension of Maoist influence. This was also a time when the Maoists more and more identified with the intentions and demands of disadvantaged sections of society such as Janajatis, Dalits, Madhesis and women.

The attack on Dunai, the headquarter of Rolpa district, marked another level of the conflict. Prime Minister Koirala wanted to mobilize the army but he was obviously prevented to do so by King Birendra, the supreme commander of the army. The year 2001 marked another escalation. Shortly after the palace massacre of 1 June in which the whole family of King Birendra was extinguished, Koirala had to resign and was replaced by Sher Bahadur Deuba. The latter initiated a direct dialogue with the Maoists which meant a ceasefire for about four months. But contrary to the Maoists, the government did not have a clear agenda and so the talks failed. Severe Maoists attacks on Gorahi, Syangja and Salleri caused the government to declare a state of emergence and to directly involve the army.

---

[14] Most of these demands were similar to the principles of state politics as they were mentioned in the constitution. Hardly any of the governments after 1990 has ever tried to adjust its politics to these principles.

[15] Officially, this had been declared part of their second plan (March 1996 to June 1997).

It was then that the conflict had to be called a civil war. Those who suffered most was the civil society that had to fear Maoist attacks in the same way as brutal excesses by the army.[16] There was hardly any district that was not affected by the conflict. Both parties in conflict acted with brute force and totally disregarded basic human rights. Until the end of the peace dialogue, 1700 people had been killed, 976 of them by security forces and 724 by the Maoists. Between 23 November 2001 and 30 November 2005 alone, another 11165 persons were killed, 7307 by the army and 3858 by the Maoists.[17] This meant that the army was to blame for most of the victims. Many people were simply killed purely on suspicion to be Maoists or to support the Maoists in one or the other way. This often happened after being arrested.

Sources on other kinds of victims were unreliable. The great number of land mines as used by the Maoists were a great danger for the civil society, especially the children. Besides, Nepal became one of the countries with most disappearances worldwide. Once again, the security forces were most responsible.[18] There was also a great number of conflict refugees. These people mainly migrated to urban centres inside Nepal, most of all to the Kathmandu valley, but also to bordering Indian towns. The Nepali human rights organization Informal Sector Service Centre (INSEC) counted 38,191 such refugees[19] but it is believed that a lot more persons were affected.[20] Youths and young adults ran the greatest risk because the Maoists wanted them as cadres and the army generally suspected them to be Maoist sympathizers.[21]

Though the Maoist guerilla units were spread over the whole country and may have faced a number of communication problems, they nevertheless exactly followed the guidelines as they had been laid down in Mao's book on guerilla warfare.[22] One of the clever moves of the Maoists was that they adopted the arguments of the elites of the disadvantaged population groups whose organizations had started a peaceful dialogue for equal rights and participation with the central government in Kathmandu.[23] Part of this politics was the division of the Nepali territory into so-called autonomous regions along ethnic lines. The Maoists installed 'autonomous governments' in these 'autonomous regions' and, thus, ran some kind of parallel

---

[16] International Crisis Group, Nepal's Royal Coup: Making a Bad Situation Worse, Asia Report N°91, 9 February 2005, p. 4, http://www.crisisgroup.org/home/index.cfm?l=1&id=3260

[17] Evaluations by Informal Sector Service Centre (INSEC) in Kathmandu, http://www.inseconline.org/download/Killings_Data.html (viewed on 25 December 2005)

[18] Amnesty International, Nepal: Escalating "disappearances" amid a culture of impunity, ASA 31/155/2004, 30 August 2004, http://web.amnesty.org/library/Index/ENGASA311552004?open&of=ENG-NPL. Human Rights Watch, Clear Culpability: "Disappearances" by Security Forces in Nepal, February 2005, http://hrw.org/reports/2005/nepal0205/

[19] INSEC website: http://www.inseconline.org/download/Killings_Data.html#Conflict-induced_Displacement

[20] Walter Kälin who had been sent to Nepal as a special envoy for human rights by the UN General Secretary in April 2005 estimated their number at 100-200,000 persons. The Kathmandu based Community Study and Welfare Centre (CSWC) even spoke of about 0.5 – 1.2 million internal refugees, see Pradhan, Suman. Refugee Crisis Builds Up as Civil War Rages On, Inter Press Service, 12 July 2005, http://ipsnews.org/news.asp?idnews=29465

[21] Amnesty International, Nepal: Children caught in the conflict, AI Index: ASA 31/054/2005, 26 July 2005, http://web.amnesty.org/library/Index/ENGASA310542005

[22] Mao Tse-tung, On Guerilla Warfare, 1937, http://www.marxists.org/reference/archive/mao/works/ 1937/guerrilla-warfare/index.htm

[23] Krämer, Karl-Heinz. 1996. Ethnizität und nationale Integration in Nepal: Eine Untersuchung zur Politisierung der ethnischen Gruppen im modernen Nepal. Stuttgart: Franz Steiner. In recent years, the Dalits have adopted a similar approach, see http://www.nepaldalitinfo.20m.com/

state. They tried to influence the run of development projects by demanding that the NGOs and INGOs registered with the 'autonomous governments'.[24]

Many Maoist steps dragged a great number of people into the conflict, like forced recruitment mainly of young persons, extortion of 'donations' from private persons as well as businessmen, forced food and shelter for Maoist fighters in private homes, and spying on civil society. The latter faced Maoist accusations they would cooperate with the security forces. The consequence was beating, torture and even murder by the Maoists. But the reaction of the army towards persons who had been forced to cooperate with the Maoists was not different. In the final phase, the Maoists abducted students and teachers of rural schools, sometimes in thousands, and indoctrinated them in special camps for days or even weeks. In the worst case, they forced children to join their army as fighters.[25]

The Maoists only changed their tactics in 2005 after King Gyanendra had concluded his coup d'état . The pressure of civil society groups brought the CPN (Maoist) and the other political parties closer to each other. The one-sided ceasefire, that was declared by the Maoists in early September 2005 and that was not joint by the royal army, opened the way for direct talks with the other parties in New Delhi, obviously with approval of the Indian government. On 22 November 2005 they concluded an agreement with seven parties[26] that had joined against the royal autocracy with the aim to fight the royal regime unitedly.[27] This meant a departure from the Maoist path of militancy which they had followed for almost ten years.[28]

[24] International Crisis Group, 9 February 2005, p. 5. As an example for conflict related problems of development organizations see: Joint Assessment of Selected Sectors of Development Work in Nepal and its Impact on Conflict and Peace. Published by the Commissioning Agencies EED, FES, GTZ, MISEREOR, SEQUA, June 2005,
http://fesportal.fes.de/pls/portal30/docs/FOLDER/WORLDWIDE/ASIEN/BERICHTE/BERICHTE2005/NEPAL0605_KONFLIKTSTUDIE.PDF

[25] See, for example, http://www.reliefweb.int/rw/RWB.NSF/db900SID/DPAS-6KCDSH?OpenDocument. It must be mentioned in this context that the security forces, as well, employed youths. see „NGO helps end child soldier hire in Nepal", http://news.webindia123.com/news/showdetails.asp?id=192791&cat=Asia

[26] Nepali Congress, Nepali Congress (Democratic), CPN (UML), Nepal Majdur Kisan Party, Nepal Sadbhavana Party (Ananda Devi), Jana Morcha Nepal, Samyukta Bam Morcha

[27] http://nepalresearch.org/coup_2005/papers/maoists_parties_agreement_051122.pdf

[28] International Crisis Group, Nepal's New Alliance: The Mainstream Parties and the Maoists, Asia Report N°106, 28 November 2005, http://www.crisisgroup.org/library/documents/asia/south_asia/ 106_nepal_s_ new_alliance_the_mainstream_parties_and_the_maoists.pdf. The are numerous books and reports that deal with the Maoists and their insurgency in Nepal. As outstanding examples shall be mentioned: Hutt, Michael (ed.), *Himalayan people's war: Nepal's Maoist rebellion*, London: Hurst and Co., 2004. Thapa, Deepak (ed.), *Understanding the Maoist movement of Nepal*, Kathmandu: Martin Chautari, 2003. Thapa, Deepak with Bandita Sijapati, *A kingdom under siege: Nepal's Maoist insurgency, 1996-2003*, Kathmandu: The Printhouse, 2003. Shrestha, Chuda Bahadur, *Nepal: coping with Maoist insurgency*, Kathmandu: Chetana Lokshum, 2004. Karki, Arjun and David Seddon (eds.), *The people's war in Nepal: left perspectives*, New Delhi: Adroit, 2003. Upreti, Bishnu Raj, *The price of neglect: from resource conflict to Maoist insurgency in the Himalayan kingdom*, Kathmandu: Bhrikuti Academic Publications, 2004. Karki, Arjun and Binod Bhattarai (eds.), *Whose war? Economic and socio-cultural impacts of Nepal's Maoist-government conflict*, Kathmandu: NGO Federation of Nepal, 2004. Pyakurel, Uddhab P. Maoist movement in Nepal: a sociological perspective. New Delhi: Adroit Publishers 2007. A detailed analysis of the CPN (Maoist) at the end of their militant phase is provided by International Crisis Group, Nepal's Maoists: Their Arms, Structure and Strategy. Asia Report N°104, 27 October 2005, http://www.crisisgroup.org/library/documents/asia/south_asia/ 104_nepal_s_ maoists_their_aims_structure_and_strategy.pdf

Failure of the Parties after 1999 and the Royal Putsch

The institution of monarchy had been in the focus of politics ever since the Rana system had been abolished in 1951. Four kings have been in responsibility during this little bit more than half a century. King Tribhuvan had already been ill in the last four years of his reign. In 1955, he was followed on the throne by his eldest son Mahendra who had the 'honour' to finish the process of democratic experiments for three decades through a coup d'état that was supported by the royal army. He and, after 1972, his son Birendra controlled the land with a strong hand suppressing liberal democratic ideas and many fundamental rights.

Birendra seems to have become milder and wiser after he had been forced to give up his absolutist power after the Jana Andolan of 1990. I would even say that he has fulfilled his tasks of a constitutional monarch in a good way. The failure of the 1990 system has not been caused by the monarchy but by the leaders of the political parties.

The palace massacre of 1 June 2001 must be seen as the beginning of the end of monarchy. It's useless to discuss this event here in detail. Many books and articles have been published with the official story that Crown Prince Dipendra has killed his parents, brother and sister as well as some other relatives and that he later died of the injuries he had caused himself. But there are as many other versions that speculate on possible conspiracies. The truth will probably never come out because those who were in responsible position when the massacre took place, never tried to bring the truth to light or even prevented this specifically. Mentioned must be in this context the new king Gyanendra, his son Paras and other royal relatives who were present and survived, the army leadership whose soldiers were also present in the palace in very great number, and the government under Prime Minister Koirala who failed to have a thorough examination of the event.

Today, we must speak of the seven years of King Gyanendra as monarch as an epilogue of monarchy. Gyanendra. who was rather unpopular compared to his brother Birendra, obviously tried to stop the course of history and to return to the 'glorious' days of royal power under his father Mahendra. He even repeated his father's way by staging a coup d'état in two steps.

The royal massacre of 2001 and its aftermath further complicated the already critical situation. Right from his accession to the throne, King Gyanendra claimed that he wanted to be an active monarch. After the previous government of Sher Bahadur Deuba had dissolved parliament and local bodies, King Gyanendra finally finished the constitution on 4 October 2002 by grabbing sovereignty and executive powers. The illegitimate and incompetent government, installed by him one week later, was neither able to solve the Maoist conflict nor to restore democratic structures. Instead, the conflict was now between three forces: Maoists, other political parties and monarchy/security forces.

I have already mentioned the lack of participation and integration of greater sections of society. This has to do with the history and ways of state formation in Nepal. The stratified social system has once been applied and legalized by the ancestors of King Gyanendra and their high caste supporters. It still exists in the minds of many of the political leaders[29], and it

---

[29] This is proved by many of their behaviour patterns and attitudes, e.g. their total disregard of Dalits when positions within the party, the government or any other state institutions are to be filled; their missing understanding for the arguments and demands of the disadvantaged groups of society; their incredible argumentation why women cannot have the same rights as men; or their almost complete failure to identify social inequalities as one of the most important reasons for political turmoil.

is reflected by some articles of the 1990 constitution and numerous subordinate laws. Those affected most are the members of ethnic groups, Dalits, Madhesis and the women in general.

The continuously high growth rate of population combined with better education has given rise to further tensions. Every year, hundreds of thousands of young people leave schools with their SLC dreaming of a better live, and many others leave with a failed SLC, which is even worse. For many of them, there are no jobs and perspectives, especially for those of disadvantaged population groups. Thanks to their education, they are aware of their rights and of the deplorable state of affairs in Nepal. These young folks have become a fertile breeding ground for revolutionary movements like that of the Maoists after 1990.

At this point, we must also mention the consequences of September 11 on Nepal. On the one hand, used then Prime Minister Deuba the chance to jump on the American bandwagon and tried to get foreign support for a forceful suppression of the Maoist insurgency. On the other hand, misunderstood the American government that this conflict had nothing to do with international terrorism, but that it was homemade because of the numerous reasons mentioned above. The obvious American pressure not to take the movement as a political but as a terrorist issue further complicated ways to a solution.

Nepal was in a state of lawlessness in early October 2002 with a more and more violent and escalating Maoist conflict, and power striving and irresponsible politicians that had brought all democratic institutions to a standstill. There was neither a democratically elected parliament nor were there local bodies nor was it possible to hold elections to these institutions in a foreseeable time. In other words, the people could no longer be called sovereign. The constitution of 1990 was already almost dead when King Gyanendra finally delivered the deathblow on October 4, 2002. There has been a heated debate in the following months with the king claiming to have acted on the basis of the constitution and the party leaders calling the royal step unconstitutional. I think that both were partly right and partly wrong, and I will explain this a little bit more.

In his October 4 proclamation, Gyanendra claimed that monarchy has always been guided by the wishes and aspirations of the people. This was a simple phrase as it has often been used by Nepali monarchs to justify their steps. It had to do with the Hindu tradition of monarchy. According to this tradition, the king may be absolute in his aspects of power but he is bound to the well-being of his subjects. This is part of his royal duty (*rajadharma*)[30]. In modern times, Nepali kings have used such kind of phrase at very critical moments, e. g. King Tribhuvan in 1951 after the ousting of the Rana system, King Mahendra at the time of his putsch of December 15, 1960, King Birendra when he announced a referendum on May 24, 1979, and King Gyanendra after the royal massacre of June 1, 2001. So, this phrase as such did not have the meaning it pretended. First of all, it was a hint that the institution of monarchy was under high pressure to undertake steps that might influence this institution in the long run.

In the same way did the commitment to democracy mean little. This phrase had also been in use during *panchayat* times when monarchy played an absolute role of representing and

[30] Hacker, Paul. Der Dharma-Begriff des Neuhinduismus. Zeitschrift für Missions- und Religionswissenschaft 42:1-15 (1958). Hacker, Paul. Dharma im Hinduismus. Zeitschrift für Missions- und Religionswissenschaft 49:93-106 (1965). Krämer, Karl-Heinz. Der politische Hinduismus von Nepal unter besonderer Berücksichtigung des Königtums. Unpublished M.A. thesis, University of Bonn 1978. Krämer, Karl-Heinz. Das Königtum in der modernen nepalischen Geschichte: Ein Beitrag zum Verständnis hinduistischer Politik in Nepal. Sankt Augustin: VGH Wissenschaftsverlag 1981.

controlling executive, legislative and judicial powers. The use of plural forms when the king was talking about himself, finally reminded of the traditional absolute position of the monarch. This may be explained by grammatical rules of the Nepali language, but these seem to have their reason in this kind of traditional thinking.

In the second paragraph of his October 4 address, King Gyanendra repeated his claim of solidarity with the aspect of welfare and promotion of the Nepali citizens but, this time, it became specifically connected to his Shah dynasty, which united Nepal in her current form by military expansion and subjugation of other territories between 1743 and 1816.[31] Following this pretended tradition of 'benevolent' Shah kings, King Gyanendra described the introduction of democracy in 1990[32] as one such benevolent act of the Shah kings. All those who observed the events of 1990 carefully found this interpretation quite disconcerting when they remembered how the institution of monarchy had come under pressure during the people's movement in spring 1990, especially during the great demonstration in front of the royal palace on April 6, 1990. Gyanendra's statement was further contradicting to the numerous attempts of the palace to save as much power as possible under the constitution promulgated on November 9, 1990. So, the institutional democratization of Nepal in 1990 was, in fact, not a benevolent and farsighted act of the Nepali monarchy, but it had to be forced out of monarchy by those who demonstrated on the streets, partly loosing their lives, and by their self-claimed representatives who organized the demonstrations and later entered into negotiations with the palace.

In his further statements, King Gyanendra correctly mentioned that, during the twelve years after 1990, a number of political exercises had been adopted for the consolidation of democracy. In some of these cases, the institution of monarchy had in so far been involved as it had been defined as royal executive and legislative tasks by the constitution of 1990. But contrary to the regulations of the Panchayat constitution of 1962, the king's executive and legislative rights and duties were exclusively those of a constitutional monarch. The king could only exercise executive power on the recommendation and advice, and with the consent of the council of ministers. In the same way could the king no longer completely refuse his assent to bills or even change such bills at his own discretion as it was normal during Panchayat days.

In his address of October 4, King Gyanendra referred to the dissolution of the House of Representatives which was accepted by him on the recommendation of Prime Minister Sher Bahadur Deuba. And also the setting of November 13 as election day happened on the recommendation of the prime minister. On August 6, the Supreme Court (SC) decided that

---

[31] Without any doubt, Nepal owes her independent existence to the military actions of Prithvinarayan Shah and his successors. But as every other ruler in history, he had first of all his own power and affluence in mind and not the farsightedness of a benevolent king who does everything for his subjects, as it has time and again been pretended by the Nepali kings and their supporters.

[32] The events of 1990 are usually called the reinstatement of democracy. During the 1950s Nepal had already faced a number of democratic experiments with young political parties favouring the introduction of a western type of democracy and a monarchy that, at the same time, managed to restore more and more of the absolute powers it had lost to the Ranas after 1846. There was only a small interval of democracy in 1959/60 with first general parliamentary elections and one and a half years of Nepali Congress government. But all this happened under a strong monarch Mahendra who still hold key positions of power under a constitution introduced by him in February 1959 only six days before the elections.

such kind of recommendation was a political prerogative of the prime minister.[33] In other words: the king had no other choice but to dissolve parliament.

Against this background, King Gyanendra was right when he denied any personal responsibility for the dissolution of parliament and the setting of the election date. The correct holding of these elections became the main task of Sher Bahadur Deuba who, after the dissolution of parliament, was no more than the leader of a caretaker government. King Gyanendra was further right in his claim that this caretaker prime minister had asked him to remove difficulties that had arisen in connection with the implementation of the constitutional rules according to article 127 of the constitution. The question is, if this situation justified the procedure of King Gyanendra in early October 2002.

First, it had to be decided in which way article 127 was to be applied. Naturally, this article could only be applied in cases that could not be solved by other regulations of the constitution. The article simply mentioned the king, i. e. the head of state, who could issue necessary orders to remove difficulties in the implementation of the constitution. Such orders had then to be laid before parliament. This already made clear that the king could not act independently from other constitutional bodies. Since the application of article 127 was an executive function, the fundamental rules of executive procedures had to be observed. This meant according to article 35 (2) that the king could only act on the advice and recommendation and with the consent of the Council of Ministers.[34] Besides, three conditions had to be fulfilled: the application of this power had to be objectively necessary and not subjectively desirable; the order to remove the difficulty had to be no more than necessary to remove it; the order should not have been incompatible with any other provision of the constitution.[35]

King Gyanendra, in application of article 127, removed caretaker Prime Minister Sher Bahadur Deuba and his Council of Ministers out of office. But this was neither the recommendation of the prime minister nor was it the constitutional difficulty that had arisen. The problem as forwarded by Deuba was simply that he could not fulfil the constitutional regulation to hold general elections within six months after the dissolution of the house of representatives as prescribed by article 53 (4). The reasons for this shortcoming were manifold. First, the situation of law and order in face of the Maoist insurgency was not so to hold elections in November 2002. Secondly, the SC took about two and a half months to decide on the correctness of the dissolution of the house of representatives. Thirdly, the three member Election Commission (EC), itself a constitutional body, delayed the important decision on the recognition of the split NC groups by more than three months. Fourthly, many oppositional politicians, especially Deuba's estranged former party president Girija Prasad Koirala who simply rejected the decision of the SC, did everything to hinder preparations for the elections.

---

[33] This decision of the Supreme Court came after contradictory decisions by the same institution in similar cases during the 1990s. In these earlier cases, the Supreme Court had gone into detail before it decided for one or the other side. In this way, the earlier decisions became strongly influenced by the political affiliation of the judges. With its recent decision, the Supreme Court has finally forged about the matter defining it as a political decision of the prime minister and thus keeping it out of future judicial quarrels.

[34] This view is confirmed by the most comprehensive commentary on the constitution (Dhungel, Surya P.S. / Adhikari, Bipin / Bhandari, B.P. / Murgatroyd, Chris. Commentary on the Nepalese constitution, p. 679. Kathmandu: DeLF 1998).

[35] Ibid., p. 680

Thus, a constitutional application of article 127 would have meant, for example, that the period of time for the holding of elections was extended by some months. And this was exactly what Deuba had recommended when he approached king Gyanendra. This would have been a strong intervention into the regulations of the constitution but, against the background of the circumstances, it would have been justified. Gyanendra fulfilled this recommendation, but only in the second position and not mentioning a time limit, which is regarded as necessary for the application of article 127.[36]

In the first position, King Gyanendra mentioned the removal of caretaker Prime Minister Sher Bahadur Deuba and his Council of Ministers. This brings us to the question if the monarch had any constitutional right to remove a prime minister from office. The answer was given by article 36 (5) of the constitution which mentions four reasons:

a) if he submits his resignation to the king,
b) if a no-confidence resolution has been passed by a majority of the total number of members of the House of Representatives
c) if he ceases to be a member of the House of Representatives
d) if he dies.

None of this happened, and other regulations were not found in the constitution. This leads to the conclusion that the removal of Prime Minister Sher Bahadur Deuba and his Council of Ministers was an unconstitutional act. Either King Gyanendra had been misguided concerning the monarch's constitutional role or he had acted fully aware of this breach of the constitution. In the latter case, his procedure would have been a putsch similar to that of his father in December 1960.

The final remarks of Gyanendra's address already had little to do with constitutional monarchy. He mentioned that he himself wanted to undertake the responsibility of governance and that he himself would exercise the executive powers. He asked the political parties for cooperation and recommendations concerning the composition of an interim council of ministers, and already set the conditions for the composition of this council. In other words, this was the end of constitutional monarchy and democracy. The council of ministers and political parties were treated as executive instruments that could be used by the king on his own discretion. Leaving the existence of political parties aside, we seemed to be back in Panchayat times. In contradiction to this, Gyanendra claimed that he would never allow any compromise on the commitment to constitutional monarchy and multiparty democracy.

In the end, Gyanendra left open how he wanted to make adequate arrangements for peace and security and to conduct the elections. More than ten months of mobilization of the army, whose supreme commander the king was, had brought nothing to improve the situation in the country. On the contrary, the political, social and cultural conditions in Nepal had never been worse than in the early years of the second millennium. If the state of emergency had proved anything, then that the conflict could never be solved by force.

But it would have been too easy to use King Gyanendra as a scapegoat for Nepal's political disaster, for he was not the only one who has broken constitutional rules after 1990. Unconstitutional behaviour and demanding had a tradition in institutionally democratized

[36] Ibid., pp. 680-1

Nepal. This could only partly be excused by the inexperience of the party politicians and the miserable conditions of the country. Personal ambitions and power hunger of party leaders, short-sightedness dependent on cultural and traditional conceptions, lacking participation of and missing understanding for disadvantaged sections of Nepal's multicultural society, all these were further reasons that had hampered the democratization process in Nepal.

Thus, I would claim that the constitution of 1990 and its political system was already dead when King Gyanendra took his step of October 4, 2002. And for this was not the king responsible but all the political parties including the CPN (Maoist). For the latter, it may have been some kind of success since they had fought to oust this system. Against this background, King Gyanendra's step could have been seen as a final stroke to allow a new beginning if he had interpreted his step in this way. In this case, his breaking of the constitution would have been to safeguard the interests and the well being of the people. But he did not explain it in this way. Instead, he claimed to act on the basis of the 1990 constitution in the interest of democracy. Besides, he used every chance to have the institution of monarchy being celebrated in an unacceptable way as it last happened in Panchayat times.

After this royal putsch, the crisis lingered for 28 months with only one phase of hope when Prime Minister Lokendra Bahadur Chand began a dialogue with the Maoists on 29 January 2003. But Chand soon lost the backing by king and army who obviously still believed in a military solution of the Maoist insurgency. Chand's successor Surya Bahadur Thapa was not even able to form a viable government. On 2 June 2004, King Gyanendra reinstalled Sher Bahadur Deuba as prime minister of a coalition government. The only success of this government was the fading of the street demonstrations that had been organized by the political parties in spring 2004.

This led King Gyanendra to tighten his assumption of power. On 1 February 2005, he dismissed the second Deuba led government within 28 months and took direct executive power in his own hands. This conclusion of his putsch was supported by the declaration of a state of emergency with a drastic restriction of fundamental and freedom rights, the arrest of numerous politicians, journalists, human rights activists, students and academicians. Police and army patrolled the streets of Kathmandu. All media were brought under state control with army officers censoring all important dailies and weeklies. The radio stations were hit especially hard. They were only allowed to transmit folk music; news and political comments were strictly prohibited. The royal government claimed that this would be normal in all free and democratic states. It took until August before the Supreme Court re-allowed the transmission of news by an interim order. All communication systems of the country were cut immediately after the royal putsch address that was transmitted through all channels. For one week, the people could get information only through foreign media like the BBC.

The new government was directly led by King Gyanendra. Once again, he declared that this happened on the basis of the constitution of 1990 and in the interest of the people to end the Maoists insurgency and to reinstate democracy within three years. Among his ministers, there were a number of former Panchas who had never joined any political party after 1990 and who had made no secret of the fact that they rejected a multiparty system of democracy and wished the return to royal non-party regime. Gyanendra nominated two of the greatest hardliners of the Panchayat system, Kirti Nidhi Bista and Tulsi Giri, as his representatives in the council of ministers. Both had served as prime ministers several times between 1961 and 1990, whenever the monarchy felt that it was necessary to tighten its grip.

The extension of the cabinet on 14 July 2005 resulted in new criticism from his opponents. Among other things, the king had justified the way he handled many party leaders with their corruption practices. He claimed that this was a special feature of the system of 1990 though it was well-known that the Panchayat system had not been less corrupt; on the contrary, the system of 1990 was more transparent so that many corruption cases became public. Interestingly, Gyanendra nominated a number of persons as ministers in July 2005, that had been convicted and punished for corruption and other criminal offences, up to attempted murder. This reduced the king's 'clean' politics to absurdity.

The solution of the Maoist conflict was Gyanendra's declared aim. Contrary to Deuba and his predecessors, the king was in total command of the security forces. Before, the army leadership had always made clear that it would accept orders only from the king. So, Gyanendra could have offered a direct dialogue with the Maoists while ordering the army to behave cautiously. But the king rejected all expert critics and exclusively backed a military solution of the conflict.

Under the constant army control and pressure, the strikes and demonstrations in the Kathmandu valley may have come to an end, but the rural situation was different. The army may have been successful with some of its initiatives against the Maoists but it could not prevent that the latter crippled the everyday life in other regions of the country at the same time. The Maoists also continued massive attacks against civil and military facilities. Also the grave human rights violations by army and Maoists did not change. While the majority of 95% living in rural areas still did not have any glimmer of hope for peace, had the 5% of the total population who lived in Kathmandu felt some kind of relief but they had to pay for it with the limitation of their freedom rights.

The most effective part of the democratization process of 1990, the excellent catalogue of guaranteed fundamental rights, became most affected after 1 Februar 2005. The constitution of 1990 not only guaranteed these rights but it also provided tools to force their implementation through an independent judiciary. The annulment or limitation of numerous fundamental rights was part of the state of emergency that was declared by King Gyanendra on 1 February 2005. In principle, this meant a return to the situation of fundamental rights during Panchayat times. It also did not change when the state of emergency was formally ended at the end of April. Every kind of opposition against the royal putsch was punished adamantly. At times, several thousand persons were in detention or under house arrest, often as a preventive measure. More than ever were people who had come into contact to the Maoists in danger to be arrested, tortured or even disappeared by the army.

Especially serious was the suppression of the freedom to press and information. Already before, journalists had been threatened by both Maoists and army whenever they had tried to report on their misbehaviour and crimes. The royal ban to report on events that had to do with the Maoist insurgency was a dilemma for the journalists. Gyanendra wanted that only government owned media reported on violent clashes between army and Maoists in the way that he liked. Journalists who resisted this royal ban and even commented and analyzed the royal steps and the politics of his government ran into trouble. This was just the maxim of the Panchayat era: The king is infallible; he must not be criticized.

The civil society, as well, became a target of royal suppression. Human rights activists and graduates came in a similar way under attack as the politicians. Not even the official National Human Rights Commission (NHRC) could investigate the numerous registered human rights violations independently. The freedom of movement of its members even within

Nepal became limited time and again, not to talk of their participation in international meetings. Political scientists, whose academic task is the critical analysis of political developments, were threatened and sometimes even arrested.

King Gyanendra tried to infiltrate constitutional commissions and institutions by installing parallel facilities or by replacing their members with persons that were loyal to him. An outstanding example was the formation of the Royal Commission for Control of Corruption (RCCC) that looked after the tasks of the Commission for the Investigation of Abuse of Authority (CIAA) without having any legitimacy. Its obvious task was the defamation of party leaders and rights activists.

According to the constitution of 1990, the king was nominally participated in executive and legislative but he did not have any authority. Concerning the judiciary, he was not even participated at all. This was no hindrance for Gyanendra to nominate a new Chief Justice in 2005. In the same way, he nominated the new members of the NHRC and only renewed the office of its chairman Nayan Bahadur Khatri. All of the new mwmbers were known to be loyal to the monarchy. The NHRC was meant as a controlling body for the government as well. So, national and international human rights organizations called Gyanendra's procedure a farce.

Gyanendra's seizure of direct power on 1 February 2005 shocked the international community of states. The events in Nepal became known worldwide despite the cutting off of the media. Nepal of 2005 could not be compared to the same country in December 1960 when Gyanendra's father Mahendra seized power with a similar coup d'état. Gyanendra obviously underestimated not only the democratic and civil forces inside Nepal but also the reaction of states he thought to be his close allies.

Most of all the USA, United Kingdom and India had supported the royal army in its fight against the Maoists insurgents without reservation. This may have led the king to believe that these countries would also respect his seizure of power. But these states, all of them functioning democracies, had had varying motives for their military support of Nepal. The USA, for example, had not been able to analyse the reasons of conflict in Nepal adequately for years. For their president, the Maoists were nothing else but an integral part of international terrorism, and that could be defeated only by the military way according to President Bush. A research into the causes of the Maoist conflict and and their removal had no place in this strategy. Consequently, the US government supported the royal army in its fight against the Maoist insurgents even after Gyanendra had seized sovereignty and destroyed the foundations of the constitution in October 2002. As a close ally of the USA in their fight against international terrorism, the United Kingdom followed similar politics towards Nepal.

But Gyanendra's final putsch of 1 February 2008 was too much for these states as well. In case of the USA, the growing disaster in Iraq may also have played a part. Military experts had explained for long that the royal army could not win its fight against the Maoists. Besides, it was still true that many Americans still saw their country as the worldwide defender of democracy and human rights, irrespective of the politics of their government. It did not fit to this American self-image to support a king and his army that misused the Maoist insurgency for anti-democratic and human rights ignoring politics.

The Indian view was different. Nepal's territory has always been an integral part of India's security politics. The Indo-Nepalese relations after 1947 are a product of this outlook. India regarded the Maoist insurgency in Nepal not as part of international terrorism but of a regional one. Similar to Nepal had India problems with Maoist movements in a number of its federal states. These movements, as well, had been caused by similar socio-political injustices and they had developed into a threat to the Indian Union. There seemed to be contacts between the Maoist groups in India and Nepal. A Maoist success in Nepal was not in India's interest, and so it's government supported the royal army even after 4 October 2002.

But India did not want an authoritarian royal regime with which it had had a number of problems between 1960 and 1990. A party political system similar to the Indian one was better to control by India than an absolutist royal regime that sought China's closer company. Besides depended India's ruling Congress Party upon its left allies, and these had signalled support to Nepal's democratic parties and asked the Indian government to stop its support of the royal army.

The European countries other than the United Kingdom stopped every kind of military support to the royal army after 1 February 2005. Besides, they made clear that development aid would only be continued if Nepal immediately returned to a democratic system of government. This approach was followed by most international aid organizations.

The royal regime countered this hard western and Indian attitude with harsh and partly aggressive statements and threats. Development aid was called an obligation of the donor countries that had to be continued. The donors' critics in Gyanendra's politics and the grave human rights violations by his army and his government were referred to as Nepal's internal affairs. Only a few countries shared this view of King Gyanendra, e. g. China, Pakistan, Cuba and North Korea. Most of all the support by China and Pakistan was used by Gyanendra against India and western nations, a procedure that was similar to that of his father Mahendra after his coup d'état in the early 1960s. Gyanendra had ensnared China already a few days ahead of his coup when he forced the closure of the Dalai Lama's office in Kathmandu. Nevertheless reacted China and Pakistan with restraint. Both were on a reconciling course with India that had priority. Neither China nor Pakistan wanted to deliver deadly weapons to the royal army, but China at least intensified its general support to Nepal.

The already mentioned pressure from donor countries had consequences for many development projects. Countries like the Netherlands even stopped the development cooperation at all. Others refused new agreements before the return to democracy and peace. Some countries bowed out of running major projects putting these projects at risk. But also NGO projects faced danger because of the further escalating Maoist insurgency. Times and again, the Maoists had declared that they did not hinder development projects and tourism, but the reality was different in a continued state of war.

The growing pressure from civil society provided a glimmer of hope. A civil movement evolved in the urban areas of the Kathmandu valley that tackled the problems not from those interested in power but from the interest of the affected civil society. In the beginning, this movement had been prevented by the suppression of the royal regime. The first public function of this 'Citizens' Movement for Democracy and Peace' on 25 July 2005 still faced the brutality of the regime with the arrest of many of its leaders but the security forces soon became more lenient.

The leaders of the political parties saw that civil society was becoming a new power and showed presence. But they remained observers; the main speakers were others. These did not talk about the return to democracy, a word that is usually translated as 'prajatantra' in Nepali, but about 'loktantra', the power of the people. They made clear that they wished a political order under which power and sovereignty remained in the hands of the people once and for all; they should never again be granted by one king and taken away by another one.

Many activists from civil society shared the view of the majority of students and the younger reform-minded generation of party politicians that the time was ripe for the introduction of a republican system. Besides, there were also civil circles that still stood for a future, though only ceremonial role of the monarchy. The discussion about the abolition or preservation of monarchy was sparked off by Gyanendra's seizure of power on 4 October 2002, and it became a key issue after 1 February 2005. The nation was formally split. All those who did not accept the steps and orders of the king without any discussion, were termed anti-nationalists or even public enemies by the royal government. This was the reason that many people could think about a Nepal without the institution of monarchy. After the democracy movement of 1990, this has still been unthinkable. Not even communist parties had then called for the abolition of monarchy. After all, one must say that Gyanendra's behaviour ever since his accession to the throne in June 2001 has been main responsible for this change of mind. King Gyanendra's steps after 1 February 2005 did not aim at restoration of democracy and human rights but more at their abolition or restriction. King Gyanendra obviously wanted to use the continued Maoist insurgency to implement his own power interests.

For Peace and Inclusion: Jana Andolan II and Its Consequences

In April 2006, a second people's movement (Jana Andolan II) literally washed the authoritarian royal regime away. This movement was less the work of the political parties than that of civil society. It seemed the latter was formally fed up with the continued power fighting of the Tagadhari elite at the top of the state and with the ten years of Maoist "people's war". But it is true that the rapprochement of the CPN (Maoist) and the parties joined in a Seven Party Alliance (SPA) since November 2005 encouraged the development of this movement.

King Gyanendra's dropping out of power on 24 April 2006 was coupled with the reinstatement of the 1999 parliament that had been dissolved in May 2002 on intention of then Prime Minister Sher Bahadur Deuba.[37] An interim government with SPA politicians was formed under the new Prime Minister Girija Prasad Koirala. It was followed by a peace agreement with the CPN (Maoist) and a number of important decisions in the parliament. The most important of these were the gradual toppling of political and cultural royal powers, the agreement to introduce an inclusive state, and the upgrading of women's rights. Besides, a commission of inquiry was installed, the so-called Rayamajhi Commission, that had the task to investigate the crimes of the royal government against the people, especially those of Jana Andolan II. The commission presented its report in autumn 2006 but, as similar reports in the past, it was not published and did not have any consequences for those persons who had been mentioned as most responsible, like King Gyanendra, his home minister Kamal Thapa and the other ministers of the royal cabinet as well as the leadership of the army.

The slow-moving peace process lingered on until late 2006. In November, the government concluded a comprehensive peace agreement with the CPN (Maoist). Its most

[37] Only MPs who had openly supported the royal putsch were excluded.

important features were: implementation of an interim constitution within a few weeks, dissolution of the parliament and its replacement by a new interim parliament with participation of the Maoists, installation of a new interim government with Maoist participation, and preparation of elections for a constituent assembly which were scheduled for June 2007. An other important agreement was the control of the army and the Maoist People's Liberation Army (PLA) through the UN. The formation of this United Nations Mission in Nepal (UNMIN) was delayed until early 2007.

The new interim constitution was implemented by the parliament on 15 January 2007. It shall be valid until a new constitution is written by the constituent assembly. The reinstated 1999 parliament was dissolved and replaced by a new parliament with 330 members who were all nominated by the leaders of the parties of the Eight Party Alliance (EPA), i. e. the SPA parties and the CPN (Maoist). The party leaders had been struggling over the composition of the new parliament till the very last moment. The SPA leaders insisted in a system that guaranteed the mandates of all those MPs who had been sitting in the previous interim parliament because they had been elected almost eight years ago. They knew that the 1999 parliament had been everything else but inclusive in respect to disadvantaged population groups, but they did not even try to participate these groups while nominating a few additional MPs. This was also in contradiction to their decision in the first interim parliament to participate all groups adequately. Only the Maoists respected this parliamentary decision when they nominated their 83 MPs. With this step, the Maoists were participated in parliament; their inclusion in the government followed in April 2007. Already far behind their schedule, government and parties were not able to hold the elections for the constituent assembly in June 2007. Thus, the elections were rescheduled for 22 November 2007.

The renewed exclusion of traditionally not participated population groups led to their acts of annoyance in different parts of the country. Most hit was the Tarai region where groups with different background came out with great militancy. But also Janajatis, Dalits, women organizations and Muslims rebelled against the state that was continuously dominated by male Tagadharis. This caused a climate that was not favourable for holding elections.

Nevertheless did the Election Commission its best to prepare the elections in time. But obvious was the lack of election statements from the political parties. Especially the NC had more to do with internal things like the re-unification of its two groups. It took until 25 September 2007 until Sher Bahadur Deuba's NC (Democratic) rejoined the mother party. After weeks of discussions, the party also professed its belief in a republican Nepal and distanced from its principle constitutional monarchy. The party defection by its old leader Krishna Prasad Bhattarai over this issue symbolized the continued conflict within the NC.

But there was also a lot of dissension within the CPN (Maoist). Too often had the party leadership been willing to compromise with the other parties even in regard to fundamental Maoist demands. Besides, the Maoists seemed not really prepared for elections. Their leaders took this excuse to call former agreements that had even been included in the interim constitution into question. The immediate abolition of the institution of monarchy may have been of minor importance at this moment. But they laid greater emphasis on their demand for a purely proportional election system with adequate reservation of all population groups. Obviously, the CPN (Maoist) hoped for votes from the disadvantaged population groups to gain a majority in the constituent assembly. Their proposal was rejected by the NC; as a compromise was the number of persons elected by the proportional system risen to 335 in relation 240 directly elected MPs of the constituent assembly. Nevertheless had this struggle the consequence that the elections had once again to be delayed till 10 April 2008.

Before I turn to the discussion of the elections and their results, I will shortly analyse the position and behaviour of the most important parties in the peace process after April 2006. This analysis will will be helpful to understand the election results.

Nepali Congress (NC): The leaders of the NC like to see themselves and their party as the personification of democracy as such. From this they derive their fundamental legitimacy of leadership. Nevertheless is their way of political thinking and behaviour very often following to same old formula that has to do with their traditionalist cultural and social environment as well as their education. Politics, according to this way of thinking, is predominantly the job of male Tagadharis. They identify Nepal's state and society with their own outlook that is very closely tied to Hindu culture and traditional views of Hindu politics. It was only after 1990 that they finally made up their mind to lip services concerning the country's multiethnicity and multilingual composition, in more recent times also to its multireligious aspects. But they still do not really identify with these facts.

Another feature of the traditionalist outlook of the male Tagadhari elite, who dominates almost all political parties, is the upholding of old networks. They see it as some kind of duty to provide their own people (*aphno manche*), i. e. relatives, friends and close party members, with special positions. Coupled with the lack of internal democratic party structures has this guaranteed that the NC top-level has remained a closed circle for a few families into which members of other groups only accidentally found access.

In this respect have the NC leaders totally failed to understand the sign of the times after April 2006. They obviously believed that they could fall back into their old ways of the 1990s after the dethronement of the king. They misunderstood the clear message of the people's movement of April 2006: introduce fundamental changes of the traditionalist state and its social order and build up an inclusive system of state in which all social groups can feel at home. It was a condition of these demands that all social groups were participated in this process of change right from the beginning. This would have meant for the NC that the party began with its internal democratization immediately in May 2006, but it has not done so even in late 2008.

The formation of the interim parliament in January 2007 is an ideal issue to prove this failure. It was the explicit politics of the then still two NC groups that all those MPs who had been elected into parliament in 1999 (and who had been selected as candidates by the party leadership and not by the basis) should remain their mandates in the 2007 interim parliament as well. Both NC groups were allowed to nominate together 16 additional members but even here the party leaders were not interested to include the traditionally disadvantaged groups. Ten of these 16 additional members were Tagadharis, among them the daughter of Prime Minister Girija Prasad Koirala. In the same way did the NC leaders handle the filling of offices, commissions, ambassador positions, etc. The party did not show any effort to make the state inclusive. This gave the politically conscious people the impression that the NC was not in a condition to provide a decisive contribution for conflict solution. It appeared more as a hindrance.

At the same time provided this situation a fertile soil for internal disputes that have less to do with different ideologies than with the power struggle of particular party leaders. The reunification of the two NC groups in autumn 2007 did not mean real unity within the party, as the resignation of Krishna Prasad Bhattarai showed. Since its foundation in the late 1940s has the NC never been a closed unity and there are many reasons to doubt that it will ever be.

CPN (UML): The leadership of this centre left party shows strong parallels to the NC. Just like the NC, it is dominated by male Tagadharis and members of other groups find only limited access. But the UML seems to be less traditionalist than the NC. This may have to do with its left orientation and its historical background. As a consequence is it easier for the UML leaders to change their political outlook for necessary changes of state and society than it is for the NC politicians. The CPN (UML) may have formally shared the concept of constitutional monarchy though the party statute stood for the introduction of a republican state ever since the UML was founded in January 1991. So, the system change after April 2006 should have been a mere formality, if this 'communist' party did not have a number of leaders who are deeply rooted in their traditional Tagadhari social order and thinking as well; K.P. Oli may be mentioned here as an outstanding example.

Since 1991, the CPN (UML) has continuously improved in parliamentary as well as in local elections. If the party had not split in 1998, it would have been the clear winner in the 1999 parliamentary elections, according to votes as well as according to seats. This fact was reflected by the party leaders' convictions that they would become the strongest party in the constituent assembly.

But a major problem had grown up with the now democratized CPN (Maoist). As long as this extreme left party had presented itself as a militant opponent of the state that did not participate in elections, as long could the CPN (UML) be sure of the majority of the left oriented voters. Ahead of the elections for the constituent assembly, it was hard to say how many left voters would give their vote for the CPN (Maoist). So, the UML leaders were torn between a closer cooperation with the Maoists that would also have been reasonable from the ideological point of view and a clear dissociation to preserve their own identity.

The potential of a closer cooperation between UML and Maoists became clear on 4 November 2007 when both parties brought their proposals for the immediate abolition of monarchy respectively the introduction of a pure proportional election system through parliament. But this meant little since it would have required a change of the interim constitution and this needed a two thirds majority that was not possible without the votes of the NC MPs.

CPN-Maoist: This left extremist party has changed its tactics sharply after April 2006, The termination as 'terror organization' seems to be inappropriate. The party has joined the democratic process, became a member party of the interim Parliament in January 2007 and later even joined the interim government. Thus, it should be treated with the same respect as any other political party of Nepal. In the international sphere, it was only the US government that still classified the Nepali Maoists as a terrorist organization.[38]

But in many respects did the CPN (Maoist) still not follow the rules of law. Especially the Maoist youth organization, the Young Communist League (YCL), was deliberately used to continue well-known negative practices like abductions, extortions, beatings and sometimes even murders. There was a wide gap between the manner and the statements of the Maoist leaders on the one side and the behaviour of the party cadres on the other. Often, one had to ask if the Maoist leaders were still in control of their party basis.

[38] In late 2008, the US government is just about to change this.

One example may stand for many: In early October 2007, the journalist Birendra Shah was abducted in Bara district. In the beginning, the Maoist leaders denied that their party had anything to do with this incident, only to call it into question soon. In late October, the Maoist chairman Pushpa Kamal Dahal admitted that the journalist had been abducted by Maoist cadres. Later it became known that they even had murdered him. With the comprehensive peace agreement of November 2006 and again by signing the interim constitution of January 2007, the CPN (Maoist) has committed itself to the rule of law. Nevertheless has the party broken this commitment at least as often as the other parties have ignored their own pledge of political and social changes.

Other parties: The other EPA parties[39] played only a minor role in the interim period between Jana Andolan II and the elections to a constituent assembly. It became obvious that their future role would be similar to that of the smaller parties in the 1990s, i. e. they would only be useful to provide necessary majorities. The leaders of the only party with regional importance, the Nepal Sadbhavana Party (NSP), had fallen out with each other leading to several splits of the party ahead of the elections to the constituent assembly.

Outside EPA, the conservative parties have to be mentioned. The moderate forces of the erstwhile royal Panchayat system had gathered in the Rastriya Prajatantra Party (RPP, National Democratic Party) in 1991. This party had already split and reunified several times in the 1990s. After the royal putsch of 1 February 2005, the RPP broke up in several groups. The mother party under the leadership of Pashupati Shamsher Rana and the Rastriya Janashakti Party (RJP) of Surya Bahadur Thapa still presented themselves as moderate parties. Both groups claimed to distance themselves from the monarchy, though they still stood for the preservation of a constitutional form of monarchy.

Besides, there were some smaller extreme right wing parties, among them some splinter groups of the original RPP, which stood for a strong monarchy. Here we found all those politicians who had favoured the putsch of King Gyanendra and who had been involved in the suppression of the people in 2005/6. Needless to say that this group also included former Panchayat hardliners like Tulsi Giri and Kirti Nidhi Bista, who had avoided contacts to any political party after 1990. Since the interim government failed to make these persons responsible for their crimes despite the existence of a corresponding inquiry report, it became possible that politicians like Kamal Thapa could take part in the elections to the constituent assembly by order of the court. Some of the extreme right wing parties did not rule out even militant activities to save the monarchy.

New Madhesi parties: One of the outstanding effects of the non-inclusive politics of the Nepali state after Jana Andolan II have been growing tendencies of separatism. This was most felt in the Tarai, the flatland along the southern border to India. Many disadvantaged groups like Janajatis, Dalits, Madhesis, Muslims and women in general had intensified their demand for adequate participation and their share of the natural resources of the country. The failure of the political leaders even to begin to fulfil sich demands had caused a number of movements and strikes. Nepal's transformation into a federal republic was a fundamental demand of all such movements. There was a difference between the groups from the mountains and those from the plains. The former seemed to be more willing to compromise

[39] I still use the term Eight Party Alliance here, even though the number of parties has been reduced to seven after the reunification of the two Nepali Congress groups. This grouping dissolved after the elections for the constituent assembly, either.

and hardly threatened to begin separatist movements. Their main demand was a federal system on the basis of ethnicity.

This was totally different in the Tarai where the conflict turned more and more violent in 2007 with the expulsion of members of hill groups living in the Tarai. Power brokers of such movements were Madhesi leaders who partly distorted historical facts by claiming that their groups were the original settlers of the Tarai region. But in fact, the Tarai was only inhabited by a number of ethnic groups, like the Tharus, until the middle of the 19th century. The Rana rulers called in population from the adjoining Indian areas after they could not get the hill groups to settle in the Tarai.[40] Neither the Ranas nor the royal or democratic governments after 1950 ever tried to integrate the immigrated Indian population into the Nepali state. So, it is a very widely-held opinion among the hill population that the Madhesis are not Nepalis but foreigners. It makes no wonder that the Madhesis, on the other hand, never developed a Nepali identity and instead kept up their private, cultural and partly also political Indian relations.

Such Madhesi feelings became in recent years more and more misused by a number of militant groups which partly had split off from the CPN (Maoist). The latter lost a lot of support in the Tarai after its leaders entered the peace dialogue with the political mainstream parties in Kathmandu. The fixed anti Indian position of the Maoists may have further intensified this tendency. The best known of such groups were the two Janatantrik Tarai Mukti Morcha (JTMM, Republican Tarai Liberation Front) groups as well as the Madhesi Janadhikar Manch (Madhesi Peoples Rights Forum, MPRF). Besides, there are a number of small militant groups spreading terror and unrest in the Tarai, among them also the already mentioned militant pro-monarchist parties.

In December 2007, a number of well-known Madhesi politicians, including ministers, left the leading political parties in Kathmandu and formed the Tarai-Madhes Loktantrik Party (Tarai-Madhes Democratic Party, TMDP). In February 2008, they formed a wider alliance with the MPRF and the Nepal Sadbhavana Party under the name United Democratic Madhesi Front (UDMF) but this front was not able to table a common candidate list for the elections to the constituent assembly.

Elections for a Constituent Assembly: Evaluation and Prospects

The elections for a constituent assembly (CA) took place on 10 April 2008. The people of Nepal had been waiting long for this day. Elections for a CA had been promised by the monarchy in early 1951 but it took only place 57 years later and two years after the toppling of royal power by an impressive people's movement. So far, the elections have been the most important step on the way to durable peace and an inclusive system of state. Compared to the extremely difficult preconditions, the elections were comparatively peaceful and fair; negative aspects will be discussed later. After a break of almost six years, politics once again got authority by the people. This alone was a highly important step. It was a pity that the first reactions of the leading politicians proved their misunderstanding that it had not been regular

[40] There were two reasons for the hill groups not to do so: There was still enough land in the hills, i. e. there was no land pressure, and hill groups could not bare the Tarai climate. The intention of the Ranas to call the Indian population was their greed to exploit the fertile Tarai land for their own pockets.

parliamentary elections but first of all elections for a constituent assembly. If Nepal shall be transformed into a fully democratic and inclusive modern state with hopeful perspectives for a prosperous future, it is essential that the close cooperation of the political parties is continued until first parliamentary elections take place under the future constitution.

As the elections were approaching, there had been a number of moves for cooperation within the camp of the SPA. It became obvious that the NC represented a more and more conservative line. This had also to do with the fact that most of the other parties within the alliance followed left-wing ideologies. But it could be no excuse that a number of politicians tried to turn the wheel back, obviously with the intention to win conservative voters. So pleaded Sujata Koirala, the PM's daughter, suddenly for the preservation of the institution of monarchy. Even her father sometimes made statements in this direction.

The way to the elections was cleared after the bigger disputes had been solved in late February 2008. There were only a few small militant parties who were against the holding of the elections. Even the ultra-monarchist RPP (Nepal) of Kamal Thapa registered for the elections.

It followed a very short but intensive election campaign. The common appearances of the SPA politicians soon got less and all parties tried to do their own thing. Time and again, there were discussions about the formation of electoral alliances but only to make sure that the leading politicians of the parties did not neutralise each other by contesting in the same constituencies. In the end, the leaders all major parties expressed the confidence that their respective pary would be the clear winner of the elections.

Altogether 575 persons had to be elected into the the constituent assembly on 10 April 2008. 240 of the seats fell to the winning candidates of the 240 constituencies of the country according to the first past the post (FPTP) electoral system. Another 335 were elected through a system of proportional representation (PR). Each voter had two votes, one to elect the FPTP candidate and one for the PR lists of the parties. The composition of the party lists for the PR system had to follow strict rules so that it was guaranteed that the different population groups would be represented in the CA according to their respective share in the total population of the country. But concerning the nomination of the FPTP candidates the parties were not bound to similar rules. In addition to these 575 elected members of the CA, the government had to nominate another 26 members on the basis of understanding from amongst the persons of high reputation who have rendered significant contribution in national life.[41] This meant that there would be 601 MPs in the CA. Many were afraid that this number would be to high for constructive working on the new constitution and saw it as another negative consequence of the continued power struggles between and within the different parties.

Only nine parties could win FPTP mandates. It soon became clear that the CPN (Maoist) was the outstanding winner. In the end, this party had won 120, i. e. exactly 50%, of the FPTP mandates. The two parties that had dominated the 1990 system, the NC and the CPN (UML), were the great losers; the NC won only 37 seats and the UML 30. Two new parties from the Tarai had also to be regarded as big winners. The Madheshi People's Rights Forum (MPRF) won 30 direct mandates und the Tarai Madesh Democratic Party (TMDP) 9 seats.

[41] Election to Members of the Constituent Assembly Act, 2064 B.S. (2007), § 3

Table 2. Inclusive system for PR lists

Group to be represented	Gender	Percentage of candidates
Madhesis	women	15.6%
	men	15.6%
Dalits	women	6.5%
	men	6.5%
Oppressed tribes / indigenous tribes[1]	women	18.9%
	men	18.9%
Backward region[2]	women	2.0%
	man	2.0%
Others[3]	men	15.1%
	women	15.1%

[1] The ethnic groups which term themselves as Janajatis.

[2] The districts of Achham, Kalikot, Jajarkot, Jumla, Dolpa, Bajahang, Bajura, Mugu and Humla.

[3] The Tagadhari castes.

Source: Election to Members of the Constituent Assembly Act, 2064 (2007), Schedule 1.

The differences of results for the elections under the PR system were less significant. The CPN (Maoist) was also the winner under this system but it got only about 30% of the votes. Runners-up were the NC (21%) and CPN (UML) (20%). MPRF and TMDP were far behind with 6% respectively 3%. In seats, this meant another 100 for the CPN (Maoist), 73 for the NC, 70 for the UML, 22 for the MPRF and 11 for the TMDP.

Table 3. Results of the CA elections of 10 April 2008

S.no	Party Name	PR Votes	Percentage	PR Seats	FTPT Seats	Total Seats	Votes in 1999	% in 1999	Seats in 1999
1	Communist Party of Nepal (Maoists)	3144204	29.28	100	120	220	0	0.0	0
2	Nepali Congress	2269883	21.14	73	37	110	3214786	37.2	111
3	Communist Party of Nepal (UML)	2183370	20.33	70	33	103	2734568	31.6	71
4	Madhesi People's Rights Forum, Nepal	678327	6.32	22	30	52	0	0.0	0
5	Tarai Madhes Loktantrik Party	338930	3.16	11	9	20	0	0.0	0
6	Rastriya Prajatantra Party	263431	2.45	8		8	1198140	13.9	11

Table 3. (Continued)

S.no	Party Name	PR Votes	Percentage	PR Seats	FTPT Seats	Total Seats	Votes in 1999	% in 1999	Seats in 1999
7	Communist Party of Nepal (ML)	243545	2.27	8		8	567760	6.6	0
8	Sadbhawana Party	167517	1.56	5	4	9	278435	3.2	5
9	Janamorcha Nepal	164381	1.53	5	2	7	74669	0.5	1
10	Communist Party of Nepal (United)	154968	1.44	5		5			
11	Rastriya Prajatantra Party Nepal	110519	1.03	4		4			
12	Rastriya Janamorcha	106224	0.99	3	1	4	121426	1.4	5
13	Rastriya Janshakti Party	102147	0.95	3		3			
14	Nepal Workers and Peasants Party	74089	0.69	2	2	4	48685	0.6	1
15	Federal Democratic National Forum	71958	0.67	2		2			
16	Nepal Sadbhawana Party (Anandidevi)	55671	0.52	2		2			
17	Rastriya Janamukti Party	53910	0.50	2		2	94860	1.1	0
20	Nepali Janata Dal	48990	0.46	2		2			
18	Communist Party of Nepal (Unified)	48600	0.45	2		2			
19	Dalit Janajati Party	40348	0.38	1		1			
21	Nepa: Rastriya Party	37757	0.35	1		1			
22	Samajwadi Prajatantrik. Janata Party, Nepal	35752	0.33	1		1			

S.no	Party Name	PR Votes	Percentage	PR Seats	FTPT Seats	Total Seats	Votes in 1999	% in 1999	Seats in 1999
23	Chure Bhawar Rastriya Ekata Party Nepal	28575	0.27	1		1			
24	Nepal Lokatantrik Samajbadi Dal	25022	0.23	1		1			
25	Nepal Pariwar Dal	23512	0.22	1		1			
26	Communist Party of Nepal (Marxist)	21234	0.20						
27	Tamsaling Nepal Rastriya Dal	20657	0.19						
28	Rastriya Janata Dal	19305	0.18						
29	Communist Party of Nepal (United Marxist)	18717	0.17						
30	Lok Kalyankari Janata Party Nepal	18123	0.17						
31	Others (24 parties)	168714	1.57						
	Independents				2	2			
	Nominated by Council of Ministers			26		26			
	Total	10739078	100.00	361	240	601			205

Quelle: Election Commission, Nepal: http://www.election.gov.np/reports/CAResults/reportBody.php?selectedMenu1=Party wise(PR-SEATS)Distribution (in Nepali, last viewed 18 September 2008).

Altogether, the CPN (Maoist) could send 220 MPs into the CA, i. e. 36.6% of the total seats. The so far dominating parties of NC (110) und UML (103) together have less seats than the CPN (Maoist). Both parties were severely shocked by this result. They first of all explained their defeat by the behaviour of Maoist cadres before and during the elections. Indeed had there been some irregularities, militant activities and intimidations in a number of constituencies. Maoist cadres, especially the Maoist youth organization, the Young Communist League (YCL), has often been mentioned in this context. But other parties had been the cause of such incidents as well. According to most national and international election observers, the elections have been rather peaceful in most areas. This means that the countrywide election result cannot be explained by some negative incidents that have happened without any doubt.

It will be better to testify political maturity to the Nepali voters and ask why they have voted in this way. Then we may understand, that the voting behaviour of the people had a lot to do with all the things that have happened after 1990 and, most of all, after 2006, with lip services and empty promises, with the longing for peace and the understanding of its preconditions, with raised hopes and, especially, with practiced inclusion.

The political system of 1990 was not bad but it was incomplete and had some grave mistakes. It has failed because it did not develop further after its birth and because it has been misused by the leaders of the established parties in the way of corruption, nepotism and power struggles. No party has introduced parliamentary politics that was oriented along the interests and the prosperity of the people. No party has broken up its traditional non-inclusive structures and has striven for internal democracy and the participation of all population groups. Since the early 1990s, a number of Janajati organizations have criticized this injustice and they have demanded rights and inclusion. They were soon followed by activists of women, Dalits and Madhesis who rose similar demands. The two leading parties of the 1990 system, NC and UML, made only lip services concerning such demands; the latter may have found access into their election manifestos but they were forgotten soon after the elections. Careful observers of the political developments in Nepal have pointed out for long that the issue of inclusion has got highest priority over the years, only the established party leaders obviously did not understand.[42]

So, if the voters wanted to punish someone for failed politics after 1990, they had first of all to call to account those parties and politicians that had born political responsibility. And this was especially the NC that had been in government for most of the time after 1990, either in form of single party governments or as biggest party of coalition governments. Thus, the bad result of the NC in the CA elections can simply be seen as democratic punishment for its politics after 1990. It was a peaceful democratic behaviour of responsible adult citizens as it happens everywhere in the world in democratic states.

The CPN (UML), as well, did not win many laurels after 1990. This party may have been in opposition for most of the time, but it failed to work for reasonable opposition politics in parliament. Instead, it already turned to the streets in the early 1990s. Its politics of general strikes (*bandh* or *banda*) soon became an excessively used tool by all kinds of political and social groups to enforce demands. Such strikes have paralysed the economy and the everyday life of the people for years. Concerning non-inclusiveness, the CPN (UML) does not differ much from the NC.

But the defeat of the UML in the CA elections still has another reason. With the participation of the CPN (Maoist) in democratic elections, the CPN (UML) has got a serious rival among the left group of voters. It can be taken for sure that the UML has lost many voters to the Maoists, not only because they were dissatisfied with UML politics but also simply because there is now a strong political party left of the UML. A voting trend towards the left has been visible since 1991. It has definitely been intensified in the CA elections. In the 1990s, the CPN (UML) has been the main profiteer of this trend. As already mentioned above, the party would have won a clear majority of seats and a relative majority of votes in the 1999 parliamentary elections if it had not split in 1998.

---

[42] Krämer, Karl-Heinz. Samanta ra sahabhagita: sangkatbata mukta hunka lagi purvasarta. [Equality and participation: preconditions for ways out of crisis]. In: Mohan Mainali (ed.), Samaveshi loktantraka adharharu, pp. 38-47. Lalitpur: Himal Books 2004

If one sees the votes for left parties in total, it becomes clear that the trend towards the left has been intensified with the CA elections. The CA is overwhelmingly dominated by left oriented parties. Today, the NC is on the right wing of the leading parties in parliament. The so far only conservative democratic party, the RPP, and its several splinter groups have become more or less insignificant after the CA elections. Even the conservative sections of society seem to have given up their hopes in the institution of monarchy. Parties in favour or support of any monarchist form of government have been totally disregarded in the CA elections.

But the success of the CPN (Maoist) cannot only be explained by the failure of the established parties and monarchy after 1990. It also has a lot to do with the political developments after April 2006. With Jana Andolan II, the people had given clear signals concerning their demands for the abolition of monarchy, an inclusive system of state, a durable peace and the return to law and order. With this in mind, the parliament made a number of far-reaching decisions shortly after it had been reinstated. But this positive outlook changed as soon as new functionaries had to be appointed to offices. Now the parties, especially the NC with its majority in the reinstated parliament, returned to their non-inclusive nomination politics and forgot what had been decided before in parliament.

This trend was intensified when the discussions over the interim constitution and the composition of the new interim parliament began. It was the intension of NC and CPN (UML), the two dominating parties in the reinstated parliament, that their MPs who had been elected in 1999 should keep their positions as well in the interim parliament that was to be nominated by the party leaders in January 2007 on the basis of the interim constitution. This was a special kind of nomination because these persons had been elected in May 1999 for a term of five years, i. e. until May 2004 latest. Besides it was well known that the 1999 parliament had been everything else but inclusive with male Bahuns specially dominating the parliamentary parties of NC and UML. So, the insistence of these parties to uphold the non-inclusive composition of the parliament was a severe violation of the decision of the first interim parliament to participate all population groups in an adequate way whenever new positions or functions had to be filled. So had the reinstated parliament decided on 30 May 2006 that women should have a share of at least 33% in all functions and positions. While NC and UML followed their traditional way of non-inclusive politics, the CPN (Maoist) nominated 40% women into the new interim parliament in January 2007. This meant a moral setback for NC and UML in the eyes of the people which was not forgotten when the voting for the CA took place on 10 April 2008.

Similar games were played as the CA elections approached. In vain, the CPN (Maoist) had fought for a purely proportional election system. We know today, that such system would have been for the disadvantage of the CPN (Maoist) because they would have won only 30% and not 36.6% of the seats. The dual election system for the CA not only prescribed an adequate inclusion of all population groups for the PR lists but it also ordered the parties to include the different groups adequately while nominating their FPTP candidates. Here we could observe shortcomings from all parties but once again it was the CPN (Maoist) that came by far closest to these guidelines. This time, it was not only a moral advantage but it had direct effects on the election result. In many constituencies, women, Dalit and Janajati candidates of the Maoists were able win against well known Tagadhari canditates of NC and CPN (UML).

Table 4. Candidates of leading parties: ethnic and gender inclusion

Party	Bahun	Chhetri	Dalit	Janajati	Madhesi	Women
CPN (Maoist)	28%	14%	5%	45%	8%	18%
Nepali Congress	36%	22%	0%	28%	14%	11%
CPN (UML)	36%	16%	0%	35%	13%	11%
Tarai-Parties	7%	2%	0%	10%	81%	4%
Percent of the total polulation	13%	16%	13%	39%	19%	50%

Source: The Kathmandu Post, 9 May 2008. Percent of total popluation according to Population Census of 2001, rounded off (Central Bureau of Statistics. Nepal in Figures 2007, p. 2. Kathmandu). See also tables of the Population Census 2001: http://www.cbs.gov.np/national_report_tables.php (last viewed: 18 September 2008).

Though more detailed analyses are necessary to evaluate other aspects of the results of the CA elections, one can already say that the overall victory of the CPN (Maoist) under the FPTP system has a lot to do with their greater participation of the different social groups. Obviously, this has been further intensified by the fact that the Maoist programs and aims have reflected the interests and issues of the so far disadvantaged sections of society in a better way than the programs of NC and UML have done. Thanks to this Maoist politics and thanks to the PR system is the composition of the CA far more inclusive than any of the parliaments of the 1990s have been.

Nepal's Future in the 21st Century

Preconditions for a new Nepal have been set. But the first months after the elections have already proved how difficult this task will be. It took more than three months before the party politicians settled on the procedure of government change. Missing majorities proved to be problematic just as in the chaotic phase between 1994 and 1999. On the one side, there were the personal losers of the elections, i. e. the established party leaders who had dominated party politics after 1990 and who now had been rejected by the people's FPTP votes. Most of them belonged to the NC or the CPN (UML). They had great difficulties to understand their defeat in the elections and, instead, sticked to their functions and positions. On the other side, there was the winner in the elections, the CPN (Maoist), whose leaders misunderstood that they had won only a relative majority of seats and had to find coalition partners if they wanted to form a new government. This meant that they would have to cooperate with either the NC or the CPN (UML) if they did not want to form a coalition government with a great number of small partners. And the Maoist leaders had great problems to make concessions towards the demands of the bigger parties whose leaders already felt humiliated by the election results. It took weeks before both, NC und UML, gave in to the Maoist demand to get the position of prime minister. Both parties threatened not to join a Maoist led government though all SPA parties had agreed before the elections that they would continue their cooperation independent of the election result.

Another discussion was over the posts of president and vice-president. The country was in need of a new head of state after the Constituent Assembly had formally abolished the institution of monarchy on 28 May 2008. De facto, Prime Minister Koirala had also filled the position of head of state after April 2006 but Koirala and his party colleagues did not want Pushpa Kamal Dahal to have the same great power. A further problem was that the functions of the future president and the formalities of his/her election had not been clearly defined by the interim constitution. So, the Constituent Assembly, that also functions as parliament, had to include such regulations into the constitution, the fifth amendment within only one and a half years.

After they Maoists could not reach an agreement with the CPN (UML) on a common candidate,[43] they were up against a coalition of NC, CPN (UML) and MPRF in the very last moment. This coalition agreed on the distribution of the offices of president and vice-president among each other. The ballot on 20 July was on three Tarai politicians. The Maoists had nominated Ram Raja Prasad Singh,[44] the NC Ram Baran Yadav, and the CPN (UML) Ram Prit Paswan. Yadav became the winner at the second ballot. Parmanand Jha (MPRF) had already been elected vice-president at the first ballot. This meant that both positions were filled by Madhesi politicians what, hopefully would calm down the regional Tarai movements. A few months later, one can already say that Ram Baran Yadav has proved to be a moderate and integrative politician, obviously a good choice for a new beginning. The general acceptance of Vice-President Parmanand Jha was more complicated right from the beginning. He took his oath of office in Hindi what caused militant riots in the country for several days.[45] The situation calmed down when Jha apologized for his procedure.[46]

Other problems arose with the formation of the new government. Till the very end, the NC had hoped to push their power interests through. Based on the successful election of an NC politician as president through the alliance with CPN (UML) and MPRF, the party had even hoped to select its old and ailing chairman Girija Prasad Koirala for another time as prime minister, even though he had not even taken part in the elections for the CA and also did not become a member over the proportional lists. The NC even ran the risk of putting the peace process at danger by excluding the Maoists once again. The CPN (Maoist), on the other side, tried to establish a common government of all bigger parties under its leadership. After all efforts failed, a strike ballot over the office of prime minister took place on 15 August 2008 between the Maoist chairman Pushpa Kamal Dahal and the NC leader Sher Bahadur Deuba. This time, CPN (UML),and MPRF as well as most of the small parties supported Dahal who won with a two thirds majority. CPN (Maoist), CPN (UML), MPRF and a number of small parties have formed a coalition government that is confronted with a number of internal problems and dissent even more than two months after its formation. Dahal still tries to bring the NC into the government as well but the latter establishes more and more as a strong opposition party. This can be fruitful for Nepal's process of renewal. The late 1990s

---

[43] The UML ha recommended its longstanding general secretary Madhav Kumar Nepal who had been defeated in the April elections in two constituencies. As a consequence, he had resigned from his party post.

[44] Singh had first become famous in 1971 when he managed to be elected into the parliament, the Rastriya Panchayat, even though he was a well-known anti-monarchist. Later, he was made responsible for the bomb attacks that rocked Kathmandu and other towns in June 1985 and left eight persons dead and many others injured.

[45] Jha's mother tongue is Maithili, Nepal's second commonest langue with 12,3% mother tongue speakers. Though a small number of Madhesis have mentioned Hindi as their mother tongue in the census of 2001, the latter is not officially recognised as a national language. Many Nepalis still see it as a symbol of Indian influence exertion, though they hardly have any problems to watch the Hindi films that swamp the cinema halls.

[46] It is to question why Nepal needs the office of a vice president at all. With a president that has more or less only representative functions, there is no need for a vice president as can be seen, for example, from the German presidential system.

have proved that it is almost impossible to reach reasonable consent within big coalition governments. The opposition is an integral and important part of every democratic system. The NC has hardly 17% in the CA, and as such it is only a small opposition group, but it can provide an important contribution to Nepal's renewal process, as long as its leaders forget their traditional power ambitions and attend this process a kind of watchdog. This means, the NC must support the steps taken by the government as long as they are necessary for the process and it must vehemently oppose steps that are against the interest of Nepal. So far, the NC still seems to have problems to find its new role. This may have to do with the fact that the party is still dominated by not elected old leaders. A process of internal reform is urgent but it has just been delayed for another year.

The greatest problem is currently the CA. More than half a year after the elections, the MPs have not started the work for which they have been elected by the people. So far, the CA has only fulfilled its subsidiary function as a parliament and this also only in a limited way. Necessary by-elections in several constituencies have also not taken place, yet. Instead, the new government is trying to establish a Ministry of State Restructuring. This is a grave misunderstanding of the interim constitution and the tasks of the CA. The restructuring of the state is the exclusive task of the Constituent Assembly and not that of the government. All institutions and commissions that guide this process have to be initiated and formed from within the CA.[47]

So far, there have been hardly any discussions how the future Nepal should look like. Discussion on important issues like the system of state, the integration of population groups and regions, the question of the integration of the Maoists PLA into the Nepal Army and the latter's future role only take place outside the CA, i. e. within and between the parties. And the opinions are extremely divergent. The elections have provided a great diversity of participation of different population groups and regions within the CA. But those who are now discussing the future of Nepal are not the newly elected representatives but the old party elites who have never been inclusive and who, to a greater part, have been rejected by the people in the CA elections. The old party elites had great problems with the understanding of the concerns of the people in the past and they still have not changed much.

The party leaders spend most of their time for critically observing and commenting every step and statement of the Maoist leaders and the latter irritate by contradicting statements that often go against their previous agreements with the other parties and rises fears that the Maoists could misuse the current process to bring their revolution to an end. This misbehaviour from all sides must stop immediately. The government has to concentrate on its executive tasks, carefully watched by the opposition and civil society, and all discussions on the future political system have to be transferred to the CA.

It is not easy to summarise the aspects of future Nepal in a few sentences. I will only mention a few things that should be foundations of Nepal in the 21st century. Democracy may have a lot of shortcomings but their can be no doubt that it is the best of all forms of state and it also has a chance to function well in Nepal. There are a number of ways how to run democracy. Some preconditions have already been set in Nepal. The institution of monarchy

---

47 This conflict is further intensified by the fact that only the CA members can be regarded as elected representatives of the people. In the government, there are even ministers that have been rejected by the people's vote in April. The outstanding example may be Home Minister and Deputy Prime Minister Bam Dev Gautam (CPN (UML)) who lost the election in his constituency against a female candidate of the CPN Maoists).

has been abolished and will not play any role in the future. A president has already been elected and his current role is that of merely representative head of state. Of course, this can be changed by the CA though it does not seem to be reasonable. The past has proved that party leaders develop a tendency to become too dominant if too much powers is concentrated in the hands of a single person. So, distribution of power should by a guiding principle for future Nepal.

This brings us to another dominating issue. The interim constitution has already defined Nepal a a federal republic. Modern Nepal, i. e. Nepal after the unification by the Shah dynasty, has been built up as an extremely centralized state. This tendency has been further intensifies during Rana times. Till today, there are many party of Nepal that have been more or less neglected by the state elite in Kathmandu. The current crisis has a lot to do with this deplorable state of affairs. The discussions of decentralisation in the past have been more or less lip services.

So, it is a good idea to transform future Nepal into a federal system with well-defined rights to autonomy for its member states and clear demarcation of central state authority. All member states must get a chance to run their own internal development projects and, at the same time, they must be represented in the central government as an integral part of the Nepali nation. At least the bigger parties seem to agree on such kind of federal state system. Their differences have to do with the foundations of such system. Two systems are favoured, one based on region and one based on ethnicity. The latter is especially favoured by the Janajati groups. Hardly participated by the central elite in the past, they see a federal system that is based on ethnicity as the only chance for their inclusion into the main process. The Janajati elites have more or less clear conceptions of a number of federal states that are based on the traditional settlement regions of the different major ethnic groups. They leave out of view that migration has been a feature of modern Nepal ever since its inception. Not only has the forceful unification process caused the migration of members of the Tagadhari castes into every nook and corner of the country but it has also led to the migration of Janajati groups, especially into the urban centers and the Tarai. As a consequence, there are hardly any areas of Nepal that are only populated by a special ethnic group. There is a great danger that the failed politics of dominating elites at the center will be transferred to the various federal states if the latter are built up on the basis of language, culture and tradition of special groups that may have a simple majority in these new federal states but not more.

A better solution would be the formation of federal states under regional aspects, but it should be avoided to cut traditional settlement areas of any ethnic groups.[48] The result would be a combination of ethnic and regional aspects. The former could be stressed, for example, by making the the mother tongue of the dominant group of the federal state the lingua franca in this state, en par with Nepali which should remain national language in all federal states.

Of special importance will be the handling of the Tarai, where militancy is still an unsolved problem. Traditionally, the Tarai has been the settlement area of the Tharus and some minor ethnic groups. A greater immigration of caste population from across the Indian border only started in the mid 19th century when the Rana rulers tried to exploit the fertile Tarai region. These immigrants grew in number over the years and now constitute about 40%

---

[48] The cutting of traditional ethnic areas has been part of unitarian royal politics in Panchayat times. For example, the transformation of the originally 35 districts into the current 75 districts in the early 1960s was part of such politics. But the Shah rulers had already split ethnic areas in the 19th century by changing the district boundaries. The main objective had been to avoid greater ethnic majorities in any of the districts.

of the total Tarai population according to the census of 2001. This group, also called Madhesi,[49] has always been treated as second class people or even foreigners by the central elites in Kathmandu. In vain, these Madhesis had tried to get recognition as a group from the central elite. "A major factor is the refusal of the state, academia and media dominated by the hill group to recognize the Madhesi and their movement."[50] The Madhesis have been very successful in introducing a great number of representatives into the CA, and they have also become part of the current Maoist led government. They still have a great bulk of demands that will have to be carefully discussed in the CA during the constitution formation process. A special problem is the great diversity of Madhesi parties and organisations, of which many have a militant outlook. The demand for a federal Madhes state that comprises the whole Tarai is a common demand of all these Madhesi groups. This demand is in conflict to the interests of indigenous Tarai groups like the Tharus who do not want to be included in a Madhesi state. But this is only one aspect of numerous problems in the Tarai, the discussion of which would go beyond the scope of this article. The Tarai has become the economic heart of Nepal. All populations groups depend on its resources. So, it will be one of the most important tasks of the CA to find a solution that satisfies all groups in future Nepal, including the Madhesis and the Tharus.

One of the most urgent tasks is the integration of the Maoist PLA into the Nepal Army. This should not only be a question of formal integration but it also touches on definition and sense of the army in general. From economic reasons, Nepal cannot afford to have two parallel armies, one of which is idly sitting in camps under UN observation. Besides has the former Royal Nepal Army been extended several time when it had to fight against the PLA. In other words, the integration of the Maoist army into the Nepal Army would mean the further enlargement of forces that are already too numerous. It must be the task of the CA to redefine the mission and strength of the Nepal Army, Armed Police Force and the police in general. The army makes little sense as a defensive force against external aggression. Nepal has only two direct neighbours. Good and friendly relations to both, India and China, are the task of diplomatic procedure. In case of open conflict, the Nepal Army would not have any chance either. On the other side has there been a constant growth of internal problems of law and order. Here could the army make good contributions in the interest of the general public. Besides has the army already been involved in support actions in case of natural disasters or generally in development projects. Both tasks should be intensified.

I have just mentioned India and China. This brings us to the issue of foreign policy in general. It is not so much a field of the CA but of the executive. There have been lot of apprehensions what might happen if the government is led by a Maoist prime minister. It seems these fears have been exaggerated. The relations to both big neighbours are balanced. Towards China, Nepal is facing one problem that already existed before, and this is the Tibet factor. Of course, Nepal must support China's politics of Tibet being an integral part of China. But it should respect the fundamental rights of Tibetan refugees along international standards as well. It will not harm Nepal's relations to China if refugees are not handed over to Chinese authorities. And it will also be no problem if Nepal allows peaceful demonstrations of Tibetan refugees as long as Chinese institutions in Nepal are not threatened. During the Olympic

---

[49] In some statistics, the ethnic groups of the Tarai are also included into this Madhesi group but it should be respected, that the former see themselves as part of the indigenous population of the country and, so, want be counted as Janajati groups.

[50] Mahendra Lawoti. Problems in knowledge generation. The Kathmandu Post, 24 October 2008

Games in Beijing, the Nepali police has brutally clubbed down Tibetan demonstrations in Kathmandu time and again. Such scenes were hardly seen in any other democratic country all over the world.

The relations to India have been changeable ever since India became independent. It seems, they are currently on a good course. India has supported the democratization process in Nepal but it has also always given highest priority to her own interests. For longer times, India regarded the Maoist insurgency in Nepal as part of her own problems with similar movements in India. This view has obviously changed in recent years. It seems, India would be happy if their Maoist groups would follow the example of the CPN (Maoist) and join the democratic mainstream in India. Prime Minister Dahal's visit to India in September 2008 was successful as far as it contributed to further destroy Indian prejudices. For the first time, the Indian government is even willing to review the Treaty of Peace and Friendship that had been concluded in the last days of Rana oligarchy in July 1950. Neither NC nor UML led governments of the 1990s had been able to get this Indian concession.

Finally, the issue of human rights has to be mentioned. Nepal is still far behind international standards of human rights, though a lot has changed after 1990 and once again after April 2006. Many Nepali laws still disregard equal fundamental rights to all people, irrespective of gender, social group and behaviour, age, region, etc. Changes of the corresponding laws have to be introduced by the CA urgently, and the equality of all Nepali citizens must be made one of the foundations of the new constitution. But it's not enough to provide the legal basis. Such equal fundamental rights have also to be implemented. This requires extensive changes in the general social thinking and behaviour. The political leaders could be of exemplary character, but most them still are not. Thus, it must be the task of a strong civil society to demand these changes. Civil society has been very strong during the times of the royal putsch, but after April 2006 it has almost disappeared. It's time for a revival of this movement. Civil society has to play its role in the process of renewal of Nepal at the beginning of the 21st century. There is great danger that the current ethnic and social conflicts intensify in the years to come, if the CA is not successful in developing an inclusive concept for a new Nepal with which all social groups can identify.[51]

[51] See Dahal, Dev Raj, Nepal: The Constituent Assembly Election and Challenges Ahead. Bonn: Friedrich-Ebert-Stiftung, June 2008 [http://library.fes.de/pdf-files/iez/05481.pdf].

In: Nepal in the 21st Century
Editor: Surendra R. Devkota, pp. 85-96
ISBN 978-1-60741-348-6

Chapter 3

PROSPECTS FOR DEMOCRATIC CONSOLIDATION IN NEPAL

Hari Bansha Dulal[1] and Roberto Foa[2]
[1]World Bank, Washington, DC, USA
[2]Harvard University, MA, USA

INTRODUCTION

Since 1990, Nepal has embarked upon a difficult process of democratic consolidation. This chapter reflects on Nepal's history of transition over the past two decades, and identifies the factors relevant for the country's evolution toward a peaceful and stable democracy. We argue that Nepal represents a failing democracy in which the prospects for consolidation have narrowed considerably since the outbreak of civil war. Advocates for stable democracy in Nepal must now see this as a generational challenge, requiring a long-term process of locally embedded civil society development, party institutionalization, and the disarmament of insurgency groups.

I. THE THEORY OF DEMOCRATIC CONSOLIDATION

Historically, most states fail during their first attempt at democratic transition. This is equally true of the now established democracies of Western Europe - where initial forms of representative governance failed in early 20th century France, Germany, and Italy - as it is in contemporary Bangladesh, Thailand, or Pakistan, where periods of multiparty democracy have been punctuated by instability and military intervention. However, while instances of democratic reversal are fairly common, comparative studies have shown that they are most frequent during the first years of a fledgling new democracy (Alexander 2002, Diamond 1999). Very few democracies revert to authoritarian rule after a generation or so into a period of representative governance, and of the 74 recorded cases of democratic failure, only three occurred following 32 or more years of democratic rule[1] (Svolik 2007).

The term democratic *consolidation* refers to this process by which democracy becomes entrenched in such a way that reversion to authoritarian rule becomes inconceivable. In their hallmark essay on the subject, Linz and Stepan have summarized this as the condition under which democracy becomes 'the only game in town', as all actors within the political system acknowledge the norm of competing through free and fair elections as the only legitimate strategy for acquiring power (Linz and Stepan 1996). In a consolidated democracy, no significant political group is seriously able to overthrow the democratic regime or secede from the state, and in the face of severe political and economic crises, the overwhelming majority of the public retain the view that further political change must emerge via the democratic process.

Closely related to the concept of democratic consolidation is that of democratic *transition*, which refers to the institutionalization of the set of norms that characterize a liberal democracy. As benchmarks of how far a country has progressed down the path of democratic transition, many political scientists refer to the seven characteristics identified by Dahl (1971): the freedom to form and join associations; freedom of expression; the right to vote in elections; eligibility for public office; the right of political leaders to compete for electoral support; the existence of diverse sources of information; free and fair elections; and the dependence of government policy-making institutions on votes and other expressions of electoral preferences. To the extent that countries have failed to consolidate democratically, they often exhibit an incomplete transition, with democratic norms being violated by actors within the political system that reject the rules of free and fair competition for public office.

Democracies in which the seven above features are not collectively present, that is, countries in which certain norms of democratic rule are repeatedly violated by actors in the political system, may be termed *failing* democracies. Due to the prevalence of regimes in the world today which exhibit an attempted yet imperfect adherence to democratic process, political scientists have developed a range of additional terms to refer to such polities, including hybrid regimes, semi-democracies, and illiberal democracies (Diamond 2002, Case 1996, Zakaria 1997, Collier and Levitsky 1997). While the range of potential infringements upon democratic norms is very wide, examples of such violations include intimidation of candidates, the electorate, or the media; bribery of voters or electoral officials; or the use of state coercion in order to ban parties, publications, or political movements. Likewise, a range of actors within the political system may be responsible for violating democratic norms, including but not limited to the dominant political party, the military, or a paramilitary organization.

The purpose of this chapter is to reflect on the history of democratic transition in Nepal since 1990. In so doing, we aim to assess the prospects for eventual democratic consolidation. We argue that the language of democratic consolidation is especially useful in assessing the political system in a country such as Nepal, which since 1990 has occupied a range of positions on the continuum from authoritarianism to democracy, without achieving a consolidated regime at either end of the spectrum. While Nepal remains very far from achieving any kind of democratic consolidation at the present time, not least of all due to ongoing guerrilla insurgency, the unclear commitment of the Communist Party of Nepal (Maoist) to the multiparty system, and the prospect of a *coup d'état* by one player in the political system, by offering an overview of the evolution of Nepalese democracy since 1990 we seek to identify the factors which have prevented consolidation thus far, and help identify the possible factors that could help advance further consolidation in future. Section II therefore offers a chronological overview of Nepal's democratization trajectory, while Section III explores some of the factors that will determine the success of future consolidation.

II. Nepal's Transition Since 1990

It is possible to distinguish four phases in Nepal's democratization trajectory since 1990. In a first phase, from 1990-1996, Nepalese democracy ran comparatively smoothly, with fair elections and, for the first four years, a workable government. In a second phase, from 1996 to 2002, Nepal experienced the onset of civil war, together with a protracted political crisis in which successive coalition governments were unable to rule coherently. A third phase openly sharply in 2002, when King Gyanendra suspended the democratic process and governed autocratically for the ensuing four years. Finally, since 2006 Nepal has entered a fourth phase, with the proclamation of a constitutional republic and the re-launching of the country's democratic experiment. However, this period has also been marked by renewed insurgency, intimidation, deadlock and uncertainties regarding the ultimate outcome of the constitutional process.

The first phase began in 1990, with the end of the royal autocratic regime and the beginning of democratic transition in Nepal. Unlike many countries, where royal regimes were toppled by radical movements seeking a comprehensive overhaul of the status quo, in Nepal, both the late King Birendra Bir Bikram Shah Dev and the leaders of the democratic parties exhibited restraint and accommodation. Parties such as the Nepali Congress (NC) and a series of communist party clustered into United Left Front and, which had led the democratic struggle against King Mahendra since the 1960s, were legalized, and multi-party democracy was restored.

The first years of democratic transition began comparatively smoothly. An interim government was sworn in on April 19, 1990, headed by the Nepali Congress President Krishna Prasad Bhattarai, and comprised of members of the Nepali Congress Party, the Communist parties of Nepal, royal appointees, and independents. A new constitution was drafted the same year, the first concrete step towards institutionalizing democracy in Nepal. This constitution established a Hindu constitutional monarchy and parliamentary democracy. A bicameral legislature was provisioned by the newly crafted constitution, consisting of a House of Representatives with 205 directly elected members, and an Upper House with 60 members elected on the basis of proportional representation.

Nepal then had its first democratic elections for 30 years on May 12, 1991. The results produced a clear verdict for change and demonstrated widespread public support for a multi-party parliamentary democracy. The NC emerged as the largest party, securing 37 percent of the total votes, and 110 seats in parliament, 7 more than the 103 required for a majority. With 28 percent of the total votes cast, the Communist Party of Nepal Unified Marxist Leninist (CPN-UML) party came second. With 69 seats in the lower house, the UML emerged as the main opposition party; other Communist parties such as United People's Front, Nepal Communist Party (Democratic) and the Nepal Workers' and Peasant Party each won less than 10 seats. The members of former royal regime, also known as 'Panchas', did not perform well, securing only four seats collectively. Likewise, the Nepal Sadbhawana Party (NSP), a

Terai-based party that represented the Southern flat plains, fared poorly in the first general elections, securing just 6 seats. The result of the democratic elections of 1991 therefore reflected a vote against ethnicism, regionalism, and cultural parochialism. Sixty five percent of votes were cast in favor of the two largest parties - the NC and the CPN-UML – raising hopes that Nepal was on its way to becoming a stable democracy with two dominant parties.

From the mid-1990s until 2002, however, these hopes were dashed, as Nepal entered a second phase of democratic transition, under which the country began to exhibit the traits of a failing democracy. The first of these attributes was a breakdown in the mechanism linking public preferences with political outcomes. Although the first parliamentary and local elections were free and fair, personality clashes within the Nepali Congress Party during its first years in office pulled the party in different directions, and Prime Minister Girija Prasad Koirala dissolved parliament in 1994. In the ensuing elections held on the 15th November, 1994, no party was successful in gaining an absolute majority. Since the CPN-UML had emerged as the largest party, veteran UML leader, Man Mohan Adhikari, led a coalition government, making Nepal the world's first communist monarchy. The CPN-UML-led government lasted for only nine months, however, and several years of unstable coalition governments followed. Prime Minister Adhikari recommended the dissolution of the parliament, yet his prerogatives were challenged in the Supreme Court, which upheld the status quo. After the dissolution of the CPN-UML-led government, an NC-led coalition took over, but it too could not last more than 18 months. Former royalists Lokendra Bahadur Chand and Surya Bahadur Thapa, of the National Democratic Party (NDP), then took turns in heading a coalition government, with the help of the NC and CPN-UML. Between 1995 and 1999, several coalition governments were formed, but they could not last due to the political insincerity among the members of parliament, dissidences within the political parties, and a culture of horse-trading which had emerged due to the weakness of the party system and a lack of stringent anti-defection laws.

Hopes for a return to bipolar politics returned following the general election that was finally held in May of 1999, and the NC once again reemerged with an absolute majority in parliament. In that election the NC won 113 seats; the CPN-UML 69; and the National Democratic Party 11. However, though the NC was once again able to form a majority government, dissent within the party led to repeated challenges to the party leadership. Between the 1999 elections and 2003 there were therefore three Nepali Congress party Prime Ministers: Krishna Prasad Bhattarai, Girija Prasad Koirala, and Sher Bahadur Deuba. With the dissident activities within the NC reaching a new high in 2003, the NC witnessed a vertical split. G. P. Koirala led the NC, whereas Sher Bahadur Deuba formed a breakaway party, Nepali Congress (Democratic), containing disgruntled politicians from the NC.

Concurrent with the instability of the party system, Nepal confronted a further and more serious challenge to its democratic consolidation, in the form of an armed insurgency, the People's War, which explicitly rejected the existing democratic order and challenged the legitimacy of the state. More than any other single factor, this guerrilla conflict undermined the prospects for peaceful transition in Nepal, by threatening the legitimacy of the multiparty state, and bringing the military apparatus to the forefront of the political system.

The insurgency began on February 13, 1996, with the declaration of a People’s War by the Communist Party of Nepal (Maoist), who attacked a police post at Halleri, Rolpa district. During its formative stages, the CPN (Maoist) consciously modeled itself on the Peruvian *Sendero Luminoso* (Shining Path) movement, and mimicked their strategy of rural insurgency and sporadic attacks on government infrastructure. Declaring that an end to Indian imperialism, capitalist exploitation, and discrimination against caste, ethnic, religious, and linguistic minorities would not be possible within the existing political order, it launched a 'people's war' to demolish that system. The main aim of the CPN (Maoist) was to declare the country a republic and draft a new constitution through an elected Constituent Assembly (CA). Rolpa and Rukum districts were used as a base to initiate the 'people's war' because it had been a fertile ground of leftwing politics.

During the 1991 general elections, out of the nine seats won by the United People's Front, to which the present day Maoist ideologues Puspa Kamal Dahal and Babu Ram Bhattarai belonged to, two were from the district of Rolpa and one from Rukum. In order to achieve its goal, the CPN (Maoist) created a parallel society through the construction of a state within the state. Solutions to the socioeconomic grievances of the poor were connected to the success of the People's War. Although the CPN (M) reiterated its commitment towards a political solution to the issues in dispute, "peace talks" with the government were primarily used as cover for military preparations prior to launching attacks on security forces. As the war became even deeper entrenched, security forces were attacked with steadily greater frequency while security posts were destroyed. In response to these attacks, in November of 2001 the government passed anti-terrorism legislation and reinforced the overwhelmed police force by committing 54,000 troops of the Royal Nepalese Army (RNA) to the counter-insurgency.

May 2002 marks a shift to the third phase in the history of Nepal's democratic transition, as the basis for executive power moved from the party system to royal fiat. With the increased intensity of the Maoist insurgency and infighting within the political parties, the middle ground occupied by parliamentary democracy and constitutional monarchy eroded steadily, and in May 2002, the sitting Prime Minister Sher Bahadur Deuba dissolved the House of Representatives. In October 2002, King Gyanendra dismissed then Prime Minister Sher Bahadur Deuba for his inability to conduct fresh elections, and from that point forth, assumed personal responsibility to appoint and dismiss new Prime Ministers. Before taking all executive power on 1 February 2005, King Gyanendra appointed and dismissed three different Prime Ministers were appointed and then dismissed in this way, before finally taking over all executive powers on February 1st, 2005. Although most of the major political parties took to the streets in protest against his action, King Gyanendra held his ground, and appointed a government made up of former royalists and the trusted aides of his father. From this point forward, Nepal was widely considered to be a failed democracy, having reverted, in essence, to royal autocratic rule.

Nonetheless, this did not prove to be the end of Nepalese democracy for two reasons. First, under Indian sponsorship, the opposition parties and the Maoists were able to form a joint platform. In late November 2005, the Maoists concluded a 12-point agreement in Delhi with the seven principal political parties that were evicted from the power by King Gyanendra, providing a united front against the Nepalese monarchy, and taking away the ability of the King to make selective political alliances from within the country. Second, Nepalese civil society, hitherto a minor player in the struggle to consolidate democracy, led the calls to restore representative governance. In April 2006, the streets of Kathmandu and other major cities across the country were filled by tens of thousands of demonstrators participating in anti-monarchy rallies. The regime was also suffering from international legitimacy crisis as donors began to set political preconditions for aid. On April 28, King

Gyanendra bowed to this pressure, and reinstated the previously dissolved House of Representatives. The House subsequently removed the words 'His Majesty's' and 'Royal' from every body of the state, placed the former Royal Nepalese Army (now simply 'the Nepal Army') under civilian control, and transferred the right to make laws, and amend or to nullify arrangements regarding succession to the throne, to the House of Representatives. It was further announced that the private property of the king would be taxed as per the law. Finally, Nepal was declared to be a secular state, bringing to an end Nepal's status as the world's only Hindu kingdom.

The fourth stage of Nepal's post-1990 democratization process began in 2007, with the reconvening of the parliament and the subsequent parliamentary decision to abolish the Nepalese monarchy to be implemented by the newly elected members of the Constituent Assembly. While this period has ushered in the promise of renewed democratic transition in Nepal, it has also been marked by two factors that now seriously compromise the medium-term prospects for democracy in the country. The first of these is the eruption of renewed insurgency, led this time not simply by Maoist guerrillas, but by ethnic movements and the activities of over two-dozen non-state armed actors seeking autonomy, self-determination and even some claiming secession from the state of Nepal. The second is the legitimacy crisis surrounding the Constitutional Assembly (CA) process, charged with the responsibility of drafting a new Nepalese constitution, which has led to a state of political anomie in which an extra-constitutional move by one player in the political system, such as a *coup d'etat*, becomes increasingly plausible.

Ethnic insurgency began in Nepal following the announcement of the interim constitution in mid-January 2007. Radical Tarai activists declared their intention to intensify their armed campaign against the Nepali state on grounds that the interim constitution made no specific reference to ethnic autonomy and federalism, but rather only committed itself to ending the unitary state. This seriously undermined Maoist credibility among the indigenous groups, including the Madhesis of the Tarai. At the news of the interim constitution's failure to enshrine a ethnic basis for a future federal Nepali state, the Madhesis erupted into a mass protest movement, bringing together a combination of ex-Maoist leaders, the Nepal Congress, and the Hindu right, backed by its Indian counterparts, who saw an opportunity to undermine popular support for the Maoists [2]. In early 2007, forty people were killed by police gunfire during the 21-day mass uprising in the Tarai. The protests were led by an ex-Maoist, Upendra Yadav, who had formed the Madhesi Jan Adhikar Forum (Madhesi People's Rights Forum) as the main rival to the Maoists' own Madhesi Mukti Morcha (Madhesi Liberation Front). The Janatantrik Mukti Morcha (Jwala Group) in the Terai (southern plains) ordered state officials hailing from the hills to leave the Terai plains, thereby exacerbating an environemnt already made tense by the hills versus plains division. Some of these groups had violent conflicts among themselves and also with the Maoist affiliated Madhesi groups. On the other hand the Chure Bhawar Ekta Samaj has been demanding security and protection of rights of people of the hilly region living in the Madhes region and an autonomous status for the Chure Bhawar region.

If the Maoists were embittered by these 'pretenders' now usurping their agenda, they hardly helped matters by advocating a tough law-and-order line by the central government against these and subsequent Madhesi mobilizations. In the following months the Tarai was largely to escape Kathmandu's control. With a defunct administration, a political vacuum had opened up which was quickly filled by some twenty-two armed groups, many of them criminal. Armed clashes, which included the killing of activists, took place between the Maoist organizations and other groups. Other sources of tension were between the state and the Madhesis, among Madhesi groups themselves, and between Madhesis and settlers of hill origin, especially as there also emerged extreme Madhesi groups demanding expulsion of these settlers from the Tarai and even independence from Nepal. India's hand was a visible influence, keen to promote forces to contain the Maoists. After inordinate delay Kathmandu finally agreed in September 2007 to some key Madhesi demands: a commission of inquiry into the police shootings, compensation payments, and an assurance that it would be constitutionally sensitive to the Madhesis' desire for respect and equality. But there has been no forward movement on this score, and the Tarai continues to simmer. Indeed, three new Tarai parties- Madhesi Jana Adhikar Forum, Tarai-Madhesh Loktantrik Party and Sadbhavana Party- have been formed led by a few parliamentary defectors from the NC, CPN-UML, NDP and Rastriya Janashakri Party (RJP) while violence continued to escalate towards the close of 2007.

Meanwhile, the chaos surrounding the Constitutional Assembly (CA) process continues to undermine the legitimacy of Nepal's democratic transition, thereby increasing the justification and support for actors to seeking to challenge the movement toward a consolidated Nepalese democracy, including secessionist and non-democratic movements. An election for a Constituent Assembly, charged with drafting a new constitution, was held in Nepal on 10 April 2008, after having been postponed on two occasions earlier (20 June 2007 and 22 November 2007). The first delay for holding the elections occurred due to the lack of preparation on behalf of the Election Commission as well as the seven parties that were at the helm of the government. The second delay, on 5 October 2007, occurred because the Maoists demanded that a republic be declared before the election, and that a fully proportional system be used in the election instead of a mixed system. A compromise was agreed to on 4 November: the election would use a fully proportional system, but the republic would only be declared after the CA election. On November 4, most parties in the interim parliament voted in favor of a Maoist proposal calling for a fully proportional election system. However, an absolute majority could not be achieved because the Nepali Congress, the largest party in the parliament vehemently opposed the idea. Later, the problem was resolved when all of the parties agreed to an election where 60% of the electoral seats would be allocated through a proportional system, and the remaining 40% by the direct system of election.

On 15 December, the government considered an amendment to the constitution. This amendment moved the deadline for CA elections from 15 December 2007 to 12 April 2008, and changed the membership of the CA: the seats for the proportional representation system were increased to 335 and the members nominated by the cabinet were increased to 26 from 17. As specified in the Election to Members of the Constituent Assembly Act (2007), party list representation will be calculated using a result divisor method, the Sainte-Laguë method. The seats for first-past-the-post elections remained at 240, making the total number 601 seats instead of the earlier 497. The word 'republic' was also included, but will have to be confirmed by the newly elected CA. The agreement was officially adopted on December 23, 2007 by the government and the Maoists stated they would rejoin the government shortly. The interim parliament approved the deal on December 28, with 270 in favor and three opposed. The Election Commission gave the parties which wished to register for the polls a new deadline of 14 January 2008; parties which had previously registered did not have to re-register. On 11 January, the Cabinet decided to hold the election on 10 April.

The election of the 601-seat Constituent Assembly to write a new constitution was touted as the cornerstone of a 2006 peace deal struck with the Maoists-rebels, ending the Nepalese Civil War in 2006 that forced Nepal's king Gyanendra to cede power, which he had seized in the year 2005. The election held great symbolic value for many in the impoverished Himalayan nation, where over 60 percent of the 27 million people are under age 35 and many voted for the first time.

The Communist Party of Nepal (Maoist) emerged as the largest party in the election with 220 out of 575 elected seats, and it became the largest party in the CA. It was followed by the NC with 110 seats and the CPN-UML with 103 seats. The official and final list of members elected under the PR system was released on 8 May 2008; this meant the first meeting of the CA (which has to be held within 21 days of the publication of the final result) would be held before the end of May 2008. At its very first session held on may 28, 2008. The newly elected Constituent Assembly voted to declare Nepal a federal democratic republic, thereby abolishing the monarchy. 564 members of the CA voted on this motion, with 560 in favor and four opposed. Of all the parties represented in the Constituent Assembly, only the Rastriya Prajatantra Party Nepal (RPP-Nepal) opposed the motion. On 29 May, the royal standard was removed from Narayanhity Palace and replaced with the national flag. King Gyanendra reportedly said on 2 June that he accepted the CA's decision.

III. Factors Relevant to Future Democratic Consolidation in Nepal

In general, it is possible to distinguish three approaches to democratic consolidation. The first approach, known as the institutional perspective, stresses the role of secondary institutions in ensuring consolidation, such as the role of the bureaucracy and judiciary apparatus in generating rule of law (Linz and Stepan 1996). The second approach focuses upon informal rules among elites (O'Donnell 1971). A third approach focuses upon informal participatory norms among the general public, also known as the ‘civic culture’ (Almond and Verba 1963; Putnam 1993; Inglehart and Welzel, 2005). Nepal's democratic consolidation depends upon the further institutionalization in each of these areas.

Rule of Law and the Democratic Process

The rule of law is an essential precondition for democratic consolidation, as formally democracy itself is nothing more than a particular set of laws governing the competition for political power. For example, parties are bound by law to respect the outcome of elections; journalists are guaranteed the right of free expression; and civic organizations have the legal right to form, petition, and lobby their political leaders. To the extent that these rules are not respected or enforced, democracy can be said to be compromised.

If a democracy is to exist, therefore, there must be some means of enforcing the rules upon which the political order is based. Should candidates attempt to cheat in elections by stuffing ballot boxes or by intimidating voters, the judiciary must be capable of bringing them before the courts and reprimanding them. Should a leader attempts to outstay his term of office, there must be a constitutional court, sovereign, or parliament capable of holding such moves in check.

In Nepal, however, the rule of law is very poorly consolidated, such that the main political contenders have increasingly been able to flaunt the rules of democratic competition. As an indicator of the extent to which this is the case, the World Bank's *Worldwide Governance Indicators* give Nepal a rating of -0.06 for *Voice and Accountability* in 1996, yet only -0.89 in 2007. This decline is exactly paralled by the decline in the indicator for *Rule of Law*, which has fallen from -0.15 in 1996, to -0.64 in 2007 - a steady deterioration from 51st to 31st percentile rank, or from about average to the lowest third of countries (Kaufman and Kraay 2008). Likewise, other data testifies to the lack of stability and lawlessness in the Nepalese state. For example estimates from the World Health Organisation, published in 2004, reveal Nepal to have a homicide rate of 15 per 100,000, among the highest rates in Asia. The detection of such a high homicide rate is concerning, as it indicates that the Nepalese police and judiciary system has essentially failed to contain the violence unleashed by political insurgency, ethnic conflict, and organized criminal activity. Until there is rule of law and access to justice for all, Nepal will continue to witness unchecked corruption, the intimidation of journalists, and the repression of civil society activists.

Informal Norms among Elites

Democracy requires the acceptance by all parties of the legitimacy of electoral competition as a means of allocating power. As yet it is not clear whether the CPN (Maoist) truly respect this principle. A key test will arise when the CPN (Maoist) lose an election, and are required to hand over power peacefully to their opponents. Many of their leaders argue that the party's ultimate goal is the formation of a People's Republic rather than a democratic republic.

It is further not evident that other players in the Nepali political system, such as the Nepali army, have accepted the terms of democratic competition. These norms were overturned in 2002 by King Gyanendra, who delegated the military full responsibility to combat the insurgency. Though the King has departed the political scene, it is not inconceivable that the military could take on the role of government of last resort, as it has done repeated in contemporary Pakistan or Thailand. An improvement in civil-military relations is therefore a must for democracy consolidation. This also requires the integration of the UN verified 19,602 Maoist combatants into productive life.

Ultimately, it will only become clear whether Nepali elites are prepared to share power through the democratic process once there has been a peaceful back-and-forth turnover of power between the leading parties (known as the two-turnover test), without postponement or annulation of the election, military intervention, or the use of paramilitary forces. With the interchange of power between NC and the CPN (UNL) in the 1990s, Nepal appeared to have reached an informal consensus among elites; the Maoist insurgency and the palace coup of 2002, however, introduced new actors to the political game with differing strategies and tactics.

Civic Culture

A developed civil society is essential for making democratic institutions function (Almond and Verba 1963, Putnam 1993). Civil society organizations do this in four ways: firstly, by help to monitor the practices of local officials, thereby increasing the possibility that corruption is detected and sanctioned; secondly, by serving as a conduit between citizens and their representatives, ensuring that the latter are made aware of the concerns and interests of the former; thirdly, by forming cross-cutting ties that bridge across religious, ethnic, or caste divides; and finally by direct street mobilization which aims at demanding democratic reform. Of these, the latter has the most direct effect upon democratic consolidation. Firstly democratic transition often begins as a response by elites to direct public action, as in Eastern Europe in 1989 or South Africa in the final years of apartheid, and secondly the threat of popular mobilization often prevents actual or potential coup d'etats from occurring, as has occurred in the Philippines in 1986, the Soviet Union in 1991, or more recently Venezuela in 2002. Inglehart and Welzel (2005) have found an active and expressive citizenry to be one of the preconditions for successful democratization worldwide, on the basis of World Values Survey data which covers a sample of over 80 societies in Europe, the Americas, Africa, and from across Asia and Australasia. Likewise, using this and other data sources Paxton (2002) also reports a strong association between strength of civil society and the level of democracy. In Nepal itself, civil society protests are widely credited playing a key role in forcing King Gyanendra to reinstate the multiparty system in 2006.

A comprehensive review of the state of civil society in Nepal was conducted in 2006 by the international civil society network, *Civicus* (Civicus 2006). Their report gave Nepalese civil society a very low rating, in particular in the areas of civil society environment and impact. For the most part, the structure of civil society remains clientelistic in nature, with organizations existing in order to draw resources from political parties or donor agencies and distribute these to members. Lack of transparency and corruption are cited as major problems and CSOs were also found to be unrepresentative of Nepali society in general. Meanwhile the values of civil society do not encourage activism, as Nepal's political culture remains hierarchical and patrimonial, with civic associations constructed around personalities rather than shared beliefs and commitments.

Unfortunately, the development of civil society is a long process and rapid change in the structure or values of Nepali civil society is unlikely to be forthcoming in the immediate future. Scholarship on the development of civil society has tended to focus on the impact of socioeconomic change, in particular the spread of literacy, urbanization, and economic development, as contributors to its rise. Nepal by and large remains a rural, poor society with a very low level of literacy (48 per cent), widespread poverty (24 per cent of the population live on less than $1 a day, and nominal income per capita is just $234), and an overwhelmingly rural, agrarian population (87 per cent live in rural areas, and 93 per cent of the labor force are employed in agriculture): these factors are likely to constrain the development of a nationally representative civil society for many years to come. There is also substantial evidence that the political insecurity of recent years has further hindered the emergence of civil society, as civil society activists have been threatened, and citizens have cowed to pressure by insurgents and the police.

CONCLUSION: PROSPECTS FOR DEMOCRATIC CONSOLIDATION IN NEPAL

Over the past two decades, Nepal has embarked upon a democratization trajectory in which the social, institutional, and economic preconditions for democracy have been at best weak or absent. Notably, Nepal has lacked the existence of a high quality bureaucracy and police apparatus, capable of maintaining the rule of law, and a vibrant civil society, capable of holding politicians accountable for their actions. If Nepal is to avoid the path of countries such as Pakistan or Bangladesh, which have become mired within endemic instability and military rule, the country must look upon its democratic consolidation not simply a constitutional settlement but as a generational challenge. Just as Nepal's southern neighbor India has been formally democratic for sixty years but only step-by-step improved the performance and functioning of its state and civil society, likewise Nepal must look to the long and difficult task of raising its literacy rate, overcoming caste and ethnic discrimination, and building a meritocratic civil service, so that over time the country will develop a vibrant civil society within a state governed by the rule of law.

All of these challenges, however, require that stability and peace first be restored to Nepal. For only once there is a state that is capable of maintaining order and delivering basic services can policies be pursued to reduce poverty and illiteracy, protect civil rights to free speech and association, and overcome group-based disadvantages through redistributive and welfare measures. Nepal must therefore enact measures to foster reconciliation and peace, restoring the state's monopoly on core functions such as the classic public goods of national security and law and order, if there is to be any hope of eventually building the other preconditions for democratic governance. In the medium term, this will require the formation of a police force, judiciary and bureaucracy based on principles of merit and executive competence, but for the immediate future the country requires a constitutional settlement binding all political actors to the rules of the democratic game. With the abdication of the king, the country now no longer has any absolute political authority, and it is now urgent that a constitutional agreement be settled which will allow the main political factions, the regions, and the military to cooperate according to principles based on the human rights, democracy and rule of law. In this regard, the outcome of the Constituent Assembly in the next two years is thus likely to have a critical bearing on the success of Nepalese democracy over the coming two decades and beyond.

REFERENCES

Alexander, G. (2002) Sources of Democratic Consolidation. Ithaca: Cornell University Press.

Almond, G. and Verba, S. (1963). The Civic Culture: Political Attitudes and Democracy in Five Nations. Princeton, NJ: Princeton University Press.

Case, (1996). "Can the 'Halfway House' Stand? Semidemocracy and Elite Theory in Three Southeast Asian Countries", *Comparative Politics*, Vol. 28, No. 4.

Collier, D. and Levitsky, S. (1997). "Democracy with Adjectives: Conceptual Innovation in Comparative Research", *World Politics*, 49:3.

Dahal, D. and Timsina, T. (2006). "Civil Society in Nepal: Searching for a Viable Role", Institute for Cultural Affairs.

Dahl, R. (1971). Polyarchy: Participation and Opposition. New Haven: Yale University Press.

Diamond, L. (1999). Developing Democracy: Toward Consolidation. Baltimore, MD: Johns Hopkins University Press.

Diamond, L. (2002) "Elections Without Democracy: Thinking About Hybrid Regimes", *Journal of Democracy*, Vol. 13 no. 2.

Inglehart, R. and Welzel, C. (2005). Modernization, Cultural Change and Democracy. Cambridge: Cambridge University Press.

Kaufman, D. Kraay, A. and Mastruzzi, M. (2008). "Governance Matters VII: Aggregate and Individual Governance Indicators, 1996-2007", World Bank Policy Research Working Paper No. 4654.

Linz, J. and Stepan, A. (1996). Problems of Democratic Transition and Consolidation. Baltimore, MD: Johns Hopkins University Press.

O'Donnell, G. (1973). Modernization and Bureaucratic Authoritarianism. New York: Cambridge University Press.

Paxton, P. (2002). "Social Capital and Democracy: An Interdependent Relationship", *American Sociological Review*, 67:254-277.

Putnam, R., Leonardi, R. and Nanetti, R. (1993). Making Democracy Work: Civic Traditions in Modern Italy. Princeton: Princeton University Press.

Svolik, M. (2008), "Authoritarian Reversals and Democratic Consolidation", *American Political Science Review*, 102:153-168.

Zakaria, F. (1997). "The Rise of Illiberal Democracy", Foreign Affairs, November.

In: Nepal in the 21st Century
Editor: Surendra R. Devkota., pp. 97-126
ISBN 978-1-60741-348-6

Chapter 4

A SOCIAL ACCOUNTING ANALYSIS OF POVERTY IN NEPAL: HUMAN CAPITAL FOR 21ST CENTURY

Surendra R. Devkota
Department of Economics University of Albany, Albany, NY, USA

ABSTRACT

In the past five decades, Nepal has followed the standard modernization path with mixed results. The country witnessed the growth of rent seeking elites and increased income inequality, in spite of huge national and international expenditures. This paper attempts to examine the socioeconomic structure of Nepal based on social accounting matrices (SAM) that utilizes some available macroeconomic information. Nepal is struggling to meet basic human needs such as an adequate supply of food, water, health care, shelter, and minimum education to majority of population. At least one fourth of households deprived of basic endowments like land, or skills (education). As the SAM coefficients reveal, investment in household sectors have high multipliers, and it is imperative to intervene at the household level to enrich human capital in order to alleviate poverty particularly at the socio-economically deprived households. Poverty alleviation through a trickle down approach has been a major planning theme since few decades, but it is yet to reach to the needy households. Planners and policy makers should realize that least developed country like Nepal does not need to follow an exact economic growth model adopted by the developed countries; they would rather focus on indigenous needs, skills, and resources and build a sustainable system.

Keywords: poverty, economic structure, sustainability, Nepal.

Introduction

The modern socioeconomic development in Nepal started only after 1950s from a very low level socioeconomic capital endowment. For example, only 2 per cent of people were literate out of nearly 8.2 million population in 1951. Prior to that Nepal lacked any systems of civil service, national accounting, records of public welfare, or basic social, economic and demographic indicators, such as schools and hospitals. Development planning began with the establishment of a central planning agency, the National Planning Commission, in 1956, and the Tenth Five Year Plan completed by 2007. During the past 50 years of socio-economic development, the process incurred many ups and downs. The country witnessed different political regimes and many economic growth philosophies including modernization, state monopoly and free market approaches. Nevertheless, socio-economic development in Nepal has been disappointing because:

- It has one of the highest per capita debt in the world and nearly two-thirds of its population struggles to meet basic needs.
- It is dependent upon outside donors for more than 50 per cent of its annual government budget.
- It has a long history of failed attempts at land reform, and one-fourth of the population is landless in an agrarian society where agricultural productivity has been stagnant for decades.
- The state has undefined rights over the resources and a lack of accountability.
- Human settlements in cities emerged without any proper planning and are full of environmental problems like pollution of air and water, and municipal solid wastes as well as shortages of basic needs for human survival. Meanwhile, the country lost a tremendous amount of forest resources under government control.

Socioeconomic development of past decades has not turned out as expected, particularly if compared to neighboring countries. Nepal has the highest poverty level in South Asia, which suggests an insignificant improvement in the average living standards. The Nepal Living Standard Survey (NLSS) of 2003/04 conducted by the Central Bureau of Statistics (CBS) reveals that about 31 percent of the population (26.4 million in 2007) is poor compared to 42 percent in 1995/96. Though the incidence of poverty declined mainly due to remittance money, Gini coefficient between these two periods increased from 0.34 to 0.41. Poverty in rural areas is about 35 percent, while that in urban area is limited to 10 percent of the population.

Nepal is still in the web of a vicious cycle of poverty and a low level of social, economic and political development. In spite of national and international efforts over the past 50 years, why has development yet to reach the majority of the people?

This paper aims to examine the structure of the Nepalese economy in order to find the answers of above mentioned question and also analyses whether the 10th Five Year Plan of Nepal achieved its goal of poverty reduction. First, a general overview the economy is discussed and socio-economic development problems incurred in modern Nepal, and followed by social accounting matrix model that is used to examine the economic structure and to forecast income level after the Plan is accomplished by 2007.

OVERVIEW OF THE NEPALI ECONOMY

Majority of population (78 percent according the NLSS) are dependent upon subsistence agriculture, though its contribution to gross domestic product (GDP) is declining. For instance, share of agriculture to GDP was nearly 65 percent in 1964, and that is reduced to 39 percent in 2004. Since 70 percent employment is dependent upon agriculture, an agrarian economy is still prevalent, but country entered into market economy only in early nineties. Prior to that, a mixed economy of centrally planned Marxist type was enforced by the then King Mahendra in 1961 after overthrowing an elected government, which was known as Panchayati system. Khadka (1994) discussed about the Panchayati economics, and Mahat (2005) presents an elaborative picture of economic growth after the introduction of multiparty polity in 1990. Different politico-economic philosophies introduced by different regimes in Nepal are also discussed by Pandey (1999) and Devkota (2007 and 2005).

Bhattarai (2003) by studying sectoral (agriculture, industry, and trade) and spatial differentiation of the Nepali economy claimed that the spatial unevenness in development in Nepal can be seen as the function of both the conservative monopolistic structure and uneven penetration of the capitals. Blaikie, Cameron, and Seddon (1979, 2001) after studying Nepal's economic growth over the decades concluded "far reaching structural change is required if the mass of people in Nepal are to be assured of their basic needs."

In earlier days, the "basic needs strategy" endorsed by the United Nations was a very routine political rhetoric in Nepal, though majority of people still lack of it. Subsequently, different governments in Nepal attempted to incorporate the Program for the Fulfillment of Basic Needs during the Seventh Plan period (1985–1990), but political upheavals interrupted its implementation. After restoration of democracy in 1990, poverty became a principal objective of the National Planning Commission. The Ninth Plan (1997–2002) mentioned poverty as the sole development objective. Likewise, the Tenth Plan (2002-2007) reiterates the emphasis on poverty alleviation. Despite more than two decades of development planning about poverty, the results are not encouraging. The 2003/04 Household Survey reported that the bottom fifty percent of the population has consumes less than 20 percent of total output, while the top 30 percent consumes more than 60 percent of the total. The situation in South Asia is like in India where the top 10 percent consumes about 33 percent of the total. Likewise, in Bangladesh the highest 10 percent consumes about 29 percent, Pakistan 27.6 percent, and Sri Lanka 28 percent (World Bank, 2002).

Following the philosophy of modernization, the government of Nepal is determined to increase the rate of economic growth so that the poor will benefit as directly as possible from economic development. To promote the growth agenda, a variety of strategies, polices, plans were put forward, although no one is really clear about how to achieve the kind of economic growth outlined in the five-year plans. What is the difference between the new Plan and old versions? The old Plans also had the same goals of socioeconomic development, but they failed. For example, in the last five decades, despite the investment of billions, if not trillions of Rupees on population stabilization efforts, unsatisfactory. the population growth rate has not declined since the 1950s he population growth rate was 2.3 percent 1950sand the latest Census of 2001 shows it is 2.24 percent, which means that the annual population stabilization efforts had insignificant impact. The actual population growth rates are in stark contrast to the aims of the Five Year Plans. The Sixth Five-year Plan of Nepal (1980-85) aimed to reduce population growth rate to 1.6 percent in 1990, and 1.2 percent in the year of 2000. The Seventh Five-year Plan (1985-90) reiterated the same objective of population stabilization. Further, at the end of the Ninth Five-year Plan (1997-2002), population growth rate was still above two percent. By this account, it can be inferred that the Plans were unsuccessful.

Some other major tribulations that hinder socio-economic development in Nepal discussed in the following sections.

i. Failure to Stabilize the Population Growth

As discussed earlier, population stabilization has been one of the top priorities of different plans since the seventies. The latest census 2001 of Nepal reveals that the population grew at the rate of 2.24 per cent per year and now totals 23.15 million people (Central Bureau of Statistics 2001). The general population trend in different ecological regions dhows that the influx of people to the plains is increasing. Compared with the 1991 Population Census, in the Kathmandu valley and the plains districts (Terai) the population increased by more than 2 per cent annually, whereas in the hilly districts it was less than 2 per cent, and in the mountain districts around 1 per cent per year. This indicates that people are still leaving the hilly or mountain areas for the plains or valleys. (Further details will be available on chapters 1 and 12). The other most striking attribute of the recent census of 2001 is the increase in landless families. Out of a total of 4.2 million families, the census reveals that nearly 1.02 million families do not have any land, which means one- fourth of the total families in the country are absolutely landless. The Census shows clearly the faulty planning practices in Nepal, a fact already discussed by Wildavsky (1972).

In the last five decades, despite the investment of billions of rupees on population stabilization efforts, the population growth rate has not declined since the fifties. The population growth rate was 2.3 in 1951–52 and 2.24 in 2001, which means that the annual population stabilization efforts had insignificant impact. The actual population growth rates are in stark contrast to the aims of the Five Year Plans. The Sixth Five-Year Plan of Nepal (1980–85) aimed to reduce population growth rate to 1.6 per cent in 1990 and 1.2 per cent in 2000. The Seventh Five Year Plan (1985–90) reiterated the same objective of population stabilization. Further, at the end of the Ninth Five-Year Plan (1997–2002), population growth rate was still above 2 per cent. By this account, it can be inferred that the Plans were unsuccessful. One of the main reasons for this magnitude of failures of the central planning exercise could be lack of appropriate institutions and strategies to complement the planning objectives at the local/village level where the crux of the problem lies (also see Box 1 in Chapter 13).

ii. Low Productivity

Earlier, Shah (1988) discussed economic growth in Nepal and observed that low productivity is one of the major impediments rather than a paucity of resources. The Labour Force Survey (Central Bureau of Statistics 1999) reveals that out of the 9.5 million employed people, 6.4 million were engaged in subsistence agriculture and agricultural productivity has been more or less stagnant— growing at about 2 per cent—in the last five decades.

Entrepreneurs at the national level are not capable of absorbing the growing number of unemployed (18 per cent in 2004–05). This may be due to lack of capital or skills or both. Since economic opportunity in the rural areas is very limited, the so-called economically active population is increasingly interested in working in foreign countries. Laborers from Nepal are spreading over the East, Southeast, South and West Asia in search of jobs—mostly unskilled. The official figure of the Nepali labor force working abroad, except India, as of March 2006 was 714,679 (Ministry of Finance 2006), but unofficially, it is estimated that about 9 million people are working outside the country. For example, about 8 million Nepalis are in India and half-a-million in the Gulf countries (Phuyal 2006), and the rest in Asia, Europe and America. Consequently, remittance money is the backbone of the current economy. The Nepal Rastra Bank (2006) estimates that the Nepali economy in 2004–05 earned over US$ 922 million in remittances from overseas workers—accounting for 12.4 per cent of national gross domestic product (GDP).

About two-thirds of the total work force in the country is absorbed by agriculture, which itself is constrained by limited land resources. It is not uncommon to see a large number of economically active people living without any real prospects for the future. For example, in the history of school leaving certificate examination, that is, Class X graduation, the pass rate is barely 50 per cent. (Chapter five elaborates on this aspect). In recent years, the annual number of failed students exceeds 100 thousand. Those who fail in the examination are mostly from the rural areas and they have limited options to be economically active, such as either to work in the farmland or to assist in a parental business. On the other side, the same Labor Force Survey showed that out of the total population of 11.2 million (aged 15 and over), 6.8 million have never attended school and about 4 million people never completed high school, which indicates a huge waste of human capital. Had either the government or donor communities spent their efforts to enhance the skills of human resources in rural/village areas, resources would have been used in productive and beneficial means. Implicitly, the general education system in Nepal is anti-development (Bista 1994) and lacks a recognition of the dignity of the value of labor.

iii. Donors as Suppliers of Development

Nepal prides itself in being a politically non-colonized state since the historic period, but this image is tarnished by economic dependency. After Nepal became a member of the Colombo Plan (Benham 1954), a gateway was opened for foreign financial and technical assistance. Since the fifties, Nepal's dependency upon foreign aid has been heavy and even in recent years about two-thirds of the annual budget is supported by foreign donations, including loans and grants.

Before 1990, foreign aid was primarily invested in industry and power, transportation and communication, and agriculture; whereas after 1990, the major recipients are transport, irrigation, communication, education and agriculture. It is estimated that the total foreign debt had reached to US$ 3.12 billion in 2005. The debt to GDP ratio—an indicator of the country's ability to pay back its debt—was 45.3 per cent in 2004–05 (Ministry of Finance 2006).

Foreign aid, rather than enhancing productivity in Nepal has become an economic burden due to the unsustainability of the projects (Schwartz and Paulhare 2000). Shrestha (1993) and

Mihaly (1965) articulated some negative aspects of foreign aid in Nepal. For instance, it has destroyed the indigenous economic system, such as local knowledge and cooperative spirit that were sustainable, though not necessarily 'modern'. Pant (1991) discussed foreign aid's major contributions and its problems and policy aspects. One of the major arguments for foreign aid is that it enhanced the level of investment in Nepal because the country had a very low domestic saving rate. Although foreign aid to Nepal is being streamlined through the Nepal Aid Group—a World Bank aegis—in general, it seems that the Nepal government is still lagging behind in its effort to use aid resources efficiently in terms of needs and capacity.

The Auditor General's annual report mentions that the trend of misuse of foreign aid and loans is on the rise. There is no record of how the devaluation of the Nepalese rupee against the dollar has added to the burden. Further, donors are able to bypass the government and initiate projects or programs of their own. There are no records of this foreign money inflow. In the words of the Auditor General[1]:

> "It is a serious matter that there are no records of how much aid and loans are brought into the country. We have repeatedly demanded that the government come up with a mechanism to keep track of these amounts to avoid irregularities and misuse of funds but this has not happened."

iv. Corruption and Lack of Fiscal Discipline

Corruption affects different aspects of economic development, such as the level of investment, making and enforcing property rights, income distribution, access to resources and assets within the country (Jain 2001). Corruption is rampant in Nepal, and it spreads from different executive levels to primary units of political, bureaucratic and legislative bodies. Mieko Nishimizu[2] (2002), the World Bank's Vice President for the South Asia region, explicitly stated: 'Nepal has a serious crisis of governance, and high level of corruption'. In March 2002, the Nepal Government constituted a high-level Property Probe Commission to find out the property owned by government officials and politicians holding key public offices, compared to their incomes. But this probe became a tool of political revenge and was later aborted. At the national level, one can estimate the fiscal discipline of the Nepalese bureaucrats by examining the un-audited amounts of national spending. For example, the 2005–06 annual report of the Auditor General accounted nearly Rs. 30 billion of inappropriate expenditures. Although all unaccounted expenses may not represent corruption, it indicates a lack of fiscal discipline of the State. No one knows when such a huge amount will be reimbursed to the national treasury. It is ironic that this un-audited amount has increased since the Panchayat regime, and corruption during the Panchayati system was simply excused by dumping off investigative reports, such as the Mallik Commission[3] report.

---

[1] Auditor General quoted in The Kathmandu Post, 1 October 2001. Available at www.kantipuronline.com (accessed on 10 September 2008).

[2] Mieko Nishimizu quoted in The Kathmandu Post, 11 September 2002. Available at www.kantipuronline.com (accessed on 10 September 2008).

[3] A three-member investigation committee under the chairmanship of the Supreme Court Justice Janardhan Mallik was set up after the 1990's movement. One of its main tasks was to find irresponsible persons and their extrajudicial activities during the 1990 People's movement. But its recommendations including action against two Prime Ministers were never implemented.

The relationship between or among different money laundering stakeholders cannot be ignored. It also signifies a lack of accountability in the present politico-administrative set up.

Socio-economic development crises are intertwined with politico-economics, and means and ends of governance, because Nepal is a victim of underdevelopment and poor policies (Meier 2001). Henceforth, it is necessary to examine the economic structure that lies behind economic production, consumption, and investment, which will help to devise appropriate policy measures in order to follow a sustainable development path. There is a general consensus that the social accounting matrix is an appropriate tool to explore the socioeconomic structure and transactions of a circular flow economy that will be discussed in following chapter.

THE SOCIAL ACCOUNTING MATRIX

The social accounting matrix (SAM) analyzes the structure of an economy. Richard Stone, a Noble Laureate in Economics in 1984, pioneered work on social accounting in the sixties and paved the way for the SAM. Stone (1986) perceived that social accounting is a systematic quantitative description of a socioeconomic system. Earlier, Pyatt and Thorbecke (1976) formalized the concept of the social accounting into social accounting matrix. Now, SAM is practiced in many disciplines of humanities and social science such as demography, education, economics, regional sciences and health (Hewings and Madden, 1995).

SAM is an expanded version of the input-output (IO) model. IO analysis focuses on the structure of production, the activity taking place in the upper left corner of Figure 1, but does not provide much detail about final users.

Final demand describes only in terms of the major components household consumption of final products, government consumption, trade (consumption by out-of area users), and investment. While the IO table describes production in terms of hundreds of industries, households are presented by a single sector in final demand, even though they account for most of final demand and are the driving force in the economy. This restricted treatment of households limited the ability of the IO model to address such issues as income distribution or environmental impacts of changing economic patterns.

The need for a more detailed treatment of households led researchers, beginning with the work of Richard Stone in the 1960s, to expand the IO system (Pyatt and Round 1985) to a Social Accounting Matrix (SAM). Figure 2 provides a simplified version of a SAM. The purpose of a SAM is to provide within the IO framework a more detailed description of the dual role that households play as consumers and as suppliers of labor and capital. Households are disaggregated into many columns according to criteria relevant to the policy question at hand. Often, households are disaggregated according to income category. As suppliers of labor and capital, the value-added block may also be disaggregated for different categories of labor according to wage group or by occupation. The connections between the source of income (household supply of labor and capital) and consumption (household purchases of final demand) are represented by another matrix showing the flows between final demand and value added.

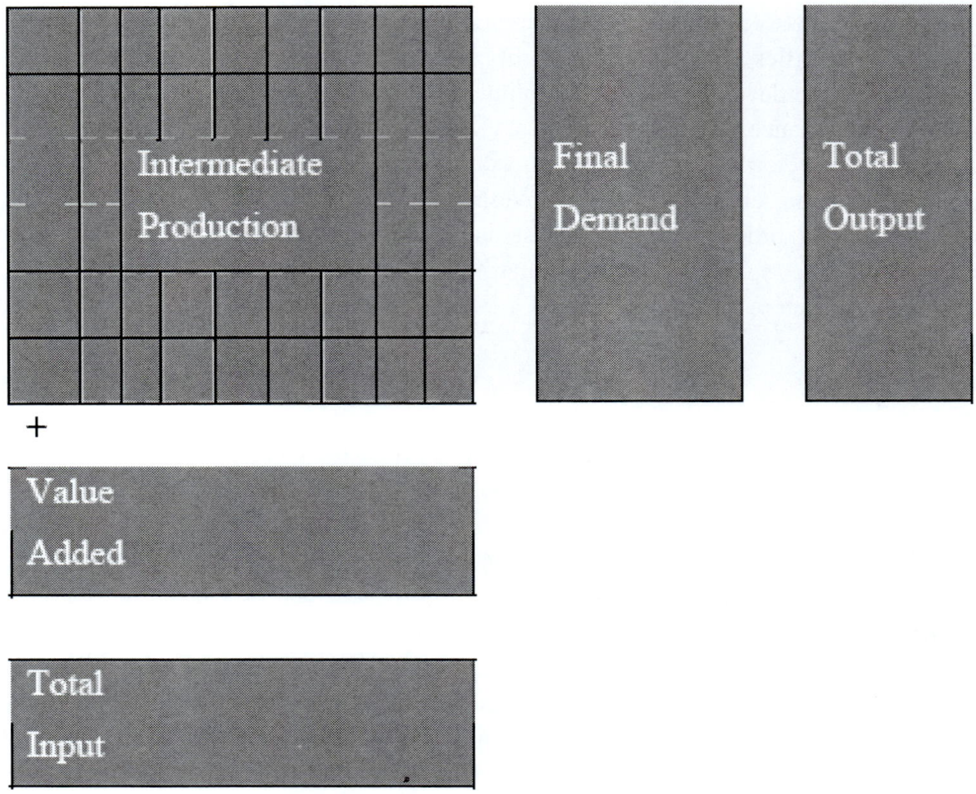

Figure 1. The basic Input-Output system.

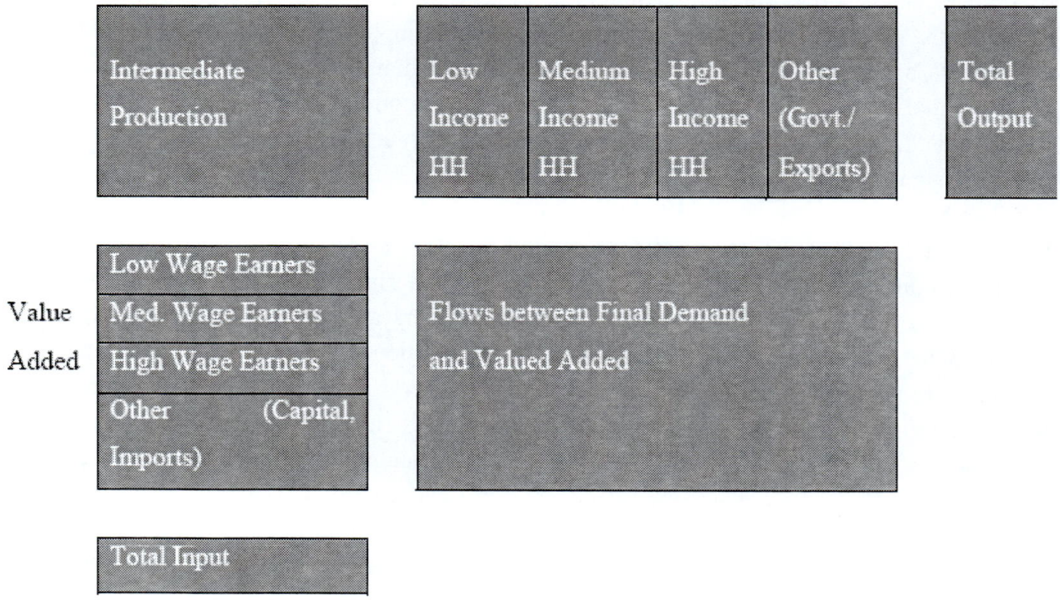

Figure 2. A general structure of a Social Accounting Matrix.

With a growing need for analysis linking economic and environmental effects, the basic IO/SAM framework has been expanded to incorporate environmental and natural resource accounts (United Nations, 1993; Lange, 1999). Thorbecke (1998) describes SAM as a comprehensive, consistent, complete and disaggregated data system that is useful for policy analyses. SAM depicts a static image of the country's economic structure. Its double entry bookkeeping system reveals incoming and outgoing accounts (King, 1985).

SAM is an efficient way of presenting a fundamental law of economics: every income has corresponding expenditure (Pyatt, 1988). It is a square matrix in which rows represent income and columns reveal expenditure. Structurally, a SAM is comprised of institutes, assets, and transactions to describe the factors of production, factor income, and consumption (Pyatt, 1991; Thorbecke 1998). Pyatt further says that SAM is a framework both for models of how the economy works as well as for data, which can be used to monitor its workings. Pyatt (1990 and 1999) discusses how statistics over time can be integrated into a social accounting matrix representation of economic activity. A further advancement of SAM is the exploration of the relationship between commodity balances and input-output tables. Robinson, Cattaneo, and El-Said (2001) used a "cross entropy" approach to estimate a consistent SAM starting from inconsistent data estimated with error, a common experience in many countries. Golan and Vogel (2000) developed a framework for estimating the entries of a SAM, or any large matrix of expenditures, and trade or income flows. SAM is used to develop a price-model that captures the interdependence among activities, households and factors to provide a complete set of accounting prices (Roland-Holst and Sancho,1995). Keuning (1991) discussed how flow accounts, which could be a part of the next system of national accounts, can be embedded easily in a SAM framework. Defourny and Thorbecke, (1994) reviewed the SAM framework as a basis for multiplier analysis, multiplier decomposition, element of structural analysis and, more particularly, the transmission of economic influence within a structure. SAM is helpful for uniform valuation of inputs for meaningful manipulation of the input-output table contained in a SAM, as well as to assess the real effects of changes in demand (Greenfield and Fell, 1979. A general guideline for building a SAM is suggested by Keuning and de Ruijter (1988) who suggest the steps of overall design of the system, identification of sources, choice of base year, defining classification, preparation of tabulation plans, derivation of initial estimates, correction of errors, and reconciliation.

SAM's strength to integrate national income and resource and environmental accounting offers a good insight of policy analysis. One of the problems with integrating social, ecological, and economic indicators is the lack of compatibility between the monetary and physical values. This may hinder analysis of the complex interaction between these indicators. However, SAM can make this task easier because it can include both monetary and non-monetary values. Alarcon, Heemst and de Jong (2000) concluded that it is feasible to extend the SAM using both physical and monetary indicators. They also observed that addressing the problem of sustainability requires detailed information about stocks and flows along with social indicators.

A SOCIAL ACCOUNTING MATRIX FOR NEPAL

The SAM for Nepal is constructed based on 1999 the Input-Output database (Shrestha and Sapkota, 1999) for the 10th Plan. In addition to the IO table, other required supplementary information is taken from the publications of the Ministry of Finance (www.mof.gov.np), and the Central Bureau of Statistics (CBS) (www.cbs.gov.np). A thematic SAM structure is presented in Table 1. Since there is no universal standard format for SAM, it is customary to build a SAM with respect to the availability of information and the objective of analysis. To this regard, a SAM model developed for developing countries (Cohen, 2002a) is followed. In general, the SAM system includes following major accounts.

- Wants include basic needs such as food, non-food, and housing.
- Factors of production include land, labor, and capital.
- Accounts of economic agents such as households, firms, government, and rest of the world are grouped as institutions.
- Products accounts are structured according to taxonomy of sectors.
- National capital accounts record the flow of savings and investment of the economy.

Since the main objective of the present SAM is to investigate the extent and magnitude of poverty, primary emphasis is on wants and the household sectors. Both wants and households are further disaggregated (Table 2). The general objective of disaggregating the SAM is to explore the relation between production and consumption in the economy, and particularly the wants of different deciles of households and factors of production. Although government of Nepal pursued different development policies in order to enhance economic growth and to alleviate poverty, income disparity is widening. Hence it is necessary to examine the economic structure lying behind the economic transactions between production, consumption, and investment. This will help to guide appropriate policy measures so that a sustainable development path could be followed.

To construct the SAM, it is assumed that the latest survey on per capita average consumption in deciles also reflects the households' average income. So wants are expanded into food, non-food, housing and other sectors, and households are categorized by income deciles. A disaggregated SAM (26 x 26) is computed based on the information available in the IO table, economic surveys, and CBS sources. Since there is a discrepancy in import and export data, a residual method is employed to balance them. Likewise, there is a lack of complete recording of incoming as well as outlays of donor agencies, residual techniques are used to balance them. That's why the exact matching of income rows and expenditure columns is lacking in Table 2.

Likewise, another of major problem with the economic data in Nepal is the incomplete accounting of remittances from abroad. Dahal (2000), and Nepal (2002) discussed the opportunity cost of the flow of remittance in Nepal sent by Nepalis working abroad. They estimated about Rs. 75 billion (1 USD = Rs. 71) in currency could have entered Nepal in 1999/2000, and this SAM also complements that estimation (Table 2). The Nepal Rastra Bank (2006) estimates that the Nepali economy in 2004/05 earned over US Dollars 922 million in remittances from overseas workers – accounting for 12.4 percent of national gross domestic product.

Table 1. Thematic SAM structure

Wants	Wants	Factors	Households	Firms	Government	Capital	Production	Rest of world
Factors			HH spending					
Households		Wages			Transfer to HH		Value added	Factor pay
Firms		Profit						Transfer
Government		Profit PE	HH direct tax	Direct tax			Indirect tax	Transfer
National capital			HH saving	Saving	Public saving		Depreciation	Deficit
Gross production	Consumption				Public Consumption	Investment	Intermediate	Export
Rest of world			Transfer		Transfer		Imports	

Table 2. Disaggregated SAM for Nepal

			Housing			HH deciles			
Food	Non-food		& other	Factors	1	2	3	4	5
1 Food	0	0	0	0	9324	11703	13563	15256	17268
2 Non-food	0	0	0	0	2723	3820	4950	6138.5	6893
3 Housing /others	0	0	0	0	1527	2218	2316	2551	3062
4 Factors	0	0	0	0	0	0	0	0	0
5 1st Deciles	0	0	0	5260	0	0	0	0	0
6 2th deciles	0	0	0	6873	0	0	0	0	0
7 3rd deciles	0	0	0	8069	0	0	0	0	0
8 4th deciles	0	0	0	9277	0	0	0	0	0
9 5th deciles	0	0	0	10545	0	0	0	0	0
10 6th deciles	0	0	0	11986	0	0	0	0	0
11 7th deciles	0	0	0	13739		0	0	0	0

Table 2. (Continued)

		Housing			HH deciles				
Food	Non-food	& other	Factors	1	2	3	4	5	
12 8th deciles	0	0	0	16075	0	0	0	0	0
13 9th deciles	0	0	0	19599	0	0	0	0	0
14 10th deciles	0	0	0	31085	0	0	0	0	0
15 Firms	0	0	0	182774.4	0	0	0	0	0
16 Agriculture	87520	39231	8528	0	0	0	0	0	0
17 Manufacturing industries	58633.2	29317	9773	0	0	0	0	0	0
18 Construction	0	0	0	0	0	0	0	0	0
19 Gas, electricity, water	1647	823.5	274.5	0	0	0	0	0	0
20 Trade, Hotel, Resturant	21460	10730	3577	0	0	0	0	0	0
21 Transport &Communication	20299.8	10150	3383.3	0	0	0	0	0	0
22 Banking & real estate	17293	8505	2551	0	0	0	0	0	0
23 Community, Social service	5006	2503	835	0	0	0	0	0	0
24 Government	0	0	0	-572.7	327	427	501	576	655
25 National capital	0	0	0	0	2222	2904	3409	3919	4455
26 Rest of world	0	0	7208.7	0	0	0	0	0	0
Total	211859	101259.5	36130.5	314709.7	16123	21072	24739	28440.5	32333

THE SAM MODEL AND MULTIPLIER ANALYSIS

Since a SAM documents the circular flow of the income and expenditures of an economy, a change in the income of one sector will affect households and other sectors both directly and indirectly because of inter and intra transactions of different kinds of sectors and demands such as factor demand, intermediate demand, household demand, and government demands.

Hence, it reveals a link between production activities and household consumption. To this regard, a SAM needs to be divided into endogenous and exogenous accounts. In general, government, capital, and rest of the world are exogenous accounts, and the other parameters such as households and their consumption (wants), and production and its factors become endogenous accounts.

Exogenous accounts are assumed as fixed for the analysis. So, the model behaves like a demand driven Keynesian model as supplies are assumed to adjust to the demand. It also satisfies Walras' Law that total income is equal to the total expenditure in the system (Pradhan, and Sahoo, 1996).

The disaggregated SAM Table 2 is further simplified as Table 3. The exogenous sectors are denoted by X and are comprised of flows of export, investment demands, income transfers from abroad, and government.

The endogenous accounts of the 23 x 23 sub-matrix show the flows from endogenous to endogenous sectors (Table 3). In Table 3, T13 is the matrix of household spending, T24 reveals a matrix of value added generated by the various production sectors, T32 reflects institutional income, T41 shows household consumption, and T44 is the input-output transaction matrix.

Each flow of the endogenous account of 23 x 23 matrices is divided by its respective column in order to obtain the SAM multipliers.

Table 3. A schematic SAM

						Exogenous	
		Wants	Factors	Institutes	Activities	Govt., Capital, ROW	Total
Endogenous	Wants			T_{13}		X_1	Y_1
	Factors				T_{24}	X_2	Y_2
	Institutes		T_{32}	T_{33}		X_3	Y_3
	Activities	T_{41}			T_{44}	X_4	Y_4
Exogenous							
	Total	Y_1	Y_2	Y_3	Y_4		

Table 3 can be interpreted in a simple matrix format as follows. A matrix of coefficients is derived by dividing each element in the *Tij* by the corresponding sum of the column vector *Yj*.

$$\begin{matrix} Y_1 & & 0 & 0 & A_{13} & 0 & Y_1 & & X_1 \\ Y_2 & = & A_{21} & 0 & 0 & 0 & Y_2 & & X_2 \\ Y_3 & & 0 & A_{32} & A_{33} & 0 & Y_3 & + & X_3 \\ Y_4 & & A_{41} & 0 & 0 & A_{44} & Y_4 & & X_4 \end{matrix}$$

$A\ ij = Tij\ Y^{-1}$, j = 1, 2, 3, 4

X is the vector of row sum of respective sub-matrix.
It can be written as;

$$Y = AY + X$$

$Y = (I-A)^{-1} X$, which is analogous to input-output model. Now, Y1, Y2, Y3, and Y4 can be derived through the inverse of $(I-A)^{-1}$.

The equation $Y = (I-A)^{-1} X$, $(I-A)^{-1}$ gives an aggregate or total multiplier of SAM (23 x 23 matrix), which can be expressed as;

$$(I-A)^{-1} = Ma\ X$$

This total or aggregate multiplier is further decomposed into sub-matrices (Table 4) as

$$Ma\ X = M_3\ M_2\ M_1\ X.$$

M_1 is called the "transfer multiplier", M_2 is known as the "own effect multiplier", and M_3 is the "cross-effect multiplier." The transfer multiplier, M1, depicts the effects of direct transfers within the production activities. M2, also known as open loop effect, indicates interactions from production to institutions, wants, and factors. M3, the closed loop effect, insures the circular flow of income from production to factors to institutions to wants and back to activities in the form of consumption demand (Cohen, 2002 a, b).

Based on above discussion of the SAM model, complete SAM multipliers are presented in Table 4, which is further decomposed and discussed below.

Table 4. SAM Multipliers

	1	2	3	4	5	6	7	8	9	10
1 Food	1.463312	0.463918	0.466217	0.449401	1.150662	1.123464	1.114938	1.10089	1.098109	1.107505
2 Non-food	0.221047	1.221337	0.222433	0.21441	0.421865	0.436603	0.45892	0.477622	0.474481	0.467526
3 Housing /others	0.08083	0.080936	1.081337	0.078403	0.193403	0.205937	0.192103	0.187445	0.193392	0.190933
4 Factors	1.82065	1.823033	1.832065	1.765985	1.822412	1.82259	1.822486	1.822477	1.822537	1.822493
5 1st Decile Household	0.030375	0.030414	0.030565	0.029463	1.030404	0.030407	0.030405	0.030405	0.030406	0.030405
6 2nd decile	0.039689	0.039741	0.039938	0.038498	0.039728	1.039732	0.039729	0.039729	0.03973	0.039729
7 3rd decile	0.046596	0.046657	0.046888	0.045197	0.046641	0.046645	1.046643	0.046643	0.046644	0.046643
8 4th decile	0.053572	0.053642	0.053907	0.051963	0.053623	0.053629	0.053626	1.053625	0.053627	0.053626
9 5th decile	0.060894	0.060974	0.061276	0.059066	0.060953	0.060959	0.060955	0.060955	1.060957	0.060955
10 6th decile	0.069215	0.069306	0.069649	0.067137	0.069282	0.069289	0.069285	0.069285	0.069287	1.069285
11 7th decile	0.079338	0.079442	0.079836	0.076956	0.079415	0.079423	0.079418	0.079418	0.07942	0.079418
12 8th decile	0.092828	0.092949	0.09341	0.090041	0.092918	0.092927	0.092921	0.092921	0.092924	0.092922
13 9th decile	0.113178	0.113326	0.113887	0.10978	0.113287	0.113298	0.113292	0.113291	0.113295	0.113292
14 10th decile	0.179505	0.17974	0.180631	0.174116	0.179679	0.179697	0.179686	0.179686	0.179692	0.179687
15 Firms	1.055461	1.056842	1.062078	1.023771	1.056482	1.056586	1.056525	1.05652	1.056555	1.056529
16 Agriculture	0.883775	0.85978	0.773494	0.363627	0.866556	0.864821	0.865811	0.865875	0.865295	0.865733
17 Manufacturing industries	0.621971	0.636677	0.69284	0.266336	0.632893	0.633997	0.633346	0.633291	0.633666	0.633389
18 Construction	0	0	0	0	0	0	0	0	0	0
19 Gas, electricity, water	0.023264	0.02385	0.026075	0.009974	0.023698	0.023742	0.023716	0.023714	0.023729	0.023718
20 Trade, Hotel, Restaurant	0.312839	0.319873	0.346704	0.133839	0.31806	0.318587	0.318276	0.31825	0.318429	0.318297
21 Transport &Communication	0.314088	0.320771	0.346298	0.134247	0.319052	0.319554	0.319258	0.319233	0.319403	0.319278
22 Banking & real estate	0.296457	0.300302	0.310134	0.12567	0.298767	0.298995	0.298891	0.2989	0.298969	0.298908
23 Community, Social service	0.055461	0.056842	0.062078	0.023771	0.056482	0.056586	0.056525	0.05652	0.056555	0.056529

HOUSEHOLDS INCOME AND PRODUCTION ACTIVITIES

Household income inequality and distribution is analyzed through the SAM multipliers: namely aggregate, transfer, open, and closed multipliers. The overall equation can be written as;

$M_{a,34}$	$= [M_{3,\ 33}]$	$[M_{2,\ 34}]$	$[M_{1,\ 44}]$
Total multipliers	= (Closed)	(Open)	(Transfer) multipliers

The algebraic derivation of the above mentioned decomposed multiplier is also found in Thorbecke and Jung (1996), and Cohen (2002 a, b). The aggregate (total) SAM multipliers presented in Table 4 indicate demand thrust in the production activities. This implies that a unit of demand injection in certain production activities will have total multiplier effects.

The wants sub-matrix in Table 4, i.e., rows 1 to 3 indicates the effects of an injection from activities on wants. Impacts of injections in agriculture, and households are high on food items compared to injection in production sectors (see rows 1 to 3). SAM propensities for food for low-income households are higher than those for high-income households. The latter has high coefficients on non-food items. 8th deciles households have high saving and housing coefficients, among others.

The impact of injections on the factor accounts (row 4) show that both construction (1.908) and community and social services (1.830) have high multiplier effects. Agriculture has minimal impacts (1.769) on the factor accounts. It should be noted that agriculture is the main activity for subsistence for about 90 percent of the population.

Rows 5 through 14 show the impact of injections in activities on households (this is separately discussed below). However, rows 5 to 10 reveal interesting multiplier effects. Low-income households retain high multiplier values in construction and social services. Injection into other production sectors has a smaller multiplier impact than found in the food and households sectors. Altogether, rows 1 through 15 reveal aggregate income multipliers, whereas rows 16 to 23 indicate aggregate output multipliers.

Agriculture has the lowest (1.769), and the construction sector has the highest income multiplier effects (1.908). Interestingly, banking and real estate have the lowest output impact (2.201) compared to all other production sectors. Both construction and manufacturing industries are the leading sectors having high output multipliers (Table 6). Injection in production sectors, on the average, will add to income by an additional 40 percent and output by 60 percent. Agriculture sectors' aggregate income multiplier (1.769) and output multiplier (2.294) are smaller than those found in Korea, Pakistan, India, Sri Lanka, and Indonesia. These income and output multipliers for the Nepali economy (Table 5) are comparable with those of an African country. Similarly, the average income multiplier (1.801) and output multiplier (2.458) is more or less equal with Kenya, Surinam, and Egypt, but less than India (income = 3.684; output = 5.946), Pakistan (income = 4.028; output = 8.770), Sri Lanka (income = 2.055; output =3.090), and Indonesia (income = 2.119; output = 3.390) (Cohen, 2002 a). It might be noticed that the output multipliers for Nepal are relatively homogeneous. Cohen also found a homogeneous pattern of output multipliers in the less developed countries he studied.

Table 5. SAM multipliers by production sectors

1 Food	0.450351752	0.45296453	0.485599954	0.4516548	0.453645382	0.452485608	0.454960073	0.465799951
2 Non-food	0.214864063	0.21611063	0.231681078	0.215485751	0.216435463	0.215882132	0.217062706	0.222234442
3 Housing /others	0.078569154	0.07902498	0.084718617	0.078796486	0.079143766	0.07894143	0.079373129	0.081264274
4 Factors	1.769721905	1.77998918	1.908234779	1.774842418	1.782664696	1.778107199	1.787830963	1.830427821
5 1st Deciles Household	0.029525077	0.02969637	0.031835951	0.029610505	0.029741008	0.029664973	0.029827199	0.030537862
6 2nd Deciles HH	0.03857906	0.03880288	0.041598572	0.038690685	0.038861207	0.038761855	0.038973829	0.039902419
7 3rd Deciles HH	0.045292367	0.04555514	0.048837317	0.045423416	0.045623611	0.045506971	0.04575583	0.046846009
8 4th Deciles HH	0.052073031	0.05237514	0.056148691	0.052223699	0.052453865	0.052319763	0.052605879	0.053859267
9 5th Deciles HH	0.059190483	0.05953388	0.063823213	0.059361745	0.05962337	0.059470939	0.059796162	0.061220865
10 6th Deciles HH	0.067279007	0.06766933	0.072544811	0.067473672	0.067771049	0.067597788	0.067967454	0.069586846
11 7th Deciles HH	0.077118828	0.07756624	0.083154777	0.077341964	0.077682834	0.077484233	0.077907963	0.079764198
12 8th Deciles HH	0.090231106	0.09075459	0.097293328	0.090492181	0.090891008	0.090658639	0.091154415	0.09332626
13 9th Deciles HH	0.110011785	0.11065003	0.118622205	0.110330093	0.110816352	0.110533043	0.111137504	0.113785466
14 10th Deciles HH	0.174484226	0.17549652	0.188140785	0.174989078	0.175760309	0.175310967	0.176269673	0.180469474
15 Firms	1.025936936	1.03188904	1.10623513	1.028905382	1.033440085	1.030798029	1.036435055	1.061129155
Total income multiplier	1.769721905	1.77998918	1.908234779	1.774842418	1.782664696	1.778107199	1.787830963	1.830427821
16 Agriculture	1.42295374	0.5763816	0.445428144	0.367984692	0.372761509	0.36815245	0.372234113	0.392247469
17 Manufacturing industries	0.311779613	1.40846758	0.528998287	0.280610686	0.277928532	0.275207013	0.288674904	0.355855711
18 Construction	0	0	1	0	0	0	0	0
19 Gas, electricity, water	0.010815996	0.02155681	0.014118462	1.026796707	0.016646915	0.012966103	0.012595016	0.014447941
20 Trade, Hotel, Restaurant	0.164155548	0.22633462	0.222240089	0.15476546	1.239840762	0.314552756	0.161938663	0.205025918
21 Transport and Communication	0.173214536	0.25843783	0.237470796	0.156874215	0.23152787	1.259120847	0.159864175	0.220929061
22 Banking & real estate	0.185343476	0.22619835	0.206335072	0.292573133	0.201171866	0.292337215	1.169361716	0.176552641
23 Community, Social service	0.025936936	0.03188904	0.10623513	0.028905382	0.033440085	0.030798029	0.036435055	1.061129155
Total output multiplier	2.294199844	2.74926582	2.760825979	2.308510275	2.373317539	2.553134414	2.201103641	2.426187895

Table 6. Transfer multipliers

	Agriculture	Manufacturing industries	Construction	Gas, Water Electricity	Trade, Hotel, Resturant	Transport Communication	Banking Real estate	Community, Social service
Agriculture	1.42295374	0.576381595	0.445428144	0.367984692	0.372761509	0.36815245	0.372234113	0.39224747
Manufacturing industries	0.311779613	1.408467577	0.528998287	0.280610686	0.277928532	0.275207013	0.288674904	0.35585571
Construction	0	0	1	0	0	0	0	0
Gas, electricity, water	0.010815996	0.021556808	0.014118462	1.026796707	0.016646915	0.012966103	0.012595016	0.01444794
Trade, Hotel, Resturant	0.164155548	0.226334622	0.222240089	0.15476546	1.239840762	0.314552756	0.161938663	0.20502592
Transport and Communication	0.173214536	0.258437827	0.237470796	0.156874215	0.23152787	1.259120847	0.159864175	0.22092906
Banking & real estate	0.185343476	0.226198352	0.206335072	0.292573133	0.201171866	0.292337215	1.169361716	0.17655264
Community, Social service	0.025936936	0.031889042	0.10623513	0.028905382	0.033440085	0.030798029	0.036435055	1.06112916
Total	2.294199844	2.749265824	2.760825979	2.308510275	2.373317539	2.553134414	2.201103641	2.4261879

Table 7. Open-loop multipliers

	Agriculture	Manufacturing industries	Construction	Gas, Water Electricity	Trade, Hotel, Resturant	Transport Communication	Banking Real estate	Community, Social service
1st Decile	0.029525077	0.029696371	0.031835951	0.029610505	0.029741008	0.029664973	0.029827199	0.03053786
2nd decile	0.03857906	0.038802882	0.041598572	0.038690685	0.038861207	0.038761855	0.038973829	0.03990242
3rd decile	0.045292367	0.045555136	0.048837317	0.045423416	0.045623611	0.045506971	0.04575583	0.04684601
4th decile	0.052073031	0.052375139	0.056148691	0.052223699	0.052453865	0.052319763	0.052605879	0.05385927
5th decile	0.059190483	0.059533884	0.063823213	0.059361745	0.05962337	0.059470939	0.059796162	0.06122087
6th decile	0.067279007	0.067669335	0.072544811	0.067473672	0.067771049	0.067597788	0.067967454	0.06958685
7th decile	0.077118828	0.077566243	0.083154777	0.077341964	0.077682834	0.077484233	0.077907963	0.0797642
8th decile	0.090231106	0.090754593	0.097293328	0.090492181	0.090891008	0.090658639	0.091154415	0.09332626
9th decile	0.110011785	0.110650033	0.118622205	0.110330093	0.110816352	0.110533043	0.111137504	0.11378547
10th decile	0.174484226	0.175496519	0.188140785	0.174989078	0.175760309	0.175310967	0.176269673	0.18046947
Firms	1.025936936	1.031889042	1.10623513	1.028905382	1.033440085	1.030798029	1.036435055	1.06112916
Total	1.769721905	1.779989177	1.908234779	1.774842418	1.782664696	1.778107199	1.787830963	1.83042782

Transfer Multipliers

As discussed earlier, transfer multipliers capture impacts resulting from direct transfers within the endogenous accounts, that is, between production sectors. Table 6 shows the transfer multipliers. Manufacturing industries (2.749) and construction sectors (2.761) have high transfer effects, whereas banking and real estate (2.201), and agriculture (2.294) are at the bottom of transfer multiplier impact in the Nepalese economy.

An addition of 1 unit in agriculture will lead to a multiplier effect of 2.294, out of which 62 percent adds to agriculture, 13.5 percent manufacturing, 8 percent banking, 7.5 percent transport, and 7 percent in the trade, hotel, and restaurant sector.

Likewise, out of total transfer effects of manufacturing industries (2.749), an injection of 1 unit will lead to impact industries (61 percent), agriculture (25 percent), transport (11 percent), banking (10 percent), and trade, hotel and restaurant (10 percent).

The construction sector has the highest transfer multiplier (2.761); an introduction of 1 unit will add 43.5 percent to construction, 23 percent to industries, 19 percent to agriculture, 10 percent to transport, 9 percent on banking, and 10 percent on trade, hotel, and restaurant.

An injection of 1 unit into banking results in a transfer impact by 2.201, out of which 51 percent adds to the banking sector, 16 percent to agricultural sector, 12.5 industries, and 7 percent on the trade, hotel, restaurant and transportation sectors.

Open-Loop Multipliers

The open loop multiplier, or cross multiplier effect, describes the transactions from production to households, factor and wants. Table 7 depicts the open loop multipliers. As the table indicates, agriculture has the lowest effect (1.769), whereas construction, and community and social services have high cross multiplier effects, 1.908 and 1.830 respectively. Only these two sectors have high multiplier effects on the lower deciles households compared to other sectors.

Injection of one unit into any of the production sectors will have differentiated impacts. Based on table 8, a comparison is drawn between the low-income and high-income households.

Table 8. Impact of injection on household

	Households	
	Lower 50%	Upper 20%
Agriculture	22.46	28.45
Manufacturing industries	22.59	28.61
Construction	24.22	30.67
Gas, electricity, water	22.53	28.53
Trade, Hotel, Restaurant	22.63	28.65
Transport andCommunication	22.57	28.58
Banking and real estate	22.69	28.74
Community, Social service	23.23	29.42

A one unit introduction in any of the production sectors will have only nominal multiplier effects on the low-income households. For example, investment of one million Rupees in the agriculture sector will increase the average income of the upper 20 percent of households by 28.45 percent whereas 50 percent lower income households' average income will add only 22.46 percent (Table 8).

Closed-Loop Multipliers

Closed- loop multipliers capture the inequality of household income. These multipliers catch the effects resulting from production activities to households to wants to factor and back to production activities through consumption demand. Then, it completes the circular flow of income. Table 9 depicts the closed-loop multipliers, which are closely related to the consumption patterns of households. Cohen (2002 a) describes the closed-loop effect phenomena: "the increase in income resulting from open loop effects are used mainly to purchase consumer goods, which increase output, and increase factor income, that is paid out as institutional income, which is again spent mainly on consumption, and so on." In general, closed loop multipliers are fairly constant which may be due to a similar pattern of household consumption and savings. Cohen (2002 a, b) also observed a similar relationship in developed and developing countries such as the Netherlands, Colombia, Surinam, and Pakistan. But these are higher than open loop multipliers, which indicate that consumption is larger than other categories of final demand (Table 9). It shows that an increase of income of one unit by any type of household will add to total income from 2.8224 to 2.8226 through the closed-loop effects which are higher than the open–loop multiplication.

Closed loop effects are also known as indirect effects. They capture the value added generated with each type of household by a one unit increase in disposal income exogenously generated. Each column total is equivalent to a Keynesian multiplier that implies an increase in the overall income of each group of households if their disposal incomes are increased by one unit. Row totals (Table 9) indicate the multiplier effect on the income of each class of household due to a one-unit increase in income of all groups of households. For example, if all ten types of household income increased by one unit initially, then, finally, their income would increase by the row total multipliers. Based on this notion, firms have a high-income redistribution potential (10.565). If income redistribution potential is compared among the households, there is only an 8 percent difference of multipliers (1.493) between the lowest and the highest income households. Hence it can be inferred that if the government wishes to redistribute the land from households, say 10th deciles to 1st deciles, it may not deliver a significant change in the income of poor households. Further, the other factor to note is the multiplier effects of the agriculture sector, which has the lowest multipliers (Tables 4, 5, 6 and 7).

If the investment projection requirements for the 10th plan are fulfilled as planned, that will boost the production sectors vis-à-vis income of households and firms. In fact, open-loop effects portray the interaction between production sectors and institutions. Now, if all estimated investment requirements are injected until 2007, Table 10 depicts changed nominal income scenarios of households and firms.

Table 9. Closed-loop multipliers

	1st Decile	2nd Decile	3rd Decile	4th Decile	5th Decile	6th Decile	7th Decile	8th Decile	9th Decile	10th Decile	Total
1st Decile	1.030404135	0.030407106	0.03040536	0.03040522	0.030406223	0.030405479	0.030404	0.03040757	0.030406386	0.03040778	1.304059
2nd decile	0.039727685	1.039731566	0.03972928	0.0397291	0.039730413	0.03972944	0.039728	0.03973218	0.039730625	0.03973245	1.3973
3rd decile	0.046640868	0.046645425	1.04664275	0.04664253	0.046644071	0.046642929	0.046641	0.04664614	0.04664432	0.04664646	1.466436
4th decile	0.053623415	0.053628654	0.05362557	1.05362532	0.053627097	0.053625784	0.053624	0.05362948	0.053627384	0.05362984	1.536266
5th decile	0.060952777	0.060958732	0.06095523	0.06095494	1.060956962	0.06095547	0.060953	0.06095967	0.060957288	0.06096008	1.609564
6th decile	0.069282123	0.069288891	0.06928491	0.06928459	0.06928688	1.069285184	0.069282	0.06928996	0.06928725	0.06929043	1.692862
7th decile	0.079414908	0.079422666	0.07941811	0.07941773	0.07942036	0.079418417	1.079415	0.07942389	0.079420785	0.07942443	1.794196
8th decile	0.092917581	0.092926658	0.09292132	0.09292088	0.092923961	0.092921686	0.092918	1.09292809	0.092924458	0.09292872	1.929231
9th decile	0.113287195	0.113298263	0.11329176	0.11329122	0.113294974	0.113292201	0.113287	0.11330001	1.11329558	0.11330078	2.132939
10th decile	0.179679191	0.179696745	0.17968643	0.17968558	0.179691528	0.17968713	0.179679	0.17969952	0.17969249	1.17970073	2.796899
Firms	1.056482428	1.056585645	1.05652497	1.05651998	1.05655497	1.05652911	1.056484	1.05660194	1.056560623	1.05660907	10.56545
Total	2.822412304	2.822590352	2.82248568	2.82247708	2.822537437	2.82249283	2.822415	2.82261846	2.82254719	2.82263077	28.22521

Table 10. Changed income of institutes due to investment injection in the 10th Plan

	Agriculture	Manuf. industries	Construction	Gas, Water Electricity	Trade, Hotel, Restaurant	Transport Communication	Banking Real estate	Community, Social service	Total income
1st Deciles	2566.6	1074.62	2377.85	328.25	1392.36	3243.71	2766.35	4237.003	17986.74
2nd deciles	3353.6	1404.16	3107.05	428.912	1819.33	4238.41	3614.67	5536.29	23502.42
3rd deciles	3937.2	1648.5	3647.72	503.55	2135.92	4975.96	4243.67	6499.69	27592.21
4th deciles	4526.7	1895.3	4193.81	578.93	2455.69	5720.91	4878.99	7472.75	31723.08
5th deciles	5145.4	2154.35	4767.03	658.06	2791.34	6502.85	5545.86	8494.14	36059.03
6th deciles	5848.5	2448.75	5418.46	747.99	3172.78	7391.48	6303.71	9654.89	40986.56
7th deciles	6703.9	2806.89	6210.93	857.38	3636.81	8472.52	7225.66	11066.96	46981.05
8th deciles	7843.7	3284.14	7266.96	1003.16	4255.17	9913.07	8454.21	12948.64	54969.05
9th deciles	9563.3	4004.1	8860.046	1223.08	5188	12086.25	10307.57	15787.27	67019.62
10th deciles	15167.9	6350.71	14052.47	1939.87	8228.43	19169.4	16348.32	25039.4	106296.5
Firms	89184.6	37341.07	82626.14	11406.13	48381.74	112712.7	96125.31	147227.3	625005
Total Output	153841.4	64412.59	142528.466	19675.312	83457.57	194427.26	165814.32	253964.333	1078121

The column sums indicate the output of each sector (Figure 3), and sum of the rows gives each group of household total income due to investment as planned in all sectors (Figure 4).

As Figure 3 illustrates, community and social sectors have a large share of output compared to other sectors, which also receive a high investment priority. Agriculture, though it receives 14.57 percent of total planned investment, ranks third as a contributor to total output (Figure 4). Out of the total estimated income due to the open multiplier effect, firms will share 58 percent of it (Table 10), and the rest will be allocated among the classes of households. The overall impact is a rise in the income level of households (Figure 4) with nearly five times difference between the lowest and the highest income households.

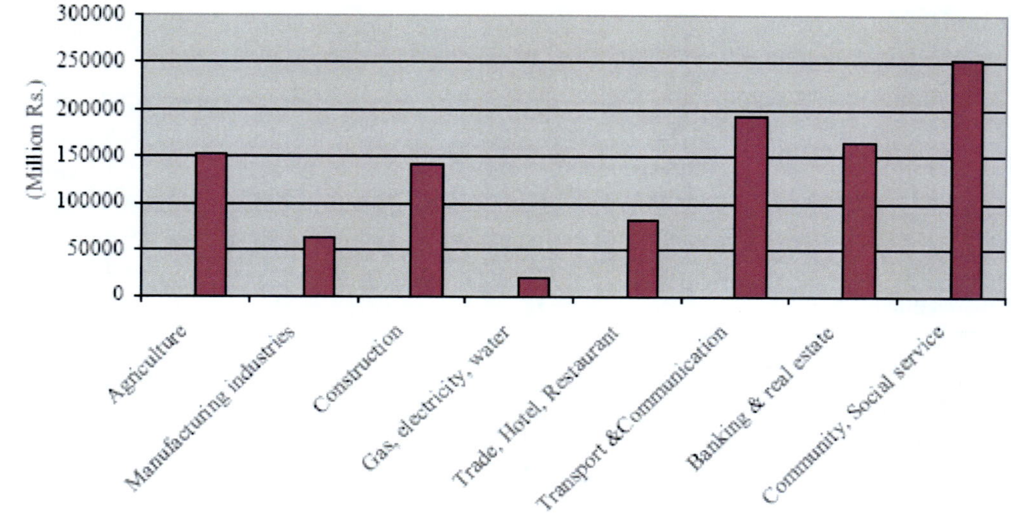

Figure 3. Sectoral output due to the total investment during the 10th Plan period.

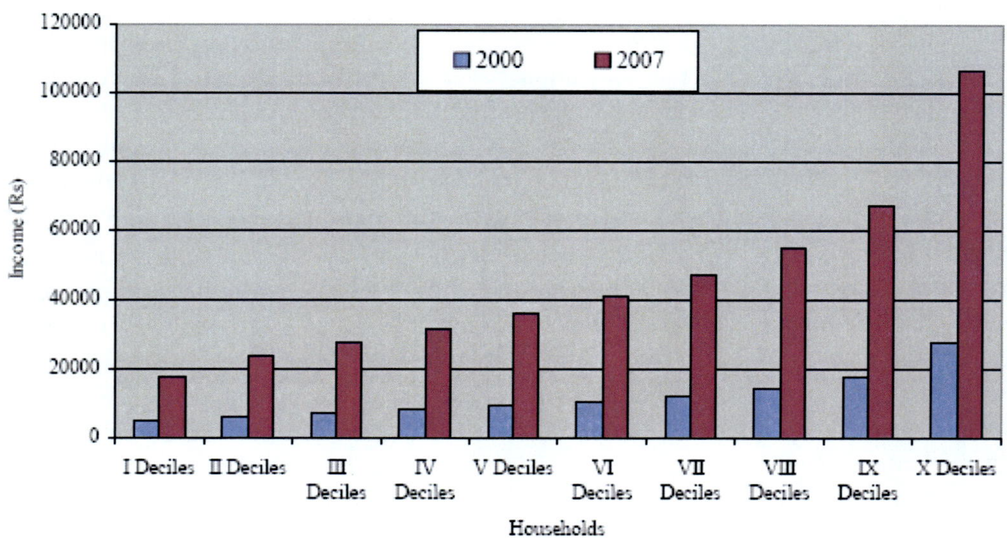

Figure 4. Projected income rise of household due to total investment in the 10th Plan period.

Investment obviously will have multiplier effects, but there are a few noteworthy considerations. For example, nearly two-thirds of Nepal's annual budget is supported by the kindness of donors or by different types of loans, which may or may not be available as expected to meet the targeted level of investment. Further, there are certain barriers to socioeconomic development like political conflict, corruption, lack of institutional support and donor driven psyche (Devkota, 2007). Although the country is on last lap of the 10th Plan, it seems that it has already lost its base due to political instability (Pyakuryal, 2006) that started in mid-nineties, which, in fact, has affected the implementation of both 9th and 10th plans. In 2005, NPC in its second assessment of the Plan realized that several factors such as absence of elected bodies at the local level and ongoing conflict and political instability hindered the accomplishment of its goals (see details on http://www.npc.gov.np/ tenthplan/assessment.htm as of August 30 2008).

Emergency, insurgency, instability, and lack of a credible government advanced the politico-economic crisis. The Asian Development Bank (2005) estimated an account of cost of conflict in Nepal. For example, economic growth slowed to an average of 1.9 percent over the period of 2002-2004, and if it will be the trend for future years (2005-2009) then the country will lose about 57 percent of the economic growth due to decline in development expenditure. Local production of goods and services were far below the potential level. The World Bank in its Global Economic Prospects 2007 report cites Nepal economic growth rate for 2006 was 1.9 percent. This is less then population growth rate and indicates a return to the situation of the 1970s. Further direct and indirect consequences of the insurgency such as cost of displaced people, damages of infrastructure, forgone opportunities, and lost of thousands of lives are yet to be accounted for. In fact, a valid figure of people who lost (15,000 is an average estimation) their lives in ten years insurgency including Maoists is still to be accounted for.

Additionally, the fundamental problem is whether the increased nominal income level will alleviate poverty in real terms. There are a few factors like price level changes that always pose problems to low-income households. It is expected that from 2000 to 2007 the GDP deflator will rise by 76 percent, which will obviously impact investment. Further, between 1995/1996 to 1999/2000 the national average inflation rate was 35 percent. These facts will obviously set back real income growth, particularly for low-income families.

There are a few additional factors that may hamper the investment – income multiplier scenarios. For instance, investment in agriculture demands a high priority due to the fact that 90 percent of the people depend on agriculture, and it contributes 40 percent of GDP. The Labor Force Survey of 1998/1999 estimated that out of 9.5 million employed people, the agriculture sector employs 6.4 million people. The problem is further complicated by households' land holding capacity. The average land hold size in 1991/1992 was 0.68 hectare in mountain, areas 0.77 in hills, and 1.26 hectare in the Terai. About 69.5 percent of the landholdings are less than one hectare and agricultural productivity has been stagnant for decades. The total cultivated land in the country is 2.6 million hectares, and 30 per cent of the cultivated area is comprised of farms less than one ha. The latest Population Census of 2001 reveals about 24.4 percent of population does not have any land. The prevailing land holding pattern means no or low possibility for income generating chances for poor households. The cumulative impacts of such factors will reduce the investment-income multipliers, and will increase income disparity. Government initiated land reform measures in the past did not deliver any significant results.

Since land is one of the resource constraints, an alternative option is to intervene at the household level. To this regard, human capital enrichment strategies could the most useful option as the closed–loop multipliers indicate. Human capital theory of Mincer (1958), Becker (1962), and Schultz (1962) comprises mainly skills, knowledge, and talent of an individual as well as some extra complementary attributes such as personality, behavior, and credentials will collectively enhance the quality and productivity of labor force, which is one of the factors of the production.

Human capital development strategy for 21st century in Nepal requires revision of existing education policy at both secondary and tertiary education levels. (Please also refer to Ganesh Signh's article Chapter 5.) Primary focus should be paid towards vocational education and training opportunities for low income households because according to the latest NLSS survey of 2003/04 only 51 percent of population (63 percent male and 39 percent female) can read and write. Further, it also reveals that literacy rate amongst the poor households is limited to 25 percent. Likewise, 31 percent of male and 56 percent of female population never attended school. Rural areas have much high rate of un-attending school (48 percent) than urban areas (25 percent). According to the Survey, reasons such as 'too expensive' for 27 percent and 'parents did not allow' for 38 percent are noteworthy. Nearly 60 percent of girls and 40 percent of boys both under-19 are not attending the school. In such prevailing context, it is highly imperative to invest primarily on vocational education and training targeting to the households that fail to complete secondary school. Thorbecke and Jung (1996) used a multiplier decomposition method to analyze poverty in Indonesia and concluded that, "human capital of the poor must be enhanced through education and vocational training." Khan (1999) also reiterated that both economic growth and increasing the capital stock of the poor by appropriate skill enhancement may help to alleviate poverty. As Ramacharan (2004) argues that wrong type of education have little impact on development, so investment on both secondary and tertiary schooling is important. Nepal has already faced a crisis of waste of human resources as indicated by Bista (1994), so an equal opportunity should be provided to socio-economically deprived households in order to break the poverty cycle and reduce the income inequality gaps. Because human capital is the fundamental key of economic growth, and a vast majority of literature reveals a strong correlation between human capital and rise of employment, productivity and income (Wheeler, 2006; Jolliffe, 2002). Barro and Lee (2000) conclude that human capital is the main engine of economic growth, which is further justified by the findings of Jones and Schneider (2006) "A 1 point increase in a nation's average IQ is associated with a persistent 0.11 percent annual increase in GDP per capita." Based on the U.S. study, Krueger (2003) observed that education and training of disadvantaged could reduce inequality. He further suggests to investing in low income areas that may result high pay off, and such a task could be executed by the local government. Skar and Cederroth (1997) observed that the greatest challenge for the government of Nepal is the provision of occupational training for national self-sufficiency that in turn can help to alleviate unemployment - a strategy of enriching human capital.

CONCLUSION

The economic structure of Nepal examined through the SAM multipliers, namely aggregate, transfer, open-loop, and closed-loop multipliers indicates a huge gap of household income disparity as also justified by the NLSS survey. Among the production activities, the agriculture sector has the lowest income coefficients where as community and social services, and construction activities have high total income multipliers. Regarding the output coefficients, the banking sector has the lowest, and industries and construction activities have high aggregate output multipliers. Investment in the community and social sectors will deliver a high output due to these sectors' high multiplier values.

Economic growth is, of course, a basis to augment the income level of people. But that may not necessarily be the sole, or even the most important, factor in reducing poverty. In addition, there exist many households deprived of basic endowments like land, or skills (education), and even economic sustainability would be impossible for them. As the SAM coefficients reveal, investment in household sectors have high multipliers, and it is imperative to intervene at the household level to enhance human capital. To this end, investment in community and social services at least the 1st, 2nd , 3rd , and 4th deciles households seems an urgent need. That may include households socio-economically discriminated against – *Dalits,* which are the so-called untouchables as well as some indigenous ethnic minorities. In other words, poverty alleviation programs should exclusively target these households, say all types of *Dalits,* to enrich their human skill and knowledge as well as quality of life, and break the vicious circle of poverty.

Nepal is struggling to meet basic human needs such as an adequate supply of food, water, health care, shelter, and minimum education, which needs to be sustained economically, environmentally, and socially. Repetition of past successive five-year development plans would be futile, since these plans are based on unsuccessful development models. Henceforth, development plans, policies, and programs should emphasize other pillars of development — human and social capitals as well as ecological capital — because sustainability cannot be achieved in parts, it should address the whole system (Gowdy and O'Hara, 1997). Economic growth could be complemented by human, social and ecological capitals development. Augmentation of social capital is possible by focusing on enriching human capital, particularly focusing on the deprived classes of society who will ultimately determine the future of sustainability. In the words of the late visionary leader of the Nepali Congress Shree B. P. Koirala "Our capital is the people. We don't have machinery, and we don't have financial capital, we have labor. So we have got to motivate our people for development purposes. And that motivation can be provided only by institutions that are democratic and responsible to the people and reflective of the aspirations of the people[1] ." In the 21st Century, Nepal would be better off had she been able to enrich human capital vis-à-vis social sustainability to complement sustainable development.

[1] B P Koirala, Worldview Jan/Feb, 1978 (also see on http://www.nepalicongress.org.np/contents/general/ about_bp nav.php?show=interview#). (As of March 10 2007).

REFERENCES

Alarcon, J. Van Heemst, J. De Jong, N., (2000), Extending the SAM with Social and Environmental Indicators: An Application to Bolivia, *Economic Systems Research*, 12(4), 473-497.

Asian Devlopment Bank (2005), Measuring the Economic Cost of Conflict: The effect of Declining Development Expenditure, Working Paper No. 2, Kathmandu: Asian Development Bank.

Barro, R. J. and J.-W. Lee, (2000), International Data on Educational Attainment: Updates and Implications, CID Working Papers 42, Center for International Development at Harvard University. http://www.economics.harvard.edu/faculty/barro/papers/p_jwha.pdf.

Becker, G.S., (1962), Investment in Human Capital: A theoretical Analysis, *Journal of Political Economy,* 70, 9-49.

Benham, F. (1954), The Colombo Plan, *Economica,* 21(82): 93–112.

Bhattarai, B.R. (2003), The Nature of Underdevelopment and Regional Structure of Nepal: A Marxist analysis, Delhi: Adroit Publishers.

Bista, D. B. (1994), Fatalism and Development, Calcutta: Orient Longman.

Blaikie P.M., Cameron, J., Seddon, J., (1979), Crisis in Nepal: Growth and Stagnation at the Periphery, Oxford: Oxford University Press.

Blaikie P.M., Cameron, J., Seddon, J., (2001), Nepal in Crisis: Growth and Stagnation at the Periphery, Delhi: Adroit Publishers.

Central Bureau of Statistics (1999), Nepal Labor Force Survey, Kathmandu.

Central Bureau of Statistics (2004), Nepal Living Standard Survey, Kathmandu. (www.cbs.gov.np).

Central Bureau of Statistics (2006), Statistical Year Book of Nepal, Kathmandu.

Cohen, S. I., (2002 a), Social Accounting and Economic Modeling for Developing Countries: Analysis, Policy and Planning Application, Burlington: Ashgate.

Cohen, S. I., (2002b), Social Accounting for Industrial and Transition Economics: Economy-wide Models for Analysis and Policy, Burlington: Ashgate.

Dahal, R., (2000), Nepal's Remittance Bonanza, *Himal South* Asia, 13, 3.

Defourny, J., Thorbecke, E., (1984), Structural Path Analysis and Multiplier Decomposition within an Accounting Matrix Framework, *Economic Journal*, 94 (373), 111 - 137.

Devkota, S. R. (2007), Socioeconomic Development in Nepal: Past Mistakes and Future Possibilities, *South Asia Economic Journal*, 8 (2), 285–315.

Devkota, S.R. (2005), 'Politics of Poverty in Nepal: Structural Analysis of Socioeconomic Development in Nepal', Heidelberg Papers in South Asian and Comparative Politics, Working Paper no 25, South Asian Institute, University of Heidelberg, Germany. (URL: http://www.ub.uni-heidelberg.de/archiv/5294).

Golan, A., Vogel, S. J., (2000), Estimation of Non-stationary Social Accounting matrix Coefficients with Supply side Information, *Economic Systems Research*, 12(4), 447 -472.

Gowdy, J., O'Hara, S. (1997), Weak Sustainability and Viable Technologies, *Ecological Economics*, 22(3): 239-247.

Greenfield, C.C., Fell, H.A., (1979), The Estimation of Price Effects in A Social Accounting Matrix, *Review of Income and Wealth*, 25(1), 64 - 82.

Hewings, G.J.D., Madden, M., (1995), *Social and Demographic Accounting*, New York: Cambridge University Press.

Jain, A.K. (2001), Corruption: A Review', *Journal of Economic Surveys*, 15(1): 72–107.

Jolliffe, D., (2002), Whose Education Matters in the Determination of Household Income? Evidence from a Developing Country, *Economic Development and Cultural Change*, 51: 287-312.

Jones, G., Schneider, W.J., (2006), Intelligence, Human Capital, and Economic Growth: A Bayesian Averaging of Classical Estimates Approach, *Journal of Economic Growth*, 11, 71-93.

Keuning, S. J, (1991), Proposal for a Social Accounting Matrix, *Economic System Research*, 3 (3), 233-249.

Keuning, S. J., De Ruijter, W. A., (1988), Guidelines to the Construction of a Social Accounting Matrix, *Review of Income and Wealth*, 34(1), 71-101.

Khadka, N. (1994), Politics and The Economy during Nepal's Partyless Panchayat System (1961-1990): A Study in Retrospect, *Asian Affairs*, 94: 25 (1): 47-59.

Khan, H.A. (1999), Sectoral Growth and Poverty Alleviation: A Multiplier Decomposition Technique Applied to South Africa, *World Development*, 27(3): 521 – 530.

King, B. B., (1985), What is SAM? In Pyatt and Round (editors) Social Accounting Matrices: A Basis for Planning, A World Bank Symposium, Washington, D.C.

Krueger, A. B. (2003), Inequality, Too Much of a Good Thing, In Heckman, J.J. and Krueger, A.B., (Editors) Inequality in America: What Role for Human Capital, p. 1-75, Cambridge: The MIT Press.

Lange, G. M., (1998), Applying an Integrated Natural Resource Accounts and Input –Output Model to Development Planning in Indonesia, *Economic System Research*, 10 (2), 113-134.

Mahat, R. S. (2005), In Defense of Democracy: Dynamics and Fault Lines of Nepal's Political Economy, New Delhi: Adroit Publishers.

Meier, G.M. (2001), The Old Generation of Development Economists and the New, in G.M. Meier and J.E. Stiglitz (eds) Frontiers of Development Economists: The Future Perspectives, pp. 13–50. Washington D.C.: Oxford University Press.

Mihaly, E.B. (1965), Foreign Aid and Politics in Nepal: A Case Study. London: Oxford University Press.

Mincer, J., (1958), Investment in Human Capital and Personal Income Distribution, *Journal of Political Economy*, 66, 281-302.

Ministry of Finance (2006), *Economic Survey* 2005/06, Kathmandu.

National Planning Commission (1998), The Ninth Plan (1997-2002), Kathmandu.

National Planning Commission (2002), Concept Paper on Tenth Plan/ Poverty Reduction Strategy Paper, NPC, Kathmandu (http://www.ndf2002.gov.np/

Nepal Rastra Bank (2006), A Glimpse of Nepal's Macroeconomic Situation, Paper presented at the 35th Meeting of the board of the governors, *Asian Clearing Union*, (May 22-23 2006) Kathmandu. (www.nrb.org.np).

Nepal, K, (2002), Remittance Economy, *The Nepali Times*, 104, 4.

Pandey, D. R. (1999), Nepal's Failed Development: Reflections on the Mission and the Maladies, Kathmandu: Nepal South Asia Center.

Pant, G.P. (1991), Foreign Aid, Economic Growth and Social Cost Benefit Analysis. Avebury: Academic Publishing Group.

Phuyal, S. (2006), Reversing "Lahure" legacy in "New Nepal", The Kathmandu Post, 2 August.Available at http://www.kantipuronline.com/kolnews.php?andnid=81512 (accessed 10 March 2008).

Pradhan, B.K., Sahoo, A., (1996), Social Accounting Matrix and Its Multipliers for India, MARGIN, 28 (2), 153 – 169.

Pyakuryal, B. (2006), Dimensions of economic restructuring, The Kathmandu Post, November03 2006. (http://www.kantipuronline.com/kolnews.php?andnid=90315).

Pyatt, G. (1991), Fundamentals of Social Accounting, *Economic Systems Research*, 3(3), 315 –342.

Pyatt, G., (1988), A SAM Approach to Modeling, *Journal of Policy Modeling*, 10(3), 327-352.

Pyatt, G., (1990), Accounting for Time Use, *Review of Income and Wealth*, 36(1), 33-53.

Pyatt, G., (1999), Some Relationship between T Accounts, Input –Output Tables, and Social Accounting Matrices, *Economic Systems Research*, 11(4), 365-388.

Pyatt, G., Round, J.I., (1985), Social Accounting Matrices: A Basis for Planning, A World Bank Symposium, Washington, D.C.

Pyatt, G., Thorbecke, E., (1976), Planning Techniques for Better Future, Geneva: International Labor Office.

Ramacharan, R., (2004), Higher or Basic Education? The Composition of Human Capital and Economic Development, *IMF Staff Paper*, 51(2), 309-326.

Robinson, S., Cattaneo, A., El-said, M., (2001), Updating and Estimating Social Accounting Matrix Using Cross Entropy Methods, *Economic Systems Research*, 13(1), 47-64.

Roland-Holst, D. W, Sancho, F., (1995), Modeling Prices in à SAM Structure, *Review of Economics and Statistics*, 77(2), 361-372.

Schultz, T.W., (1961), Investment in Human Capital, American Economic Review, 21, 1017.

Shah, S. (1988), Nepal's Economic Development: Problems and Prospectus, Asian Survey, 28(10): 945–57.

Shrestha, D. L., Sapkota, P. (2002), Integrated Macroeconometric and Input Output Model of Nepal, Report Developed for the Formulation of the Tenth Plan, National Planning Commission/ Nepal.

Shrestha, N.R. (1993), Enchanted by the Mantra of Bikas: A Self-respective Perspective on Nepalese Elites and Development, *South Asia Bulletin*, XIII (1and2): 5–22.

Skar, H.O., Cederroth, S. (1997), Development Aid to Nepal, Nordic *Institute of Asian Studies*, Report no 35. Curzon.

Stone, R., (1986), Social Accounting: The State of Play, *Scandinavian Journal of Economics*, 88(3), 453-472.

The World Bank (2002), Nepal Development Forum: *Economic Update*. Washington D.C.

The World Bank, (2002), *World Development Indicators* 2002, Washington, D.C.

Thorbecke, E., (1998), Social Accounting Matrices and Social Accounting Analysis, in Isard W. et al., (eds.) Methods of Interregional and Regional Analysis, Vermont: Ashgate Publishing Company.

Thorbecke, E., Hong-Sang J. (1996), A Multiplier Decomposition Method to Analyze Poverty Alleviation, *Journal of Development Economics*, 48: 279 – 300.

Wheeler, C.H. (2006) Human Capital Growth in a Cross Section of U.S. Metropolitan Areas, *Federal Reserve Bank of St Louis Review*, 88 (2), 1130132.

Wildavsky, A. (1972), Why Planning Fails in Nepal, *Administrative Science Quarterly*, 17(4): 508–28.

In: Nepal in the 21st Century
Editor: Surendra R. Devkota, pp. 127-152
ISBN 978-1-60741-348-6

Chapter 5

QUALITY SCHOOL EDUCATION FOR ALL IN 21ST CENTURY NEPAL

Ganesh Bahadur Singh
Faculty of Education, Tribhuvan University, Kathmaamndu

ABSTRACT

Education has been recognized as most important aspect for national development in Nepal. People's aspiration has been increasing with political changes at different times in Nepal. Public aspiration has been instrumental in opening of the new schools which received government support at some times and faced restriction at other times. Public aspiration has been mostly focused maximizing access to education to Nepalese children. At present quality education is being aspired for. Thus access to quality education for all is the major concern in 21st century Nepal. This article narrates developmental of education in Nepal, analyzes Nepalese school education in terms of purpose, access, quality, and discusses rendering issues, future prospect and further requirements to achieve quality school education for all in Nepal.

DEVELOPMENT OF EDUCATION IN NEPAL

Religious education, rivalry among competing religions, and opening modern education to the royalties makes the educational history before Nepalese people's struggle for democratic Nepal in 1951. Education for people was limited due to restricted access and aspiration was low due to lack of relevance.

Buddhism and Hinduism system of education remained for a longer period in Nepal. Though both were founded on religious base, Buddhism was more scientific (NNEPC, 1956). Buddhist monastery was build on a three level organization La-Chi, Dra-Chhang and Khamjen which correspond to University board, college and a boarding hostel respectively. Theoretically monastery was open to all and curriculum embraced all aspects of religious ties of catering to the daily needs of the people. Education lead one to specialize in vocal training, engage in business or trade, be a painter, a dreamer, a fighter, or be just a hanger-on. Though

Buddhist education in Nepal can be traced back to B.C. dates, it was not widespread and universal. But the influence of the Buddhist education can be seen intact in Nepal such as in the Vihars and Gompas at present.

Buddhism came under attack in Nepal with the advent of the Sankaracharya in the eleventh century. Buddhist institutions were attacked and religious texts, literature, grammar, dictionary books were burned. This brought Nepal to the point where Nepali literary history beings only in the fourteenth century as most of the works before that period were destroyed (Bista, 1990). Hindu system of education was of Gurukul model where Guru (teacher) disseminated knowledge to his students. Education mainly assumed learning of rituals, prayer and the reading of religious texts. Eventually Sanskrit schools were introduced where medium of instruction was in Sanskrit language. Gradually Sanskrit language became difficult and rigid with stiff rules of grammar. This made Sanskrit language inaccessible to the common people. Mastering the grammatical forms took six of the most productive years of a candidate after eight years of lower level education. Like language of learning, method of learning was equally injudicious. Students had to learn by rote the Vedas, the Meemansas, literature, astrology or whatever text or course they want to specialize in. The result of this entire endeavor was that students committed to rote memorize huge amount of text with so much devotion and painstaking, but their studies were without understanding the meaning and the context of what they were reading about (NNEPC, 1956).

Religious type of education system dominated Nepal for longer period of time. Another influencing factor was Indian system of education. Modern education system paved way in Nepal after Rana Prime Minister Jung Bahadur Rana returned from his visit to Britain and France. He established the first English high school in 1853. Modernization of education system in Nepal was influenced by the British system of education as practiced in India, but the modernization process was very slow in Nepal. Though a high school was operating in Nepal, School Leaving Certificate (SLC) examination was conducted by Indian Universities – Calcutta University and later by Patna University until 1934.

Opening of a modern school in 1853 was in no way an impetus for opening an educational opportunity to Nepalese people. This school was in the vicinity of Rana's palace and education was accessible only to Rana children. A few of the later Rana prime ministers were more liberal to make education more accessible to more children or open more schools, but the development was erratic and also disrupted by other autocratic Ranas. About two hundred schools were opened by Dev Shamsher Rana after he became prime minister in 1901. But his younger brother, Chandra Shamsher exiled him after four months of Dev Shamsher's rule and these schools were closed down.

The first college in Nepal was established in 1918 which was like the high school operating with the curriculum developed in Indian University and accredited by them. After independence of India in 1947, Gandhian schools were also opened in Nepal as it was in India. Though Gandhian education system was more life oriented and practical, public aspiration was on English model schools. Nepalese education system as others aspects of Nepal U-turned towards expansion and development after Ranas were overthrown by the democratic movement in 1951.

EDUCATION COMMISSIONS AND PLANS IN NEPAL

Nepal, a land-locked and predominantly agricultural country, lacked both political will as well as adequate planning for overall development of education until the establishment of democracy in 1951. Democratic Nepal required educated and qualified human resources to take her to the modern world from the 100 years of Rana's darkness era. People even with marginal qualification could get attractive jobs due to shortage of qualified persons. This aspired people to be educated. Enrollment at the schools swelled up. More new schools were opened mostly from public initiatives, but planning was lacking. Nepal needed a planned and insightful educational development initiative. The first overall educational development initiative was taken by forming Nepal National Education Planning Commission (NNEPC) whose work was inaugurated on March 22, 1954 and submitted its report on March 1, 1955.

NNEPC marked the beginning of the planned development of the education sector in Nepal. This Commission initiated a comprehensive national education system in vogue (MOES, 2000). This report described the Nepalese historical, geographical and societal contexts; narrated educational developments and analyzed requirements; and put forth plans for school and University education. The Commission faced several difficulties such as unavailability of accurate school level data; difficulty in defining a school and the pupil attending in it; etc. A number of innovative concepts were also brought up in the report such as free education; universalization of education; multi-purpose secondary schooling; graded standards at the primary level; credit certification, etc. The commission also undertook research to generate data and information required for proper planning.

Interim governments were in function until 1959 after democratic movement and fall of Ranas in 1951. Nepal's first general election, held in the spring of 1959, gave Nepali Congress a vast majority and Nepal was under the prime ministership of B. P. Koirala. This government was paving way to modernization and development within a short period. At the same time intrigue against Nepali Congress government was started from the royal palace and some of the opposition parties. There was protest against taxation, land reform and other progressive measures of the Nepali Congress government (Shaha, 1982). Royal cope on 15 December 1960 took over and clamped down the first elected government after 19 months of its being in the office. Partyless Panchayat System was established. Since then like other spheres of government, education was used to strengthen monarchy in Nepal.

'All Round National Education Commission' (ARNEC), the second education commission in Nepal, commenced its work in 1961. The rigor and comprehensiveness established by the first education commission in Nepal started to erode from ARNEC. This commission worked for nine days, set out fifteen meetings and worked for a total of sixty two and half hours. As could be assumed the commission prepared its report based on the ideas and judgments of the commission members. Some of the proposal of the NNEPC was reiterated in the ARNEC report such as universal and free primary education, vocational education (MOE, 1961). But what had been done and accomplished during the period of first commission and the second one had not been analyzed nor there were any lessons drawn.

Lack of consolidation effort and working from the scratch continued in following education commissions as well. But what remained intact was to promote education for safeguarding monarchism. The third education commission, 'The National Education System Plan' (NESP) in 1971 stated objective of the education as, "... to produce citizens who, with full faith in the country and the Crown, will conduct themselves in accordance with the Panchayat system and to meet the manpower requirement of the development through the spread of scientific and technical education" (MOE, 1971). Two of the striking features of this commission were compulsory vocational education at grades 8, 9 and 10 and nationalization of the schools. Though some of the intentions seemed to be good, implementation was devastating. Both political system and educational system arrested development of Nepal. Panchayat system restricted people participation in the governance and nationalization of the school restricted opening of the new schools which in turn restricted access to education to many Nepalese children.

There was a gap of more than twenty years in commissioning another education system plan in Nepal. 'National Education Commission' (NEC) was formed in 1990 after the reinstatement of democracy in Nepal in that year. This commission organized interaction sessions, study tours and sharing sessions. There were some ambitious plans such as 'to raise the school-going population from the present 64 percent to 100 percent' and promises such as there is 'need of formulating clear plans and policies for the provision of primary education to the various linguistic groups' (NEC, 1992). This commission report tried to set quantitative targets and pointed out specific needs to achieve certain goals as well.

The report of the 'Higher-Level National Education Commission' (HLNEC, 1999) reflected on the plans of the NEC, analyzed the progress and shortfalls in some respects and tried to formulate further plans. This report highlighted some pertinent aspects such as low quality of education; need of incorporating pre-primary education in the school education system; bilingual education; contribution of private sector in education.

After HLNEC no other national education commission has been formed in Nepal. However there are various national education plans which play important role in the development of school education in Nepal such Education for All (EFA) and School Sector Reform (SSR). Based on the plans forwarded by the national education commissions some of the important aspects of the school education are analyzed and presented under the sub-headings of focus, access and quality in the following sections. Relevant data, information are also drawn from other educational documents, research and evaluation reports, and relevant references.

Focus of Educational Plan

Universal, free, compulsory education underlining quality was envisioned in most of the education commissions in Nepal. Visioning is the first step to development. NNEPC (1956, p. 81) envisioned:

> ... the first goal of education in Nepal should be universal primary education. It suggested as targets: at least one primary school for each 1000 people by 1965; 300,000 children in primary schools by 1965 (this is one-fourth the number of children of primary school age at present); voluntary universal primary education by 1975; compulsory universal primary education by 1985 (i.e. all children of primary school age in school).

ARNEC reemphasized free and compulsory education through out the country. According to the 1956 NNEPC plan voluntary universal primary education should have been implemented during NESP period. NESP rather brought up the issue that effort at quantitative increase alone had unfavorably influenced the standard of education. Consequently NESP in 1971 lowered the target to provide primary education facilities to 64 percent of 6 to 8 years of children in the next five years. NEC brought back universal primary education as educational focuses on the backdrop of 'World Conference on Education for All' in Thailand and 'World Summit on Children', USA – both in 1990. NEC in 1992 report (p. 20) envisaged a target to be accomplished by 2000:

> ... increasing the primary school enrollment from the present 67 percent to 100 percent, and to raise the enrollment of girls from the present 31 percent to 100 percent by the year 2000. Another target is to raise the percentage of the children completing primary education from the present 27 percent to 70 percent.

A sanguine dream of schooling all the Nepalese children has been pushed back further and farther, but its worthwhile intention has been reiterated for the good. HLNEC in 1999 (p. 14) envisaged, "compulsory and free primary education will be introduced in the country within the next 10 years". This commission report set the target to provide primary education to 90 percent of children of 6 to 10 years by the end of the Ninth Plan, i.e. by 2002 and to all primary age children by the Tenth Plan, i.e. by 2007. Whereas according to the 1956 NNEPC plan universal primary education was to be achieved by 1985.

Another important emphasis of the education commissions was on single, national system of education with national level curriculum, examination system and control. NEC and NESP even emphasized on Nepali language as the medium of instruction. NESP suggested assimilating words and phrases from different regional languages into the national language (i.e. Nepali) so that Nepali language might be further enriched and so developed into a more effective medium of instruction (MOE, 1971, p. 10). The education commission set up by the democratic ideology led government in 1992 recognized use of a language other than Nepali as the medium of instruction in the areas where Nepali is not the mother tongue (MOE, p. 27). Mother tongue as medium of instruction has been given emphasis since then.

Besides these two focuses education commissions in Nepal have intended other general aspects in the curriculum objectives such as citizenship, socialization, culture, environment, vocational and technical education, human resource development, etc. NEC also emphasized addressing backward section of the society as one of the focuses of education.

In the education system of Nepal pronounced initiatives for the development of primary education that has direct bearing at present could be traced back to 1984 initiatives with Primary Education Development Project (PEDP) and Primary Education Project (PEP). PEP had three major areas of activities – primary schools, the examination system, and administrative capacity at the central level and it was designed to a) achieve a low-cost qualitative improvement in primary education and b) strengthen the administrative and technical capacity of the sector (CERID, 1989). Master Plan for Basic and Primary Education (BPEP) sub-sector 1992-2001, under which BPEP 1992-1996 was implemented, had four main objectives: a) improving quality (through new curriculum, new set of textbooks, teacher training, improved and continuous student assessment, improved physical and learning environment); b) improving access to and participation in basic and primary education; c) improving system efficiency; and d) enhancing the relevance of basic and primary education (MOE, 1997a). Building upon and learning from BPEP I, BPEP II 1997-2002 had slightly modified objectives – a) to enhance the relevance of Basic and Primary Education (BPE), b) to improve the efficiency of BPE, c) to improve the quality of BPE, and d) to improve the access to and participation in BPE. Next program in the educational lane that precedes is Education for All (EFA) 2004-2009. EFA has three main objectives – a) ensuring access and equity in primary education, b) enhancing quality and relevance of primary education, and c) improving efficiency and institutional capacity of schools and institutions at all levels providing technical backstopping to schools. During one quarter of the century from PEP to EFA spanning from 1984 to 2009 the focus of the educational endeavors has been access, quality, relevancy, efficiency. The emphases for quality improvement were into curriculum revision, curricular materials development and distribution, teacher training, management, etc.

Though program focus was more inclined towards Primary Education since 1980s, there were several projects/programmes focusing the secondary education. Science Education Development Project, 1983-1991 aimed at strengthening Science, Mathematics and English education at secondary level. These subjects are still poorly performed subjects in the secondary level in Nepalese secondary education. Secondary education received similar prominence as primary level with the work on Secondary Education Perspective Plan (SEPP) prepared in 1997. SEPP (MOE, 1997b) prepared a 15 years (1996-2011) plan for secondary education development with four objectives: to enhance quality; to ensure equity; to enhance efficiency; and to promote relevance. SEPP covered period of three 5 year national plans – 9th, 10th and 11th plans. Secondary Education Action Plan (MOE, 1998) for the period of 1997-2002 in the context of 9th Plan was prepared. The focus of the secondary education has been developing the talents and values of the individual; modernize the society and develop the human resources in consonance with national interest; prepare self dependent citizens; communicate articulately and be industrious etc. (MOE, 1997b; MOE, 2000). SEPP set targets to achieve 70% GER in lower secondary and 50% GER in secondary levels; 80% fully trained teachers; class size of minimum 20 students and maximum 45 students; and 80% or more at grade 8 and 60% or above pass rate in the School Leaving Certificate (SLC) examination at grade 10 (MOE, 1997b). Secondary Education Support Programme (SESP) was prepared in 2002 which reiterated target to increase access and pass rate in grade 8 and SLC. By the end of SESP primary education and secondary education was seen and embraced in a holistic way into School Sector Reform (SSR) to be implemented in 2009.

Access to Education

Unfulfilled commitment to the universal primary education still makes about 11% of the primarily school age children out of the school system in Nepal in 2007 (DOE, 2007). Government of Nepal has been putting its efforts to increase the number of schools, students and teachers from year to year, but even universalization of primary education has not been achieved and set target are far from being achieved. When increase in the number of schools, students and teachers are considered at the primary, lower secondary and secondary levels an improvement trend can be seen as shown in the following figures:

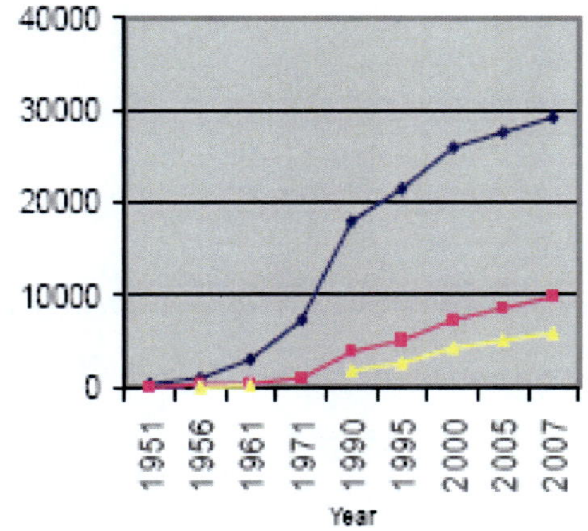

Figure 1. Increase in the number of schools.

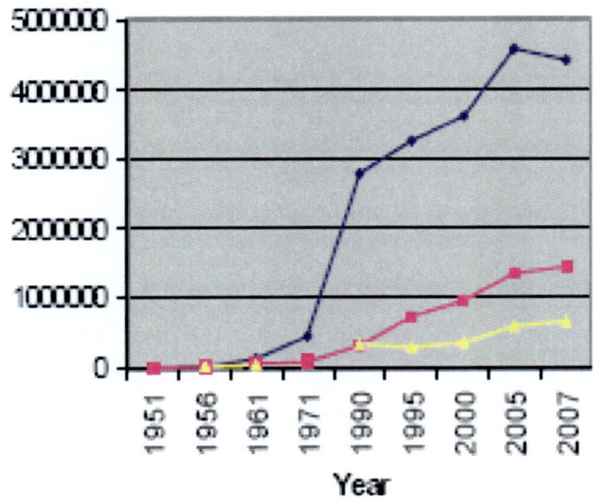

Figure 2. Increase in the number of students.

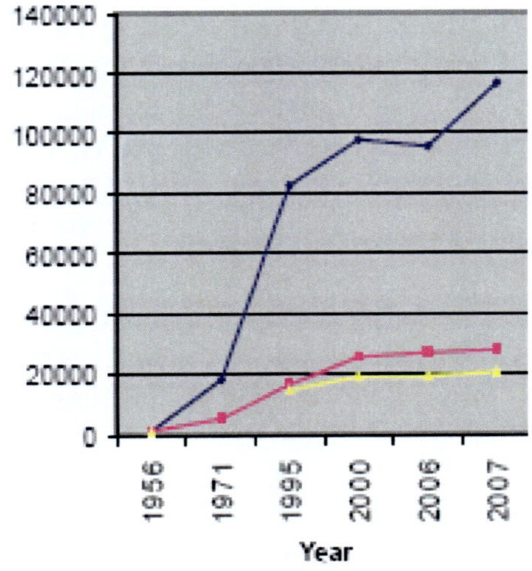

Figure 3. Increase in the number of teachers.

However when these improvements are compared with the target set for universal access or increased access to the primary education then the pictures becomes dismal. Commitment for the universal primary education has been pushed down several times and even lowered down sometimes as presented in the following figure:

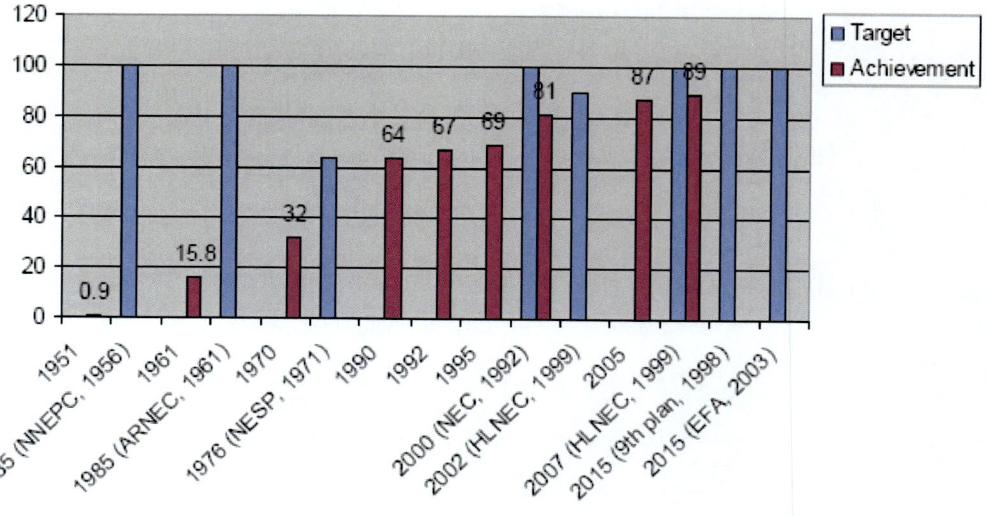

Figure 4. Percentage of Primary School Age Children in the School.

Above figure indicates – 1) that universal primary education has been envisioned in 1956 and Nepal, in more than 50 years, is still far from it; 2) that though a promise for the universal primary education has been kept most of the times, the fulfillment of the promise has been pushed further and farther – sometimes even lowering promises to provide primary education to only certain percentages of the children and to certain lower grades only; and 3) that if target 2015 will be achieved is questionable as the uphill becomes steep the task becomes harder and difficult.

Secondary level plans, perhaps not to repeat similar story of the gap between set target and achievement in the access, set manageable targets. To give an example Gross Enrollment Ratio (GER) for grades 6-10 was 40% in 1997. SEPP set targets to achieve 70% GER in lower secondary and 50% GER in secondary levels by 2011. The achievement in the GER in 2002 was 55% and 35% in the lower secondary and secondary level respectively. SESP in 2002 set target to achieve GER in lower secondary from 55% to 65% and in secondary from 35% to 55% by 2007.

The achievement in 2007 in GER is 78.8% and 55.9% in the lower secondary and secondary level respectively.

Countries with resource crunch face dilemma whether to focus on meeting quantlitative target or improve quality of education because both require financial investment. Opposing the target of 100% universal primary education of the previous two education commissions, NESP (MOE, 1971) viewed that:

> The rapid expansion of education, devoid of specific objectives, has produced a number of problems. The investment of the limited financial resources available for the development of education, therefore appears to have been unproductive and unsatisfactory (p. 3).... Effort at quantitative increase alone has resulted in a wide diffusion of the available financial

> resources and has unfavorable influenced the education standard (p. 4).... (Such analysis led the commission to set target that)... in the next five years 64 percent of boys and girls in the age-group between 6 and 8 will be given primary education facilities (p. v).

HLNEC saw how to increase student's participation and attendance in the school as the main challenge rather than to increase accessibility. The argument was that by 1999 the schools for 89 percent of children of primary age were situated in a distance taking the walk of half an hour or less than that. Proximity is a necessary condition, but not a guarantee to attend a school.

Another point raised by HLNEC itself is that schools are opened under the political pressure rather than on the basis of a scientific mapping. This is largely responsible for the distribution of schools un-proportionally and a number of needy and backward hamlets without a primary school within half an hour walking distance. SEPP (MOE, 1997b) gives the picture of the access to secondary education scenario:

> The current (1994) GER for grades 6-10 is 40%, but this average hides marked inequalities in access and opportunity. There are twice as many boys in school as girls. Children in remote and rural areas have much less opportunity to attend school than those in towns and the Kathmandu valley.... Regional inequalities in student participation rates are very high and tend to increase at higher grades. On average, there are 39 secondary schools for every 100 primary school in Kathmandu, this ratio falls to 15:100 in the Central Mountain and the Mid-Western Hill districts. (pp. i and A4-1).

SESP (MOES, 2002a) also highlights inequalities in the educational participation which are striking in terms of gender, geographical situation, socio-economic strata and ethnicity. Girls, rural and mountain region, lower socio-economic strata, ethnic minorities are deprived of education in many ways.

Access to education should also be analyzed in terms of access to what level of education. This implies the structure of education. Though the number of the schools, students and teachers show the increasing trend, the progress made remained inadequate – firstly the target made has never been met and secondly the minimum level of the education expected to a Nepalese child to have has been changing.

Majority of the Nepalese parents use to express expectation of maximum level of education for their wards as the highest grade the school runs in their community or near to them. Therefore the highest grade at the lowest structure is important condition for what level of education a common Nepalese child could have. There have been changes in the educational structure in the Nepalese education system time to time. The change in the structure of school education seems to have been forwarded either what the government expected to provide as minimum level education or due to changes at the global education scenario.

However the logic for the frequent structural changes in Nepalese education system has not been plausible. The education system in Nepal has been periodically restructured as shown in the following figure:

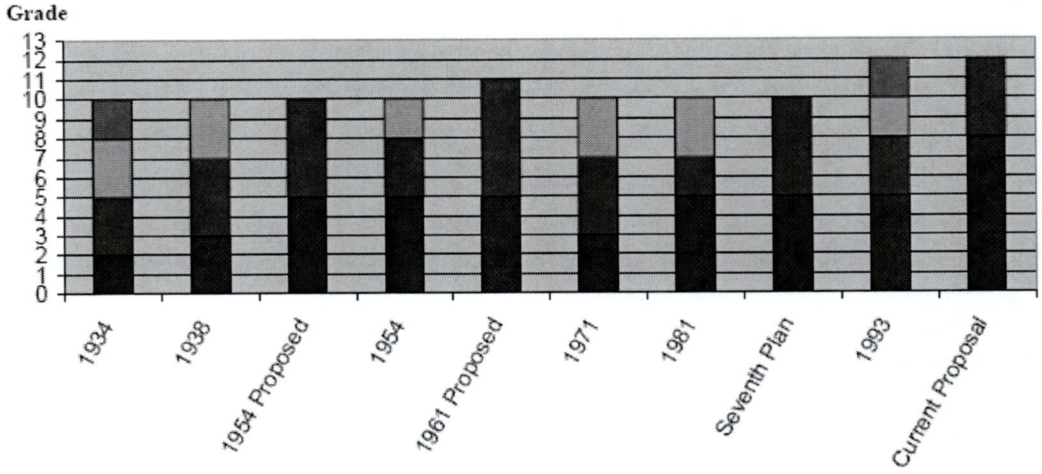

Figure 5. Structure of Schooling in Nepal.

Changes come one after another and there has been lack of lesson learning and building upon the past. Like a new administrative head rearranging chairs, desks and cupboards of the office to show off a change has been made, educational committees set up usually suggest a change in education structure. Changes for the sake of a change do not automatically bring about a change in the quality. Nepalese education system has rather suffered from frequent structural changes. Varieties of combinations that have been tried out gives an impression that we are not yet tired with this probability game. Another important aspect of the school structure is educational provision of at least the lowest level of the structure to all children of the country. This aspect has not been contented – in 1994 there were even one classroom schools and promise was five grades and there are a number of schools with less than five rooms at present as well and promise is grade 8. Unfulfilled structural promise will again depilate the access to the education to all.

Quality of Education

Another important question is access to what kind of education. This implies quality of education and motivation to the children to come to school. This is also largely related to awareness about and relevancy of education. Access to education has been focused mostly, but it has not entirely shadowed the concern for quality in education. In the Nepalese education system, concerns for the quality started with the implementation of the PEP. Regarding quality of education need for improving physical infrastructure, provision of instructional materials, improving classroom pedagogy, providing trained teachers, etc. have been emphasized.

Physical Infrastructure: NNEPC described many schools to be of the 'one-room type with one or two teachers'. Schools were even under a tree or a thatched roof. These conditions can be seen in few cases at present as well in Nepal as are reported in the media time to time. SSR in 2007 re-promised that 'there will be a separate classroom for each grade, well furnished, properly ventilated with a writing board, desk and benches, and book corner' (MOES). Comparisons of the conditions as described at the time of NNEPC in 1956 and plans of SSR in 2007 could give the sense of the meager achievement made in improving physical conditions of the schools. Gap in the between can be discerned.

Instructional Materials: NNEPC pointed out serious shortage of instructional materials – equipments for teaching nature study and science, fine arts and music, geography and history, etc. were almost non-existent. Book written in Nepali were seriously lacking. Even the simplest audio-visual aids were missing. To give an example of depilated condition the report writes, "frequently there is no chalk-board; the teacher and children write in the dust of the floor". NNEPC devoted almost a chapter in 20 chapter report and recognized the 'physical and material environment of learning' to be one of the three factors to be considered in the educational experiences of children – other two being 'the learner' and 'the teacher' (p. 179). NNEPC detailed out the types of the materials that would be required for effective classroom teaching learning and the ways these materials should be used. ARNEC, 1961 mentions mostly about the books rather than instructional materials. NESP, 1971 recommended Ministry of Education to issue detailed instructions on the nature of school buildings, furniture and other physical facilities. The report also emphasized that every school should have one classroom for each class and secondary schools to have a workshop, a laboratory and a library as well. Along with the textbook NESP suggested provision of various educational materials for effective teaching learning. Educational Materials Organization established in 1958 was named as Janak Education Materials Center in 1971 which NESP envisioned as the Center to undertake writing, printing and distribution of textbooks; produce and distribute educational materials or provide schools with model sets along with guidebooks. Scarcity of instructional materials in one hand and non-use of those available or provided to the school on the other hand is still general scenario in the school at present as well. Above all is the lack of clarity on what is required and expectation often does not translate into action. SSR in 2007 also devises expectation:

> Minimum enabling conditions include: an environment for equitable participation, appropriate facilities, adequate instructional process and materials, and sufficient number of qualified teachers.... The Government will develop a national framework of norms and standards for enabling conditions. The government will develop a mechanism for defining minimum enabling conditions and for assuring that they are met. (MOES, 2007, p. 36).

Teacher Training: NNEPC in 1956 recognized 'the teacher' as one of the three important factors for the quality education. This report outlined objectives, organization, curricula, evaluation, etc. for the teacher training. This commission estimated requirement of 40,000 to 60,000 trained teachers in order to enforce compulsory primary education. According to the recommendation of this commission report College of Education was established in 1957 to train the teachers. NESP in 1971 pointed out two problems in the teacher training – 1) how to increase the number of trained teachers and 2) how to improve the standard of training. These two are the vital questions relevant at the present context of Nepal as well. A five year Teacher Education Project ending in 2009 due to extension of one more year focused to clear backlog of untrained teachers in the primary schools of Nepal. Now about 87% of the primary teachers are trained. But quality of the training and performance of the trained teacher at the classroom has been often of the poor quality.

The impact of teacher training has not so far been found to be up to the desired level in classroom practices in Nepal. Until the end of BPEP I, teacher training had been, "a one-way traffic of unknown emphases and unseen practices" (MOE, 1999). BPEP II master plan (1997-2002) raises concerns over the gap between the content and the intent of the teacher-training curriculum, and the teacher-training endeavors for producing under-trained teachers at large (MOE, 1997a). PEDP (1993) pointed out that trained teachers were not inclined to use appropriate teaching skills in the classroom. It has also been reported that there is no significant differences between the classroom delivery practices of the trained and untrained teachers as well as in the achievement of students taught by these two groups of teachers have been pointed out by the studies in Nepal. Studies on the impact of training have pointed out shortcomings related to various aspects such as trainers not being able to become role models for teachers; lack of conducive classroom environment due to large class size and poor facilities (NCED, July 2000a); teachers not being competent enough to use student-centered methods properly (NCED, July 2000b; NCED, 2002a); shortcomings in the training packages such as lack of activity base (NCED, 2002b). These aspects are to be appropriately addressed to ensure effective transfer of training skills.

Classroom Pedagogy: The main aspect in the quality of education is classroom pedagogy that ensures student's learning and achievement. Improving classroom delivery/classroom pedagogy and enhancing students' learning have been major features in the educational plans in Nepal. NNEPC in 1956 emphasized both expansion of the education in terms of access and qualitative improvement of delivery. Quality of education has been a major educational focus since this commission. This commission's report clearly demands respect for the individual differences and intelligent adaptation of the curriculum to various local conditions and to the individual differences of children. In effect this is related to child/student-centered principles. ARNEC also recognized that there exist differences among individuals physically, mentally and affectively. Like a doctor diagnoses a disease on the basis of history and tests and then prescribes treatment, teaching should also be based on the diagnosis of student's history, physique, feeling, and mental development (MOE, 1961). This statement implies a diagnostic and individualized approach in teaching. NESP was not explicit on classroom pedagogical approaches. It just indented to conduct research to improve teaching methods for each subject. The intention was on use of scientific methods (MOE, 1971).

The better prospects with regard to classroom pedagogical approaches as intended in 1956 and 1961 education commission reports seems to have not been implemented into classroom practices. The common classroom pedagogical practices seemed to be not effective as pointed out by the NEC in 1992. This commission's report stated, "The teaching-learning situation in primary schools is rather depressing.... Students are encouraged to learn by rote, and assessments are made on the same basis." HLNEC in 1999 also raised some issues related to diversity education. This report pointed out inability of primary level education to represent various language groups, cultural diversity and regional needs. This commission suggested reformative teaching at the primary level.

One better prospect that could be observed in these commissions' report is a progressive refinement in defining and linking quality education to children's learning. To take recent examples 'Basic and Primary Education' emphasized, "Teachers will be able to use appropriate method of teaching to achieve the objectives of the lesson." (MOE, 1997a). 'Concept paper for further support on Basic and Primary Education in Nepal 2004-2009' (MOES, 2002b) pointed out a need to deemphasize rote learning and a need to develop further away from treating the students in classes as homogeneous units and away from rote learning. Core document of EFA (MOES, 2003b) envisioned a classroom by 2015 as:

> The classroom is a stimulating learning environment, deigned to meet the learning need of all students, thus ensuring that each student develops to their full potential. This recognizes that children learn in different ways at different rates and will achieve different levels of attainment. It is a caring environment, in which there is mutual respect between teacher and students, and from student to student. It is a safe and happy environment, to which students look forward to coming each day.
>
> ... The curriculum and educational materials are designed so as to ensure active, child-centered learning delivered through a wide range of teaching-learning methodologies. Teachers evaluate students through a range of formal and informal techniques, using these assessments to identify each student's strengths and weaknesses so that they may adapt their teaching methodology to cater for the needs of students as individuals, and so improve the quality of each student's learning.

Thus EFA documents pointed out emphasis on rote learning and teacher-centered approach as dominant pedagogical practices in the Nepalese schools. Child-centered approach, individualized instruction, formative assessments are pointed out to be practices for reforming classroom pedagogical practices. It also necessary education takes all children into its consideration as emphasized by 'Education for All', "Inclusion of cultural, linguistic and other social values of the local communities in the education system." (MOES, 2003b). SSR also accords students' learning as most important aspect and proposes, "... promote independent learning by students being educated under diverse situations... Local curriculum, content and materials will be developed... A child's mother tongue will be employed as the medium of instruction up to grade three... Flexible instructional arrangements will be developed and employed..." (MOES, 2007).

Thus for the qualitative improvement child-centered education has been forwarded as vision and intention. Another emerging concern in relation to classroom pedagogy is education for diversity. Nepal is a diverse country with great physiographical, environment, and cultural variations. Topographically Nepal has plain Terai region in South boarding India and highest mountain peak in North boarding China and environment varies from South to North. Population census, 2001 registered 101 different caste groups, 92 language groups, and 10 religious groups indicating cultural diversity of the country (DOE, 2003). Interim constitution of Nepal respects this diversity with educational provisions such as, "Each community will have right to receive basic education in mother language as provided by the law" (MOES, 2007). The findings of the studies on the practices in the Nepalese classrooms are not so encouraging. It is still a long way to have improved classroom practices.

Intention and commitment for the 'quality primary education' is being reiterated from one project/program to another in Nepal. There is progressive refinement in defining and linking quality education to children's learning. For example 'Basic and Primary Education' emphasized, "Teachers will be able to use appropriate method of teaching to achieve the objectives of the lesson." (MOE, 1997). 'Concept paper for further support on Basic and Primary Education in Nepal 2004-2009' (MOES, 2003a) pointed out a need to deemphasize rote learning and a need to develop further away from treating the students in classes as homogeneous units and away from rote learning.

CLASSROOM TEACHING LEARNING PRACTICES

Study on classroom teaching learning practices are very few in Nepal. EDSC (1997) study points out almost non-existent of the research studies which investigated into the impact of the training on classroom performance of teachers. EDSC in its 1999 study on national assessment of grade 5 students pointed out that appropriate classroom practices for learning are not taking place in primary schools. The report views that the efforts so far made in improving classroom teaching learning had not been transferred into classroom practices. Studies on transfer of training skills which is presented in the next section below also indicated poor transfer of training skills in the classroom teaching learning. Formative Research (FR) undertaken by CERID for Ministry of Education covered classroom teaching learning practices as one of its major research area from 2001. Its 7th study on classroom teaching learning has been completed in 2008. FR study shows that a slow pace of improvement in the classroom teaching learning has been found and clarity in visioning the classroom pedagogy in terms of child-centeredness has been emerging.

Studies related to classroom practices mainly found classroom delivery teacher dominated and emphasis on rote learning. Teacher lecturing, paraphrasing, drill, reading and repeating from textbook, memorizing question/answer were dominant approaches. Another important aspect, the classroom process which is envisioned to be a child-centered, was found largely confounded to the whole class teaching and leaving the weaker ones behind. Single language, single session, same material (if used), same method (usually lecture, paraphrase) were the general practices in the classroom delivery. CERID (2002) pointed out classroom delivery teacher dominated and textbook based and the dominant classroom practices were as following:

- On entering the classroom, teacher asks students for a copy of the textbook if he/she has not carried one with him/her.
- He/she asks students where they were (page number or lesson number) in the sequential order of the lessons or ask students to turn to such and such page number.
- Teacher asks one of the students to read the text or the teacher himself/herself reads it adding his/her own interpretations here and there – mainly in a paraphrasing manner.
- In lower grades chorus repeating of the text is the usual practice and in the upper grades memorization of the question answer is done.
- Translation method is used most in the English language classes.

FR study also found a small number of teachers (in about 12% of the classes in 153 observed classes) who involved students actively in teaching learning demonstrated better practices. The classroom practices of the better performing teachers were as following:

- Used real objects (pebbles for multiplication).
- Explained and demonstrated first (protector), then asked one of the students to demonstrate the same and then got the whole class to practice it. Teacher went around and provided feedback individually.

- Used objects in the classroom and around the school in teaching English words rather than by telling their meanings in Nepali.
- Teacher encouraged students to ask questions in English among themselves.

The common practice found was that the textbook was used by the teachers more often than curriculum, teacher guide or other curricular materials even though these might be available in the school or could be easily arranged if needed. Analysis of the curriculum and teacher guide related to the concerned lesson of the classroom delivery indicate that if the teacher would have consulted curriculum and followed the suggestions provided in the teacher guide, classroom delivery would have been better than the existing ones. But classroom teaching learning practices indicated curriculum and teacher guide being used very less. Better classroom delivery in the cases where curriculum and/or teacher guide were consulted compared to the cases of non-consultation also supports this statement. Analysis of teacher guide and training manual showed that most of the teaching methods suggested in the teacher guide are covered in the training manual and materials suggested in teacher guide are explained in the training manual. Thus, skill learned during training would be supportive in implementing teacher guide effectively in the classroom delivery. However, such transfer was lacking largely in the classroom delivery. (CERID, 2002 and 2003).

Assessment is another major component of the effective classroom learning. FR study (CERID, 2004) assessed classroom delivery with major focus on assessment practices as used to enhancing student's learning. This study found that assessment practices in the form of homework, class work, classroom questions, and periodic examinations were mainly based on low level of cognitive domain. Again emphasis was on rote learning and memorization of answers to the questions to do better in the examination. Assessment fed in rote learning strategy. Even in the schools/classes where Continuous Assessment System (CAS) was piloted, CAS was used as an assessment tool than a tool for continuous support for the learning of the students. Use of assessment to provide feedback to the students to improve learning was done in about one fifth of the observed classes and these were found to be helpful in enhancing students' learning. Evaluation of the CAS piloting by Nyachhyon and Webber (2001) found gaps between the intention of the CAS and its practice at the schools such as 'intention: student's assessment during teaching, no periodical examination – practice: teachers used to conduct end-of-trimester tests in order to justify the allocation of ratings in the portfolio'. To take another example 'intention: teacher applies various informal methods appropriate for CAS – practice: use of formal paper and pencil test'.

A study by CDC (2003) on the practice of CAS in the pilot districts brings forth several finding which negate with the intention of CAS. For example the study found out that the schools were conducting the periodic examination as they used before the introduction of the CAS. The achievement indicated in the portfolio was higher compared with the achievement test score of the students that there was no correspondence in the portfolio score and achievement score. The study also pointed out other reasons on the way of effective implementation of the CAS -- overcrowded class; difficulty for the teachers to match lesson goals with that of the students' progress report; maximum use of textbook and less use of other curriculum materials; teachers not using outcome of assessment for improving instruction.

Use of the mother tongue has been emphasized in the classroom to enhance children's learning. FR Study done by CERID (2005) reported that though use of mother tongue as medium of instruction at the primary level was found to be politically, emotionally, and pedagogically correct, several practical issues emerged at the field. In the three schools and their communities visited, there was general consensus for using mother tongue at the classroom teaching learning for the purpose of supporting children's learning when he/she cannot understand the word, term in Nepali. There was refutation in general for using mother tongue textbook and mother tongue only as medium of instruction. There were several reasons for giving priority to the Nepali language such as it facilitates exposure; children learn mother tongue at home so that school time need to be used to learn other important aspects; learning another language from beginning would be helpful especially for those children who dropout early. There were also other practical issues such as variety of dialects in a mother tongue language group such as in Tharu and Tamang. Generally children's learning and language learning were not differentiated. In such situation where educational policy and student and parent expectation mismatch classroom teaching learning as it is intended can not take place properly.

Similar situation was found in the classroom where life skills education has been piloted (CERID, 2006). Teacher who received life skill related training and had access to support materials in the project supported districts, there was transfer of training skills in some extent, but a number of gaps were visible. There was lack of proper working coordination and learning from each other among concerned agencies viz. CDC, NCED and UNICEF. Seeking synergic effect/impact would have been fruitful. Use of textbook, emphasizing rote learning, teacher domination was still the common classroom process. In Health Education class teachers were also found using children for making comparisons by setting one child as good example and another as bad. This practice was found to be discouraging and harassing the child set as bad example. Another common practice in Health Education class was to list down 'don'ts' than highlighting existing positive behaviors/aspects. Such blaming practices were found not to be child friendly.

A study conducted by VSO (2005) pointed out fragile morale of the teachers and their low motivation to be major factor in depilated performance of the teacher in the classroom. This study reported that teachers, in general, felt that much was expected of them in the classroom, but that their roles in educational development had been disregarded by the educational authorities. Teachers in Nepal are found to be working in very difficult situations and with limited resources. The teachers also had the feeling of powerlessness that teachers experience about their inability to create positive learning experiences for their students. There is also severe lack of the instructional materials in the schools which hampered classroom teaching learning.

In case of secondary classrooms heavy backwash effect of SLC examination is easily discernible in the classroom teaching learning such as practicing with old questions, revisions of important topics in the classroom in terms of examination, rampant practice of taking help from guidebooks and guess papers that provide important question and answer (CERID, 1997; MOES, 2005). In many schools preparation for the SLC examination starts from grade 8 itself. A good school will be expected to complete grade 10 courses by grade 9 and repeat the course at grade 10. SLC is main criteria of success for a school and a student – a school gets its reputation and name and for a student the opening of the door of opportunity for higher education and success. Doing better in the SLC is important.

Another example of the backwash effect of the SLC examination is on the practical courses. There is provision of practical in the Science and Social Studies subjects in the curriculum, but practical classes in these subjects are not done in the schools. The main reason for not doing practical in these subjects is that there is no weightage for the practical works in these subjects in the SLC examination. There is also provision of listening and speaking component practical in the English language subject. There was no practical in listening and speaking component as well few years back. After practical examination in the listening and speaking component in English language started in the SLC examination, schools managed materials and spend certain periods for practical in listening and speaking component as well. This indicates that schools never realized that listening and speaking components are important in English language, what they realized is listening and speaking components are important to do better in SLC examination.

Existing pedagogical practices as shown from the review related to the classroom practices indicates following as common classroom teaching learning practices in the Nepalese schools:

Knowledge accumulation and rote memorization: There is emphasis on knowledge accumulation and rote memorization in the classroom teaching learning. Usual classroom delivery takes the repetitive mode of textual content or paraphrasing teaching by the teacher or bulk of classroom time on task spend on exercising question and answer important for the examination.

Limitations due to single textbook: In Nepalese education system national level of curriculum is used and there are also prescribed textbook for each subjects included in the curriculum. The practice is to publish a textbook for a subject on the basis of course content given in the curriculum. Most of the schools use single textbook for whole of the course. Provision of single textbook is also thought to have restricted the teacher as well as the student in discovering, exploration, comparison activities. Provision of the single textbook unduly gives the message that knowing the content thoroughly is important which ultimately promotes rote learning.

Textbook rather than the curriculum guiding the classroom teaching learning: Due to sole use of textbook in the classroom teaching learning without consulting the curriculum several gaps could be found. Due to this curriculum objectives not covered in the textbook lessons were ignored and left out. Usually these happen to be higher level objectives and those requiring habit formative and affective ones in the curriculum, but not adequately covered in the textbook content.

Dominance of whole class technique: Existing classroom teaching learning activities/processes consider whole class as a unit. Whole class is taught together and the class moves together along the lessons in the textbook as if all the students have same ability, interest, needs, learning styles, achievement, etc. Neither the curriculum nor the classroom activities take student's need, learning styles, ability, etc. into consideration. Due to such teaching strategy the weaker students fall further behind and develop learning difficulties. Group work, individual work, project work and other innovative approaches are rarely employed in the classroom in most of the schools.

Emphasis on finishing textbook and preparation for examination: Teachers take it as their most important duty to complete textbook lessons on time whether or not the students are ready for the next lesson. Due to emphasis on completing textbook lessons, individualization and learning differentiation is not given any value to sought for. Completing the textbook lesson and preparing students for the examination dominates the teachers' activities. A good teacher is thought to be one who completes the textbook lesson and prepares the students to score high in the examination. Due to this Hence backwash effect of examination could be seen in the classroom teaching learning such as practicing with old questions, revisions of important topics in the classroom in terms of examination.

Scarcity of resources: Classroom teaching learning practices are also affected due to scarcity of the physical and material resources. Crowded class, lack of adequate space for activities and materials, even lack of required materials are often pointed out to retorting teaching learning with the help of textbook alone.

DISCUSSION ON ENDURING ISSUES – ACCESS AND QUALITY

Increasing access and improving quality of education have always been focused in the education plan in Nepal. But both of these focuses are still far away to be achieved. Quality education is must if Nepal is to stand at a par to its neighbors. First step is to provide at least quality school education for all the Nepalese children that also in a fixed time interval. What NNEPC in 1956 observed for the Nepal of that time is still true to Nepal today, "The mud is thick, the pull is long, and the load is heavy".

Access to Education

Universal, free and compulsory education committed time and again at the primary or more is still far to achieve. The latest time set for 2015 for universal primary education is also unlikely to be achieved if present trends of school enrollment, retention and completion continue (UNCTN, 2007). The big issue is promises are repeated, but seldom fulfilled. It has become a tragedy that pushing fulfillment of the promises not by year but by decade has become a common and regular practice. No one is accountable and no one takes the responsibility if something does not happen. The issue is to set a time frame and make the concerned personnel accountable for the tasks. There is no option but to provide quality education to all Nepalese children as early as can be. Commitment and fulfillment of commitment as a mission is required. Government commitments could be seen, but fulfillment is still to happen.

Time to time it has been seen that planning was done without proper understanding of the situation and needs analysis. Suggestion of the SSR (MOES, 2007) for restructuring of the school education to 8 plus 4 school system is such an example. SSR observes that 'five years of schooling is not sufficient given the global and regional norms as well as rising national expectations'. That's fine we want to make first 8 years, the basic education, universal. But the question is when we are not likely to attend five years of primary education to all the Nepalese children by 2015, what plans do we have to make education universal up to grade 8. If five years of compulsory education fails, on what basis can we assert eight years of compulsory education will be a success? Action to translate vision is important. So the question is – how we will be able to fulfill the vision of 8 plus 4 system? False claim should be avoided like that made in Eighth Plan – the achievement was satisfactory because 3524 additional primary schools were opened against the target of 2025 additional primary schools; 14883 additional primary level teachers were recruited against the target of 8000. This claim defies the real target not being achieved that the gross enrollment achieved was 69.4 against the target of 90 (NPC, 1998). On the face of grade 5 not yet universal, a large number of children still out of school, and lack of policy and plan, will it be feasible to enforce 8 years of compulsory schooling?

Or is it schooling for mass and higher education for selective few? Multi-streams after basic education envisages majority of the students will take up vocational education in which they are interested and in which they are more likely to success. General stream leading to higher education will be open for selective few. But in a system where other things rather than students achievement and capacity plays more determining role, will not there be a danger to the poor family end up in the vocational stream? Will it not establish the wrong concept vocational stream is for the poor and give false impression it is good to go to the general stream even if the student is not fit for that? What kind of counseling facilities will be available which is important for the success of the vocationalization?

Basic education to increase relevancy? SSR claims that the structural integration of 1 to 5 with 6 to 8 schools improves students' performance by easing curricular integration and consolidating the competency-based learning programme. The argument is that restructuring will help to ensure relevant and quality education to the children. On the contrary it can be argued that isn't it appropriate to focus on curriculum development and classroom teaching learning, rather than restructuring grades in numerical sense, to make the education relevant to the children? Another question that comes up is it more years in the school or quality of education that plays more important role what children learn? Is it not possible to increase relevancy and quality of education to the lives of the children in the existing structure – at least to get started?

Changes in other countries or local need? It often happens that when a new thing is adopted it is adopted on the premises that the program has been a success elsewhere. It is good to adopt what has worked out good. But when a program fails there will be hue and cry that program was not suitable for the local need and the country has been subjected to another futile experimentation. In case of restructuring as well, success of basic education in other countries should not be taken as a foolproof that qualifies Nepal to adopt it. More thoughts should go on this.

It is extremely essential to have a more or less complete picture and a long-term vision if restructuring is going to be implemented. Restructuring decision should be based on firm grounds that restructuring will indeed benefit the educational system. It should not be decided in an abrupt manner. Also the option of slow start and gradual implementation strategy should be considered. Restructuring should be linked with access to quality school education to all the Nepalese children in reality, not just a plan that would not to be fulfilled.

Quality Education

Classroom teaching-learning improvements requires myriad of aspects to be considered and should be looked upon in wider context. For example: setting classroom standards and roles expected from teacher and students -- …demanding, informing, teaching, negotiating, and arising… (Kordalewski, 2000). Best use of time for preparation time helps teachers to improve the inventiveness and appropriateness of the pedagogy (Hargreaves, 1994). Using space more intelligently for space is essentially a learning resource and a vital skill for the teachers to manage (Cohen, Manion and Morrison, 1996). Similarly classroom environment need to be managed for the environment in the school classroom should be aesthetically pleasing; should stimulate children's interest; should set high standard in the display and presentation of the children's work; and should be created in such a way that is practical to maintain (Pollard, 2006). The considerations for institutionalization of classroom teaching-learning process and development of such a framework need to pay attention to various important aspects such as stages of innovation process such as three overlapping stages suggested by Kinsler and Gamble (2001): initiation, implementation, and institutionalization or abandonment. How each stage is handled is crucial and can significantly affect the outcomes of both the succeeding stages and the innovation as a whole. Similarly building collaborative cultures is also equally important in developing framework for effective collaboration operate in the world of idea, examining existing practices critically, seeking better alternatives and working hard together at bringing about improvements and assessing their worth (Fullan and Hargreaves, 1992).

There is also need to conceptually clarify indented pedagogical vision in terms of classroom practices such as child centeredness, joyful learning, individualized instruction, project work, etc. These terms are still loosely defined in the training manuals and educational documents in Nepal and also lacks concrete activities to achieve these in the classroom level.

Rousseau emphasized the fact that the child should be free to learn from direct experience. Dewey advocated that children pursuing their own studies would be motivated to speculate, observe, gather information, and test out guesses or hypotheses to solve their own problems. (Pollard, A and Bourne, J, 1994). It has also been advocated if it is not children's experiences and interests that direct the curriculum content, their experiences and interests need to be considered by the teacher. A child-considered pedagogy takes account of children's experiences and interests, but decision is made by the teacher (Collins, Insley and Soler, 2001).

Individualized instruction requires teacher to work on a personal, one to one basis with each student; tailor instruction to specific needs and abilities of the learner; learners be free to work alone at their own pace; and pace, medium of presentation, study style, context, evaluation technique are adopted to the needs of each individual students. (Chauhan, 1979, p. 59). When individual work is in progress the teacher is almost bound to favour individual attention as well because no two children are doing the same thing (Boydell, 1978).

Better classroom practices are intended in the educational documents in Nepal. If implemented according to the plan a Nepalese school classroom practices would have been improved a lot than what it is now. But the existing practice in the Nepalese schools is that teachers teach according to their assigned classes on the basis of the class routine planned for the year at the beginning of the school session. The content to be covered is already fixed in the textbook. Teachers follow the content and the sequence of the lesson as provided and arranged in the textbook. Two or three periodic examinations are the main evaluation tools used by the schools and these tools are used for summative purpose. Single national level of curriculum, whole class teaching and mainly paper and pencil method of assessment is in practice. From such teacher centered educational approach we are aiming (if we mean child centered education) towards "an educational theory or system that emphasizes the pupil and his or her individual characteristics as central in conducting instruction instead of focusing on subject matter, external authority, and educational requirements" (Hawes and Hawes, 1932).

It is not easy to change teacher centered practices to child centered one in a short duration and in an easy way. Child centered education need to be a long-term vision with a number of intermediary steps. This will require starting with what is immediately possible such as providing assess to the materials (blackboard, learning materials, reference books/reading materials etc.) to the students and progressively increasing involvement/participation of the students in learning to employing student's interest, ability and need as the basis for teaching learning activities. Such changes also need to be furnished with the required expertise in the teachers, suitable physical environment in the schools and parental support. This requires to clarify: 1) what we are aiming to achieve (by stating child centered education); 2) what will be the best possible time frame to achieve a child centered education system; 3) what intermediary steps should be there; 4) what support need to be provided to the teachers; 5) what physical/infrastructure developments and materials need to be provided to the schools to adopt child centered education successfully.

Another issue is consolidation of the efforts to improve quality of education in the classrooms. The efforts needed to put into and providing needed support for achieving quality education such as a child centered education will be largely determined when the vision is clearly stated. Clarifying what we are aspiring for would be helpful to develop action steps and consolidate efforts towards achieving the vision. At present there are discrepancies present in a number of supports provided to the teachers and practices if these supports and practices are to be analyzed in terms of child centered education vision. The main discrepancies are related to these aspects: 1) provision of single national level curriculum and single textbook while in a child centered education curriculum is constructed according to the interests and needs of the pupils (Hawes and Hawes, 1932) with variety of resources and activities; 2) emphasis on norm referenced test while in a child centered approach criterion refverenced test is used with formative emphasis (Craft, 1996); 3) dominance of whole class teaching while individualized or group teaching is to be used in case of differentiated levels of students learning (Craft, 1996); student promotion on the basis of periodic, summative evaluation while students are to be provided with support on continuous basis to maximize learning.

There is a need for streamlining the efforts and supports to achieve a child centered education. For this a revision or development in curriculum, curricular materials, teacher training, and support to the school/teacher support might be required. For example a number of objectives of "Primary Teacher Training Curriculum" (NECD, 2000) are related to child centered approach, but some of these objectives are not explicit with respect to the child centered approach as well such as: *Objective:* Teach primary school subjects following a systematic process of planning lesson, selecting appropriate methods, selecting and preparing relevant materials and using continuous assessment schemes (CAS). *Remarks:* This objective seems to emphasis lesson preparation for the whole class teaching. It is also useful to prepare a lesson for planning instruction according to the need and capability of the individual child while it is required. Planning unit with individual child is important. To take second example – *objective:* Construct and use evaluation tools to assess students' progress vis-à-vis expected learning outcomes, and provide feedback to the students, and the parents. *Remark:* 'Construct and use evaluation tools' might imply developing formal written test only. While it is necessary to emphasize informal method and spontaneous evaluation opportunities as well for evaluation in the CAS. It is necessary for the teachers to be able to use diagnostic method to identify learning difficulties of the students. Teachers need to be provided evaluation/testing skills related to criterion referenced than norm referenced. To take even a third example – *objective:* Use reward and punishment in reinforcing children's learning. *Remark:* PUNISHMENT! that too in the primary level? Punishment should not the objective of a teacher training program.

It is necessary to provide training focused on the teaching learning approach we want to employee in our system. That will lead to identifying required skills in the teachers to provide them skills through discussion, demonstration and practice for lasting impact.

Another issue is over-burdened teacher with full period teaching responsibilities. It is necessary to mitigate teacher with over burden of the period per day or week, which is commonly 7/8 periods per day. It is also necessary to mange size of students in a class where it is over crowded. In this respect teacher rationalization is important. It is also important to try out alternative solution to make a class in a manageable size such as alternative days school, multiple shift with longer hour school and charter hour teaching learning. The long term vision should be provision of adequate number of classes with appropriate students teacher ratio.

PROBLEMS IN TRANSLATING INTENTIONS INTO IMPLEMENTATION

A brief account of the intention of the educational system to improve quality of education and existing classroom teaching learning practices indicates that classroom pedagogy to this end has not been effectively translated. There has been several repeated suggestion to use better teaching methods; involve and engage students in the classroom process; cater needs, interests, ability, individuality, background, etc. of the students; update curriculum; provide required materials; involve stakeholders in the reform process and so on. There might have been several barriers and challenges that impede translation of intention into implementation. Some of such probable barriers/challenges are discussed here:

Quality vs. quantity: Nepal has a commitment to 'Education for All'. Providing educational opportunity to those who are out of education system needs a greater effort and investment. Quantitative expansion has been in progress, but meeting qualitative standard at the same time has been hampered. Maintaining a balance between quantitative expansion and qualitative standard has been a challenge. But planning should address both at the same time, not separate them into two different tasks.

Dominance of the examination: Backwash effect of the examination at all level of education in Nepal has been tremendous. Importance of the learning would be measured in terms of its worth in helping get higher score in the examination. As examinations are dominated by lower level of test items of the cognitive area knowledge accumulation through rote learning has been accorded higher importance.

Conceptual clarity lack: It is usual practice to suggest measures for improvement in the educational reports without adequately discussing the related concepts. Due to lack of clarity of the concepts implementation becomes weak. Clarifying concepts, preparing guidelines on translating these concepts in classroom practices, and preparing teachers adequately with required skills, and providing required resources have not been done properly.

Inadequate teacher preparation: There have been several initiatives such as provision of local curriculum, teaching learning in mother tongue, curriculum revision, development of new textbooks, life skill education, etc. recently, but all of these lack one important aspect that teachers were not prepared in advance. Though the curriculum was revised recently and new textbooks introduced, most teachers knew about it when they had new textbook in the class when the new session started in the school. Prior orientation/training about the revised curriculum and new textbook was not done in most of the schools. Introducing revised and new textbooks at the classroom level without adequately preparing the teachers should be taken as a serious fault in the curriculum revision process. This was the similar case in other initiatives as well.

Transfer of training skills low: Transfer of training skills in the classroom has been weak in Nepal. Teachers would be provided with classroom delivery skills; construction and use of instructional materials; classroom management; lesson plan; motivating and involving students in the classroom teaching learning, etc. in the training. But use of these skills in the classroom has been found to be very weak. Maximizing transfer of training skills in the classroom teaching learning has been emphasized, but it is still a great challenge.

Low motivation and morale of the teachers: It has been found that teachers, in general, felt that much was expected of them in the classroom, but that their roles in educational development had been disregarded by the educational authorities (VSO, 2005). Due to this teachers are experiencing low morale. When teachers are unmotivated and they feel low in morale classroom teaching learning is affected.

Lack of consolidation of efforts: Suggestions from national commissions and plans developed are usually found to start from the scratch. There is usually lack of reflection on the past endeavors and build upon them. Study by VSO (2005) even stated that national education policies do not explicitly spell out anything about the interaction between teachers and students at the classroom. Just mentioning 'quality of education need to be improved' is not sufficient to improve classroom pedagogy. Reform can not be accomplished through events, it should be a process where small steps are tried out, effective ones are taken in and ineffective ones are left out and success is build upon gradually. There should be some transformation or continual development of initial ideas of the reform (Fullan, 1991).

Lack of coordination: One of the main reasons for the lack of preparation of the teacher in advance and creation of confusion regarding the changes brought is due to lack of coordination among the concerned institutions mainly teacher training institution NCED and curriculum development institution CDC. For example revised curriculum in 2003 emphasized teaching learning in mother tongue where necessary, life skill education in the health education subject and more structured textbook were also developed. Based on those revision and improvements made teacher were not oriented/trained in advance which should have been under the purview of NCED as teacher training institution. Such lack of coordination is often prevalent among educational institutions under ministry of education.

PROSPECT

Nepal has been fortunate enough to receive financial and professional support to develop educational plans and programs from international community. Due to such professional support the plans developed are well thought and sound. But what lacks is the implementation of the 'implementation'. Plan and program documents draw out the implementation strategy but while these are in the implementation then either these are not implemented or not implemented appropriately. In some cases such as CAS the innovation itself is blamed for rather than learning lesson from the failure. Therefore to ensure quality education for all Nepalese children as is envisaged in SSR to be implemented in 2009, implementation counts most.

As we can see the commitment for universal, free and compulsory primary education first made in 1956 has been pushed back to 2015 and is still uncertain to be fulfilled. It would be wise not to make new commitments. First previous commitments should be fulfilled and then build upon the success. Nepal, with two giant countries making rapid developments, should not enjoy lethargy to making commitment, fail and recommit. Even if we fail in some aspects these should be lessons to learn. Therefore previous target and achievement should be analyzed and lessons drawn. Failures should not be shadowed and forgotten.

Clarity on the vision, concepts, strategy, and implementation steps would be helpful to achieve success. It is necessary to be clear what we want to say and do, jargons will only confuse and delay. In this respect SSR seems to have left open a number of aspects that might delay its implementation. For example after more than a year's planning which involved best professional group, still left open to set ministry the minimum standards for the schools. This mean such several more studies would be required after 2009. If so when will the actual implementation be undertaken? Planning itself should be complete.

For the implementation slow start, build upon successes step by step, retain successes, drop those aspects which do not work or improve where it lacks would also be helpful in the reform process. It is also equally important to set timeline what should be achieved when and who is responsible for it. There should be a person and/or an institution accountable for each of the tasks. A transparent and strict accountability is necessary in Nepalese system. Working coordination, sharing, among the related institutions need to be established so that proactive steps could be taken on time. A shared vision and understanding among all the concerned stakeholders should be established for the success of the reform.

REFERENCES

Bista, D. B. (1990). Fatalism and Development: Nepal's struggle for modernization. Patna: Orient Longman Limited.

Boydell, D. (1978). The Primary Teacher in Action. London: Open Books Publishing Ltd.

CDC (2003). Effect of CAS on students' achievement, dropouts and attendance. Sanothimi: Author.

CERID (1989). Primary Education Project: an interim evaluation study report. Kathmandu: Author.

CERID (1997). SLC Examination and Classroom Practice. Kathmandu: Author.

CERID (2002). Effective Classroom Teaching Learning (Phase 1: Classroom Delivery). Kathmandu: FRP for BPEP: Author.

CERID (2003). Effective Classroom Teaching Learning: Transfer of Training Skills in the Classroom Delivery. *Kathmandu:* FRP for BPEP: Author.

CERID (2004). Effective Classroom Teaching Learning: School Based Assessment. Kathmandu: FRP for BPEP: Author.

CERID (2005). Meeting Learning Needs of Children of Indigenous Peoples and Linguistic Minorities. FRP for BPEP, Kathmandu: Author.

CERID (2006). Life Skill Education: Nature of Issues and their Linkage to System Provisions. FRP for BPEP, Kathmandu: Author.

Chauhan, S. S. (1979). Innovations in Teaching-Learning Process. New Delhi: Vikas Publishing House Pvt. Ltd.

Cohen, L; Manion, L and Morrison, K. (1996). *A Guide to Teaching Practice* (4th Edition). London and New York: Routledge.

Collins, J., Insley, K., Soler, J. (2001). Developing Pedagogy: Researching Practice. London: The Open University, Paul Chapman Publishing Ltd.

Craft, A. (ed.) (1996). Primary Education: Assessing and Planning Learning. London: The Open University.

DOE (2003). *Education in Nepal*. Sanothimi: Author.

DOE (2006). Status Report I – 2006. Sanothimi: Author.

DOE (2006-07). Flash Report I, 2006-077. Sanothimi: Author.

DOE (2007). Flash Report I, 2007. Sanothimi: Author.

EDSC (1997). National Assessment of Grade 3 Studetns. Kathmandu: Author.

Fullan, M. G. (1993). Change Forces: probing the depths of education reform. UK: The Falmer Press.

Fullan, M. G. and Hargreaves, A. (1992). *What's worth fighting for in your school?* UK: Open University Press.

Hargreaves, A. (1994). Changing Teachers, Changing Times. London: Teacher College Press.

Hawes, G. R. and Hawes, L. S. (1932). The Concise Dictionary of Education.

HLNEC (1999). The Report of Higher-Level National Education Commission. Kathmandu: Author.

Kinsler, K and Gamble, M. (2001). Reforming Schools. London and New York: Continuum.

Kordalewski, J (2000). Standards in the Classroom. New York and London: Teacher College Press.

MOE (1961). Report of All Round National Education Commission. Kathmandu: Author.

MOE (1971). Report of the National Education System Plan. Kathmandu: Author.

MOE (1997a). The Basic and Primary Education: Master Plan 1997-2002. Kathmandu: Author.

MOE (1997b). Secondary Education Perspective Plan. Kathmandu: Author.

MOE (1998). Secondary Education Action Plan (1997-2002). Kathmandu: Author.

MOE (1999). BPEP (1992-1998): A synthesis of Experiences. Kathmandu: Author.

MOES (2000). Education Information of Nepal 2000. Kathmandu: Author.

MOES (2002a). Secondary Education Support Programme. Kathmandu: Author.

MOES (2002b). Concept paper for further support on Basic and Primary Educations in Nepal. MOES: Author.

MOES (2003). Education for All 2004-2009 Core Document. Kathmandu: Author.

MOES (2005). National Curriculum Framework for School Education (pre-primary to 12) in Nepal.. Kathmandu: Author.

MOES (2007). School Sector Reform: Core document. Kathmandu: Author.

Nyachhyon, M. G. and Webber, R. (2001). School Based Assessment in Nepali Primary Schools. Kathmandu: Opifer Ltd./MOES.

NCED (2000). Primary Teacher Training Curriculum. Sanothimi: Author.

NCED (2000a). Training of Teachers: Factors Contributing to the Effectiveness of Training in Classroom Practice. MOES, NCED, Sanothimi, Bhaktapur.

NCED (2000b). Teacher Training Follow-up: A Study Report. MOES, NCED, Sanothimi, Bhaktapur.

NCED (2002a). Follow-up Study of Teacher Training Program. MOES, NCED, Sanothimi, Bhaktapur. Submitted by ICS Education Campus, Minbhawan, Kathmandu.

NCED (2002b). Teacher Training Follow-up: A Study Report. MOES, NCED, Sanothimi, Bhaktapur.

NEC (1992). Report of National Education Commission. Kathmandu: NEC.

NNEPC (1956). Education in Nepal. Kathmandu: Bureau of publications, College of Education.

NPC (1998). The Ninth Plan. Kathmandu: Author.

PEDP (1993). Policy Options in Primary Teacher Training and Career Development of Primary Teachers. Kathmandu: PEDP.

Pollard, A. (2006). Reflective Teaching (2nd Edition). London and New York: Viva-Continuum Edition.

Pollard, A., and Bourne, J. (1994). Teaching and Learning in the Primary School. London: Routledge.

Shaha, R. (1982). Essays in the Practice of Government in Nepal. New Delhi: Manohar Publications.

UNCTN (2007). Common Country Assessment for Nepal. Kathmandu: Author.

VSO (2005). Lessons from the Classroom. London: Author.

In: Nepal in the 21st Century
Editor: Surendra R. Devkota, pp. 153-167
ISBN 978-1-60741-348-6

Chapter 6

ENERGY PERSPECTIVES: 2030

Shaligram Pokharel*
School of Mechanical and Aerospace Engineering
Nanyang Technological University, Singapore

Energy sources in Nepal are broadly categorized under three main categories: Traditional, commercial and Alternative. Traditional energy sources refer to fuelwood, crop residues and animal manure. Commercial energy sources refer to sources that need modern technologies to extract and use such as coal, petroleum products and electricity. Alternative energy category refers to those sources which are renewable in nature, for example, wind, solar, biogas and small scale hydropower generation.

The major use of traditional energy, for example, fuelwood and agricultural residues is in the residential sector. Due to the availability of traditional energy sources close to their home, as much as 90% of the total energy requirements in residential sector are met by traditional sources. Although this percentage has declined considerably since the Eighties, mainly due to the use of commercial energy sources in urban areas, the share of traditional energy sources is still very high and the rate of its growth in the consumption is still positive.

In rural areas, fuelwood is the primary energy source that meets almost all of the household energy needs. However, for some parts in the rural areas, where there is a constraint in fuelwood supply, people are forced to move to the lower step in the energy ladder, that is, to the use of crop residue or even further down to the use of dried animal manure. Although dependency in biomass is good in the current context of clean energy generation and use, the same at a large scale beyond the capability for regeneration is not. While carbon emission through regenerated biomass is very small, non replaceable carbon due to overexploitation of biomass would have a significant and detrimental negative long term environmental impact.

In the shorter term, the use of fuelwood in households has been linked to land denudation, and loss in the fertility of downstream agricultural land. In the longer term however, loss in the regenerative capacity of forests would lead to loss in the source of perennial water and degradation of land productivity. Diversion of agricultural residues, crop

---

* Email: Shaligram.pokharel@gmail.com

residues and livestock manure for fuel can also have significant impact on land productivity since field manure is the only source of fertilizer in many parts of the country. Unsustainable use of traditional energy sources would have a detetrimental effect in climate change.

In terms of commercial energy sources, coal is imported and used mainly in cement, brick and steel industries. The use of coal has been fluctuating mainly because of poor import situation, increasing prices and non continuous operation of industries due to political and social unrest in the country for the past 12 years (since 1996).

The use of petroleum products has also faced similar problems. The increase in the oil price in the international market has created supply hurdles in the country. This, coupled with political and social unrest, has disrupted the supply line and has severely impacted the growth in transport and industrial sectors.

Electricity generation is not much of a relief either. Although Nepal had its first hydropower station of 500kW installed about a century earlier (in 1911), the current hydropower generation capacity is less than 700 MW and currently peak power deficit is more than 20% of total system availability. On one hand electricity distribution capability is limited due to very low spatial coverage by transmission lines, on the other hand, due to low industrialization, the extension of transmission and distribution system would further add the load of residential sector, which peaks in the evenings. The extension of transmission system, without the extension of electricity generation capacity is causing as much as 40 hours per week of load shedding. This does not promote a positive growth of the economy.

At present, the country has neither the technical capability to produce large turbines, nor has the expertise or money needed for investments in large scale hydropower projects. While small investments in hydropower are generally made locally on small and micro-hydropower generation, large investments are generally at the mercy of donor countries and multilateral agencies. These small hydropower generations, however, contribute to less than 3% of total electricity generation.

There have been attempts to attract foreign direct investments in power generation, but owing to the lack of persistent demand of electricity in industrial sector and difficulties in setting a favorable pricing policy to access national transmission grid, these attempts have not been very fruitful. Persistent base load demand is attractive for investing in run-of-the-river projects. Therefore the progress on increasing hydropower generation capacity is very small and the current transmission system fulfils about 1.5% of energy consumption of which 25-30% is lost largely due to technical and non technical leakages..

About 15% of the electricity used in Nepal is either imported or generated by using petroleum products. While the country boasts a very high technological potential to develop large scale hydropower generation, its supply situation is also marred by non technical electrical loss, caused by either its inability to recover the costs of used electricity or large scale leakages, which amounts to about 25-30% of electricity generation.

1. Energy Resource Base

1.1. Fuelwood

Fuelwood extraction from forests is rampant in non-protected forest areas thereby causing localized deforestation, which causes fuelwood crisis in rural areas. This requires people to travel long distances or to climb steep slopes in the hills to collect fuelwood.

Forest related adverse environmental impacts are the consequences of agriculture land expansion and fuelwood extraction. Between 1964 and 1985, natural forests were reduced by 570,000 ha, of which about 380,000 ha are used for cultivation (Bhadra, 1990). During the same period, only about 70,000 ha were reclaimed through plantations.

Recent estimates show that forests cover about 5.6 million hectares (DFRS, 1997) and it has declined at the rate of about 4% annually over the past two decades. It is not known as to the current rate of deforestation.

Sustainability of forests becomes more important for a continued supply of fuelwood mostly in rural areas. Table 1 shows that out of about 12.6 million MT of fuelwood produced on a sustainable basis, only about half is accessible (reachable) for collection. Data further shows that about half of the sustainable supply is contributed by existing forest supplies followed by one fifth of the supply contributed by farm lands. The rest of the supply comes from matured plantation, shrub and other areas. Data also shows that much of the contribution to reachable fuelwood supply comes from the Hills. Reachable fuelwood supply in Tarai (southern plains) is less that the gross supply due to the protection of forests in many areas in Tarai. This supply demand situation of fuelwood would change in the future as more forests would become accessible and more of them would be denuded thus reinforcing an acute energy poverty cycle in rural areas.

Table 1. Estimates of sustainable fuelwood supply scenario in Nepal (in '000 MT)

Forest Type	Physiographic Regions						All Regions	
	Tarai		Hills		Mountains			
	Gross	Reachable	Gross	Reachable	Gross	Reachable	Gross	Reachable
Existing forests	1085	488	5712	1870	2239	1019	9037	3378
Plantation	108	108	172	172	69	69	350	350
Sub-Total	1193	596	5884	2042	2308	1088	9387	3728
Shrub	29	13	628	283	351	158	1076	454
Grass Land	19	2	32	14	140	63	191	79
On farm supply	512	512	637	637	165	165	1314	1314
Other	71	71	491	491	107	107	670	670
Sub-Total	631	598	1788	1425	763	493	3251	2517
Grand Total	1826	1194	7672	3467	3071	1581	12638	6245

Source: RWEDP (2001).

The energy balance shows that even if Nepal is to promote only sustainable fuelwood supply, it cannot meet half of the current fuelwood demand. This clearly indicates that there is an encroachment of forest areas encroachment in Nepal for energy purpose. Such encroachment for fuel and cultivation has resulted in degrading forest supply capability, decreasing water retaining capacity of soil and increasing soil erosion. Energy conservation for fuelwood might be one of the options to reduce the impact of such consequence.

1.2. Hydropower

Nepal is the major contributor of the Ganga Basin and the annual discharge of out-flowing rivers from Nepal is about 224 billion cubic meters (Yogacharya, 1998). In a distance of about 100 km from the North to the South, rivers lose a potential height of about 4,000 meters, thus providing a very high power average linear power density (33 MW/km) and large hydropower potential as shown in Table 2. However, current generation compared to the economic potential is very small as shown in the table.

Table 2. Basin-wise hydropower potential in Nepal (Shrestha, 1966)

Basin	Theoretical Potential (GW)			Economic Potential (GW)	Generation (GW) by 2010
	Major rivers	Small rivers	Total	Total	
Koshi	19	4	23	11	0.11
Gandaki	18	3	21	5	0.48
Karnali and Mahakali	32	3	35	25	0.03
Others	3	1	4	1	0.05
Total	72	11	83	42	0.67

1.3. Petroleum Products

Table 3 shows a significant growth in the consumption of petroleum products between 1988 and 2002 and in 2006.

There is a decline in the use of kerosene but a significant increase in LPG in recent years. As kerosene is primarily used in urban areas for cooking, fuel switching to LPG can be a reason for decreased consumption in kerosene. This can also be corroborated with the increased number of LPG bottlers in Nepal after 1990. In the long run, at the current prices, it is less expensive to use LPG for cooking than to use any other marketed fuels (Pokharel, 2004).

Table 3. Import of Petroleum Products in Nepal (in KL)

Fuel Type	1988	2002	Average	2006	Average
			Annual growth		annual growth
			(1988 -2002)		(2002 -2006)
Petrol	15609	63271	10.5%	80989	6.4%
Diesel	73321	286223	10.2%	294329	0.7%
Kerosene	51835	386593	15.4%	226637	-12.5%
Fuel Oil	7435	18225	6.6%	3695	-32.9%
Aircraft Turbine Oil	19698	47453	6.5%	64335	7.9%
Liquefied Petroleum Gas (in MT)	2304	48757	24.4%	81005	13.5%
Gas (in MT)					
Value in Rs. (Million)	972.3	18117	23.2%	32449	15.7%
Import as a	24%	39%		54%	
percentage of					
Merchandize Export					

Source: Ministry of Finance (2004,2008).

1.4. Other Traditional Fuels

Agricultural residues (crop residues and livestock manure) are considered as other traditional fuels.

1.4.1. Crop Residues

Estimates show that about 11 million metric tons of crop residues are produced in Nepal, more than 60% of this in Tarai alone (RWEDP, 2001). This value however, fluctuates from year to year due to variations in crop production. For the purpose of analysis, only paddy, maize and sugarcane residues are considered for use as energy. However, it should be noted that all of the available residues cannot be collected economically and they are often left over in the farm land to maintain soil texture. Nevertheless, the use of crop residues is widespread in Tarai region of Nepal.

1.4.2. Livestock Manure

Livestock manure is the major fertilizer in the hills and mountains and is the major energy source in the rural areas in Tarai. About 30 million MT of dry livestock manure is estimated to be available for energy use. Surveys by the author shows that although dried manure is primarily considered as fuel in Tarai and Kathmandu Valley, its use in hills and mountains is increasing as well mainly due to fuelwood scarcity in those areas. This is alarming because diversion of field manure to fuel will reduce crop productivity in those areas and it can bring about food scarcity.

1.5. Resource and Status of Alternative Energy

1.5.1. Biogas Technology

Biogas technology was first introduced in 1955 but it was widely disseminated only in 1977, after the establishment of Biogas Company. The main growth in biogas plants started around 1993 when almost half of the biogas installation costs were provided as subsidy by the government. To date, there are more than about 150,000 biogas plants installed in Nepal but it is estimated that only about 70-80% of these plants are in operation. This is mainly due to the end of operating life of biogas plants or conversion of land occupied by biogas and livestock to other economical uses, such as house construction or vegetable gardening particularly in urban and suburban areas. Considering the high temperature requirement for biogas generation based on current technology and minimum number of livestock required to operate a biogas plant, about 640,000 biogas plants are estimated as potential number that can be operated in any given year (Pokharel et al 1991).. However, actual number of plants that would be operating is likely to be much less as all livestock owners may not prefer to install biogas plants and biogas generated from the plants during the winter in the hills and mountains may make biogas unattractive in those places.

1.5.2. Small Hydro Turbines

Ten companies produce and market micro hydro turbines ($\leq$100 kW capacity). The combined installed capacity of these units (installed by individual entrepreneurs and the Nepal Electricity Authority) is less than 15 MW. Most of the smaller units are installed for grain processing. However, electrification with these units is increasing due to the government's effort to provide electricity in rural areas through subsidies for coupling electric generators in these units.

1.5.3. Solar Energy

Utilization of solar energy using modern equipment began mainly in early seventies through the introduction of domestic solar water heaters (DSWH). Today there are more than 30 DSWH fabricators and the total installed capacity is estimated at 100,000 m^2 of solar panels (equivalent to about 10,000,000 litres per day of heated water).

The worst case for solar energy availability is between 3-5 $kWh/m^2/day$ in Nepal (Solarex, 1992). The huge potential of solar energy is also illustrated in WECS (1984). At present, the major use of solar photovoltaic panels is for communications. The second most popular application is solar home system, a 36 Wp unit for lighting in households. It is estimated that solar generation capacity has reached to about 1 MW in Nepal. However, the installation rate of solar home systems seems to be decreasing due to its high cost compared to that of a micro hydropower plants. The market for solar home systems may be reaching a saturation point.

1.5.4. Wind Energy

There is no regular data to prove wind energy potential in Nepal. A few attempts in the past to electrify houses through wind energy have proved unsuccessful. It may not be a viable source of energy for Nepalese topography.

2. Energy Consumption Pattern

Figure 1 shows the share of primary energy consumption of various sectors in 1988 and 2002. Compared to 1988, the share of energy in residential sector has declined, whereas the share of industrial and transportation sectors have increased significantly. The decline in the share of residential sector is not due to reduced energy consumption in residential sector but due to increased energy consumption in industrial and transportation sectors. Data show that energy consumption has increased in agriculture sector, which is mainly due to the use of tractors and modern agro-processing technologies. Data also show that, during 1988-2002, total primary energy consumption grew by about 2.9%. In terms of fuel type, the growth in traditional energy was 2.1%, which is very close to the growth in the population. The growth in commercial energy is dominated by petroleum fuel consumption (10% growth rate) during the same period.

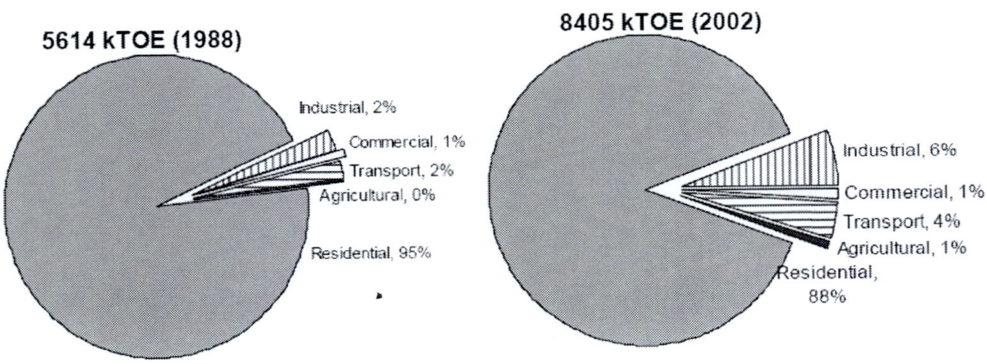

Figure 1. Share of energy consumption in different sectors.

3. Analysis of Energy Use

For the analysis of energy demand, a period between 1988 and 2000 is chosen. In this period, energy data is consistent because the assumptions for the calculation of energy demand are the same. Data presented in the later periods have either changed the basis for calculations or used different formats for presentation. Therefore, data consistency has been given priority for the development of models. Various economic and energy data were obtained from the Ministry of Finance/Government of Nepal (GON) and Water and Energy Commission Secretariat (WECS)/GON. The data reported by the two government agencies, however differ, mainly in the traditional energy consumption. When discrepancies were noticed, the author used his own discretion based on his experience in energy planning in Nepal. Econometric models for consumption sectors given in Pokharel (2007) are adopted here for energy analysis. Some changes made to those models are also discussed.

Table 4 outlines the share of various sectors in total GDP. Data shows economic restructuring in Nepal over the analysis period. In 1988, agriculture GDP accounted for about 48%, while in 2002, its share was reduced to about 40% and in 2006, the share had declined to about 35%. The shares of all other economic sectors except trade has increased during the analysis period.

Table 4. Economic parameters for various years

Share of GDP in Different sectors	1988	2002	2006
Agriculture/Forestry	48.0%	38.9%	35.3%
Industrial	6.6%	9.4%	7.9%
Construction	11.2%	11.4%	5.9%
Service	18.6%	22.3%	24.4%
Trade	10.5%	10.3%	14.7%
Transport/communications	5.1%	7.7%	11.8%

Data further show that industrial and construction activities are trailing behind trade and transportation in recent years. With changes in economic structure, the requirements for energy would also change. Therefore, it is necessary to understand the perceived growths in various sectors of economy.

Pokharel (2007) mentioned that although both fuel and energy consumption models can be developed separately by using econometric method, when all types of fuels are not considered, they may not produce similar results. Also, due to various attributes in the models and regression coefficients, this problem can be acute. This problem, however, may not appear when the models are used for a short term forecast, e.g. Pokharel (2007). Therefore, only log models for energy consumptions are discussed here. For the government, it is much easier and practical to forecast the structure of economy than to forecast energy supply and demand situation while approaching from economic point of view. For instance, energy requirements can be forecast based on the envisaged economic future. Therefore, the consumption sector models are used here to develop energy scenario for 2030.

3.1. Consumption Sector Models

Summary of consumption sector models are given in Table 5 below. The models show that rural population has as much as seven times more influence on energy consumption than urban population. Fuelwood supplies most of the energy in rural areas. Unless there is a significant change in the composition of rural and urban population, the amount of energy in residential sector would be substantially dominated by fuelwood consumption.

The model shows that industrial sector will grow if the private consumption grows. That means, if the disposable income does not increase, industrial growth will suffer and it will also reduce energy consumption. Transportation sector does not seem to depend on kilometers of road and population but on the number of total vehicles.

Vehicle population is concentrated in urban areas and given an unrestricted supply of vehicles, the transportation demand will be led only by vehicle population.

Energy consumption in service sector has no correlation with tourist arrivals, the number of hotel beds and services provided by the public utilities but on service sector GDP. In agriculture sector, energy consumption does not correlate well with the number of tractors and agriculture GDP, but it relates closely with the total land irrigated in the country.

Table 5. Models for energy consuming sectors

Variables\ Models	Residential	Industrial	Transport	Service	Agriculture
Intercept	-1.561	-5.247	-2.579	-10.999	-50.104
Rural Population	+0.946				
Urban Population	+0.164				
Service_GDP				+1.335	
Irrigation hectares					+4.698
Private Consumption	-0.021	+0.875			
Total vehicles			+1.329		
Diesel_price			-0.821		
Correlation Coefficient	0.999	0.805	0.927	0.930	0.919

4. Energy Forecasting 2030

In order to forecast energy requirements through the modeling process mentioned here, we need to define forecasting parameters carefully as well. . The parameters given in the consumption sector models must be developed by assuming a particular growth scenario. For the purpose of evaluation here, growth rates for 1988-2002 are assumed to produce a base case scenario. Some exceptions in assumptions are noted next.

It is assumed that annual growth rates for agricultural GDP, industrial, GDP, service sector GDP and construction sector GDP will grow by 2.8%, 7.1%, 5.7% and 4.5%, respectively from the year 2002 (Table 6). It is to note that GDP contribution by transportation and communication sector was about 14.7% between 2002 and 2006, mainly due to the growth in mobile phone infrastructure. Therefore, over the long run, a lower value of transportation and communications based on 1988-2002 period is assumed. Also, industrial GDP growth was about 0.5% during 2002-2006 due to socio-political turmoil in the country. In our assumption, the total GDP is expected to grow by about 4.8% during the forecast period. Although it seems to be optimistic considering the current dismal state of economy and infrastructural development, it can be assumed that the growth rate is attainable as the socio-political situation has improved and continuous thrust for the development is expected.

It is assumed that in 2030, about 30% of the population would live in urban areas. The growth in the number of total vehicles between 1988 and 2002 was 13.7%, which is assumed as the growth rate for forecasting here as control in the number of vehicles, such as that done in Singapore, through legislation is not anticipated yet.

The projected data for energy consumption by consumption categories is given in Table 7. It is seen that the energy consumption in 2030 will be about 2.7 times the energy consumption in 2002. Comparing this with energy share in 2002, it is seen that the growth of energy consumption in residential sector reduces considerably due to the decrease in consumption of fuelwood. There is a considerable growth in energy consumption in both industrial and transportation sectors.

Table 6. Growth rates in various periods needed for the model

Parameters	Assumed Growth rates (2002-2030)
Rural Population	1.03%
Urban Population	5.79%
Service_GDP	5.70%
Irrigation hectares	2.80%
Private Consumption	12.28%
Total vehicles	13.70%
Diesel_price	10.66%

Table 7. Energy forecast in '000 TOE for 2030

Sectors	Energy ('000 TOE)	Share	Growth rates 2002-2030
Industrial	6532	28.9%	9.78%
Residential	13071	57.7%	2.04%
Transportation	2077	9.2%	7.23%
Service	760	3.4%	7.40%
Agriculture	201	0.9%	3.35%
Total	22640		3.61%

5. Energy Backcasting

Backcasting is a method to envision a future based on likelihood scenarios (Robinson, 1982). Therefore the development of future scenario is an important task to understand the energy allocations in the perceived future. Given the current uncertainties in petroleum prices, companies will be looking towards improving efficiency of energy consumption so that the overall cost on energy goes down. In addition, they will attempt to reduce wasteful energy consumption through demand management. This multi-prong approach can help them to manage energy consumption effectively in the future. Therefore, following assumptions are made for assessing energy future in Nepal.

5.1. Residential Sector

i. Sixty percent of the population will live in urban areas. This is a remarkable change in the population structure, however, it is attainable. When rural areas are accessed by modern basic supplies like road, electricity and water and economic activities, people from close by areas would start moving in towards these places, swelling the population in those areas.
ii. All fuelwood consumed in urban areas for cooking will be replaced by electricity. It is assumed that the efficiency of end use device is 8% and the efficiency of commonly available electric stove is 70%. This is a possible scenario considering the fact that in Nepalese urban areas fuelwood used for cooking in urban areas is being replaced by replaced mainly by kerosene and LPG. Pricing of fuelwood, shortage in supply, increased affordability of the people to buy modern energy sources are some of the reasons for this trend. Therefore, the assumed replacement of fuelwood in urban areas is not unlikely.
iii. For fuelwood use in rural areas, 50% of the stoves would have an increased efficiency from 8% to 20% due to the use of efficient stoves. Due to decreasing forest areas, people might start planting trees in the farm land and start conserving the energy sources. Therefore, a likely scenario is that people will start using fuelwood mainly from their farm land and would conserve its use by adopting efficient methods for collection, storage and use in rural areas.
iv. Total estimated kerosene consumption in residential sector is about 364.7 TOE. Ten percent of total kerosene is assumed to be used in rural areas in 2030.
v. There would be no cooking with kerosene in urban areas in 2030. This can be considered reasonable considering that most developing urban areas either cook in LPG due to cost and convenience or switch to electricity when the family affluence rise.
vi. The use of compact fluorescent lamp in urban areas will decrease total lighting load in residential sector by 20%.
vii. The current trend of LPG use in urban areas will not change.

5.2. Industrial Sector

i. All fuelwood required by boilers are replaced by coal. When boilers are retrofitted to use coal, their efficiency will increase from 15% to 25%.
ii. Cottage industries will still require fuelwood as they operate mostly in rural areas. The efficiency of the industries that use fuelwood will increase from 8% to 20% due to technological improvements.
iii. There will be no replacement of coal, diesel, and kerosene used in industries.
iv. End-use devices running on fuel oil will be converted to run on diesel.

5.3. Transport Sector

i. As of 2002, about 66% of total transport energy is assumed to be supplied by diesel.
ii. About 16% of the transport energy is supplied by aviation turbine fuel.
iii. The remaining fuel is used by cars and motorcycles. The ratio of cars to motorcycles is expected to be ¼. It is to note that the rate of growth in the number of motorcycle is much more than the growth in the number of cars.
iv. About 5% of diesel transport will be shifted to electric transport. This could be due to electrifying of existing rail system or introducing trolley buses or mass rapid transit rail system in Kathmandu.
v. Fuel efficiency of diesel vehicles and cars will increase by 10% in 2030.
vi. Hybrid gasoline cars will make about 5% of total car population by 2030.
vii. Fuel efficiency of motorcycles will also improve by 10% by 2030.

5.4. Service Sector

i. All fuelwood requirements will be replaced by kerosene and efficiency of energy use would be increased from 8% to 30%.
ii. LPG consumed in commercial sector is replaced by electricity.
iii. Coal and fuel oil are replaced by electricity.
iv. Fifty percent of lighting energy requirements in service sector is saved due to the use of compact fluorescent lamps.

5.5. Agriculture Sector

i. Twenty percent of the energy is used by diesel for tractors and agro processing units. The efficiency of the vehicles and units using diesel will improve by 10%.
ii. Water pumping for irrigation will only be done by using electricity.

5.6. Energy Requirements 2030

Energy requirements by fuel type and demand by sector are given in Table 9. Energy forecasting given in Table 7 showed that compared to 2002, energy requirements would increase by 2.7 times in 2030.

However, if energy backcasting assumptions are used, the net increment would decrease to 1.7 times due to interfuel and intermode substitutions in various sectors. Due to this reduction, annual growth rates in energy demand would be around 1.9% only. This is a reasonable estimate if proper policies are designed to promote conservation and fuel switching. Table 8 gives the energy projections by fuel and by sector.

Data shows that in case of fuelwood, still about 9 million metric tons of fuelwood is required to meet the demand. It is to note that considerable amount of fuelwood demand is replaced by either electricity or LPG, which is shown by a negative growth in fuelwood requirements. Biogas plants can help to relieve some of the pressure on fuelwood as well.

Table 8. Energy mix in 2030 obtained through backcasting for Nepal ('000 TOE)

Fuel\ Sectors	Residential	Industrial	Transport	Service	Agriculture	Total	Share	Annual growth rate from 2002
Fuelwood	3514.8	113.2				3628.0	25.1%	-2.01%
Kerosene	36.5	746.4		272.6		1055.5	7.3%	4.64%
LPG	1160.0					1160.0	8.0%	8.92%
Petrol			341.6			341.6	2.4%	6.88%
Diesel		1789.4	1160.4		36.1	2985.8	20.7%	9.01%
ATF			328.2			328.2	2.3%	7.32%
Coal		1972.5				1972.5	13.7%	6.72%
Electricity	1096.9	1353.1	68.3	280.0	160.5	2958.7	20.5%	11.95%
Total	5808.2	5974.6	1898.4	552.6	196.6	14430.4		1.95%
Share	40.2%	41.4%	13.2%	3.8%	1.4%			
Annual growth from 2002	-0.88%	9.43%	6.89%	6.19%	3.27%	1.95%		

The analysis further shows that the country would require about 37,000 GWh of electricity in 2030. This would translate to about 9.4 GW (given 80% availability factor and 70% capacity factor) of electricity generation capacity. If the capacity factor is decreased the generation requirement would increase further. This is a substantial growth rate but only way to achieve a more sustainable energy portfolio for Nepal.

The increased reallocation biomass into coal would require the supply of coal to grow by about 6.7% annually. The increased demand for transportation would require a higher volume of petroleum products. Diesel has the largest share in energy profile and ATF has the lowest share. The use of petrol will be reduced due to increase in the efficiency of cars and shift of many people towards motorcycles. Since, there is no vehicle limiting policy in Nepal, unlike in countries like Singapore where vehicles sale is monitored and moderated in different periods, unrestricted supply of vehicles can be anticipated in the future as well.

In terms of sectoral requirements for energy, due to fuel switching, the requirements in residential sector would decrease. However, this is contingent upon the number of population living in rural areas. If there is a large proportion of people living in urban areas in 2030, and if fuelwood is not used in urban areas, fuelwood demand will reduce further. However, it is difficult to replace fuelwood demand in rural areas.

5.7. Other Fuels

Experiences have shown that decentralized alternate energy options such as the installation of biogas technology, micro hydropower units and solar system are sustainable energy sources in rural areas. Although biogas may reduce fuelwood consumption in rural areas and can make some impact in total energy consumption, the total impact on energy by other renewable energy technologies except for efficient fuelwood stoves (as mentioned above in backcasting) will not be significant and possibly hover below 5%. These technologies are being encouraged by the government through de-licensing, subsidies, and policy options.

CONCLUSIONS

This chapter started with a very bleak energy situation in Nepal, where fuelwood is the major energy supplier and residential sector is the main energy consumer. The energy consumption was dominated by inefficient energy use. The use of econometric models based on 1988-2002 period to forecast energy consumption for 2030 showed that Nepal's energy consumption will grow by 2.7 times in 2030 compared to that in 2002.

In order to promote good energy use practice, Nepal should aim at reducing the consumption of fuelwood and petroleum products. Fuelwood consumption can be decreased by increasing the efficiency of energy use, by introducing efficient fuelwood stoves, or switching to higher energy value fuels. In general, energy sources with higher energy values are traded and are used in efficient devices.

The disaggregation of energy end-use in residence, industry and service sectors as obtained from a previous report was used to come up with energy end-use shares for energy backcasting.

The assumptions show that due to high population growth in urban areas, where fuelwood is likely to be displaced by kerosene, or LPG or electricity, the energy consumption would be more efficient.

This will reduce the total primary energy consumption. However, in rural areas, unless substantial programs are implemented to increase energy use efficiency or to replace fuelwood consumption by other sources, accessible and sustainable fuelwood supply will not be sufficient to meet fuelwood demand. Therefore, further denudation of forests can take place. However, with increased community forestry for the protection of forests and for extraction of fuelwood, regeneration of forests might help to relieve this pressure in rural areas.

Nepal's richness in hydropower is yet in paper only. High investments required for hydropower generation, that ranges between USD 2000-USD 5000 per kW, can be distracting factor for future development.

However, over the long term, it is only hydropower, which can provide a major share of energy in Nepal. It can also bring national income through exports. Concerted efforts must be made for its development, if Nepal wants to see a reduced import dependency on commercial fuel and a reduced deficit in trade.

Nepal should venture first on middle level hydropower stations (up to 100 MW) to supply for internal electricity demand and then higher level power stations solely to export to India. The government should also allow hydropower generation for dedicated use, for example industrial or large scale commercial development.

This will meet electricity requirements for major industries. If small and medium scale hydropower projects could be developed to supply adequate energy in affordable prices, then there would be a possibility to reduce the current level of biomass and fossil fuel consumption even in rural areas.

After 1990s, the government promulgated a flood of acts and policies to attract foreign investments. However, owing to various reasons, including political instability, there is not much flocking of investments. For hydropower at least, poor expansion of grid, lack of continuous load and a difficult path to power purchase agreements are seen as major hurdles for business assurance.

In short, Nepal's current energy situation is not conducive to development and to the economy. However, if correct policies are implemented, Nepal can have a dependable energy scenario, that would be dominated by electricity consumption.

REFERENCES

Bhadra, B. (1990). Forest resources: Nepal. In Energy Systems and the Environment Approaches to Impact Assessment in Asian Developing countries, P. Hills and K.V. Ramani (Eds.), *Asian and Pacific Development Centre*, Malaysia.

DFRS, (1997). Forest resources of Nepal 1987-1998. Publication number 74, Department of Forest Research and Survey (DFRS), Babar Mahal, Kathmandu, Nepal.

Ministry of Finance (2004). *Economic Survey*: 2004, Kathmandu, Nepal

Ministry of Finance (2008). *Economic Survey*: 2008, Kathmandu, Nepal.

Pokharel, S., Chandrashekhar, M. and Robinson, J.B. (1991). Biogas potential and implementation issues in Nepal. *Journal of Engineering for International Development*, 1 (1): 45-57.

Pokharel, S. (2004). Energy economics of cooking in households in Nepal, *Energy* 29 (2004) 547–559.

Pokharel, S. (2007). An econometric analysis of energy consumption in Nepal. *Energy* Policy, 35:350-361.

Robinson, J.B. (1982). Energy backcasting: A proposed method of policy analysis. *Energy* Policy, 10(4):337-344.

RWEDP, (2001). Wood Energy Planning:Nepal, A Country Case Study. Sponsored by Regional Wood Energy Development Programme (RWEDP) and WECS Institutional Development Project (WIDP), Nepal and published by RWEDP, Bangkok. Available at http://www.rwedp.org/acrobat/gp_planning_nep_P1.pdf.

Shrestha, H.M. (1966). Cadastre of hydropower resources. PhD Thesis, Moscow Power Institute, Moscow, USSR.

Solarex Corporation (1992). *World Design Insulation* (Map), USA.

Water and Energy Commission Secretariat (1994). *Solar Energy Availability in Nepal*, Kathmandu, Nepal.

Yogacharya, K.S. (1998). Hydrometric measurements in Nepal. A paper presented at the Introductory Session on Project Launch Workshop on Nepal Irrigation Sector Project (NISP), Kathmandu.

In: Nepal in the 21st Century
Editor: Surendra R. Devkota, pp. 169-180
ISBN: 978-1-60741-348-6

Chapter 7

QUESTIONS FROM NEPAL'S HYDROPOWER SECTOR

Biswo Poudel
University of California at Berkeley, CA, USA

1 Introduction

Nepal's snailpaced development process often has one major hope: hydropower. In a country bereft of any major natural resource, hydropower stands out , and it is increasingly becoming more significant as two of Nepal's giant neighbors, India and China, are reeling under the pressure of their own energy crunches. There has been major policy initiatives from Nepali policy makers in the past too, from the introduction of Electricity Act (1993) to the opening up of small hydropower sector for private sectors.

According to the NEA whitepaper (2006), Nepal's total electricity generation capacity is 611 MW. However, most of the electricity production comes from run-of-the-river system, and thus is extremely unreliable during the dry season. NEA's way of addressing it is by implementing loadshedding during the peakhours. Though households often complain about unreliable electricity supply, there is rarely any public protests against it. The usual problem of high leakage (25%) also means the added burden in terms of cost and reliability of service for the law abiding consumers. The often pointed irony of Nepal's development is its reliance in fossil fuel, and almost complete ignorance of its ability to harness natural resources, while latter could have saved precious foreign reserve,and made the country strategically secure from the point of energy consumption.

Table 1: Supply of Electricity in Nepal by Producer Groups (in MW).

Nepal's Hydroelectric Production

Type of Electricity	Nepal Electricity Authority	IPP
Hydroelectric	408	148
Thermal	55	0

(Source: NEA Whitepaper,2006)

For a landlocked country like Nepal, finding the market for the hydropower and irrigation water is also a vexing problem. India virtually occupies the seat of the monopsonist, and tries to guarantee favorable terms for itself in any deal. Nepal feels squeezed in India's terms, and the problem is compounded by the politics; especially Nepal's deep rooted suspicion about India's desire to exercise maximum control over Nepal's political affairs. It has resulted in both countries having been locked in the prisoner's dilemma outcomes, where they don't make deals and don't produce anything.

In this paper, we discuss about the current state of Nepal's hydropower industry. We will then discuss about the possible evolving relationship between different groups of water users within the country. Our discussion will then proceed to the relationship between Nepal and India, and we discuss how reconfiguration of power structure within India changes the power production dynamics within Nepal. We will also discuss about other issues such as load shedding and rural electrification before we conclude the chapter.

2 Rivers and Power In Nepal

Rivers are respected in Nepali culture. Both the rivers and the mountains have their divine counterparts, and they have been accorded the status of god and goddess. People depend on them for pretty much everything in their life, and yet power generation from the rivers has been accorded the least priority so far. The first hydropower plant was set up in Pharping in 1911AD, twenty nine years after the first small hydropower plant was set up in America. But the electricity plant in Nepal remained the only plant around for long, despite the tremendous potential of power generation in Nepali terrain.

The idea that river is the sacred form of the divine power, the *Ganga*,used to mean something very different from what we see in today's effluent contaminated rivers of Nepal and northern India. Devout Hindus have traditionally been reluctant to contaminate the rivers. It was prohibited, for example, to relieve oneself in the river, and the river water was meant to clean body, clothes and more abstractly, one's sin. Ganga- a common name for all the rivers originated in the Himalayas- therefore was a lifeline, inalienably connected to the Hindus, who even at the death were incinerated right at the bank of the Ganga. Ganga gave everything, she is the supreme goddess, she supported agriculture, she washed away sins, she provided drinking water, and thus, the body, which for Hindus is an immaterial temporary adobe for the soul which in turn is eternal, is offered to the Ganga at the end of one's incarnation. Despite their understanding of Ganga as the supreme power, the Hindus of Nepal missed out on one of the most important gift of Ganga: hydropower. There was no built-in resistance against the use of Ganga for power production, it was the result of ignorance of technology.

Based on their origin, there are 3 major river systems in Nepal. In this widely recognized classification, the rivers originating from snowfed lakes in the Himalayas are in the first category, and the example of such rivers are Karnali, Koshi and Narayani. The rivers belonging to the second category are those originating from the Mahabharat range, and they include Mechi, Babai and so on. The third categories encompasses all rivers which are small, and are minor tributaries to the first two kinds of rivers. From the point of view of power production, the rivers in the first category are the best, as they flow from the high mountain, often falling at the appropriate gradation for electricity production. Studies of

Nepali hydropower has put the total potential of hydropower production of Nepal at 83000 MW, roughly half of which is considered to be economically feasible (see for example, Warnock (1989)), though this number changes as Nepal's infrastructure situation changes, and more and more sites become feasible.

Contribution of river in Nepali economy can be broadly divided into the following categories:

(i) Agriculture: Rivers are lifeline of any rural society, and Nepal is no exception. Eventhough there are no large dams in Nepal so far, rivers have been harnessed for agricultural use. Construction of wier to divert water to farmland is not rare in Nepal. To our knowledge, there is hitherto no cost benefit analysis of the contribution of river water in crop production.

(ii) Tourism: Rivers inspire two kinds of tourism: religion tourism, and secular tourism such as rafting. Hinduism regards any place where two rivers join each other as holy. There are multiple such confluence sites within the country where people flock to pay respect to their gods. The major example of such sites are Devghat (Chitwan), Tribeni, Ridi, Kagbeni(Muktinath) and so on.The second kind of tourism involves all other secular activities done for pleasure in Nepal's rapid rivers. Rafting is the major example, and it continues to draw a significant number of tourists to Nepal each year. Although exact number of tourists going for rafting is unknown, there were 64 rafting companies in 2002(Raj, PA, 2002).

(iii)Fisheries: The exact contribution of fisheries in Nepal is unknown. However, historically, there are several castes who survive by fishing on rivers, such as *bote*, *majhi* and so on. Although Nepali are not very keen on fish, there are some economic centers such as those in Dolalghat(Kabhre),and Malekhu(Dhading) which have built their reputation on fisheries.

(iv) Power production: Whether by using *panighatta*, or by modern turbines in the modern stations, the power production has been rising in Nepal. A broad discussion about this topic has been started already in the introduction, and will continue below also.

(v)Transportation: In transportation sector, the use of river has been sparse.Early Nepali rulers used Narayani river for transportation to sell the logs of famous Chitwan jungle to the British rulers of India, and it pretty much sums up the use of river as a transportation. Besides this use, rivers around the country were used as transportation very rarely. Most importantly though, river banks have been used as the convenient guiding paths that take an itinerant to his destination. Early *goretos* (walking trails) were built along the river bank, and that formula has been picked up by modern day highways too most of which are built along the rivers.

One way to adjudge the development on the river in Nepal is, therefore, how would a new development affect the existing uses? Who will benefit and who will lose? How will the above mentioned areas be affected? And often,in the past, rather than these criteria, other criteria have been used. For example, whether the beneficiary belongs to the ruling elite was one obvious criteria.

2.1 The possible sources of domestic conflict in water sharing in future

The possible sources of domestic conflict may arise from the following sectors.

1. Hill versus plain residents: Although the federalist constitution hasn't been written yet, and therefore we don't know for sure how the revenue raised will be allocated between different regions, there will be some conflict between people of Hill where most of the hydropower projects are likely to lie and the people of plain who may be left with nothing in terms of revenue. Ironically, the current leadership of regional parties from south may be contributing to their own loss by insisting that there be no north south states in the future federal republic. In such a scenario, the revenues collected from the hill state will remain in the hill, and the plains will remain more impoverished. The effects of such uneven distribution are already evident in regions such as Khumbu where life standard has been much better because of the Khumbu-bound tourists.

2. Urban versus village residents: A big city like Kathmandu has a high demand that can be met only by using the resources of the nearby villages. If the villages are not adequately compensated (however subjective this definition may be in Nepali context), there will be conflict between village users and the city users. Such conflicts are commonplace in Nepal already. For example, villages which are in proximity to the Kathmandu's waste dumping site often claim a huge compensation package for allowing the sites be used for dumping purpose.

3. Industrialists versus farmers: Though it is not a matter of immediate concern, in future, industries will be competing with the farmers for water, like they do in western Chitwan already. Also in future, The industralists may also include the power producers who might have to make a deal with the farmers about releasing water on time for their agriculture production, but might find it beneficial not to do so.In such cases, an efficient use of water is necessary in which case a proper compensation to the farmers living close to the industry may need to be calculated.

A simple model of intra-country conflict due to different valuation of involved players is given below. It is based on framework developed by Sunding(2004).

The project we look at it Melamchi like project, in which the government diverts the river to the big city, such as Kathmandu, and then allows the remaining water to go to the farmers in Terai.

In figure 1, the quantity is on the horizontal axis, and the price or related function is on the vertical axis. The line GB indicates city demand, and FC indicates the demand in the agriculture sector. The total demand of both city and agricultural sector is given by GHD. The total supply curve for water and residual supply curve are also given above. City's demand curve is higher than agricultural users' demand curve,reflecting their higher willingness to pay, which is a standard assumption.

We assume that city dwellers get the first priority, as Kathmandu and other cities in Nepal lie above fertile Terai plain. In this case, we will see the price in city to be E, and the quantity consumed by the city to be given by OA. If market rate for water is to prevail, then, farmers pay K and consume OJ.Obviously, this solution won't work for several reasons. One is that farmers will hate to see themselves paying more for water than city dwellers, something that rarely happens in the world. Second, if the city dweller's *priority rights* are to be ignored, and a competitive market is allowed to prevail, then the farmers will be paying R and consuming OX, which will make them strictly better off, (assuming free disposal of water). Even a free market, therefore, will be better for the farmers.

The case with the industralists and farmers sharing the water is similar. In some cases, if the farmers live above the industries or cities, the only difference will be that the residual

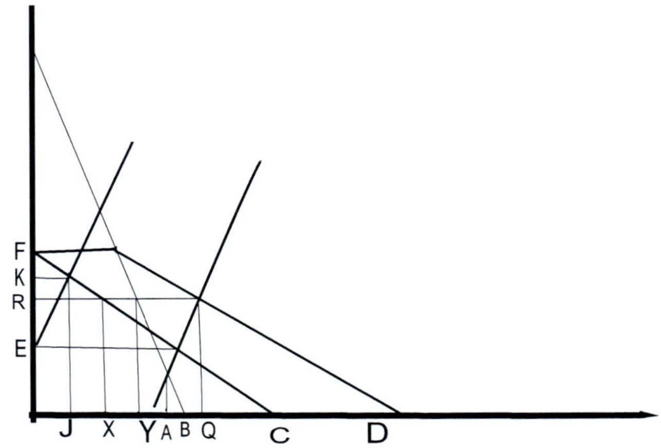

Figure 1: Illustration of problems in sharing water domestically.

demand curve in the graph above will be that of city or industrialists. The conflict will, however, be there.

There are several political economic solutions to these conflicts. One, and perhaps the most obvious, is to provide subsidy to farmers by extracting more royalty from the urban users. Another will be to provide equal water rights to all citizens, and make those rights salable. In all cases, careful and equitable solutions are necessary as not to invite conflict among users within the country.

3 Load Shedding

Load shedding is a common feature of Nepal's electricity sector. In 2008, a study done by Nepal Electricity Authority(NEA), nation's hitherto sole distributor, found that it was 41% shy of its total electricity requirement. NEA uses brute force method to solve this shortfall by implementing power outages (also called load shedding). The manufacturing sector has been hit hard due to these planned and unplanned load sheddings. A recent study puts the opportunity cost of such load shedding at as high as \$1.28/kWh with the levelized average of such cost being \$0.41/kWh (Rupjyoti et al). How will nepal cope with this in the next century?

First, in the short run, one might want to privatize a part of NEA's responsibilities, where competition will improve the performance. One immediate sector for such target is the privatization of substations and the responsibility of their maintainance that cause unscheduled power outages. Another is to jump start the production process by privatizing generation and distribution sector, and then upgrading transmission sector by using a state owned monopoly such as NEA. This will encourage entry of several firms in generation and distribution sectors and probably the introduction of differentiated services–even though electricity in itself is a homogenous product. Industries may even start to acquire electricity

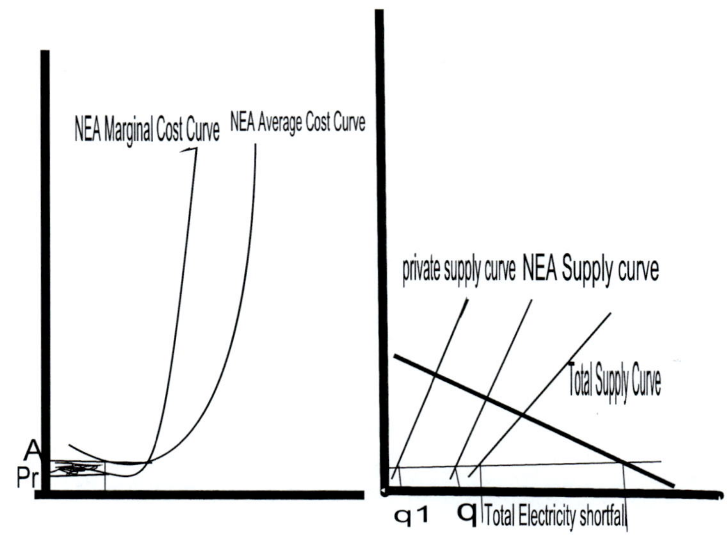

Figure 2: Illustration of the problem of load shedding.

generation plants themselves for specialized use. For example, industries and industrial sectors located in Chitwan or Makawanpur may find it more effective to produce electricity in Gorkha, and then, by hiring government owned firm's transmission service, transport it to Chitwan or Makwanpur.

Results have shown that electricity industry has a U shaped LRAC. One way to explain the loadshedding in Nepal is by the following figure.

The prevalent belief in Nepal is that the NEA is operating at the declining portion of its long run average curve, primarily because politically motivated price setting makes it operate at loss. In figure 2 above, NEA's cost functions are given in the left, and the market is given in the right. The regulators set price at Pr, and the NEA responds by producing q and incuring the loss as given in the shaded portion. Other private firms contribute q1 at that price, and , as the right part shows, the demand at the price is higher than the total supply, causing power outages.

In the next century, Nepal will be producing more electricity and will very likely get rid of load shedding but the important question is how it will achieve that goal. One answer is to assume that because of construction of roads and other related infrastructure, the industry's cost function will change, and that long run average cost will shift downward, causing NEA not to lose money, and increase the production. Other ways of producing more electricity will involve freeing electricity pricing and making it in line with the market demand. The third way is encourage the R&D sectors of firms, which will bring innovating technology and management practices to reduce the cost.

4 Issues related to the power export to India

India features prominently in any discussion related to hydroelectricity production in Nepal. Eventhough Nepal has produced electricity for only one fifth of its population so far, policy-makers are already gushing about the potential of electricity export to India. The discussion sometimes veers towards the potential of selling irrigation water, but mainly it is the hydropower that is considered the potential source of income, and a major factor in offsetting a lopsided trade imbalance with India. Despite the potential of export to India, the recent statistics actually shows Nepal is importing electricity from India. The NEA has sold 101GWH electricity to India, while it purchased 266 GWH electricity from India in the year 2005(2062/2063BS).

Except for in the case of the Karnali project, the relative absence of any talk on irrigation water as a commodity to be shared between Nepal and India is a surprising omission, as it plays a major role in efficient allocation of water in different sectors within Nepal and India.

The following chapter gives an insight into the relationship between two neighbors who are to share the water *for different purposes*. Suppose, the upstream country produces electricity to meet the demand needs of its population. The surplus energy is sold to the downstream country. The upstream country has the population of N, and individual i's utility function if he consumes H amount of electricity is given by $u_i(W, H)$,where W is the water stored in the country to produce the electricity, with the properties that $\frac{du}{dW} < 0, \frac{du}{dH} > 0$. The downstream country is a profit maximizing country, involving two sectors: crop production and manufacturing. Crop production sector has the production function given by $F_s(w_s)$,where s is the season $s \in \{1, 2\}$ and w is water used as input, and manufacturing sector, which has the production function given by $g(\tilde{}H) = B\tilde{}H^{\beta}$, where electricity,$\tilde{}H$, is an input and B and β are the production parameters. Note that the production function in crop production sector is dependent on season, whereas the production function in manufacturing sector is independent of seasons. Manipulation of water by upstream country can affect the downstream country in different ways.Upstream country's demand season of energy, for example, may not coincide with the downstream country's demand season of water in which case upstream country may collect water in a reservoir when downstream country needs it, and release it when downstream country doesn't need it.

We analyze the case in which both countries make their decision independently. In particular, the upstream country collects water in the reservoir in season 1, and then releases it in season 2, while producing electricity from it. Suppose total water available to country 1 is theoretically not binding (i.e. we are in the interval where country 1 can produce as much electricity as it wants), and the electricity production function is given by $e = E(W)$, where W is water used to produce electricity.Suppose the cost function of holding water W in season 1 is given by $c(W)$. The total utility of the country 1 is given by ${}^{N}_{i=1}u_i(W, H) + p(E(W) - NH) - c(W)$. Hence, country 1's problem is given by

$$H, W\max{}^{N}_{i=1}u_i(W, H) + p(E(W) - NH) - c(W)$$

FONCs:

$${}^{N}_{i=1}\frac{du_i(W,H)}{dH} = pN....(1)$$

$${}^{N}_{i=1}\frac{du_i(W,H)}{dW} + pE'(W) = c'(W).....(2)$$

If utility of electricity for all individuals is same, then condition (1) can be interpreted as

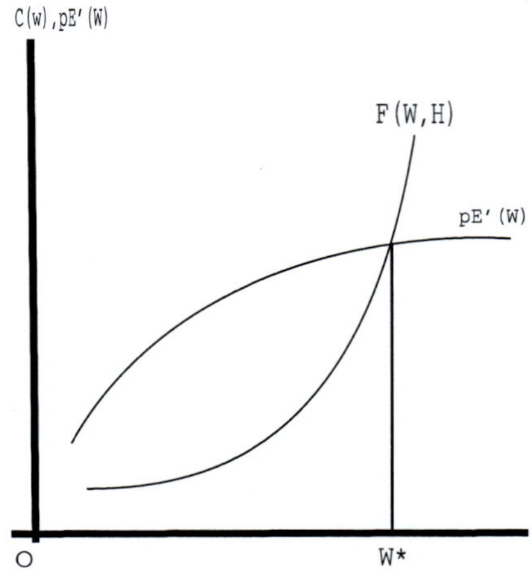

Figure 3: Illustration of optimum water storage decision.

following: the allocation of electricity to individual households is such that marginal utility of electricity for the population of country 1 is equated with the *marginal opportunity cost* of selling electricity in country 2 . Condition (2) tells us that country (2) makes reservoir, in such a way that value of electricity produced in the margin equals the sum of the marginal cost of holding water in the reservoir and the total disutility of holding one more unit of water.

Define $F(W,H) = \frac{dc(W)}{dW} -_{i=1}^{N} \frac{du_i(W,H)}{dW}$
Graphically, the condition (2) can be given as follows.
Country 2's problem is given by following:
$w_s, H\max_{s=1}^{2} p_A[F_s(w_s)] + p_H[B\tilde{\ }H^{\beta}] - p\tilde{\ }H$
FONCs:
$p_A[F_s'(w_s)] = 0, s = 1, 2$...........(3)
$p_H[B\beta\tilde{\ }H^{\beta-1}] = p$.............(4) The four equations above , from (1)-(4), provide some

insights into the nature of future negotiations between Nepal and India. In particular, (3) says that if water is provided free of cost to the country downstream, then the downstream country will want as much water as it can in both seasons. This result has two important implications: (1) free water means the downstream country will always oppose the construction of big reservoirs upstream. In particular, if the construction of big reservoirs implies less water during the season 1, and if the marginal product of water during summer for agriculture is higher than the marginal product of water during winter, then this opposition will be more fierce as given in the figure below. (2) free water also means there is no incentive for the upstream country to release water in economically efficient way, and thus there will be overall loss of welfare. Equation (4) says that the demand for electricity will be such that the value of marginal product of electricity equals the price of electricity.

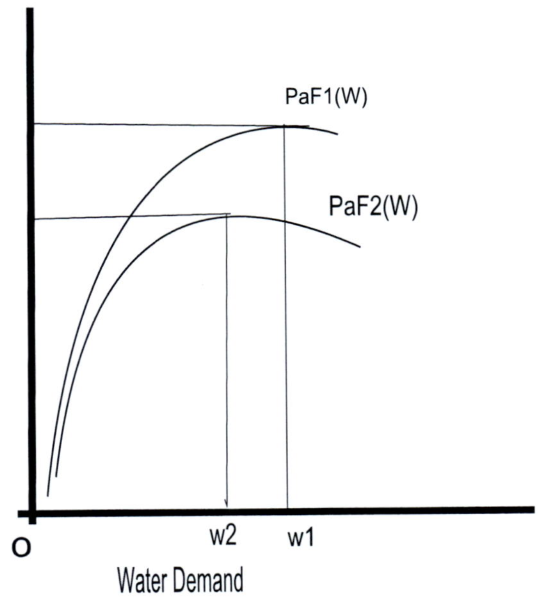

Figure 4: Seasonal Water Demand in downstream country: because of higher productivity of water, downstream country wants more water during the season 1. Here P_a denotes the price of agricultural commodity, and $F_i(w)$ denotes the production function for season i given water supply is w.

Implications for future India Nepal electricity trading from the above model are as follows:

1. When farmer's lobby is powerful in India and when supply of water in the river in season 1 (say, farming season, as opposed to winter season) is given by W_1^*, then India is likely to oppose any big hydropower project that requires the construction of reservoir in Nepal that holds more than $W_1^* - W_1$ water. Arun hydropower project was an example of this behavior. At the time when India was yet to experience the economic growth that it is recently experiencing, India opposed such big project as Arun in Nepal.

2. When "P_H" goes up, i.e. when the price of the industrial product of downstream country increases,demand for "H" increases as well. Then, the industralists in the downstream country becomes more influential in the policymaking. In that case, they lobby for higher electricity production in upstream country. If upstream country joins hand with conglomerates from downstream country (say, by starting a joint venture in electricity production), then the electricity generating activities in the upstream country really takes off, especially if the conglomerate stands to gain from the construction project itself and future sales . However, after a threshold, there comes a time when it is not economically feasible for the upstream country to "store water", in which case the price of electricity may go up in the winter.

What happens to the farmers downstream? Since the industry's demand for electricity is independent of season, it might want high amount of electricity in both seasons. In that case, there will probably be increased release of water from upstream country during the summer as well.

Recent interest in Nepali hydroelectricity by Indian firms confirms this result. After Arun, India's industrialization took place rapidly, and the firms there are in need of more power. This has resulted in the India's volte-face vis-a-vis Nepal's hydroelectricity projects, including Arun. In deed, Arun is now being restarted, with the help of an Indian company.

5 Rural Electrification

Rural electrification in Nepal presents an interesting perspective for the country: should a developing country focus on export oriented production or should it look inward and serve its destitute population first? Nepal faces challenges in its drive to gain from electricity production, as rural electrification is often deemed financially unprofitable. Social equity, rather than the rationality of a firm, is the primary motive for rural electrification drive of the NEA and Nepalese government.

Rural electrification, in Nepal, has two distinct connotation: it means serving poor people, and it also means serving a sparse population, often living far away from each other. It is, therefore, little wonder that Nepal Electricity Authority (NEA) has asked government not to force itself to be devoted for rural electrification, suggesting instead to form a special company for this purpose. Government's challenge, therefore, is to identify exact trade-off in rural electrification. The country gains by rural electrification in terms of welfare gain to population, and in terms of containment of peasant (who represents overwhelming rural population) unrest. On the other hand, construction of infrastructures to make rural electrification possible is costly, and there is a huge cost associated with this endeavor. An alternative, such as lump sum transfer of money or relocation of people near city, could be impractical solution from political point of view, but may sometimes turn out to be more economical.

One solution is to focus on microhydro in rural areas. Nepal has been cited variously as a country that has adapted microhydro technology efficiently. Nepal's weak industrial base now also includes its capability to produce and export turbines for microhydro (World Water, 1989). Nepal's hill traditionally had the system of canals and water management systems, which are basically about what people need to operate a hydropower in the villages. Therefore, micro-hydropower can be seen as a good solution for rural electrification. The problem, however, is the high cost of installations of such systems. The cost problem is exacerbated by the fact that the electricity produced during the day time is likely to be wasted, as villages without industries don't need electricity during the daytime. The government can help this situation either by helping people to develop tools to use in agriculture and other day-to-day work ("mechanisation of daily life") or by expanding national electricity grid system and buying the electricity from the villagers when they don't need it. This will reduce the overall cost of rural electrification, while simultaneously fulfilling the goal of electrification.

6 Conclusion

In this chapter, we discussed various questions related to the exploitation of water resources in Nepal in the coming century. Foremost of all is the domestic water sharing issues that may arise, as urban-rural population lock horns for their share of water. Though we didn't provide any specific policy suggestions, we indicated that market based solution might be slightly better for overall welfare. How to allocate water resources among different segment of population is as much a political question as it is an economic question, and is likely to be determined accordingly.

We then discussed the case of load shedding in Nepal, and how it affects the future of industries, and how to address this. We cited evidence that planned and unplanned load sheddings have exerted heavy toll in Nepali industries, and that regulated pricing may be one of the reasons why load shedding has been a part of Nepali electricity market. A carefully planned privatization will probably be the right answer to address the issues of load shedding in the future.

Our third topic dealt with the power trading issues with India, Nepal's southern neighbor, and only likely importer of power. Nepal's trading pattern with India will continue to evolve as the Indian power structure evolves, and relative strength of industries and industrialists improve/subside over the relative strength of agrarian northern India. A model was presented to understand this intuition.

We then briefly talked about rural electrification issues in Nepal. Nepal can't ignore rural population, and hope to be a developed country, as rural population can always be a source of political unrest. Furthermore, most of the electricity plants are likely to be located in the rural areas, and thus a fair allocation of resources is always important to ensure that rural population doesn't feel particularly aggrieved. Whether the government needs to employ NEA as a tool to achieve the goal or whether there should be a targetted firm to achieve rural electrification is an open question. We suggest that microhydro be promoted for this.

7 References

Raj, PA. 2002."Criteria for strategy for sustainable development of Nepal", http://publications.ksu.edu.sa/Conferences/Sustainable%20Development%20Strategies %202002/nep07.pdf, accessed on Nov 5th, 2008, 3:36PM.

Roop Jyoti, Ozbafli, A. , and Jenkins,G. 2006. "The Opportunity Cost of Electricity Outages and Privatization of Substations in Nepal," Working Papers 1066, Queen's University, Department of Economics.

Warnock, J.G. (1989). "The Hydroresources of Nepal" *International Water, Power and Dam Construction*.

Rai, Kavita. 2005. "Dam Development: They dynamics of social inequality in hydropower project in Nepal". Cuvilier Verlag.

Sunding, David. 2004. "Natural Resource Economics, lecture notes", UC Berkeley

World Water. 1989. "Nepal to export micro-hydropower" *World Water*(October).

Nepal Electricity Authority. 2006. *White Paper.* Kathmandu, Nepal.

In: Nepal in the 21st Century
Editor: Surendra R. Devkota., pp. 181-197
ISBN 978-1-60741-348-6

Chapter 8

ENERGY INPUT–OUTPUT MODEL FOR SUSTAINABLE SOCIO-ECONOMIC DEVELOPMENT IN NEPAL

Surendra R. Devkota[1]
Department of Economics, University at Albany, NY, USA

ABSTRACT

Energy is a crucial ingredient in the socio-economic development of any country. This paper examines whether a developing country like Nepal can achieve the development objectives specified under its tenth five-year plan in terms of energy requirements. In this regard, an IO input – output analysis was carried out to study the energy demand by the different economic sectors as outlined in the tenth five – year Plan.. This analysis indicates that Nepal's total energy demand cannot be met by the existing energy policy and the unsustainable supply sources. Alternative energy sources can play a vital role in meeting the deficit energy demand as these sources need less time and cost for installation and energy extraction and are sustainable. One of the possibilities could be community-based initiatives like small scale or micro / hydropower schemes at the local level, which would mobilize social capital and conserve ecological resources as well as enhance their sustainability in the long term.

Keywords: Energy, input-output model, sustainability policy, Nepal.

INTRODUCTION

The energy sector is fundamental to all socio-economic activities, either through its direct impact on the final demand or on the production system because energy is linked to all human

---

[1] This paper was published in "Resources, Energy, and Development 4 (1):1-16 (2007). Republsihed with permission.

activities, ecosystem services, and economic growth. The relationship between per capita energy demand and economic development has been widely studied, and it is clear that economic growth and energy consumption are strongly correlated. Georgescu-Roegen (1976) discussed that while economic growth is a dynamic and irreversible process, it is not isolated and self-sustaining. The economic process demands energy along with other factors of production such as labour, capital, and various natural resources. These inputs also require free energy for their production and maintenance. Hence, energy serves the production system both directly and indirectly. The development of production systems is also associated with the issue of energy availability. However, b in the standard production function model energy is another economic input subject to augmentation through technology and substitution. But the standard model of production ignores the dynamic interplay among energy, economy, environment, and society. Recently, Pokrovski (2003) analyzed the role of energy for US economic growth over a 100 year period and concluded that capital, labour, and productive energy are the only three production factors, and energy and labour inputs are substitutes, while capital and work (labour and productive energy) are complements.The role of energy in economic production and growth is complicated by the price structure of energy sources including varying energy content and layers of subsidy (McDaniel and Borton 2002).

Energy, along with water, health, agriculture and biodiversity is one of the specific areas set forth by the Millennium Development Goals of the United Nations (Annan 2002). The issue of energy availability is serious in terms of economic growth and sustainability. Desai (1986) claims that energy consumption reveals economic activity, capital intensity, and the structure of an economy, and at the aggregate level, GDP (gross domestic product) represents both demand and supply influences. It is claimed that technological progress till date has been driven by energy use, and economic growth over the next few years will continue to depend on increases in energy consumption accompanied by declining prices (Ayres 2001). Further, almost all energy resources have some environmental impacts. Sustainable development demands a sustainable supply of energy resources that, in the long term, is available easily, is sustainable at reasonable cost, and can be used for all required tasks without having negative societal and environmental impacts (Dincer 2000).

This paper examines the energy demand entailed by different socio-economic development activities in Nepal based on the Tenth five-year Plan (2002-07). Nepal has been following five-year development plans since the 1950s. In 2002, Government of Nepal (GN) introduced the Tenth Five-Year Plan (2002- 07). Primary aim of this paper is to assess whether this Plan is achievable in terms of energy demand and supply and its sustainability. Section 1 presents an overview of the energy consumption and supply situation followed by a discussion of the methodology employed in Section 2. Section 3 takes up results the along with the energy demand scenarios. Some macro-policy reforms are suggested in order to achieve economic growth and maintain sustainability.

Energy Use in Nepal (A Level)

Energy is a significant important constraint for the Nepalese economy. Energy sources in Nepal can broadly be classified into three groups: (1) traditional biomass, (2) modern or commercial sources, and (3) alternative energy sources like biogas and solar power. Biomass-based energy includes fuelwood, agricultural residues, and animal dung. Commercial energy includes electricity, petroleum products, and coal; the latter two fossil fuels are entirely imported. Energy consumption patterns and trends in Nepal are quite unlike those in developed countries (Table 1). The residential sector accounts for nearly 89% of the total energy demand. (Author pl. rephrase not clear). About 4% of residential energy use is sourced from petroleum products and remaining 95% from biomass. The general structure of the utilization of different petroleum products is 40% kerosene oil, 39% diesel oil, 7% gasoline, 7% aviation turbine fuel, 3% furnace oil, and 4% LPG (liquefied petroleum gas) (WECS 2002). Both kerosene and LPG are primarily used for domestic cooking in city areas.

The energy problem in Nepal arises not only from excessive reliance on non-renewable energy sources, but also from the fact that one form of energy, fuelwood, is being consumed at an unsustainable rate, while the vast potential of other forms of renewable energy, hydropower for example, remains virtually undeveloped (less than one percent of total hydro-power potential) and over priced. Though fuelwood is the primary energy source in Nepal, with forest areas being it's the main suppliers, the problems associated with forests were recognized long back. The Master Plan for the forestry sector, introduced in 1988, referred to the fuelwood deficit in Nepal. The per capita fuelwood consumption in the hill is estimated at 640 kg (kilogram)/person/year while for the terai (plains) it is 479 kg/person/year. Household and industrial biomass fuel consumption has been estimated at 14 million ton/year in 1995/96 as against 11.3 million ton/year in 1985/86, and is projected to increase to 15.4 million ton/year in 2000/01. The annual fuelwood deficit at the national level was estimated to be 3 million ton in 2000/01 (MOPE 1999). Natural forests, though a regenerative resource, simply cannot yield adequate fuelwood sustainably to satisfy the growing energy demand. This deficit supply of fuelwood can be met by either exploiting the nearby forests or by switching to agricultural residues and animal dung or other low-or no-cost alternatives. Residues of crops such as corn, paddy, and wheat straw are basically complementary energy sources of fuelwood in the hills, but these are of equal of importance in the Terai. Excessive extraction of crop residues from agricultural fields may lower the organic content of the soil and this will hamper agricultural productivity, which has been almost stagnant in the past decades. Further, burning of biomass in rural households is one of the major sources of different kinds of respiratory problems (Pandey, Hessen, and Schei 2001).

Table 1. Energy consumption pattern in Nepal (1999/20) (in 000'ToE)

	Household	Commerce	Industries	Transport	Agriculture	Total
Fuelwood	5892	34	15	0	0	5941
Agricultural residue	264	0	28	0	0	292
Animal waste	448	0	0	0	0	448
Coal	1	0	235	0	0	236
Petro-products	257	46	38	300	68	709
Electricity	39	7	43	0	1	90
Total	6901	87	359	300	69	7716

Source: WECS.

ToE – Ton of oil equivalent.

On the other hand, import of non-renewable energy products is costly and the pricing of petroleum products is a controversial issue in Nepal. For instance, in 1999/2000, about 13.3 billion rupees worth of petroleum products were consumed, which represents about 5% of the real GDP for that year or at least one-fourth of the total export earnings of the nation MoF (2002). A few anomalies exist within the pricing and distribution mechanism. NOC (Nepal Oil Corporation), a state-owned agency, has the sole authority to import, price, and distribute petroleum products. As a landlocked country, Nepal and India have an understanding on the procurement, storage, and transportation of petroleum products. Nepal purchases different products on the international market and stores them in the IOC's (Indian Oil Corporation's) facilities. These fuels are delivered to Nepal from IOC's depots in the bordering areas. Formerly, the Government of India had subsidized IOC, but in 2002 the Government of India adopted a new system of privatizing the import and export of petroleum products, which affected the Nepali market as well as NOC. Although the prices of such products are not directly linked to those in India, Nepal is compelled to raise its prices when India does. The obvious reason is the porous border between the two countries, and people hoard fuel so as to sell it on either side of the border as prices differentials arise. Further, NOC distorts prices in its own interest as it follows a fixed price system for all types of users. It cross-subsidizes the sales of kerosene and diesel with that of gasoline. During the 1990s a general pricing situation wassubsidization of 5 rupees/liter in the sales of kerosene and 3.37 rupees/liter in the sales of diesel. Though the sales of gasoline yield a profit of 5 rupees/liter, due to cross–subsidization, NOC incurs a loss of 8 rupees/liter of kerosene and 6 rupees/liter of diesel. The import tax for gasoline was fixed at 9 rupees/liter until the late 1990s. A complete and recent pricing system is unavailable since the operation of NOC is not transparent because it hardly makes public its procurement and price-fixing mechanism (New Business Age 2003). Very recently, on May 15 2006, an economic White Paper presented by the Finance Minister in the Parliament also reckoned that the Nepal Oil Corporation has suffered an oil loss of over Rs. 11 billion over the last three years. Monthly average loss of the NOC exceeds about Rs. 500 million (US $ 80 million). According to NOC, the corporation is currently incurring a loss of Rs 9.24 per liter of petrol, Rs 11.46 per liter of diesel and Rs 6.33 per liter of kerosene. Likewise, import-sales price disparity has also inflicted NOC with a loss of Rs 3.84 per liter of aviation fuel and a loss of Rs 142.71 per cylinder (14.2 kg) of cooking gas.[2]

Likewise, another state-owned agency NEA (Nepal Electricity Authority) also enjoys a monopoly in the energy business in Nepal. NEA was set up in 1985 by merging two different public agencies — Nepal Electricity Corporation and Department of Electricity. It basically deals with hydropower generation and distribution. Hydroelectricity is the main source of electricity generation in Nepal because its water resource is one of the country's major natural endowments. The average annual flow of water from the territory of Nepal is estimated to be about 225 billion cubic metres. The theoretical hydropower generation capacity is estimated to be 83000 MW (mega watt), of which the economically feasible capacity is about 44 000 MW, and out of this less than 1% is harnessed at present (Pokharel 2001). The latest Living Standard Survey of the Central Bureau of Statistics (2004) estimates that out of 4.2 million households nearly 37% have access to electricity, of which the urban – rural difference is 87% to 27%. The average cost per unit of electricity is 7.02 rupees, which may be the highest in Asia. Obvious reasons for this could be both monopoly and institutional failure. NEA

[2] http://www.kantipuronline.com/kolnews.php?nid=74023 (As of March 29 2007).

appears to be on the way to diseconomies of scale, which implies that unit cost of electricity at the consumer level goes up as its generation scales up. Further, its' major agreements are either opaque or inaccessible to the public (Pun 2003). In general, energy pricing in Nepal reflects neither the economic cost nor considers the efficiency or equity principles (Shresthacharya 2002) that is also justified by the latest financial audit report prepared by CSC and Co, an associated firm of PricewaterhouseCoopers. NEA has accumulated losses crossing over five billion rupees - one quarter of its capital - by the end of fiscal year 2004/053. The report criticized the power purchase agreements with the private sector power producers (IPP) and stated that the faulty agreement was one of the major factors responsible for hefty loss suffered by NEA. According to the report, "NEA purchases energy at an average rate of Rs 5.30 per unit and the rate becomes Rs 7.30 per unit when expenses for transmission, distribution and other costs are added. Average sales price of NEA stands at Rs 6.59, NEA incurred loss of Rs 0.71 on sale of each unit of power purchased from IPPs. During the fiscal year 2004/05, NEA suffered a loss of Rs 626 million in trade of energy purchased from the IPPs and the amount was 40 percent of the total loss of NEA." Further interesting but alarming issue as mentioned in NEA's annual report of 2004/05 that NEA owned plants were operated on an average less than 3500 hours (out of 389 MW installed capacity) whereas the IPP owned hydropower plants were reported to be operating 6000 hours/yr (out of 141 MW installed capacity).

Methodology

The introduction of theIO model by Leontief (1966) in the 1960sopened up new possibilities for the study of the structure of any economic development along with other variables such as the environmental, energy, demographic, and technological contexts of a particular society (Duchin and Hubacek 2003). IO techniques have been applied to subjects as heterogeneous as international trade, economics of the environment, and productivity issues as well as policy design, modelling, planning, and forecasting (Baumol 2000).

Hawdon and Pearson (1995) examined a complex interrelationship among the economy, energy, and environment with the aid of a 10 sector IO model of the United Kingdom. The IO model is used to analyze economic development, poverty reduction, and carbon emissions in India based on the energy consumption information (Murthy, Panda, and Parikh, 1997),and is also applied to calculate energy intensities for the different sectors of the Indian economy (Tiwari 2002). Although most of the IO applications to energy issues focused on demand relationships, Giarratani (1976) analysed the inter-industry flows from the supply perspective. Inter-industry supply constraints can be applied to the problems of allocating scare energy resources to intermediate users.

EMPIRICAL ANALYSIS

The IO model depicts the flow of goods and services among all the individual sectors of a national economy over a stated period of time. All sectors in the economy buy goods or

[3] http://www.kantipuronline.com/kolnews.php?&nid=69727 (As of March 29 2007)

services from one another and produce final products. This interdependence can be described by a set of linear equations. A detailed method is described by Miller and Blair (1985) and Miernyk (1965). The entire IO analysis is based on the Leontief inverse:

$$X = (I - A)^{-1} Y$$

where, I is an n x n identity matrix,

A is a matrix of technical coefficients or IO coefficients, and

$(I - A)^{-1}$ is the Leontief inverse.

The Leontief inverse shows the direct and indirect input requirements from a change in the final demand. It can be used to determine a variety of IO multipliers. Multipliers can be calculated to show the effects of final demand changes on output, employment, and factor (land, labour and capital) use (Hsu 1988). Multipliers reveal the difference between the initial effects of an exogenous change or final demand, and the total (direct and indirect) effects of that change. In this paper, multipliers are derived based on the above mentioned method and they are used to predict the sector-wise energy demand under the on going Tenth Plan of Nepal. Further, the IO model is employed in two ways. Firstly, it is used only for the production sector to derive energy demand scenarios, and secondly, household sectors are also included in the main model – household endogenization.

ENERGY IO MODEL AND ASSUMPTIONS

The general energy consumption pattern in Nepal (see Table 1) is further disaggregated with respect to the GDP activities (Table 2).

Table 2. Direct energy-use coefficients (TOE/ GDP in million rupees)

Sectors	Petroleum	Coal	Wood/ agriculture .	Electricity	Total
Cereal crop	0.44879	0	0	0.00526	0.45406
Cash crop	1.24263	0	0	0.02167	1.26431
Fruit/vegetable	0.31011	0	0	0.00369	0.31380
Livestock and Fisheries	0.10857	0	0	0.00201	0.11058
Forestry	0.28323	0	0	0.00977	0.29299
Mining	0.99688	2.49221	0	0.49844	3.98754
Food and Beverages	0.163	0.02296	0	0.09183	0.27779
Tobacco manufacturing	0.00561	0.44322	0	0.14774	0.59658
Textile and production	0.34121	0.1034	0	0.17233	0.61693
Leather and production	0.63785	0	0	2.28894	2.92679
Wood and production	1.11071	0	0	3.1317	4.24241

Sectors	Petroleum	Coal	Wood/ agriculture .	Electricity	Total
Paper and printing	0.59275	20.24030	0	1.73488	22.5679
Petroleum production	0.16552	0	0	0.70935	0.87487
Chemicals	0.13349	0.27243	0	0.34054	0.74646
Rubber and plastic	0.38754	0	0	0.97493	1.36247
Non-metallic production	1.09275	24.0202	6.93539	0.16916	32.2175
Basic metals	0.1517	0.31214	0	0.12485	0.58869
Electric machinery	0.13013	0	0	0.30984	0.43997
Other manufacturing	0.19955	0.22172	0	0.22172	0.643
Construction	0.029	0	0	0.029	0.058
Gas, electricity, and water	0.68588	0.36743	0	0.24496	1.29827
Trade, hotel, and restaurant	0.49059	0	0.47657	0.07008	1.03726
Transport and Communication	4.85565	0	0	0.00162	4.85727
Banking and real estate	0.14532	0	0	0.04844	0.19376
Community, and Social services	0.01792	0	0	0.00896	0.02687
Households	0.99668	0.00387	25.6113	0.15124	26.76312

ToE – tonne of oil equivalent ; GDP – gross domestic product.

This direct energy-use coefficient simply indicates energy consumption by each economic sector. A simple disaggregation of energy consumption for the year 1999 is carried out based on the available energy totals as well as the relative importance in production of the various sectors in 1999/2000. The fiscal year 1999 is also considered the base year by the Tenth Plan document and the economic scenarios envisaged therein. It is assumed that IO coefficients for a short-term analysis, i.e. for a five-year period till the end of the Tenth Plan will not change significantly. Table 2 is modelled to get energy intensity as described above and also by Herendeen (1978) and is presented in Table 3. In general, energy intensity is the function of the technical coefficients describing the economy (Casler and Wilbur 1984).

Results and Discussion

Energy Intensity

Energy intensity is a measure of how much energy is consumed, directly and indirectly, per unit of sectoral activity (Schipper, Unander, and Murtishaw 2001). The IO analysis offers a powerful framework for the calculation of both direct and indirect energy input demand effects. The production of commodities has both direct and indirect energy use implications.

Table 3. Total energy intensity (ToE per million rupees)

Sectors	Electricity	Petroleum	Coal	Wood	Total energy
Cereal crop	0.06010	0.73525	0.02391	0.01826	0.80450
Cash crop	0.07960	1.57471	0.02917	0.01841	1.66865
Fruit and vegetable	0.04170	0.48684	0.01309	0.01104	0.52726
Livestock, and Fisheries	0.02810	0.27446	0.00767	0.00964	0.30397
Forestry	0.01210	0.31239	0.00971	0.00290	0.33582
Mining	0.52270	1.12236	2.60614	0.02926	4.26788
Food and Beverages	0.16920	1.11300	0.04378	0.04727	1.32593
Tobacco manufacturing	0.17340	0.23045	0.47498	0.01061	0.88154
Textile and production	0.23430	0.79509	0.12731	0.02438	1.16053
Leather and production	2.42560	1.31254	0.02282	0.03934	3.76181
Wood and allied products	3.21860	1.86178	0.01867	0.04219	5.09989
Paper, and printing	2.01270	1.02454	23.03880	0.02137	26.12030
Petroleum product	0.77350	0.82931	0.01267	0.04125	1.61762
Chemicals	0.40850	0.56345	0.40190	0.05065	1.40636
Rubber, and plastics	1.13680	0.75128	0.05956	0.01865	1.94814
Non-metallic production	0.24960	1.53406	24.87995	7.14672	34.33001
Basic metals	0.17010	0.42595	0.39865	0.01707	0.99896
Electric machinery	0.38930	0.60382	0.09154	0.02737	1.08721
Other manufacturing	0.51680	1.24642	0.37185	0.06089	2.14074
Construction	0.12300	0.48191	1.87139	0.54959	3.55871
Gas, electricity, and water	0.32810	0.82056	0.41403	0.00957	1.50361
Trade, hotel, and restaurant	0.10800	0.89374	0.08321	0.51378	1.53905
Transport Communication	0.07300	5.37819	0.00000	0.06322	5.48319
Banking, and real estate	0.51420	0.27365	0.07730	0.00360	0.42170
Community, and social services	0.03950	0.51623	0.07150	0.03246	0.48141

ToE – Ton of oil equivalent.

For instance, the mechanical tools and inputs like fertilizers/manure for farming are the direct inputs for the agricultural sector; while energy, labor, and the material resources required to make these tools are the indirect inputs for that sector.

The major energy-intensive industries in Nepal (see Table 3) are the brick and clay industries (34.333 [ton of oil equivalent] TOE/ million rupees; paper, publishing, and printing (26.12 TOE/million rupees); wood and wood products (5.09 TOE/million rupees.), transportation (5.48 TOE/million rupees), mining and quarrying (4.27 TOE/million rupees.); leather products (3.76 TOE/million rupees), construction (3.56 TOE/ million rupees), trade, hotel, and restaurant (1.54 TOE/million rupees); food and beverages (1.32 TOE/ million rupees); and cash crops (1.66 TOE/million rupees); Energy intensity in the production sectors does not necessarily imply that Nepal has a more energy-efficient technology, because energy the losses in some industrial sectors in Nepal were as much as 30% (Devkota 1997). Other possible reasons could be the types, technologies, and the output levels of energy used by the manufacturing sectors.

ENERGY DEMAND SCENARIOS

Based on the IO analysis and Table 3, energy demand projections for Nepal's Tenth Five-Year Plan (2002 – 07) are derived (Tables 4 and 5, and Figure 1). Energy used in the fiscal year 1999, considered the base year, was 7.7 millions TOEs out of which the production sectors used only 10%. The estimated GDP for 2002 is about 711 billion rupees (10.5 billion dollar) at the 1999 prices, which demands 1.56 million TOE of energy for the production sectors (Table 4). The projected economic output at the end of Tenth Plan, the year 2007, is 967 billion rupees ($.2 billion dollars), which demands 2.17 million TOE of energy by the different production sectors (Table 5).

The major energy demanding sectors are transportand communication; trade, hotel and restaurant; non-metallic production that includes cement and bricks; paper and allied business; food and beverages; and cereal crops. These sectors will consume about 64% of the total energy demanded by different production sectors, that is, 2.17 million TOE. On average, 50% of the total demand will be for petroleum products, 31% for coal, 8% for electricity, and 10% for biomass at the end of 10th Plan.

During the Plan period, the transport sector will be a leading user of petroleum products, and will demand up to 46% of the total petroleum products imported by Nepal. This represents approximately 23% of the total national energy demand. The other major sectors demanding petroleum products are construction, trade, hotel and restaurant, banking, community services, textile production, food and beverages, and cereal crops. The agricultural sector will demand about 13% of the petroleum products.

Non-metallic industrial sectors such cement, bricks, and ceramic clay producing industries, as well as paper mills will demand 0.97 million TOE of coal energy. Cement, brick, and clay producing sectors will demand 44% of coal energy.

At the end of the Tenth Plan, the total electricity demand will be 0.17 million TOE, out of which the agricultural sector will demand 6%, hotels —7%, 21% will be demanded by different service sectors like banks, real estate, and community services, and the remaining by different types of industries. Major industries that demand electricity are food and beverages, textiles, paper, chemical, and construction.

Wood will also be a significant energy source and the key wood-demanding sectors are brick, and clay production (38%), hotel and restaurant (24%), and construction (28%). It should not be forgotten that these energy values reveal an interdependence of the industries in an economy, which includes direct energy requirement and indirect embedded energy.

The sector-wise total energy demand scenario at the end of the Plan period is projected at 24%by transport, construction — 19.2%), non-metallic production — 18.7%, trade and hotel — 7.4%, and agriculture —6.6% (see Table 5). Meeting the estimated output, at the beginning of the Tenth Plan will require 1.56 million TOEs, and at the end of that plan, the energy required by the production sectors will be 2.17 million TOEs. That indicates a 39% increase in the total energy demanded during the five–year plan period.

Table 4. Energy demand projections for 2002 (in ToE)

Sectors	GDP 2002 (million rupees)	Petroleum products	Coal	Electricity	Fuelwood Agricultural . residue	Total
Cereal crops (1)	95214	69962.3	2276.5	5720.5	1738.6	79741.7
Cash crops (2)	14838	23358.3	432.8	1181.7	273.2	25253.2
Fruit/vegetables (3)	18471	8986.9	241.7	770.8	203.9	10208.9
Livestock and Fisheries (4)	31845	8735.5	244.2	894.2	307.0	10185.6
Forestry (5)	14848	4637.8	144.2	180.1	43.1	5005.7
Mining (6)	978	1095.9	2548.8	511.2	28.6	4186.3
Food and Beverages (7)	76664	85238.9	3356.3	12972.3	3623.9	105279.6
Tobacco manufacturing (8)	5397	1242.6	2563.4	935.6	57.3	4800.1
Textile and products (9)	43201	34300.3	5499.9	10119.8	1053.2	51021.6
Leather and products (10)	946	1241.0	21.5	2294.6	37.2	3595.1
Wood and wood products (11)	2669	4965.1	49.8	8590.4	112.6	13721.8
Paper and printing (12)	2809	2873.3	64715.9	5653.5	60.0	73307.5
Petroleum products (13)	509	422.1	6.4	393.7	21.0	843.2
Chemicals (14)	13434	7559.7	5399.1	5488.3	680.4	19137.3
Rubber and plastic (15)	3635	2728.1	216.5	4132.4	67.8	7147.6
Non-metallic production (16)	8322	12759.5	207051.0	2077.3	59475.0	281369.6
Basic metals (17)	16125	6863.9	6428.2	2742.7	275.3	16314.6
Electric machinery (18)	1155	696.7	105.8	449.7	31.6	1284.4
Other manufacturing (19)	11533	14358.9	4288.5	5959.9	702.2	25325.6
Construction (20)	81181	38298.8	151921.3	9986.1	44616.0	245645.5
Gas, electricity, and water (21)	4960	4066.5	2053.5	1627.3	47.5	7798.3
Trade, hotel, and estaurant (22)	73930	65989.2	6151.7	7985.2	37984.0	118191.8
Transport communication (23)	65501	352226.4	0.0	4779.0	4141.0	361196.7
Banking, and real estate (24)	45213	12286.0	3495.1	23246.7	162.8	39277.1
Community, and Social services (25)	77874	27301.9	5568.2	3079.1	2527.8	51375.6
Sum	711252	792195.4	474780.3	121772	158270.9	1561214

ToE – Tones of oil equivalent; GDP – gross domestic product.

Table 5. Energy demand projections for 2007 (in ToE)

Sectors	GDP 2007 (M. Rs.)	Petroleum products	Coal	Electricity	Fuelwood Agri.residue	Total	Increment (%)
Cereal crops	117884	86620	2818.6	7082.5	2152.6	98727.9	23.8
Cash crops	17769	27972.3	518.3	1415.1	327.1	30241.6	19.7
Fruit and vegetables	21846	10629	285.9	911.6	241.2	12074.3	18.3
Livestock and fisheries	39327	10788	301.6	1104.3	379.1	12578.7	23.4
Forestry	17697	5527.7	171.8	214.6	51.3	5966.2	19.2
Mining	1299	1455.6	3385.3	678.9	38	5560.3	32.8
Food and beverages	102250	113686.7	4476.5	17301.7	4833.4	140415.8	33.4
Tobacco manufacturing	6850	1577.1	3253.6	1187.5	72.6	6092.4	26.9
Textile and products	59414	47172.9	7563.9	13917.7	1448.5	70169.7	37.6
Leather and products	1212	1590	27.6	2939.8	47.7	4606	28.1
Wood and wood products	3660	6808.7	68.3	11780	154.4	18816.8	37.1
Paper and printing	3626	3709	83538.6	7297.8	77.5	94629	29.1
Petroleum products	733	607.9	9.2	566.9	30.2	1214.3	44
Chemicals	17927	10088.1	7204.9	7323.9	908	25537.8	33.4
Rubber and plastic	4801	3603.2	285.9	5457.9	89.5	9440.4	32
Non-metallic production	11867	18194.8	295250.4	2962.1	84810	401227.3	42.5
Basic metals	22071	9395	8798.6	3754.1	376.7	22330.6	36.8
Electric machinery	1509	910.2	138.1	587.5	41.3	1678.1	30.6
Other manufacturing	15800	19671.5	5875.2	8164.9	962	34695.7	36.9
Construction	117510	55437.7	219907	14454.9	64582	355573.5	44.7
Gas, electricity, and water	8034	6586.7	3326.3	2635.8	76.8	12631.4	61.9
Trade, hotel, and restaurant	105157	93862.1	8750.1	11358	54028	168114.5	42.2
Transport and communication	93763	504203	0	6840.9	5927.7	517043.9	43.1
Banking, and real estate (24)	58799	15977.8	4545.2	30232.1	211.6	51079.4	30
Community and social services	115885	40628.1	8286.1	4582.1	3761.6	76452.6	48.8
Sum	966690	1096702.8	668787	164752.6	225628.9	2176898.1	

ToE - Ton of oil equivalent; GDP domestic product.

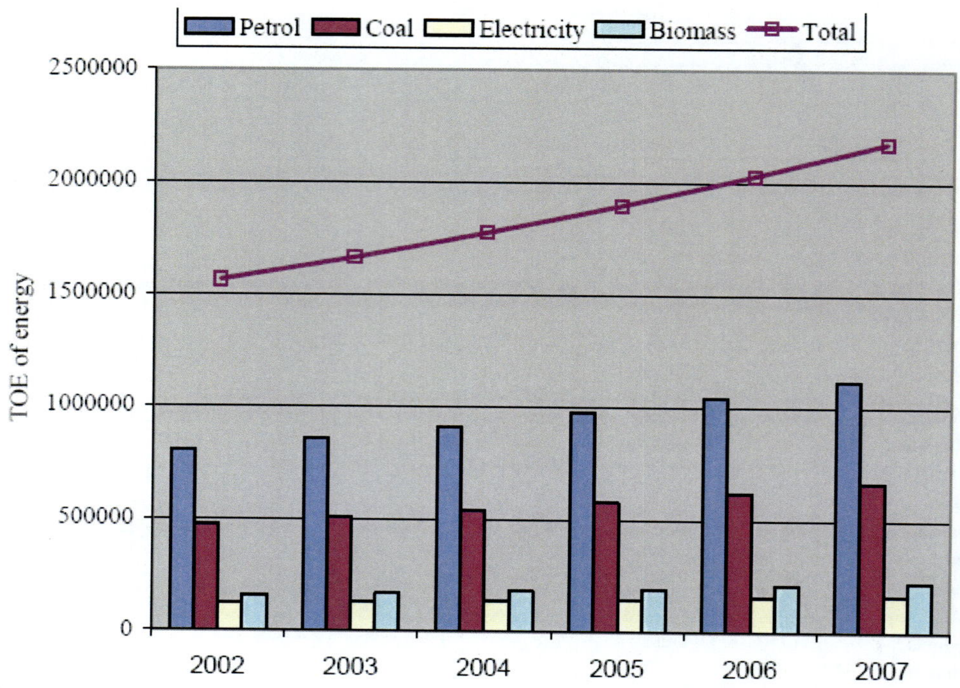

ToE – ton of oil equivalent.

Figure 1. Energy demand by the production sectors during Nepal's Five – year Plan (2002 – 07).

During the Tenth Plan period, the sector-wise energy demand of major production activities will increas: paper — 30%, cereal crops — 42%; food and beverages — 33%; brick, clay, and cement (non-metallic) — 43%; transport —43%, and construction—45%, out of which construction, paper, and food and beverages have high output multiplier values. Sector-wise, from 2002 to 2007, the total demand for electricity will rise by 35%, petroleum products — 39%, coal — 41%, and biomass — 42.5% (Table 6).

The IO analysis shows that the production activities of food and beverages, wood, leather, electric machinery, construction, textile, chemical, and paper sectors have high output multipliers. Meanwhile the Plan expects more contribution to GDP from service and utility areas like electricity, gas and water, community and social services, and transport, which have low output multipliers. In terms of production, non-metallic sectors and cement manufacturing along with construction activities are anticipated to make a higher contribution than other sectors.

Table 6. Energy consumption demand projection for production sectors

Fuel	2002 consumption (million TOE)	2007 demand (million TOE)	Increment (per cent)
Petroleum products	0.792	1.09	37.6
Coal	0.475	0.668	40.6
Electricity	0.122	0.165	35.2
Fuelwood	0.158	0.225	42.4

ToE – Ton of oil equivalent.

Based on the energy multipliers and the energy demand scenario to meet the targeted economic growth during the Tenth Plan, production sectors such as non-metallic, paper, wood, mining, transport, and construction are identified as the major energy intensive sectors. Industries like paper and allied business, leather, wood, and rubber and plastic demand more electricity. The transport sector has very high energy intensity for petroleum products—four times more than others. Non-metallic production activities have high coal and wood energy intensities. Similarly, paper industries are also as coal intensive as brick and cement manufacturing.

The Tenth Plan envisages higher value-addition from the service sectors than the production sectors. The Plan also shows that the energy demands for services sectors like community and social sectors, and utility are higher than for other activities. The agricultural sector has the lowest increase in energy demand compared to others, because the Plan anticipates that the agricultural sector will share a total of 16% of the total investment. The manufacturing sectors, particularly non-metallic production, retain a high energy demand along with construction activities. The transport sector shows the highest increase in energy demand (24%) during the Plan, which also has an average 7.7% of value added.

Regarding the sector-wise energy demand during the Plan period the following industries account for the major demand for electricity: food and beverages, textile, wood, construction, trade, hotels, and restaurants. However, banking and real estate activities have the highest electricity demand — 18.6%. The transport and food and beverages industries are the major users; petroleum products; they will require 46% and 10% of the total petroleum products respectively.

The production of brick, clay, and cement, and paper, and construction activities are primarily based on coal. Their demand will be 24% by the non-metallic sector, 33% by construction, and 12% by paper industries. Similarly, non-metallic industries will demand 37.5% of fuelwood, and hotels, and restaurants 24%. In order to meet the 2007 GDP target the production sectors will require about 5.71 million TOEs of petroleum products, 3.39 million TOEs of coal, and 0.863 million TOEs of electricity.

Household Endogenization

In general, the inter-industry part of the IO model does not include households, which are usually considered a final consumption part of the economy. Households represent a major share of consumption expenditure, and clubbing household spending with inter-industry transactions can accelerate the gross output of the country. It is estimated that for the Nepalese economy the household contribution to the final demand consumption is 56%, government expenditure — 7%, national investment — 22%, and export — 16% (Shrestha and Sapkota 2002). Energy intensity will greatly vary after the household sector is shifted from the final demand column and included in the interrelated table — endogenous, known as closing the IO inter-industry transaction matrix with respect to households. It should be noted that households account for nearly 89% of the total energy demand (see Table 1).

Based on the above mentioned technique the household sector is endogenized by including it in the IO model.After households are endogenized, the energy demand for 2007 is projected to be approximately 39.5 million TOEs, which nearly doubles that of the production sectors. If the projected energy demand is satisfied, per capita energy use would be 1.47 TOE in 2007 based on the expected population of 2007 (26.8 million), compared to 0.33 TOE in 1999. The high values reflect the fact that additional outputs are necessary to meet the expected increase in consumer spending as income increases. The household sector in both rural and urban areas demands a sustainable energy solution rather than continued reliance on traditional and costly supply sources.

Meeting Energy Demand

Based on the 1999 energy consumption patterns of the production activities, and the energy demand and supply scenarios, it appears doubtful to that the increased energy requirements can be met so as to achieve the objectives of the Tenth . Table 6 summarizes both the 2002 and 2007 situations; it does not include the household sector – the major energy user, also, it includes both direct and indirect energy use. Previous information on direct and indirect energy use is unavailable. As mentioned earlier, biomass, including fuelwood collection from forests, is being used at an unsustainable rate to meet the spurring fuel demand. Electricity production is primarily based on hydropower generation. The general trend of electricity production in the past years reveals that it took nearly one decade to double electricity production to reach the level of 1999/2000. If the requirements of electricity, and fuelwood can not be met, major industries such as the non-metallic sector, paper, construction, hotel, and restaurant, food and beverages, wood and wood products would be adversely affected and this would have a high multiplier effect on the Nepalese economy.

One of the obvious reasons for Nepal's inadequacy in meeting, the essential energy demand is the failure of the institutions and the lack of a comprehensive energy policy to address the role of energy in overall socioeconomic development. Nepal needs to overhaul of its energy policy to address poverty, gender discrimination, and community involvement in decision—making on social, economic, and environmental issues for a holistic development (McIntyre and Pradhan 2003). Although GN has theoretically adopted a 'market economy' since the early nineties, in practice a mixed economy is still prevalent as the state controls all potential businesses involving energy. Consequently, consumers are paying higher prices due to the failure of the state-owned agencies such as NEA, NOC, and Nepal Timber Corporation. The economics of the resource losses of such state-owned agencies and the externalities induced by the energy-pricing system are a subject for further research. In general, energy policies, and in particular energy-pricing policies, affect the ability of households and production sectors to switch to different fuel types. Therefore, in order to meet the target of the Plan regarding energy demand or supply, a comprehensive energy strategy is urgently needed, though some of these options have a long-term significance. Meanwhile, it is essential to focus on facilitating clean and environmentally sustainable energy sources.

1. The foremost requirement is to involve the private sector in the energy business, which includes importing non-renewable sources as well as to exploring renewable energy potential. Had the private sector been allowed to import fossil fuels from the international market, it could have played a key role in driving the fossil fuels market efficiently, since prices, and supply and demand would be determined by the market

and not the state agency. For example, if private sectors were allowed to import fossil fuels from international market that could save $ 80 million per month based on NOC's expenditure. Similarly, the private sectors' involvement needs to be extended to promotion of alternative energy sources.

2. Alternative energy sources will primarily supply the energy for households. Households should be encouraged to switch over to meet their energy needs from fuelwood/ biomass to environmentally sustainable and economically feasible alternative sources. Some viable energy alternatives are the small hydropower systems, micro hydropower systems, solar home system, solar photovoltaic system, solar water heating systems, solar dryers, solar cookers, wind systems, briquettes, biogas, efficient fuelwood stoves, and community forestry (Pokharel 2003). There are successful models of community-based sustainable socioeconomic development and resources mobilization in Nepal (Devkota 2005), which could be simulated for hydropower generation and distribution by involving local resources and capital. In this regard, a UNDP (United Nations Development Programme) supported project 'Rural Energy Development Program[4]' could actively facilitate the local people and sustain the local government, primarily in rural areas in order to meet local energy demand. By studying the strengths and weakness of the micro-hydro programmes in Nepal, Fulford, Mosley and Gill (2000) suggested that they are successful tools to help rural people develop their economic position and improve their lifestyle.

CONCLUSION

Energy is one of the main components of socio-economic development. Based on the projected IO scenarios of energy supply and demand for the Tenth Five-year Plan of Nepal and the above discussions it is inferred that the country is unlikely to achieve the goals set by the Plan. Further, the ongoing political instability in the country has already derailed the socio-economic development plan. For example, Ra and Singh (2005) reported that as a result of conflict in Nepal economic growth slowed down to an average of 1.9% over the period 2002–04 compared to 4.9%in the preceding decade, and if this is the trend for future years (2005-09) then the country will lose about 57% of its economic growth due to decline in development expenditure.

Limited supply of energy, both domestic and international, and its pricing would be the major impediment to realising the goals set by the Tenth Plan. The major energy demanding sectors are transport and communication; trade, hotel and restaurant; non-metallic production that includes cement and bricks; paper and allied business; food and beverages, and cereal crops. To meet the mounting energy demand for the future, a comprehensive policy reform is necessary that will ensure the role of the private sector in all types of energy development, i.e. renewable, non-renewable, and alternative energy resources.

State's monopoly over hydropower generation as well as distribution and import of fossil fuels is hurting to both people and national economy. People are paying high prices due to failures of state owned agencies. Private sectors' involvement also needs to be extended to promotion of alternative energy sources. Alternative energy sources will primarily supply the

[4] http://www.redp.org.np/

energy for households, which are environmentally sustainable and economically feasible. The household sector's heavy dependence on forest resources needs to be switched to other clean and environmentally benign options. Amongst different alternative sources one viable option could be community-based small-scale or micro hydropower development by granting water rights to the local people, and mobilizing local socio-ecological resources, i.e. both social and natural capital. Community-based hydropower, a replica of the community forestry model, will have a lesser environmental footprint compared to big dams, and it will be economically feasible and socially acceptable. Economic progress can be achieved through socio-ecological stewardship that will be sustainable in the long term.

ACKNOWLEDGMENTS

I am thankful to the referees. My sincere thanks go to Professor John Gowdy, Rensselaer for his insight and comment on the earlier version of the paper. This paper is taken in part from a dissertation submitted in partial fulfilment of the doctoral degree in the Department of Economics at Rensselaer Polytechnic Institute, USA.

REFERENCES

Annan K. 2002 Towards a sustainable future, *Environment* 44(7): 10–16.

Ayres R U. 2001 The energy we overlook, *World Watch* 14(6): 30–40.

Baumol W J. 2000 Leontief's great leap forward: beyond Quesnay, Marx and von Bortkiewicz *Economic Systems Research* 12: 141–153.

Casler S and Wilbur S. 1984 Energy input–output analysis: a simple guide *Resources and Energy* 6: 187–201.

Central Bureau of Statistics. 2004 *Nepal Living Standard Survey 2003/2004* Kathmandu: CBS (Central Bureau of Statistics).

Desai D. 1986 Energy–GDP relationship and capital intensity in LDCS *Energy Economics* 8(2): 113–117.

Devkota S R. 1997 *Industrial wastes survey in Nepal* Report submitted to Ministry of Industry, Government of Nepal, United Nations Development Program, and United Nations Industrial Development Program.

Devkota S R. 2005 Whether strong sustainability is operational? An example from Nepal *Sustainable Development* 13: 297–310.

Dincer I. 2000 Renewable energy and sustainable development: a crucial review *Renewable and Sustainable Energy Reviews* 4(2): 157–175.

Duchin F and Hubacek K. 2003 Linking social expenditures to household lifestyles *Futures* 35: 61–74.

Fulford D J, Mosley P and Gill A. 2000 Recommendations in the use of micro-hydro power in rural development *Journal of International Development* 12: 975–983.

Georgescu–Roegen N. 1976 *Energy and economic myths* New York: Pergamon Press.

Giarratani F. 1976 Application of an inter-industry supply model to energy issues *Environment and Planning (A)* 8: 447–454.

Hawdon D and Pearson P. 1995 Input–output simulations of energy, environment, economy Interactions in the UK *Energy Economics* 17: 73–86.

Herendeen R A. 1978 Input-output techniques and energy cost of commodities *Energy Policy* 6(2): 162–165.

Hsu G J Y. 1988 Energy multipliers for economic analysis: an input–output approach *Energy Economics* 10: 33–38.

Leontief W. 1966 *Input–output economics* New York: Oxford University Press.

McDaniel C and Borton D. 2002 Increase human energy use causes biological diversity loss and undermine prospects for sustainability *BioScience* 52(10): 929–936.

McIntyre J and Pradhan M. 2003 A systemic approach to addressing the complexity of energy problems *Systemic Practice and Action Research* 16(3): 213–223.

Miernyk W H. 1965 *The elements of input output analysis* New York: Random House.

Miller R E and Blair P D. 1985 *Input-output analysis: Foundations and extensions* Englewood Cliffs: Prentice Hall Inc.

MoF (Ministry of Finance). 2002 *Economic Surveys 2001/2002*Kathmandu: MoF.

MoPE (Ministry of Population and Environment). 1999 *State of the Environment of Nepal* Kathmandu, Nepal: MoPE.

Murthy N S, Panda M, and Parikh J. 1997 Economic development, poverty reduction and carbon emission in India *Energy Economics* 19: 327–354.

New Business Age. 2003 Special Editorial Issue about petroleum products January Issue Kathmandu See (http://www.nepalnews.com.np/ contents/ englishmonthly/ businessage/ 2003/ jan/cover.htm>, last accessed on 27 March 2007.

Pandey M R, Hessen J O, and Schei M A. 2001 Motivational factor related to improving indoor air quality in rural Nepal *Mountain Research and Development* 21(2): 148–153.

Pokharel S. 2001 Hydropower for energy in Nepal *Mountain Research and Development* 21(1): 4–9.

Pokharel S. 2003 Promotional issues on alternative energy technologies in Nepal *Energy Policy* 31: 307–318.

Pokrovski V N. 2003 Energy in the theory of production *Energy* 28: 769–788.

Pun S B. 2003 Trading off a jewel *Himal South Asia,* November issue <http://www.himalmag.com/2003/november/analysis.htm>, last accessed on 29 March 2007.

Ra S and Singh B. 2005 *Measuring the economic cost of conflict: the effects of declining development expenditure* Kathmandu: ADB (Asian Development Bank) mission.

Schipper L, Unander F, and Murtishaw S. 2001 International comparisons of sectoral carbon dioxide emissions using a cross-country decomposition technique *Energy Journal* 22(2): 35–76.

Shrestha D L and Sapkota P. 2002 *Integrated Macro-econometric and Input-Output Model of Nepal* Report developed for the formulation of the Tenth Plan Kathmandu Nepal: National Planning Commission Secretariat.

Shresthacharya A. 2002 *Energy Economics in Nepal: Issues and Options* Kathmandu: Uday Books.

Tiwari P. 2002 An analysis of sectoral energy intensity in India *Energy Policy* 8: 771–778.

WECS (Water and Energy Commission Secretariat). 2002 *Energy Balance Sheet of Nepal* Kathmandu: WECS.

In: Nepal in the 21st Century
Editor: Surendra R. Devkota, pp. 199-223
ISBN 978-1-60741-348-6

Chapter 9

IRRIGATION GOVERNANCE AND NEPALI FARMER MANAGED IRRIGATION SYSTEMS

Ashok Raj Regmi
Arizona State University, Arizona, USA

INTRODUCTION

Hydrologists have estimated a figure of 1,700 m^3 per person per year as the national threshold that is required to meet water requirements for agriculture, industry, energy, and the environment. If availability is below 1000 m^3 then a region is considered to be in a state of "water scarcity" and if below 500 m^3, absolute scarcity (UNDP, 2006). With an estimated availability of 7,600 m^3 per capita (4 x threshold) Nepal is relatively well endowed with water resources. Water availability, however, does not automatically translate into water security. The ability to use water and make it available at the right place, time, quantity and quality depends on a host of factors amongst which institutional capability appears critical. Nepal's water resource consumption, for instance, is less than 10% of an estimated 207 km^3 of water resource that is available annually (FAO, 1999; ICID, 2000). From the resource availability perspective water in Nepal is plentiful yet there is severe crisis in supplying both drinking as well as irrigation water. The national water supply corporation is able to meet only about 70% and 38% of Kathmandu's 210 million liters per day demand during the wet and dry seasons respectively (Shangraula, 2007); and year round irrigation is available to less than 20% of the 2.2 million hectares of land area that can potentially be irrigated (Shah and Singh, 2001). Accounting for water abundance at the macro level hardly reflects what is actually available locally.

The potential to expand irrigated agriculture and the need to improve agriculture productivity in Nepal can hardly be over-emphasized. With 80% of the population engaged in the agriculture sector and 40% contribution towards GDP (MOF, 2006) irrigation is obviously important. In accordance, the involvement and efforts of the national government at providing irrigation infrastructure have also been substantial. Yet, the performance of agency-managed irrigation systems (AMIS) have been far from satisfactory relative to the resources invested in the sector (NPC, 1994). Failure to provide an assured supply of water, incapacity to get water to farmers located at the tail end of canals, and the inability to achieve economies of scale in construction, operation, and maintenance are problems that have persistently dogged irrigation agencies. Interestingly, many of these problems have been observed to be outcomes of poorly designed institutions[1] rather than poorly designed infrastructure. While there is no dispute in recognizing the importance of irrigation, there are still major disagreements over who can better provide the necessary institutions to govern irrigation usage. Some believe that without government intervention resource users will not be able to provide their own institutions while there are others who think otherwise.

Small scale community managed irrigation systems have been in successful operation in many countries of Asia - the Balinese Subaks of Indonesia, the Zanzeera irrigation societies of The Philippines, and indigenous irrigation systems of Northern Thailand, China, Laos, Japan, India and Nepal. Even today they serve a third or more of the total irrigated area in Asia (Barker and Molle, 2004). In Nepal this proportion is even higher and stands at 75% (ICID, 2000). Small scale irrigation systems such as these are important because many of them are sustainable and tend to perform better in their abilities to equitably distribute water, maintain their infrastructures and even produce more agricultural yield than the larger state funded irrigation systems with better infrastructure (Lam, 1998). Despite massive injections of fund by States throughout the world (1950-1980) to expand irrigation infrastructure and their success at generating increased agricultural yields many large scale projects have not been sustainable (Ostrom, 1992). Whether it is the Jamuna project in India (Ascher and Healy, 1990), Mahaweli project of Sri Lanka (Jayawardene, 1986), Dez Pilot Irrigation Project of Iran (Levine, 1980) or the many major projects across Asia (Bromley, 1982) failures have occurred because of capital cost overruns, substandard construction/design, unrealistic productivity projections, poor system management and service provision, and poor understanding of farmer priorities (Ostrom, 2002). Given the underperformance of these larger irrigation systems and the high costs of investments ($8,000 – 15,000 per hectare) fewer inflows are expected to go into new irrigation projects. The irrigation strategy to get more irrigation water to farmers in the coming years will, therefore, have to involve the improvement and maintenance of existing systems. Strengthening existing community managed small scale irrigation systems, and organizing larger systems to capture the strengths of the smaller ones will be critical to ensure food security to millions of people who depend on farming for their livelihoods.

The potential of these small scale irrigation systems or farmer managed irrigation systems (FMIS) as they are called in Nepal is substantial but not every FMIS is successful. There are some settings where appropriators are able to self-organize and other settings where they are not. Since there are many variables that can affect benefits and costs of organizing there are also many points of external intervention that can either enhance or reduce the chance of self-organization (Ostrom, 2001). The paper, in some detail, examines how various variables affect irrigation performance, how resource settings influence cooperation and conflicts, which conditions are conducive to self-organization, and what conditions can threaten the abilities of communities to organize. An understanding of how different variables interact in different settings allows for the design of policies that can strengthen institutional and governance capabilities of FMIS. Unless government agencies are willing to recognize that

---

[1] The use of the word institution in this paper connotes rules-in-use.

local users under certain conditions are able to offer better institutional solutions and enforce rules at lower costs they run the risk of failing over and over again.

One of the key objectives of this chapter is to underscore the idea that local user groups, under certain conditions[2], are able to self-organize and successfully govern their natural resources. Successful self-organized groups are not only able to craft optimal rules and enforce them at low costs but in many instances are also able to out-perform centrally governed resource systems. Examples are presented from the Nepali irrigation sector[3] to show that farmer managed irrigation systems (FMIS) can be better at delivering water to their tail ends, maintaining their infrastructures, and realizing greater agricultural productivities than agency managed irrigation systems (AMIS). External assistance, therefore, does not necessarily have to be channeled through AMIS alone. Helping farmers to self-organize and develop their own institutions also has the potential to improve irrigation performance.

This chapter is organized in the following manner. First, a brief overview is provided of the irrigation sector and its performance in Nepal. Second, incentive structures facing farmers in self-organized and in agency-managed systems are explored to assess why farmers in the former system tend to be better motivated than those in the latter. Then, a comparison is made between the performances of FMIS and AMIS. The last section looks at the impact of resource setting on cooperation in self-organized systems before making policy recommendations.

IRRIGATION DEVELOPMENT AND PLANNING IN NEPAL

The country has a total cultivated area of 2.6 million hectares. Though 85% of this area has potential for irrigated agriculture, only 1.1 million hectares is covered by irrigation infrastructure (ICID, 2000; Shah and Singh, 2001). Surface-water is used to irrigate 900,000 ha and ground-water[4] 200,000 ha of land area. Round the year irrigation is available to only 38% of the irrigated areas. Most (75%) of the irrigated areas are serviced by farmer managed irrigation systems and the remaining (25%) by agency managed irrigation systems (ICID, 2000)

A vast majority of the irrigation infrastructure developed until the mid 1950s was constructed and managed by farmers. During this period there was some State involvement (Chandra Nahar and Juddha Nahar[5] and a few "Raj Kulos"[6]) but it was marginal (Shah and

[2] Though researchers are not able to definitely determine under what set of conditions appropriators will self-organize there is, however, consensus on the set of resource and resource user attributes that will enhance cooperation. The resource attributes are scope of feasible improvement, availability of reliable indicators of the resource condition, relative predictability of the flow of resource units, and the ability to learn and understand the dynamic patterns of the resource stock and flow. Resource user attributes conducive to self organization are salience, common understanding, low discount rate, trust and reciprocity, autonomy and prior organizational experience (Ostrom, 1999).

[3] Quantitative analyses reported in this study are primarily based on the Nepal Irrigation and Systems (NIIS) database maintained at the Workshop in Political Theory and Policy Analysis, Indiana University. The NIIS database has information on 231 irrigation systems from Nepal.

[4] Ground-water is used for irrigation mainly in the Terai

[5] Chandra Nahar was the first public sector irrigation project undertaken by the National Government in 1923. The Juddha Nahar was built in Rautahat district in the Terai in 1946.

[6] State budgets were allocated to construct and operate the "Raj Kulos" or royal canals. (Regmi M. C., 1978) calls them state operated irrigation canals.

Singh, 2001). Even today farmer managed irrigation systems contribute three times more towards irrigated agriculture than agency managed irrigation systems. It was only after 1956 that planned modes of irrigation development were initiated by the government through its five year plans.

Irrigation infrastructure development from 1956-1980 initially focused on the construction of medium and large scale projects. It then gradually moved towards the intensification of existing command areas through the expansion and rehabilitation of existing infrastructure. Program implementation during this period was very centralized. Irrigation officials assumed all planning, construction, operation and management, and maintenance responsibilities. Beneficiaries were not involved. Only after 1985 did the Government begin to take a more integrated approach to developing land and water resources and unlike earlier times more emphasis began to be placed on user involvement in the irrigation process (Angwood et. al., 2002), Shah and Singh, 2001).

The policy reforms undertaken by government to adopt a participatory approach to irrigation development are reflected in documents such as the Water Resources Act 1992, and the updated Irrigation Policy 2003. The policy sets out objectives and guidelines for irrigation interventions including FMIS development and management and transfer of Department of Irrigation (DOI) constructed systems to water user associations (WUA) (Water Aid Nepal, 2005). The irrigation policy which was initially adopted in 1992 has explicit provisions for supporting community efforts in irrigation development and encouraging more users' participation in Agency led irrigation development programs. The Water Resources Act 1992 also provides a legal basis for implementing participatory development programs as it recognizes the rights of WUAs. Another important document is the Government's 20-year Agricultural Perspective Plan (APP). Irrigation is identified as the primary input to increasing agriculture productivity and FMIS are recognized as key vehicles to deliver the inputs.

IRRIGATION PERFORMANCE

An estimated $1.2 billion has been spent in the irrigation sector from 1956-2000 (Shah and Singh, 2001). Only 20% of this amount was funded through the Government's own resources. The remaining 80% in investments has been funded by external donors[7]. Nearly 60% of these funds have been spent on constructing new irrigation infrastructure. Despite a standing policy since the mid eighties to prioritize the rehabilitation and expansion of FMIS networks the DOI has invested only about 16% in this area (Shah and Singh, 2001).

DOI investments in medium and large scale projects have been disappointing. Shah and Singh (2001) report that water volumes supplied by many large projects[8] are far below original plans and they consistently have capital cost over-runs. Some projects such as Bagmati and Babai are reported to have cost over $5000 per hectare to construct. The 1994 appraisal by the National Planning Commission's regarding irrigation development performance in the country was also negative. It reported that "irrigation development and operation in Nepal is performing dismally relative to the amount of resources poured into the

[7] The Asian Development Bank, World Bank and the Saudi Development Fund account for 60% of the investment and bilateral donors 20%.

[8] Large irrigation projects such as Sunsari-Morang, Bagmati, Bhairawa-Lumbini Groundwater, Narayani etc.

sector" (NPC, 1994). There are many reasons for such poor performance but the ones that are more frequently reported are: a) weak governance framework and enforcement in attaining effective service delivery b) unrealistic productivity projections in assessing benefit-cost ratios, c) poor system management d) insufficient operation and management due to lack of user participation, and e) poor understanding of farmer priorities (ADB, 2001). The institutional arrangements to induce realistic project planning and effective system management are, obviously, weak.

Intervention by government agencies to improve farmer managed irrigation systems have also run into difficulties. (Ostrom, 2002) points out that these difficulties often arise because irrigation agencies fail to recognize the institutional aspect of irrigation systems and focus only on improving physical capital. To emphasize her point she cites the experience of the USAID funded Chiregad Irrigation Project in Dang as reported by Hilton (2002). A new irrigation system with permanent headworks and cement lined canals was constructed in an area that was previously irrigated by a network of five farmer managed irrigation systems. Making no efforts to understand how the pre-existing water associations were organized DOI appointed a new user committee. This committee, however, did not even include the water managers of the earlier five FMIS. The outcome of this intervention was that only three of the five "maujas" received water consistently. Prior to the intervention all five "maujas" used to receive adequate water. The effort to improve agricultural productivity through investments in physical capital alone thus resulted in reduction of the service area, unreliable water deliveries, nonfunctional WUA, and a weakened older WUA. Institutional structures stand on social capital developed over many years of learning through shared experiences and are as tangible as physical capital. Their neglect as we see in this example not only resulted in weakening of farmer organizations but also led to opposite outcomes.

Why Farmers May Be Motivated to Perform Better in Self-Organized Systems Than in Agency Managed Systems

A self-organized system can be structurally superior in generating positive incentives than externally organized systems. In a self-organized system such as the FMIS it is the farmers themselves who act collectively to construct and govern their systems. They make decisions on delineating service areas, determining water allocation rules and assigning maintenance responsibilities. However, in externally designed systems such as the AMIS it is someone other than the farmers who design the physical system and assume responsibility for making rules and enforcing them. Government officials who are tasked with managing these systems, however, have to govern on shoe string budgets and with limited manpower. Without much incentive to develop long term working relationships with the farmers and faced with resource constraints many try to develop simple uniform allocation rules across the board and often neglect to enforce rules. Given the farmers' diverse cropping schedules and needs such uniform rules are mostly inadequate and without enforcement the stage is set for breaking rules. When "official rules" do not match local needs then conflicts break out, canals are breached, and physical capital is destroyed (Lam, 1998; Shivakoti and Ostrom, 2002).

In more recent times irrigation policy does encourage "turnover" and "joint management" of AMIS to formal water user groups to overcome perverse incentives. However, very little attention tends to be paid in forming these groups and they are often seen as arrangements to obtain a community's cooperation. Little is done to either encourage or develop the governing function of these organizations. Officials (professional engineers) who oversee this process are not motivated[9] and often not skilled[10] to serve the needs of the farmers. The farmers too are not confident about the transfer process and are unwilling to invest their time in operating the system. Incentives to shirk on the part of the officials and incentives to free-ride on the part of the farmers often result in the poor performance of AMIS.

Farmers in successful self-organized systems tend to overcome their collective action problems by crafting their own rules. However, the conditions that are necessary to initiate collective action do not arise spontaneously. Unless farmers have a common shared understanding of the costs and benefits of engaging in collective action, unless a secure property regime makes it possible for them to reap the benefits of their efforts in the long run, and unless they are confident that external authorities will not interfere in their rule-making, rule following and rule-enforcement activities farmers will not invest their efforts in organizing for the long term. Simply turning over systems to the farmers and expecting viable organizations to take root is expecting too much. To craft rules that suit a particular environment there has to be an understanding of the interrelationships between the combination of rules with the physical, social, and cultural environment.

GOVERNING FARMER MANAGED IRRIGATION SYSTEMS

An irrigation system can be conceptualized as a common-pool-resource. Withdrawal of water from the system means that there is less water available for others to use and once a system is constructed farmers who own land adjacent to the watercourse can potentially access water even if they have not contributed towards its provision. Farmers sharing an irrigation system have to cope with the problems of provisioning and appropriation. Unless non-contributors can be excluded from enjoying the benefits of a common system no rational actor would be willing to contribute towards its development and upkeep. Also, unless there are rules constraining resource use each user would want to maximize consumption. We see, however, that many farmer managed irrigation systems are able to resolve such cooperation dilemmas by creating effective agreements amongst themselves. I draw on my own research (Regmi, 2007) and (Shukla, et al., 1993) work on irrigation resource inventory of Chitwan to describe the structure of a FMIS and how they operate.

Irrigation Infrastructure

The key FMIS irrigation infrastructures consist mainly of headworks, canals and structures for water distribution. The headwork of an FMIS typically consists of an intake structure to divert water and a gated structure to control water flow. The intake diverts water

[9] Engineers do not regard the O&M operation highly. They are much more interested in the construction part of the process. Also promotions in the civil service are based on seniority which to a large extent discourages initiative and creativity. Promotions and transfers are strongly associated with political patronage and not to keeping an irrigation system in good condition.

[10] Institutional aspects of irrigation system design are often not a strong component of engineering training.

from the natural water course into a constructed canal. These intakes are mostly temporary structures constructed from stone and brushwood. Uses of semi-permanent gabion box structures have also been observed. The gated structures for flood control are usually observed in systems that have received external assistance. Systems that do not have gates are forced to breach their diversion structures when threatened by flood waters.

Systems consist of a main canal and a number of branch canals. The majority of systems in East Chitwan have fewer than six branch canals where mean canal lengths (sum of the main and branch canals) are less than 6200 meters. Most of the branch canals are unlined and the main canals partially cement-lined. The mean service area and households served by a typical FMIS is 124 hectares and 139 households respectively.

Quite a few systems have the cement concrete proportional weirs for dividing water shares. Most rely on piped outlets and other temporary structures. Systems without permanent water allocation structures use wooden stakes, bushes, stone and earthen materials across the main canal to ensure proportional allocation of water.

Water Sharing Arrangements

Allocation of water in a system reflects entitlements. Water is allocated only to those farmers or farmlands who have water rights and not to others. Allocation also means the quantitative division of water in the system among the entitled farmers or fields. The principle on which water is shared is decided by the irrigator community and can take a number of forms (Pradhan, 1989). The most common allocation principle observed in Chitwan is the principle of dividing water in proportion to the land owned by the farmer. There are other principles too, for instance, apportioning of water based on the paddy cultivation task[11] and on water shares[12].

Distribution of water among farmers is the implementation of the allocation principle. It involves implementing a set of agreed upon rules with the help of some physical structures. Depending upon their system characteristics water users are known to use a variety of methods to distribute water e.g. free flow, timed rotation, time-area relationship, and time required to wet/saturate a given unit of land. The most popular method of distributing water during stressful periods is timed rotation[13]. Water user associations decide the time and duration each farmer is allowed to irrigate his/her field.

---

[11] The task of paddy cultivation can be divided into two periods a) transplantation period and b) post transplantation period. During the first period water is required for preparing the seedbeds and preparing land for transplantation. During this period farmers can agree to meet the water needs of all the users irrespective of entitlements. In the post transplantation period, however, water distribution is based on entitlements.

[12] The total water supply in a system is divided into a fixed number of shares which is then apportioned to farmers based on their initial contributions towards system construction.

[13] Depending on the water availability and area entitled to be irrigated associations decide the time duration per branch canals before they rotate turns. For instance, there are four branch canals in the Baireni/Pakhdibas irrigation system which rotate turns after 24, 36, 17, and 51 hours respectively. All of the water in the system is supplied to the first branch for the first 24 hours before it is diverted to the second branch for 36 hours and so on. The fields in each branch then divide up the water among themselves based on a prior agreed allocation principle. There is quite a variation in waiting times. Farmers in some system may get their turn every 8 hours and in other systems every six days.

Maintenance and Resource Mobilization

WUAs are organized for regular as well as emergency repairs. The regular maintenance activities include de-silting of the major branch canals, repair of intake structures, and strengthening of canal dikes. These activities are undertaken prior to the rice planting season i.e. in March for the spring rice season and May for the monsoon rice season. Emergency maintenance typically involves repairs of the diversion structure and main canal embankments that get washed away by floods. In addition to the one off bi-annual maintenance activities farmers are also organized for continuous maintenance during the monsoon season. Either association members themselves or hired helpers regularly monitor the canals for early detection of canal breaches.

Cash as well as labor resources are mobilized internally to carry out repair of intake structures and de-silting of canals. While landholding is the basis for cash contributions households are the basis for mobilizing labor resources. In an emergency all members are mobilized regardless of benefits or entitlements.

Organization

All irrigation systems in Chitwan have WUAs. However, some may not be formally registered and may also not have written constitutions. Association memberships are mostly based on ownership of land in the service area. Executive officers headed by a chairperson are selected from among the members. Officials are tasked with mobilizing resources for maintenance, organizing and supervising system work, maintaining records and accounts, and resolving conflicts. Although WUA officials are permitted to take routine decisions the major ones need consensus from a general assembly. All members make compulsory contributions towards the upkeep of systems either through labor or cash contributions.

Rules are used extensively to structure irrigation activities. All systems have explicit and commonly understood rules and regulations relating to the allocation and distribution of water, contribution of resources for repair and maintenance, and sanctions for violating rules. Sanctions can take any of the following forms: a) verbal warning without monetary fines, b) monetary fines, c) cessation of water turn, and d) removal from the association. Sanctions are imposed by water user functionaries, guards, or fellow appropriators depending on the nature of the sanction imposed. About 60% of the systems in Chitwan have written rules and regulations. Many of the systems managed by the indigenous people (Tharu) do not have formally written rules yet rule following is reported to be higher in these systems than in others (Shukla, et al., 1993).

Comparing FMIS and AMIS Performance

There are many individual case study reports by authors who assert that FMIS in Nepal perform better than AMIS. Lam (1998) who undertook a systematic and comprehensive study of 127 Nepali irrigation systems also reaches the same conclusion. In the following sections I review his results and those of a few others to underscore (Ostrom, 1990) idea that self-organized resource users may be better able to resolve cooperation dilemmas (or be a major part in the resolution) when resources are local in scale. In other words, external actors may face more difficulties than local resource users in designing optimal institutional solutions and enforcing rules at lower costs.

Lam uses three measures of irrigation performance - Agricultural Productivity[14], Water Delivery[15], and Physical Condition[16] - to compare performances between FMIS and AMIS. All of his measures are composite indices that consist of multiple variables. Agricultural productivity attempts to capture the productive potential of a group resulting from their collective action efforts. Water delivery measures the ability of a system to deliver water adequately, reliably, and equitably. And, the variable physical condition is a measure of how well an irrigation system is being maintained. Comparing FMIS and AMIS along each of these three dimensions he finds that FMIS on average have higher levels of agricultural productivity, maintain their infrastructures better, and deliver water more effectively than AMIS. These differences are statistically significant at the .01 level (Table 1.1).

Two other relevant results that he reports in his study are that - rule following among appropriators is significantly greater in FMIS than AMIS, and levels of mutual trust is higher in FMIS than in AMIS. More than 50% of the FMIS are characterized by high levels of rule following whereas this is only 20% in case of AMIS; rule infractions in 9 out of 10 FMIS systems are of a minor nature compared to 1 in 2 in AMIS; and farmers trust fellow farmers nearly twice in FMIS than AMIS. The reason why FMIS are able to perform better than AMIS is probably because the rules adopted by the former are better able to distribute the benefits and costs more equitably among the users than the latter. This is reflected in the higher levels of trust and greater rule following behavior observed in FMIS than in AMIS.

Table 1.1.[17] Performance by type of governance arrangement

	FMIS (N=70)	AMIS (N=19)	F	p
Physical Condition	3.73	2.75	40.76	.00
Water Delivery	3.73	2.65	38.02	.00
Agricultural Productivity	4.36	3.40	17.25	.00

Source: Adapted from Lam (1998).

Water is generally most abundant in river courses during the monsoon season. In the spring and winter seasons, however, it tends to be scarcer. Water is the most critical agricultural input for Nepali farmlands and crop yields and cropping intensities are mostly a function of its availability. Therefore, the ability of irrigation systems to deliver water to their tail ends across the seasons is a strong indicator of irrigation performance. Comparing FMIS

[14] Agriculture Productivity consists of three variables viz. agricultural yield measured in metric tons per hectare per year, cropping intensity at head-end, and cropping intensity at tail-end. One crop per year on a plot of land equals a cropping intensity of 100%, two crops mean 200%, and three crops mean 300%.

[15] Water Delivery includes three variables i.e. water adequacy, equity and reliability. Water adequacy refers to whether a system is able to make enough water to meet farmer needs. Equity refers to fairness in distributing water between head and tail end. Reliability refers to the predictability and timeliness of water delivery.

[16] Physical condition reflects the collective maintenance efforts as well as the degree of social organization of the group. It comprises two variables viz. condition of infrastructure and the degree of perceived economic efficiency in maintaining the infrastructure.

[17] The values reported for each of the dimensions are factor scores and do not have a unit of measure. These scores can, however, be used relatively to make comparisons.

and AMIS on this measure (Ostrom and Gardner, 1993) find that FMIS consistently outperform AMIS across the seasons, more so in the scarcer seasons, in their ability to provide abundant water to their tail ends (see Table 1.2).

Table 1.2. Water abundance by type of governance arrangement and season

Season of Year	FMIS	AMIS	FMIS	AMIS
	Abundant Water at the Head End		Abundant Water at Tail end	
	% (N)	% (N)	% (N)	% (N)
Monsoon	97 (100)	91 (23)	88 (100)	44 (23)
Winter	47 (99)	43 (23)	38 (98)	13 (23)
Spring	34 (98)	26 (23)	24 (96)	9 (23)

Source: E. Ostrom and Gardner (1993:103).

Table 1.2 shows that twice the numbers of FMIS are able to deliver abundant waters to their tail ends than AMIS. During the scarcer seasons, in winter and spring, three times more FMIS than AMIS accomplish this task. There is abundant water at the head ends of more FMIS than AMIS even in the summer season; however, the differences are not as striking as in the water scarce seasons.

Studies of 160 FMIS in Tanahu by (Poudel, et. al., 1994) and 88 FMIS in Chitwan by Shukla et. al. (1993) also indicate that FMIS are able to produce more spring paddy (4 mt/ha/yr and 4.6 mt/ha/yr) than the national average (2.28 mt/ha/yr).

The above results indicate that farmers in self-organized irrigation systems are capable of performing better than their counterparts in systems that are managed by external actors. This, however, does not mean that farmers are always successful at self organization. There is general agreement that appropriators who are dependent on a resource, intend to use their resources over a long period of time, have achieved certain levels of trust, and possess some level of autonomy to make their own rules are more likely to self-organize. Whether they are actually able to do so, however, depends on how attributes of the resource and attributes of the resource users interact in specific field settings to affect the perceived costs and benefits of organizing (Ostrom, 1999a). The following sections examine how some of the resource user attributes and resource attributes may influence performance of FMIS in specific resource settings.

Farmer Managed Irrigation Systems in Chitwan

This section draws heavily on my study (Regmi, 2007) of 74 farmer managed irrigation systems from Chitwan, Nepal. In Chitwan, there are two distinct types of river systems; north-south flowing rivers and east-west flowing rivers. Rivers that flow north-south originate from the Mahabharat hills and pass through changing terrain from hills to plains. These rivers are characterized by steep gradients, seasonal flows, changing river course, low discharge volumes, and difficult terrain. Irrigation systems drawing water from these rivers tend to have longer canals, pass through landslide zones, and require frequent maintenance of diversion structures. East-west rivers on the other hand are characterized by flat terrain, mild gradients, perennial flows, and high discharge volumes. Irrigation systems on these rivers enjoy an advantage over the other systems in terms of ease with which appropriators can access resource units. The north-south and east-west groupings reflect distinct resource settings. Apart from this, system variations can also occur with respect to group size, ethnic compositions, exit options, in-group income differences and many other variables. It is within such a context that local resource users have to organize and craft rules that allow them to maintain their resources as well as ensure equitable resource distribution.

Factors that Influence FMIS Performance

One of the key results of this analysis suggests that performance of an FMIS in Chitwan is strongly associated with the orientation of the river system from which it draws its waters. As pointed out in the earlier paragraph, the characteristics of a river system have a direct bearing on the amount of efforts required to operate and maintain a system and the volume of resource units available to it. This is reflected in the ability of E-W irrigation systems to access water for more number of months in a year (Table 1-3), maintain their infrastructures better (Table 1-4) and enjoy higher cropping intensities (Table 1-5).

Table 1.3. Relationships between Average Access to Water and Orientation

	Systems on East–West running Rivers	Systems on North–South running Rivers
Access to water less than 9 months/yr	0 (0%)	35 (76%)
Access to water greater than 9 months/yr	25 (100%)	11 (24%)
TOTAL	25	46
	100%	100%
$Chi^2 = 37.52$, $p = 0.000$		

Table 1.4. Relationships between Orientation and Performance Measures

	N	Systems on East - West running Rivers (N=22)	Systems on North- South running Rivers (N=43)	F	P
Physical Condition	65	4.33	3.67	43.43	0.00
Productivity	65	5.38	4.29	44.57	0.00

Table 1.5. Orientation and Cropping Intensities

	East-West Systems	North-South Systems	F	p
Cropping Intensities at Head End	297 % (22)	245% (43)	39.9	0.000
Cropping Intensities at Tail End	275 % (22)	212 (42)	33.2	0.000

Whereas all E-W irrigation systems have access to water for more than 9 months this is true for only 1 out 4 N-S systems (Table 1-3). Not only is agricultural productivity significantly better in E-W systems than N-S systems (5.38 vs. 4.29; p=0.00) but so is the physical condition of irrigation infrastructure (4.33 vs. 3.67; p=0.00). This suggests that the average irrigation system located on E-W running rivers is more productive and also better maintained than an average system on N-S running rivers (Table1-4). Evidence of higher productivity can also be seen in Table 1-5. Cropping intensities at both the head as well as tail ends are significantly higher in E-W systems than in N-S systems. This implies that land area located at the head ends of irrigation systems tend to be more productive than those at the tail ends irrespective of the orientation of the system and E-W systems in general are more productive than N-S systems.

Irrigation systems located on N-S flowing rivers exhibit significantly higher levels of rule following behavior compared to their counterparts in the E-W Rivers (Table 1-6). However, there aren't significant differences in the monitoring and sanctioning activities (Table 1-7) and in the levels of rule infractions between the N-S and E-W groups (Table 1-8). The results suggest that less endowed resource systems (N-S) tend to be more conscious about following operational rules than the better endowed systems. But, in terms of monitoring and enforcing rules they tend to be more or less similar. The nature of rule infractions in both cases also tends to be mostly of a minor nature such as shirking "banwari"[18] duties or not showing up on time. It would be unusual to find irrigators stealing water or irrigating out of turn.

Table 1.6. Relationships between Rule Following Practices and Orientation

	Systems on East–West running Rivers	Systems on North–South running Rivers
Low/Moderate level of rule following	8 (42%)	8 (20%)
High level of rule following	11 (58%)	32 (80%)
TOTAL	19	40
	100%	100%
$Chi^2 = 3.185$, $p = 0.074$		

Table 1.7. Relationship between Monitoring/ Sanctioning and Orientation

	Systems on East–West running Rivers	Systems on North–South running Rivers
Low/Moderate Monitoring and Sanctioning Activities	5 (42%)	13 (37%)
High Monitoring and Sanctioning Activities	12 (58%)	22 (63%)
	17	35
TOTAL	100%	100%
$Chi^2 = 0.057$, $p = 0.811$		

[18] "Banwari" is a practice where each household has to contribute one able bodied person as loabor contribution towards irrigation system maintenance.

Table 1.8. Relationship between Level of Infractions and Orientation

	Systems on East–West running Rivers	Systems on North–South running Rivers
Minor Infractions	15 (83%)	34 (97%)
Major infractions	3 (17%)	1 (3%)
TOTAL	18	35
	100%	100%
Yate's $Chi^2 = 1.57$, $p = 0.21$		

Rules are used extensively to structure irrigation activities. All of the surveyed systems have water users associations and rules govern the allocation and distribution of water, resource mobilization, and monitoring and sanctioning. There is also a common understanding among users regarding principles of water entitlements, resource contributions, and fines for rule violations. The rules in use, however, vary from system to system as they are designed to cope with their own situations.

Two other factors that significantly influence irrigation performance are the willingness of individuals in groups to assume leadership or entrepreneurial activities, and the group's history of prior organizational experiences. Whereas only 1 out 5 E-W systems lack leadership activities nearly 3 out 5 do so in N-S systems (Table 1-9). The differences in leadership activities also associate positively and significantly with performance variables (Table 1-10).

This pattern is similar in the case of prior organizational experience (Tables 1-11, and 1-12). Whereas more than 8 out of 10 E-W systems have a history of cooperation in activities other than irrigation only 3 out of 10 N-S systems have such a history. Prior history of cooperation is also positively and significantly associated with performance (Table 1-12).

The results confirm that leadership abilities and prior organizational experience matter and that they significantly influence irrigation performance. Unless individuals are willing to invest substantial amounts of their personal time and energy to coordinate activities of the many users it may not be possible to craft workable institutions.

Table 1.9. Relationships between Leadership Activities and Orientation

	Systems on East–West running Rivers	Systems on North–South running Rivers
No leadership activities	3 (18%)	24 (60%)
Presence of some level of such activities	14 (72%)	16 (40%)
TOTAL	17	40
	100%	100%
$Chi^2 = 8.58$, $p = 0.003$		

Table 1.10. Relationships between Leadership Activities and Performance

	No leadership activities (N=26)	Presence of some level of such activities (N=28)	F	P
Physical Condition	3.74	4.13	14.13	0.00
Productivity	4.37	5.06	14.85	0.00

Table 1.11. Relationships between Cooperation in Other Activities besides Irrigation and Orientation

	Systems on East-West running Rivers	Systems on North–South running Rivers
No cooperation	3 (16%)	29 (69%)
Some cooperation	16 (84%)	13 (31%)
TOTAL	19 100%	42 100%
Chi^2 = 14.87, p = 0.000		

Table 1.12. Relationships between Cooperation in Other Activities besides Irrigation and Performance

	No cooperation (N = 30)	Some cooperation (N = 26)	F	P
Physical Condition	3.76	4.05	5.72	0.02
Productivity	4.45	4.91	5.01	0.03

Making, testing, fine tuning, interpreting, and monitoring and enforcing rules to structure irrigation activities is a continuous process and it requires substantial amounts time and energy. Ternstrom (2002) also finds a significant relationship between leadership abilities and performance in her study of irrigation systems. Prior organizational history also appears to be an important variable that influences performance. The reason why groups with a prior history of working together in other activities tend to also do well in governing their irrigation resources is because familiarity with various rules and strategies used to achieve various forms of regulations make the task of organization a bit easier as users are more likely to agree upon rules whose operation they understand from prior experience.

Heterogeneity and FMIS Performance

The socio-cultural differences as reflected by a group's ethnic composition are not correlated negatively with irrigation performance. Performance, rather, is correlated negatively with income variation. The results suggest that variations in incomes within groups may be a greater impediment to collective action than the number of ethnicities that comprise a group (Regmi 2007). The result of this study in regards to the socio-cultural variable is in line with the studies of Masako et. al. (2005), Gautam (2002) and Somanathan et. al. (2002).

They too do not find any association between their measures of socio-cultural heterogeneity and collective action. Similarly, in regards to heterogeneity of assets my results corroborate the results of prior studies undertaken by Tang (1992), Lam (1998), and Ternstorm (2002). All these studies of irrigation systems find a negative correlation between income inequality and collective action. The size of the irrigation system as measured by its command area is also not correlated to performance. One might expect better coordination and collective action when system size is small but this is not the case. Again, this result is similar to the results that Tang (1992) and Lam (1998) report in their studies.

The effects of engineering infrastructure - type of headwork and canal lining - on irrigation performance appears not to be uniform. The presence of a sturdier and more permanent type of headwork on a system appears to be negatively correlated with performance. A sturdier cement lined canal, on the other hand, is positively correlated to system performance. Though the results are not statistically significant their implications very much are. A truly permanent headwork, ironically, generates negative incentives for head-enders not to want to cooperate with tail-enders in system maintenance (Lam 1998). Partial or complete cement lining on the other hand appears to improve performance by minimizing system water losses thereby enabling water to reach the tail ends. The policy implication of such results is that an improvement in engineering infrastructure alone may not necessarily translate into improved system performance. Unless users are able to craft and enforce rules to cope with the asymmetries generated by improvements in irrigation infrastructure the positivee effects may well be cancelled out by the negative effects.

RESOURCE SETTING, COOPERATION AND CONFLICT

The general topography of a region can influence initial resource endowments. These conditions in turn determine the efforts that may be required to manage individual irrigation systems. Some systems may have to invest greater cooperative efforts than others to realize equivalent benefits but the fundamental cooperation dilemma for all systems is essentially similar. Intakes and canals have to be constructed and maintained on a periodic basis; rights and responsibilities have to be agreed upon; and appropriate rules have to be crafted, monitored and enforced. If multiple systems share waters from a common river course then intersystem arrangements also need to be worked out in addition to the intrasystem agreements. In the following sections I examine the response of individual irrigation systems to conditions of relative resource abundance and scarcity (Regmi, 2007).

Conditions of Relative Water Abundance

Rapti is a perennial, E-W flowing, river with a dry season mean monthly discharge greater than the estimated water requirements of 11 FMIS that draw its waters. Water in the river course is fairly abundant round the year. Systems on this river have to cope with flooding and maintaining washed out intakes, which requires considerable resource mobilization, instead of conditions of water stress arising from reduced flows. Resource abundance does away with the need to maintain inter-system water sharing agreements and opens up opportunities for cooperation. An example of cooperation between irrigation systems in Chitwan are those between Jana Kalyan "Kha' and Amrit Kulo.

Amrit Kulo's water source used to be the Kanteswori stream. It served 25 hectares of land in Kathar VDC Ward number 7. Farmers of ward number 5 in 1983 proposed to farmers in Ward number 7 to jointly construct a canal that would tap water from the Rapti River. Ward 7's cooperation was necessary because canals had to traverse their land before it could reach Ward 5. Farmers from these two Wards reached an agreement where both would jointly construct the main canal, ward 7 would grant passage by allowing ward 5 to use its existing infrastructure to transport water, and three parts of the water from the Rapti would go to Ward 5 and two parts to Ward 7. This canal named Janakalyan "Kha" was constructed in 1983. With its share of the water Amrit kulo was able to irrigate an additional 50 hectares of land raising their total irrigated area to 75 hectares.

Conditions of Relative Water Scarcity

If resource conditions are poor and there are not too many suitable sites to locate intakes then conflicts can arise not only between systems but also within a system. In some cases systems are able to resolve these conflicts while in other cases these conflicts can render the system virtually useless. An example of an intersystem conflict that was ultimately resolved is that of Pumpa Kulo (PK) and Kyampa Kulo (KK). Another example of a system that has failed to function due to the inability of users to resolve their internal conflicts is that of Bahireni-Pakhadibas Kulo (BPK). All of these three systems draw water from the N-S flowing Pumpa River.

Pumpa is a seasonal river that flows through changing terrain from hills to plains. During the dry season the flow in the river course is drastically reduced and the lower reaches dry out completely. Pumpa Kulo is upstream from Kyampa Kulo but their intakes are less than 300 meters from each other. The characteristics of both these systems are similar in terms of households and area served. Pumpa has a smaller service area than Kyampa (70 vs. 100 hectares) but serves more households (140 vs. 120 hh). Both of these systems have exerted tremendous efforts to construct their systems and their infrastructures are in top condition suggesting very high levels of cooperation within the system. However, the two systems have been involved in extensive physical and legal battles over water rights. What sparked the battle was the construction of a semi-permanent structure by Pumpa at its intake (see Shukla et al, 1996 for details). Kyampa's claim was that this construction drastically reduced their water shares. After years of conflicts an agreement has been reached which requires Pumpa to release sufficient water during winter to irrigate Kyampa's wheat crops[19]. Relative water scarcity is the source of conflict between these systems; however, they have been able to resolve their conflicts.

The intake of Baireni–Pakhadibas Kulo is located about 2 Km downstream from the intake of Kyampa Kulo. Naturally, less water is available in the river where its intake is located. Further, scouring of the river bed has lowered its elevation at the intake. Since the differences in elevation between intake and canals are becoming smaller this is reducing the natural flow of water into the canal. During the dry season when water volumes in the river

[19] Water stressed systems grow two crops, rice in the summer and wheat in the winter.

are low flow in the canals is reduced to a trickle. Relocating the intake to higher elevations is possible but requires serious investments in time and labor. Also, a significant length of the main canal passes through difficult mountain terrain prone to landslides. Given these conditions user groups are facing difficulties in operating the system. Serious conflicts have arisen among the Tharus and the Tamangs, the two major ethnic groups sharing this system, on labor contribution and water sharing issues. This has led to a decline in the condition of the infrastructure and the system in average is able to access water only for two months in a year.

Conditions That Enhance Self-Organization

Attributes of a resource that are considered important for self-organization are chances of feasible improvement, predictability of resource units and moderate size boundaries (Ostrom, 1999a). Also, unless modest levels of scarcity are apparent to users little efforts will be exerted to organize. Scholars also agree that appropriators who are dependent on a resource, intend to use their resource over a long period of time, have achieved certain levels of trust, and possess some level of autonomy to make their own rules are most likely to organize. Many of the aforementioned variables are in turn influenced by the larger political regime in which users are embedded. Whether users are actually able to organize, however, depends on the benefits and costs of changing institutional rules as perceived by those who can change them.

From the examples presented in the previous section we note that group efforts required to self-organize for irrigation are not trivial. Farmers under varying resource conditions have to define command areas, negotiate canal alignments, construct and maintain infrastructure, and coordinate efforts to design institutions that all agree to abide by. Despite the costs involved there are also benefits to be realized from cooperation. Year-around irrigation not only ensures higher crop yields but also increased cropping intensities. The ability to produce two rice crops annually instead of one is strong motivation for farmers to cooperate. Since the benefits of organizing are valued and commonly understood most user groups are able to create and sustain agreements to avoid serious problems of appropriation and provision. Under certain conditions we also see that groups can fail. For the most part, however, FMIS in Chitwan are able to overcome the basic cooperation dilemma.

Each successful self-governed common-pool resource system copes with its own settings by designing institutions that are most relevant to its own conditions. The particular rules that successful systems use may vary substantially from one another but there are common principles underlying their success. Ostrom (1990) calls them the design principles and has identified them to be a) presence of boundary rules, b) congruence, c) ability to monitor and sanction, d) right to modify rules, e) minimal recognition of rights to organize and f) mechanisms for conflict resolution. Most of these design principles can be observed in the farmer managed irrigation systems of Chitwan.

Users maintain written records and know exactly which households have the rights to withdraw resource units and which don't; there are clear commonly understood rules defining who can appropriate how much resource units and when; all are aware of what constitutes an infraction; a simple, effective and low cost monitoring[20] mechanism is in place; rule infractions attract graduated sanctions; WUAs have the power to change operational rules via the general assembly; WUAs are registered with department of irrigation and have legal standing; and informal conflict resolution mechanisms exist to resolve potential problems.

There are conditions that are conducive to self-organization and there are also conditions that can threaten the abilities of communities to manage their institutions. Ostrom (2005) cites the inability to cope with rapid exogenous changes as one of the factors that can threaten the robust governance of common-pool resources. Example of an exogenous shock that led to the breakdown of a system in Chitwan is that of Jyamire Kulo, a system on the Kair Rirver. Incessant floods washed away its intakes and flooded not only its farmlands but also those of neighboring systems. There was tremendous pressure on Jyamire Kulo to close its intake. A permanent gabion wall over hundred meters in length had to be constructed to contain the floods. Since Jyamire Kulo was a small irrigation system (55 hectares, 100 households) it was unable to generate sufficient resources to develop a diversion structure at an alternate site. Farmers now rely on the drainage waters of neighboring systems and some on private pumps fro their water needs. A well-functioning system instantly went out of commission due to its inability to cope with an exogenous shock. Such shocks can also be induced by rapid out-migration or in-migration from or into an area. Out migration can change the economic viability of a regime due to loss of those who contributed resources. In-migration can bring in new participants who do not trust and others and share extant social norms that have been established over a long period of time (Ostrom, 2005). Since collective action is based on mutual trust and reciprocity self-organized resource regimes can quickly disintegrate if population changes occur rapidly. Threats to self-organized small scale resource governance systems can also come from transmission failures from one generation to the next of the operational principles, corruption and opportunistic behavior, lack of large-scale institutional structures to support governance at the local level; and easy access to external funds (Ostrom, 2005).

FMIS face a variety of challenges. Under some set of conditions they are able to perform well and not so well in other sets of conditions. There are certain attributes that are conducive to self-organization and others that are not. They are also continuously subject to external threats some of which they are able to cope with and others that can quickly unravel long established systems. Particular examples associated with each of the above scenarios can be observed across the FMIS of Chitwan. However, in general, most perform pretty well given their particular conditions. They have effective water users' organizations with well-defined rules for water allocation, distribution, resource mobilization, and conflict resolution; they are low cost and based on local resources; and leaders of these systems are accountable to the users. Their technical deficiencies are well compensated by the managerial inputs. FMIS can be suitable vehicles for improving agricultural performance. Policies to improve irrigation performance have to be geared towards supporting these self-organized local resource management systems.

[20] In irrigation systems the cost of monitoring is relatively low. The irrigator who is about to complete his turn would like to extend his time, but the next irrigator in line is waiting for him to finish his job and would like to start early. The presence of one deters the other and additional resources do not have to be invested to monitor, one is simply waiting his turn.

POLICIES TO IMPROVE IRRIGATION PERFORMANCE

Emphasize Institution Building

Cooperation among villagers cannot be assumed. Even in instances where cooperation could have benefited all parties, there are examples from Chitwan of sophisticated agency-managed irrigation infrastructure falling in disrepair due to collective inaction in assuming responsibilities for system operation and maintenance. There are many dimensions to the basis for cooperation among individuals. Individual common-pool resource users are likely to contribute and cooperate only if they perceive that they will be able to reap the long-term benefits of engaging in collective action. They are also more likely to cooperate if they are aware of their interdependence and see mutual benefits resulting from working together. The presence of a set of credible, commonly understood, well-enforced and agreed-upon rules further helps in generating a positive incentive system for villagers to engage in collective action. Without creating the right environment, bureaucracies cannot assume that cooperation among resource users will develop naturally once an irrigation system has been handed over to the users.

The relationships between Nepali government officials, who are charged with oversight of natural resource systems, and resource users are generally based on the dominance-dependence relationship. Villagers are discouraged or disallowed from taking initiatives. The villager, therefore, sees no incentive in taking responsibility and assumes that it is the government's role to take responsibility for the operation and maintenance of the resource system. Given the non-incentives for villagers to participate, system performance hinges on the capabilities of the government officials. With inadequate resources, weak incentives to perform, and inadequate understanding of resource systems, these officials very often fail to perform. It, therefore, comes as no surprise to see agency-managed irrigation systems turning dysfunctional. Common-pool resource systems are co-production processes that perform best when both the oversight agencies and resource users cooperate in making the system work. Non-cooperation by either party results in poor performance.

Developing sustainable common-pool resource systems involves not only the application of technical skills but institutional design skills as well. Failures in most instances occur not because of deficiencies in technical skills but due to lack of knowledge in designing institutions (Ostrom, 1992). Since the most important consideration in institutional design is the process of developing a set of rules that participants in a process understand, agree upon, and are willing to follow, valuable insights can be gained by understanding them and their interrelationships. Agencies charged with oversight responsibilities need to recognize this.

Recognize Local Institutions

Policy actions that aim at facilitating the development of local institutions might have greater chances of success if existing local institutions are recognized and encouraged. Institutions are built on common understandings that take years to build (Ostrom, 1992). If such an understanding already exists in a local community, this is a source of great strength. Institutional development is a slow process based on the principles of trial and error. One cannot expect new institutions to take root merely by introducing them, that too, without the support of the community who are affected by them.

The Department of Irrigation has frequently imposed their institutional designs and organization structures on irrigation communities. Imposing these structures adversely affect the functioning of local organizations if they exist. When legitimacy of local institutions is challenged, farmers' faiths in local institutions vanish quickly. When agencies intervene to develop irrigation infrastructure in potential areas, they need to recognize the presence of existing systems.

Officials often see local organizations merely as arrangements through which to obtain a community's contributions and cooperation. Very little attention is paid either to encourage or develop the governing function of these organizations. Participation is thus frequently equated to getting the villagers to fit their efforts in the operation and management plan suggested by the officials. Policy actions, therefore, need to be strongly linked with an institutional environment where villagers are provided positive incentives to participate in crafting rules and engage in productive working relationships. Farmers have to be recognized as being intelligent with capabilities to make informed decisions and engage in collective action.

Engage Local Resource Users

Farmers are very knowledgeable about stream flows, crop preferences, stability of land, and a host of other time and space information. Such types of information are extremely valuable in operating irrigation systems under considerable amounts of uncertainty. The weather, topography, and changing needs of appropriators introduce uncertainties in assessing the volume of resource units that will be available to an irrigation system. During monsoons, the intakes and embankments are regularly breached requiring emergency action. Discharge from the rivers during winters also decreases drastically, requiring major adjustments in the appropriation rules. Unless users are able to quickly adapt to changing conditions, system operation can drastically suffer. A quick response is not possible, however, without user participation and cooperation. If local knowledge and participation can be incorporated into designing rules governing resource use, then it is more likely the systems will function successfully. Without a clear understanding of the local time and space information that users possess, designing rules to regulate forest resource use may not, again, be effective.

Efforts at helping communities to develop institutions, therefore, have to be directed towards enhancing their capabilities and willingness to relate to and work with one another rather than handing down rules or organizations to govern resources. Institutions, no matter how well designed they are in the beginning, will subsequently require adjustments to changing conditions. Unless these changes can be incorporated, institutions quickly become ineffective. It is, therefore, important that resource users who are affected by the operational rules are permitted to participate in modifying the operational rules. Since the lifestyles of resource users are closely linked to their resource systems, they are the ones who are most knowledgeable about the resource conditions. Unless they are involved resource management can be expected to be both ineffective and inefficient.

Secure Legal Standing

Historically, farmer-managed irrigation systems (FMIS) were never recognized as a legal entity. Not only did they not have legal standing but even their contribution towards irrigated agriculture was not recognized by the Irrigation Department despite their significant contributions (even today, nearly 75% of irrigated agriculture in Nepal is a result of FMIS). Developing irrigation infrastructure for the Department meant the construction of medium and large-scale systems,[21] especially in the Terai. Planning, construction, implementation, operation and management, and maintenance were all considered to be responsibilities of the Irrigation Department. The beneficiaries (resource users) did not have a role to play in any of these processes. In more recent times, however, with the adoption of the irrigation policy of 1992, provisions have been made for users' participation in the agency-led irrigation development programs. The Water Resources Act of 1992 also, for the first time, acknowledged the legal rights of duly registered water users associations with their own *bidhans* (charters). This is a significant step forward in ensuring secure property rights.

The enactment of key legislations does not instantly alter the power relationships between the bureaucracy and the users nor does it ensure ready cooperation by the users (Seymour and Rutherford, 1990). Regardless of legislations, National government and its agencies quite often fail to translate their policies into action. This inability, or rather the unwillingness, of the agencies to recognize diverse local rules governing rights and responsibilities is often a major impediment to successful self-organization. Legislations alone may not change the situation overnight, but it does provide a legal base and legitimacy to user groups to assert their rights.

Practice Nuanced Interventions

It sounds counterintuitive to assert that irrigation system efficiencies may actually decline if temporary irrigation structures are replaced by permanent ones. However, Lam's (1998) results from the study of Nepali irrigation systems point in that direction. He finds that provision of permanent headworks is not a sufficient condition to improve irrigation performance, implying that technological fixes alone may not be the solution to improve system efficiencies. The amount of labor required for operation and management activities are significantly reduced by permanent structures, therefore, labor contribution by tail-end farmers becomes unimportant to farmers at the head end. Negative incentives are thus generated for headenders to ignore the demands of the tailenders, resulting in low levels of cooperation and hence lower productivity. An important policy implication is that there must be as much emphasis on developing social capital as there is on developing physical capital when undertaking projects to assist irrigation systems. Care needs to be taken to ensure that assistance does not negatively affect cooperation.

---

[21] A command area of approximately 500-2,000 hectares is defined as a medium-scale irrigation system. Anything above 2,000 hectares is considered large scale.

CONCLUSION

Irrigation systems face a variety of challenges. The terrain can be difficult, rivers can be unruly, group members may belong to diverse cultural backgrounds, group sizes can vary, asset endowments may differ, and interests may differ within groups. Given these constraints, an irrigation system has to be able to solve the fundamental problems of provisioning and appropriation associated with common pool resources. Intakes and canals have to be constructed and maintained regularly, and working rules have to be crafted to reflect appropriation rights and responsibilities. Such activities, which consume lots of energy and require the mobilization of significant resources, might be undertaken more effectively by self-governed groups than by centralized government agencies.

The arguments for government interventions are often based on the premises that flimsy infrastructures used by farmers result in waste, group differences within a community prevent farmers from self-organizing, increasing group sizes and command areas make it more difficult for farmers to reach effective agreements among themselves, and larger integrated systems result in economies of scale. Empirical results from the field, however, suggest otherwise. Despite considerable group heterogeneity, farmers are able to organize; even with flimsy infrastructure, they are able to outperform AMIS with superior infrastructure; and they are able to reach agreements even when group size or command area is large. These results underscore Ostrom's (2002, 2005) observation that there is a strong institutional aspect to irrigation systems, and focusing only on improving physical capital may not result in improved irrigation performance.

Although FMIS potential may be substantial, not every FMIS is successful. Some resource settings tend to be more conducive to self-organization than others. Systems with difficult topography – N-S systems – face far more organizational challenges than systems with favorable topography. However, the abilities of groups to craft rules and their willingness to monitor and enforce them can, to a great extent, overcome the problems associated with initial resource endowments. The lack of leadership abilities or prior organizational history, in fact, can turn out to be more detrimental to self-organization and irrigation performance than poor initial resource endowments, ethnic differences, or even the presence of permanent irrigation infrastructure. Understanding how different variables interact in different settings can help in designing policies that can strengthen institutional and governance capabilities of FMIS.

There are many dimensions to the basis for cooperation among individuals. Individual common-pool resource users are likely to contribute and cooperate only if they perceive that they will be able to reap the long-term benefits of engaging in collective action. They are also more likely to cooperate if they are aware of their interdependence and see mutual benefits resulting from working together. The presence of a set of credible, commonly understood, well-enforced, and agreed-upon rules further helps in generating a positive incentive system for villagers to engage in collective action. Without creating the right environment, bureaucracies cannot assume that cooperation among resource users will develop naturally once an irrigation system has been handed over to them. Creating the right environment requires bureaucracy to emphasize institution building, engage local resource users in all aspects of irrigation development, and ensure their legal standing. Common pool resource systems are coproduction processes that perform best when both the oversight agencies and resource users cooperate in making the system work.

Farmers in Chitwan have been able to overcome collective action problems and are fairly successful at managing water resources in their unique settings. This implies that, even though it is difficult, it is possible for resource users with a supportive political system to locally overcome what are assumed to be severe collective-action problems. If external assistance is geared toward supporting the farmers' efforts to develop their own institutions, this could result in enhanced water security and improved irrigation performance.

REFERENCES

ADB. (2001). Technical Assistance to the Kingdom of Nepal for Preparing Community Managed Irrigation Sector Project in Central and Eastern Basins. TAR NEP:33209. Manila: ADB.

Angwood, C., Chancellor, F., Hasnip, N., Morrison, J., and Smith, L. (2002). Contribution of Irrigation to Sustaining Rural Livelihoods: Nepal Case Study. DFID. Wallingford: HR Wallingford.

Ascher, W., and Healy, R. (1990). Natural resource policymaking in developing countries. Durham, N.C.: Duke University Press.

Barker, R., and Molle, F. (2004). Evolution of Irrigation in South and Southeast Asia. Comprehensive Assessment Research Report no. 5, IWMI, Colombo.

Bromley, D. (1982). Improving irrigated agriculture: Institutional reform and the small farmer . Staff working paper no. 531, World Bank, Washington, D.C.

FAO. (1999). Aquastat Nepal. FAO's information system on water and agriculture. (Land and water development division, Rome,) Retrieved 5 10, 2007, from Food and Agriculture Organization of the United Nations: http://www.fao.org/ag/agl/aglw/aquastat/ countries/ nepal/index.stm.

Gautam, A. (2002). Forest Land Use Dynamics and Community-Based Institutions in a Mountain Watershed in Nepal: Implications for Forest Governance and Management. Ph.D. Dissertation . Bangkok, Thailand: Asian Institute of Technology.

Hilton, R. (2002). Institutional Incentives for Resource Mobilization in Farmer-Managed and Agency-Managed Irrigation Systems. In G. Shivakoti, and E. Ostrom (Eds.), Improving Irrigation Governance and Management in Nepal. Oakland, CA: ICS.

ICID. (2000). Sector Vision: Water for food and rural development - country position paper on Nepal. Retrieved 11 2007, from International Comission on Irrigation and Drainage: http://www.icid.org/v_nepal.pdf.

Jayawardene, J. (1986). The training of Mahaweli Turnout Group leaders. In Participatory management in Sri Lanka's irrigation schemes., International Irrigation Management Institute, Colombo, Sri Lanka.

Lam, W. F. (1998). Governing Irrigation Systems in Nepal: Institutions, Infrastructure, and Collective Action. Oakland, CA: ICS.

Levine, G. (1980). The relationship of design, operation, and management. In W. E. Coward (Ed.), Irrigation and agriculture development in Asia: Perspectives from the social sciences. Ithaca, N.Y.: Cornell University Press.

Masako, F., Hayami, Y., and Kikuchi, M. (2005). The conditions of collective action for local commons management: the case of irrigation in the Philippines. *Agricultural Economics* , 33 (2), 179-189.

MOF. (2006). Economic Survey. Ministry of Finance. Kathmandu: Government of Nepal.

NPC. (1994). Irrigation Development in Retrospect: Search for a breakthrough. Kathmandu: National Planning Commission.

Ostrom, E. (1999a). Self-Governance and Forest Resources . Jakarta, Indonesia: Center for International Forestry Research.

Ostrom, E. (1999). Context and Collective Action: Four Interactive Building Blocks For a Family of Explanatory Theories. Bloomington, IN: Indiana University.

Ostrom, E. (1992). Crafting Institutions for Self-Governing Irrigation Systems. San Francisco, CA: ICS.

Ostrom, E. (1990). Governing the Commons: The Evolution of Institutions for Collective Action. New York, NY: Cambridge University Press.

Ostrom, E. (2001). Reformulating the Commons. In J. Burger, E. Ostrom, R. Norgaard, D. Policansky, and B. Goldstein (Eds.), Protecting the Commons: A Framework for Resource Management in the Americas. Washington, D.C.: Island Press.

Ostrom, E. (2002). The Challenge of Underperformance. In G. Shivakoti, and E. Ostrom (Eds.), Improving Irrigation Governance and Management in Nepal. Oakland, CA: ICS.

Ostrom, E. (2005). Understanding Institutional Diversity. Princeton, NJ: Princeton University Press.

Ostrom, E., and Gardner, R. (1993). Coping with Asymmetries in the Commons: Self-Governing Irrigation Systems Can Work. *Journal of Economic Perspectives*, 7 (4), 93-112.

Poudel, R., Pandit, K., Adhikari, K., Shakya, S., Yadav, D., and Joshi, N. (1994). Inventory and Need Assessment of Irrigation Systems in North-East Tanahau (Volume-I). A report prepared for International Irrigation Management INstitute (IIMI) . Rampur, Chitwan, Nepal.

Pradhan, P. (1989). Patterns of Irrigation Organization in Nepal. A comparative Study of 21 Farmer Managed Irrigation Systems. Country paper No. 1 . Colombo, Sri Lanka: IIMI.

Regmi, A. (2007). The Role of Group Heterogeneity in Collective Action. A Look at the Intertie between Irrigation and Forests. Case Studies from Chitwan, Nepal. Ph.D. Dissertation . Bloomington, IN: Indiana University.

Regmi, M. C. (1978). Land Tenure and Taxation in Nepal. Kathmandu, Nepal: Ratna Pustak Bhandar.

Seymour, J. F., and Rutherford, D. (1990). Contractual agreements in Asian Social Forestry Programs. First Annual Meeting of the International Association for the study of Common Property, September 27-30. Durham, NC.

Shah, S. G., and Singh, G. (2001). Irrigation Development in Nepal Investment, Efficiency and Institution . Research Report Series, Series No. 47 . Kathmandu, Nepal: Winrock International.

Shangraula, B. (2007, February 5). Water Supply dips with Daily Power Cuts. Kathmandu Post . Kathmandu, Nepal.

Shivakoti, G., and Ostrom, E. (2002). Improving Irrigation Governance and Management in Nepal. Oakland, CA: ICS.

Shukla, A., Gajurel, K., Shivakoti, G., Poudel, R., Pandit, K., Adhikari, K., et al. (1993). Irrigation Resource Inventory of East Chitwan. Institute of Agriculture and Animal Science, Irrigation Management Systems Study Group, Rampur, Chitwan, Nepal.

Somanathan, E., Prabhakar, R., and Mehta, B. (2002). Collective Action for Forest Conservation: Does Heterogeneity Matter? Delhi, India: Indian Statistical Institute.

Tang, S. Y. (1992). Institutions and Collective Action: Self-Governance in Irrigation . San Francisco, CA: ICS.

Ternstrom, I. (2002). The Management of Common-Pool Resources. Theoretical Essays and Empirical Evidence. Stockholm, Sweden: Stockholm School of Economics. EFI, The Economic Research Institute.

UNDP. (2006). Human Development Report - Beyond scarcity: Power, poverty and the global water crisis. United Nations Development Program, New York, NY.

Water Aid Nepal. (2005). Water Laws in Nepal: Laws Relating to Drinking Water, Sanitation, Irrigation, Hydropower and Water Pollution. Lalitpur, Nepal: Water Aid Nepal.

In: Nepal in the 21st Century
Editor: Surendra R. Devkota, pp. 225-239
ISBN 978-1-60741-348-6

Chapter 10

FARMER MANAGED IRRIGATION SYSTEMS IN NEPAL: PEOPLE-CENTERED GOVERNANCE ALTERNATIVE

Upendra Guatam and Ganesh Khaniya
FMIS Promotion Trust, Nepal

ABSTRACT

Farmer managed irrigation units are an indigenous system. A number of these systems have been in operation since the beginning of the millennium. They manage irrigation water in more than two third of area in the country; significantly contribute to the country's food security; and act as a mainstay of farmers' livelihood. Member farmers of the farmer managed irrigation systems (FMIS) organization themselves construct, maintain, manage and rehabilitate their irrigation system. They value water as a community property. As such, equitable access to and contribution in system management by each member farmer provide sustenance to the FMIS. Equity in irrigation resource generation and distribution bolsters the FMIS's self-governance capability that is reflected in their fundamental organizational features of non-partisanship and autonomy in decision making. For their role in the country's political economy in general and irrigated agricultural production in particular, FMIS are national socio-economic heritage of Nepal. In the first decade of the 21st century when political society in Nepal has started talking about newly "restructured" and "reconstructed" Nepal, what it is essentially rediscovering are the values and fundamentals of the nation's own FMIS.

INTRODUCTION

Nepal's irrigated farming system is predominantly occupied by Farmer Managed Irrigation Systems (FMIS). In FMIS, since the dawn of the millennium, farmers are responsible for all management activities encompassing water acquisition from the source to delivery to the plant in the field [Pradhan, 1989] and shoulder themselves the tasks of canal operation and maintenance, harmonious distribution of irrigation water, conflict resolution, and decision making. According to information documented, FMIS are found in an altitude of 32 to 2500 m above the mean sea level [Devkota, 2001]. They are spread over all the ecological zones of Nepal-mountain, hill, and Tarai (flat land). They manage 70 percent of the country's irrigated area of 1.1 million hectares [Pradhan and Gautam, 2004] that constitute about 1700 farmer managed irrigation units in the Tarai and over 15,000 systems in the hills of Nepal ranging from less than 10 ha to 15,000 ha. There are numerous FMIS with an irrigation area ranging from 3,000 to 5,000 ha and they are not merely small irrigation systems [Ibid, 1989]. FMIS inventory of 7 districts, namely, Kathmandu, Bhaktapur, Dolakha, Kanchanpur, Okhaldhunga, Mugu and Bajura indicates that the average number of FMIS in districts are 414 [FMIS Promotion Trust, 2004]. These FMIS occupy special place in the national political economy in general and irrigated agriculture in particular. They are the main source of livelihood of the local farmers who constitute more than four fifth of the country's 25 million population. All FMIS taken together significantly contribute to equity in access to water, resource mobilization, ecological conservation and food security.

FMIS have been adopting their own specific management modes while diverting water from the source to the field through the dug canals, and consequently are location-specific. Within the same ecological zone too, the management patterns substantially vary from one system to another. Community and cultural practices in conjunction with local ecological management approaches play a significant role in these variations. Indigenously in operation since ancient time, they can be described as the national socio-economic heritage of the country. Their self-governing organizational autonomy at the local level is perhaps only consistent with the current advocacy of the new political forces in Nepal for the restructuring and reconstruction of the state in the 21st century (Attachment -1].

EVOLUTION OF FMIS

Community efforts in water resource management in Nepal have a long history. Customary norms have valued water as community resource with innate rights and community's self-governance structures for the management and utilization of these resources by local water users. In the olden days, the state supported the organizational autonomy of the local community in the management of the water by basically assuming a role of a promoter.

Irrigation water has served as both the spiritual and material foundations of the communities' civilization. The rich cultural tradition, arts, artifacts and architecture of Kathmandu valley are attributed for the network of irrigation systems supporting intensive agriculture activities. In the past, spiritual mission, royalty and religious trust [known as *Guthi*] coupled with community initiative for irrigated agriculture were the main driving forces in promoting FMIS. The state encouraged trusts to help develop FMIS. These trusts allocated a portion of their income out of religious performance to assist irrigated agricultural activities on which livelihood of the trust's members was also dependent.

It was rather fascinating to note that even in the ancient city planning like in the layout of Handigaun, the ancient capital of Nepal, irrigated agriculture as identified with the rural areas was incorporated in the city landscape in the manner that the available land use was maximized by appropriate zoning of land for agricultural use, human settlement, market place, water conservation ponds, pasture lands and religious sites [Tiwari, 2002].

Before 464 AD, King Shankar Dev constructed Shankhu *Rajkulo* (royal canal) tapping water from Sali Nadi (River) for the purpose of making drinking water and irrigation facilities available to the people of the Sankhu town [Pun, 2001]. During Lichchavi Period [78 to 880 AD], the indigenous water engineers developed the system of integrated water utilization by combining stone water conduit along with the ponds and canals. In the first half of the fifth century, a grave water crisis was reportedly occurred in the capital city in Kathmandu valley, popularly known as Nepal *Khaldo* (valley). Landslides caused the crisis. To resolve this crisis, the Lichchvi King commissioned a large water supply project, taking advantage of the accidentally created ponds as well as of the existing natural channels of water. This system was later called the *Rajkulo* [Tiwari, 2002].

Argeli Jethi *kulo* built around 1543-47 AD in Palpa district in western Nepal represents the example of religious *Guthi*-(religious trust) supported irrigation system [Pradhan, 2002]. As per the legend, this system was developed during the rule of King Mani Mukunda Sen I of Palpa. This irrigation system was built to cultivate rice to generate revenue to meet the worship expenses of God Rishikeshav Narayan, which is located on the bank of Kali Gandaki at Ridhi, Palpa district.

During King Baliraj of Kalyan dynasty (1400 AD), farmers were supported to build canals in Jumla district in Nepal, which is a remote district located about 2500 meters above the sea level [Devkota, 2002]. Besides the state support for the irrigation canal construction, the local communities have taken initiative in constructing irrigation channels for paddy cultivation. Along the banks of Tila and Sinja rivers, one can observe many community initiated irrigation systems. They are maintained and managed by the members farmers themselves.

State policies and practices were historically conducive to strengthen community roles in water resource management. It provided top priority to water and food security of the people under the active initiative of the local community. In the 17th century, the edict of King Ram Shah of Gorkha mandated that water resources related conflicts to be settled at the community level itself. Though such mediation had to take into account local power structures, it allowed community initiatives and governance structures to evolve. Hence, the indigenous tradition of FMIS got deeply rooted in the Nepali populace over the period of time. In the directive of King Jitamitra Malla (circa 1682 AD), a *Rajkulo* was constructed from Mahadev Danda, some 6 km far from Bhaktapur city collecting water from Mahadev Khola at Nagarkot to Sundhara of Thunthu Palace at Durbar Square in the heart of Bhaktapur city through this canal. In addition to the religious purpose of this water, it was used for irrigation, water mill operation, drinking water for the city populace as well as for fish farming. He had instituted *Guthi* and formulated rules for the maintenance of these systems as evident in a stone inscription [Khaniya, 2004; and Wright, 2000].

Under the reign of General Bhimsen Thapa, the first Prime Minister of modern Nepal, a canal was dug out from the Pokhari Tal (lake) of Raniban of Kirtipur, 20 kilometers from the heart of Kathmandu in 1829 AD. Farmer representatives or persons designated for the purpose could collect water tax for the use of water. The rate was fixed by the government. This shows that a system of water tax collection as service charge was in practice in those days too. The lake was allowed to have other functions as well. Fishery was promoted in these three lakes to generate income for the state [Nepali, 1965].

In the days of Rana regime (1846-95), they did not invest except in a few systems (Chandra Nahar and Judha Nahar in cental and eastern Nepal Tarai) for irrigation development. They allowed the private parties and communities take initiative for irrigation channel construction. Once the land got irrigation facility, the status of the land would be changed and more revenue was generated without government investment.

After 1951, however, the role of the state expanded and attempts were made to extend the state control over the community and FMIS.

FMIS in Policies and Plans

Despite the immense contribution of FMIS in Nepal's economy, they remained fully unnoticed and unrecognized till 1980. Only in 1981, the government acknowledged them and began to consider ways to enhance and expand them [WECS, 1981 as quoted in Pradhan, 1989].

Water Resources Act [WECS, 1992] envisions the ownership of the water resources available throughout the country to be vested in the state. Despite the state ownership of the water, the Act is affirmative towards the customary water rights, and has made specific provisions to recognize such rights. This Act maintains Water User Association (WUA) in irrigated areas as a corporate body with succession in perpetuity [Upadhyay, 2008].

The Irrigation Policy [DOI, 2003] highlights the importance of year round irrigation facilities by optimum utilization of existing physical infrastructures and institutional arrangements. The policy stipulates at least 33% of women participation in the WUA and asks to equally include representatives from Dalits, indigenous, oppressed and disadvantaged communities. If demand is made for the repair, renovation and rehabilitation of indigenous irrigation systems operated by farmers themselves or the systems built and operated by them by organizing themselves in WUA, the policy asks the public irrigation agency to implement the work with people's participation.

The National Water Plan [WECS, 2005] recognizes importance of FMIS well. It states, "The total irrigated land was 0.764 million ha. whereas the net irrigated area for which infrastructure available was estimated at 1.121 million ha. in 2002. Out of this, only about 0.50 million ha. of land had round-the year irrigation facilities". The plan has set the target of providing year-round-irrigation to 49%, 64% and 67% by 2007, 2017 and 2027 respectively. The plan emphasizes rehabilitation of FMIS and on-farm water management, giving priority to hill irrigation development. In addition, its action program also includes the expansion of micro-irrigation technologies for hill and mountain farmers. Acknowledging the long history of FMIS in Nepal, this plan has laid focus on the rehabilitation of FMIS as one of its key strategies to boost agricultural production.

Realizing that it has been possible to extend irrigation facility to only 66 percent land [1168144 hectares], the *Interim National Plan*, 2007 [http://ekh.unep.org] targets to extend the irrigation coverage to 1263824 ha during its three years' period. Even this post-Communist Party Nepal-Maoist (CPN-M) insurgency plan fails to specifically recognize FMIS and their contribution in the national economy. Rather this plan seems to confuse FMIS for a size it irrigates, that is, small and medium irrigation system.

CHALLENGES IN THE 21ST CENTURY'S CONTEXT

Population growth, urbanization and industrialization, and need for ecological conservation have increased demand for water. Externally induced values such as local partisan political governance and privatization increased competition and conflict for water. These new dimensions of changes have affected FMIS. They have wrought new challenges to them in the development and management of irrigation water. Integrated Water Resources Management (IWRM) concept, which claims to address the changes "in an equitable manner without compromising the sustainability of vital ecosystem" [GWP 2001], as a matter of historical fact, has been operationally practiced by FMIS. The major challenges in the realm of Nepal's FMIS pertaining to 21st century can be broadly discussed under the following issues.

Resource Availability

The demand for water for non-agricultural uses is growing in Nepal. The demands especially for domestic and industrial uses and for conservation of natural environment are on rise. It is certain that public policy will increasingly be inclined to meet these demands consequently reducing the share of water for the agricultural uses. FMIS need to adapt themselves with a less- water situation. As FMIS will increasingly face competition for water from the non-agricultural sectors, rightful protection of their part of the water share becomes a critical challenge for FMIS to maintain equitable access to water, and ensure water and food security [Pradhan and Gautam, 2002].

In addition, the restriction on the accessibility to forest resources, and rampant depletion of the this resource by sheer commercial and rent-seeking interests has affected maintenance of FMIS. Now farmers find it difficult to maintain their systems in time and with flexibility as they do not have access to river and forest resources [stones, bamboos, logs and woods]. The farmers thus have become more dependent on the external resources. Deterioration in the relationship between larger ecology and irrigated agriculture has become a major risk for FMIS, a risk FMIS only at the local level can not manage. This has led them to new types of challenges in conserving the irrigation systems [Gautam and Rana, 2001].With the excessive harnessing of water sources for competitive and even conflicting uses, there is drastic depletion in the availability of water for irrigation in many FMIS. Thus, it will invite intra-system and inter-system conflict among the water users in the same river basin/sub-basin level.

Communication and Education

Since more than 80% FMIS in Nepal are spread in hilly and mountainous terrain, there is no systematic access to any communication facilities, let alone the effective and two-way modes of communication. Thus, establishing communication among FMIS themselves and between FMIS and external agencies is really a challenging task ahead [Subedi and Gautam, 2005].

FMIS treasure rich indigenous knowledge with local know-how and practices. But their knowledge base about farming and irrigation management are not conserved, refined and progressively utilized by west-oriented centers of higher learning (colleges and universities). The traditionally available water engineers, such as Agris of Palpa, for water works construction and rehabilitation have disappeared. Earlier, their profession was handed down from one generation to another. The university graduates hold mines of theoretical knowledge. But several public assistance programs for FMIS have failed because these university graduates were not properly oriented towards the indigenous wisdom and management practices of FMIS, and they did not know how to build on them [NEC, 2001].

As lack of interest of the young people in FMIS is on the rise who perceive the agriculture endeavor as non-creative, non-enterprising, traditional and less beneficial, the young and energetic youths stay away from their villages in search of greener pastures in the city centers and abroad, FMIS are deprived of the care, service and protection of skillful and educated youths leaving the farm and irrigation systems to old people, women and children who shoulder the tasks of irrigated agricultural management [Gautam et. al. 2002]. This trend has highly been accelerated in the last two decades with the upsurge in both the brain-drain and labor drain from the country, in part, owing to long-prevailed situation of violence and insecurity. Hence, the social capital developed over a period in history is getting eroded because of western education-induced inter-generational difference between the groups of irrigators [Pradhan, 2002].

Multiple Functions

The resulting situation of decreasing water resources and unpredictability in the trend of weather as an impact of climate change has brought new challenges to FMIS which are hitherto involved in single purpose rather than taking up multiple undertakings. A study on "Diversification of Irrigation Systems in Nepal" [FMIS Promotion Trust, 2004] observed that out of 15 FMIS studied, more than 50% of the FMIS are only focused in the irrigated agricultural practices. Only 6 FMIS (40%) have been involved in other activities too. These activities include provision of water storage system for lean period (Khokana, Lalitpur district), running of community mill (Chherlung, FMIS, Palpa district), earning through water sale (Sakhuwa ground water, Rupandehi district), operation of water mill, cooperatives and continuation of environmental protection initiatives (Sardikhola-Puranchaur, Kaski district), operation of grinding mill (Gadkhar, Nuwakot district) etc.

Incompatibility in Laws and Planning

The state has been rendered weakened. It therefore can not enablingly support the autonomy of FMIS. It has been run over by the interests of powerful external market agents and from within by private sector, public sector, non-governmental and multilateral agencies. Consequently, it enacts legislations that are not compatible with the autonomy of FMIS. For example, it has enacted the Local Self-Governance Act 1999, which has empowered the local government bodies (District Development Committees, municipalities and Village

Development Committees) to manage natural resources within their respective jurisdiction. It allows them to impose royalty and taxes on the use of natural resources [Gautam 2002]. In an environment where the objective of government regulation seems more to satisfy the expedient partisan political needs than enhance the capability of indigenous institutions in the overall context of development, FMIS can not expect enabling support from laws such as the Local Self-governance Act "in a compatible manner" [Upadhyay, 1999].

The new Irrigation Regulation 2000 made mandatory to register the FMIS in the District Irrigation Office (DIO) to cause FMIS to accept its control as and when the Office deems so right [Irrigation Regulation, 2000]. This provision goes against the long-standing state policy of non-interference in the autonomous functioning of FMIS. The trend toward centralization of irrigation bureaucracy allows government-control over local community management. The centralized planning approach has resulted in temporary gains in the World Bank and Asian Development Bank funded irrigation management transfer projects and irrigation sector projects. But it has failed to create and protect a sustainable base of irrigation development at the local level. Attempt to accomplish sustainable irrigation development on the basis of centralized planning and associated administration paraphernalia has resulted in destabilizing hitherto minimally functioning FMIS [Development Research Group, 1986], and accelerated eroding their social capital base [Pradhan, 2002].

RESPONSES TO CHALLENGES

Ensuring Water Security

FMIS recognize water security as the most critical function. Food security is contingent upon water security. The FMIS condition of success in ensuring water security is an effect of three inter-dependent elements: equity, conservation and food security.

Equity: FMIS are based on equity [Abernethy, 2000]. They help induce elements of fairness and distributive justice in the not-so-equitable agrarian relations in the country. They share the available amount of water fairly among all parts of irrigation system. For them fair allocation of available water is more significant than adequacy of water. Fairness of FMIS makes their member-farmers willing to sustain them. This enhances legitimacy of FMIS as each one of the member-farmers gets a fair share. If water were not sufficient in one season, each member-farmer of FMIS would share same degree of hardship. Wider participation of the members of the system and equal distribution of stake among head, middle and tail end farmers indicate enforcement of principle of equity in the systems. Application of the principle of equity makes the member-farmers to operationally recognize that they are inter-dependent on one another in terms of cost as well as benefit of the system. However, equity of distribution does not mean equal distribution to everybody. It means distribution according to the system of rules, which everybody can understand. Sometimes, rules allow different groups to receive quite different quantities of water, but the users think it is right because they know the equity rationale behind the rules. For example, in Logain FMIS, it is considered that water lost in the canals is the loss of the farmer irrigation organization and not of the individual member-farmer who happened to be at the lower reaches of the canals. Member-farmers of the FMIS recognize this rule, which takes care of equity in the use of water across the irrigation system [Gautam, 1992].

FMIS serves equity at the national level. They support the largest percentage of small and marginal farmers in the country. Out of the four FMIS studied in mid-western region, Chhinchu FMIS served 87.5 percent, Seltada FMIS 67.86 percent, Siyari FMIS 74.60 percent and Udain Dhakeri Shallow tubewell FMIS 73.81 percent small farmers [CMS, 1997]. This is significant in view of the national average of 76, 69 and 62 percent of the marginal and small farmers who are covered by shallow tubewell, deep tubewell and surface irrigation respectively [Bhandari and Sharma, 2000].

However, FMIS have yet to perform an appropriate assessment of the potential impact of their equity principle on the social relations between upper and lower strata of farmers in the society [Gautam and Subedi 2000].

Conservation: Administration and management of the principle of equity is shaped by FMIS's adaptation to the environment and the needs of the people it serves. It shows the relationship of agro-ecology and infrastructure, physiographic and spatial factors of land, supply of water and crop choice in an agro-ecological conditions [Parajuli, 1999]. Farmers have shown their knowledge and capacity to understand and appreciate this relationship since long. Sir Richard Temple, who visited Kathmandu valley in 1876 AD, wrote:

> "The cultivation of the Nepal (Kathmandu) Valley is blessed with unequalled advantages, and is carried on with utmost industry. In May, we found a waving harvest of wheat awaiting the sickle, and I was told that almost all these lands had had already yielded an equally good rice harvest within the agriculture year, and that many of the fields would yet yield special crops, pepper, vegetables and the like. In short, most of the lands yield two harvests in the year, and some yield even three."

Farmers of the Kathmandu valley could reap the "unequalled advantage" by their knowledge of the climate and seasons, interdependence of the surface and groundwater, inter-linkages between irrigation and water supply infrastructure, and water use and drainage. Cases from Bhaktapur and other parts of Nepal provide intelligent examples of conservation, integrated and multiple acquisition and use of water [East Consult, 1983].

The tenacity of FMIS in conserving and protecting the irrigation system in contemporary times is further offered by Bhutlung FMIS (Box - 1).

Food security: Water security is pre-condition for food security. FMIS have been contributing in the national food security. FMIS produce about 50 percent of all rice grown in the country [Pradhan 1989]. The contribution of FMIS in ensuring food security of the nation is aptly illustrated through the case of Chhattis Mauja (Box-2)

The value of FMIS has much more increased in view of the dismal performance of public irrigation and agricultural sectors [Adhikari and Bharadwaj, 1999]. The government started constructing large scale capital-intensive public irrigation projects in *Terai* to feed the increasing population. But as these projects were more construction-oriented and centrally controlled, they did not have effective water user's participation in the project management, and they were mostly non-responsive to farmer's demand.

Box 1. Conservation through reconstruction

Farmers of Bhutlung village located in Ward No. 3 of Topgachi Village Development Committee in Jhapa district of eastern development region decided to build a new FMIS. They obtained a loan from the Branch Office of Agriculture Development Bank (ADB/N), Damak, Jhapa to build a system, which would serve 171 hectares of land in monsoon and 85 hectares in winter season. ADB/N conducted the preliminary survey and estimation work of construction. In accordance with the recommendation of the preliminary work, construction of the headworks was initiated. Unfortunately, due to flood and landslides the constructed structure was washed away and that investment remained only as a burden of loan to the farmers. As per the 1998 data of the ADB/N, there was NRs. 867,645 outstanding loan on the heads of the farmers which was gradually being repaid on an installment basis.

Despite the bitter experience of the irrigation development, farmers were not discouraged. They went for another loan from the ADB/N to reconstruct the head works with a smaller command area of around 88 hectares. During the second effort, farmers actively participated in the planning, design and construction of the system. They reviewed the design works from conservation point view. They very much emphasized on the drainage of excess water at the water diversion point and regular drainage maintenance. Drainage works have not only helped in reducing siltation and protecting soil quality, but also reliability of the irrigation at the water acquisition level.

Source: Farmer Managed Irrigation Systems Promotion Trust, 1999.

Box 2. FMIS Ensuring Food Security

Chhattis Mauja FMIS with a command area of 3500 ha is located in Rupandehi District of Western Nepal. Paddy, mustard, corn, potatoes and wheat are main crops produced in its command area. 90% farmers of this system have adopted improved seed varieties. On the basis of the average 181 kilograms cereal requirement per person per year in *Terai,* [plain land], it is found that the Chhattis Mauja FMIS, after meeting food needs of its member households, produces as much surplus cereal that fulfills the need of additional 58,343 population.

Source: Gautam et. al., 2001.

Knowledge Building and Reform

Increasing the quality of agricultural labor and modernizing the management of irrigation system were two suggestions coming from the farming community for attracting the young people to get them involved in FMIS. Fortunately, for increasing the quality of agricultural labor and promoting interactive learning process between academic institutions and FMIS, efforts have been under way in a university college in the country. The college has also started reviewing and improving their curriculum to incorporate indigenous knowledge and management practices relating to irrigation management in the country. These efforts are expected to bridge the knowledge and management skill gap between FMIS and the young people on the one hand, and FMIS and university products on the other [NEC, 2001].

Community Resource-Base of Water

FMIS view the incompatible state legislations as the consequence of partisan competition for water. Incompatibility in state legislations is duly corrected if water as a common property is politically recognized. For FMIS water is a common property. Water does not belong to any sectors, private, public or non-governmental. FMIS value of water as community property helps them to specify water rights to the community members. Collective decision of the community becomes the basis for water allocation and utilization. Specified water rights guide to define obligations of the community members both in terms of participation in organizational decision making and resource. Such an extension of FMIS value of water can help manage future mobilization. Common resource-base creates a unifying value for members of the community [Pradhan, 1989]. Even if water is being utilized by multiple stakeholders (agricultural, domestic, industrial or commercial), the allocation and distribution of water can be equitably managed if it is recognized as a common property without having any one's exclusive right to it. If an individual farmer violates the allocation and distribution principle he or she is subject to penalty. The community determines the conditions of the penalty. FMIS's water right based on water as a community resource can be extended to other water use conflicts due to competition and exclusive rights between water users, and builds thereby an equitable water-sharing regime.

Organizational Autonomy

FMIS represent an indigenous autonomous model of self-governance. They exist separately from the non-governmental, local government, public, private and corporate agency-administered water management units in the country. They decide for themselves. They take care of and internally harmonize plural interests that are there in the irrigation system. Naturally, their values of governance go against the monolithic central structure that forces the decision imposed from unknown center [Pradhan, 2003]. Nevertheless, there are cases in history where farmer irrigation organization can be the result of the deliberate effort of the government. In another level, there are also examples where farmer irrigation organization came into existence because of the government's sheer negligence of the system.

Location and cultural specificity of FMIS shape their indigenous governance. They guide design principles of FMIS infrastructure and their operational objectives. These objectives, which are transparent, equity-oriented and flexible, necessarily define irrigation functions in an inter-disciplinary manner, meaning irrigation functions are not only technical and hydraulic but also social and managerial [Parajuli, 2001]. The intensity of task that an irrigation organization performs is sensitive to the environment. Change in one environmental factor, whether physical or socio-economic, influences how tasks are performed by the organization. Accordingly, farmer organizations tailor the methods of water allocation, labor mobilization and water allocation and distribution to the needs of the farmers. In cases where common needs are not fairly expressed in the form of rules because of socio-political factors, FMIS have failed to govern in an equitable manner. In WUA where the election of the officials of the WUA is done on the basis of political planks [Pradhan 2002], and the authority of state is abused to polarize the water users for partisan interest, that WUA has remained plagued with the vice of politicization-fragmented, non-responsive to their member farmers' needs and thoroughly not accountable [Pradhan and Gautam, 2002].

Attachment-1. Portions of CPN-M, CPN-UML and Nepali Congress' Constituent Assembly Manifestos related to the Restructuring of the State

S.N.	Topic	Maoist	United Marxist-Leninist [UML]	Nepali Congress [NC]
1	Federal State System or Federal Democratic Republic [FDR]	Nepal consists of multi-nationality, multi-lingual, multicultural, multi-religious and geographical diversities. Federal restructuration of state shall be borne with autonomous inclusive self-determination of nationalities and regions. The first meeting of CA shall implement the FDR. Executive President shall be elected by CA members CA shall form Interim Government. Transformation of the State to Federal Structure through national and regional Autonomy with right to self-determination. Relief to the poverty line, unemployed, squatters, disabled, senior citizens, conflict-affected, martyr families, and families of the disappeared. Reintegration of PLA and Nepali Army to form a New National Army. Establishment of Truth and Reconciliation Commission and action shall be taken against the perpetrators. Scientific and practical Bases of Federalisms shall be ethnic/caste and regional identity: common language, common geography, common economy, and common psychology. Sovereignty and State power shall rest on the people in its entirety, which shall be represented through their elected representatives. . Democratic transformation of the majority of working people, poor classes, oppressed classes, regions, women and Dalit by ending the current trend of keeping democracy as a mere formality.	The federal structure shall be developed based on ethnic, linguistic, cultural and topographical specialties. The federal states shall be named to display the ethnic, linguistic, cultural and historical identity, a high level constitutional commission shall be formed to decide on it. Each federated state shall follow multiparty democratic system. Guarantee of political rights to nationalities, to their economic, social and cultural development, including ILO convention 169 relating to self-determination. A High Level Constitutional Commission shall be formed to decide the structures of FDR.	Nepal shall be a full democratic, federal republic based on Plurality. The ethnic, linguistic, cultural, religious and regional diversities are the basis of federalism. It shall be formed by transforming the unitary central system into integrated and indivisible FDR. The specialties and characters of populations in Tarai, Hills and Mountains on Madhesi, nationalities, Dalit and other groups shall be taken into account in the FDR. The FDR shall be divided into three layers: Central, Provincial and Local, their rights, duties and responsibilities shall be guaranteed in the new Constitution.

Attachment 1. (Continued)

S.N.	Topic	Maoist	United Marxist-Leninist [UML]	Nepali Congress [NC]
2	Structure of Federal Mechanism	Regional: Seti-Mahakali and Bheri-Karnali States; Ethnicity: Magarat, Tharuwan, Tamuwan, Tamang- Saling, Kirant, Limbuwan, Kochila, Newa and Madhes;Linguistic: Mithila, Bhojpura and Abadh sub-State The State borders shall be demarcated though mutual consensus considering ethnic composition, linguistic frame, economic possibilities, geographical accessibility, etc. Local Autonomous areas shall be created if dense population of other ethnicity/caste reside in an Autonomy. The nationalities registered presently in Mountain region – Byansi, Mountain– lama, Bhote, Sherpa, Thakali, etc., Hill – Baramu, Bhujel, Chepang, Chantel, Dura, Haiyu, Hulmo, Jirel, Lepcha, Sunar, Thanmi , etc. Inner-Madhes– Majhi, Bote, Danuwar, Dusahi, Kumal etc. and Tarai– Dhimal, Jhangar, Kisan, Meche, Munda, Santhal, Koch-Rajbasnhi, etc. shall have Local Autonomies.	Madhesi, nationalities, Muslim and minorities living in Tarai shall have rights to protect their language and culture including just distribution and of resources and autonomy. Equal right to development for the people living in remote places. Political participation and special privileges to people in Karnali and other remote places.	The bases of federal structure shall be territorial integrity, geographical landscape, accessibility, population, natural resources and economic feasibility, interrelationship of provinces, density of linguistic, ethnic and cultural aspects, politico-administrative viability.
3	Governance	The FDR shall be implemented according to the Interim Constitution's third amendment.	An effective mechanism developed against corruption, rule of law and transparency for good governance.	Positive discrimination with social justice shall be adopted to access and participate state mechanism and decision making process. End to immunity and full realization of rule of law, civil rights, security, fundamental rights and justice. Control Corruption shall be to control abuse of authority and power, control corruption and accountable governance.

Source: Conflict Study Center. [2008]. Situation Update 67. Unedited Version. March 28. Kathmandu, Nepal.

CONCLUSION

FMIS self-governance indigenous model of local autonomy can be a comprehensive national institutional alternative for building people-centered Nepal in the 21st century. As a national socio-economic heritage handed down by history, it provides an operational framework based on community initiatives and rights to sustanably, equitably and progressively develop and manage the invaluable water in the best interest of all the strata of irrigators.

REFERENCES

Abernethy, Charles L. [2000]. Management of Water and Irrigation Facilities in Effective Irrigators Organization for Participatory Management. Proceedings of the Workshop organized by DSE-MARD and MAF. Quy Nhon, Vietnam.

Bhandari, Ram Prasad; and Sharma, Khem Raj. [2000]. Sustainability Issue of Irrigation Development. Workshop Proceedings. Kathmandu, Nepal: Research and Technology, Department of Irrigation.

CMS [Consolidated Management Services Nepal [P] Ltd.]. [1997]. Final Report on Social Assessment Study of FMIS to be Supported for Improvement/Modernization of NISP. Kathmandu, Nepal.

Department of Irrigation, 2003. Irrigation Policy. Kathmandu, Nepal: Ministry of Water Resources, His Majesty's Government.

Department of Irrigation, 2000. Irrigation Regulation. Kathmandu, Nepal: Ministry of Water Resources, His Majesty's Government.

Development Research Group [P] Ltd. [1986]. Rapti Rural Development Project: Medium Irrigation Appraisal Study Report. Lalitpur, Nepal.

Devkota, Devi Dutta. [2002]. FMIS in the Highlands of Nepal [in Nepali] [unpublished].

East Consult. [1983]. Socio-*economic Study of Irrigation Alternatives*. Kathmandu, Nepal.

Farmer Managed Irrigation Systems Promotion Trust, [2004]. Project Proposal of FMIS Promotion Trust. Submitted to Ford Foundation, New Delhi Office, India. Unpublished Report. Kathmandu, Nepal: Farmer Managed Irrigation Systems Promotion Trust.

Farmer Managed Irrigation Systems Promotion Trust, [2004]. Diversification of Irrigation Systems in Nepal: A Case Study of 15 FMIS. Unpublished Report. Kathmandu, Nepal: Farmer Managed Irrigation Systems Promotion Trust.

Gautam, Upendra. [1992]. NGO in the Irrigated Agricultural Sector: Review of the Institutional Instrument. In Ujjwal Pradhan [ed.] Role of NGOs in Irrigation Development and Management in Nepal. Kathmandu, Nepal: IIMI-Nepal Field Operations and Udaya-Himalaya Network.

Gautam, Upendra. [2002]. Nepal Farmer Managed Irrigation Systems: The State of Higher Risk [unpublished].

Gautam, Upendra; and Rana, Shrish [eds.]. [2001]. Challenges to Farmer Managed Irrigation Systems. Kathmandu, Nepal: Farmer Managed Irrigation Systems Promotion Trust.

Gautam, Upendra; Shrestha, Ajaya Lall; and Khaniya, Ganesh. [2001]. Report on FMIS Award and Training on the Theme of Resource Mobilization for Operation and Maintenance of Irrigation System. Kathmandu, Nepal: Farmer Managed Irrigation Systems Promotion Trust.

Gautam, Upendra; and Subedi, Rajan. [2000]. Water Resources Development in Nepal: Poverty, Gender and Project Affected Person. In Peter P. Mollinga [ed.] Water for Food and Rural Development: Approach and Initiatives in South Asia,. New Delhi: Sage Publication.

GWP [Global Water Partnership]. [2001]. *Integrated Water Resources* Management.

http://ekh.unep.org/files/Nepal_InterimPlanApproachPaper.pdf visited on 1/18/2008.

Khaniya, Ganesh. [2005]. Traditional Water Management Practices: A Case Study of Bhaktapur City. Kathmandu, Nepal: Jalsrot Vikas Sanstha/Nepal Water Partnership.

NEC [Nepal Engineering College]. [2001]. Activity, and Program Proposal on Re-crafting the Role of Education for FMIS Knowledge Promotion [unpublished].

Nepali, Chittaranjan. [1965]. Shasan byabastha ra Sudhar Karya [administrative system and reform activity]. In General Bhimsen Thapa ra Tatkalin Nepal [General Bhimsen Thapa and then Nepal] [in Nepali]. Kathmandu, Nepal: Ratna Pustak Bhandar.

Parajuli, Umesh. [2001]. Irrigation Technology: Design Principles and Systems Operation. In Upendra Gautam; and Shrish Rana [eds.] Challenges to Farmer Managed Irrigation Systems. Kathmandu, Nepal. Farmer Managed Irrigation Systems Promotion Trust.

Pradhan, Prachanda. [1989]. Patterns of Irrigation Organizations in Nepal: A Comparative Study of 21 Farmer Managed Irrigation Systems. Colombo: International Irrigation Institute.

Pradhan, Prachanda. [2002]. Eroding Social Capital through Incompatible Legal and Institutional Regime: Experiences from Irrigation Systems in Nepal. Bloomington, Indiana: Workshop in Political Theory and Policy Analysis, Indiana University.

Pradhan, Prachanda; and Gautam, Upendra [eds.]. [2002]. Farmer Managed Irrigation Systems in the Changed Context: Proceedings of the International Seminar held on 9-10 September. Kathmandu, Nepal: Farmer Managed Irrigation Systems Promotion Trust.

Pradhan, Prachanda. [2003]. Farmer Managed Irrigation Systems: A Water Governance Mode. In Water Nepal: Journal of Water Resources Development, Vol. 9-10, July 2001-July 2003.

Pun, Shuku. [2001]. Role of Gender in Sali-Nadi [Shankhu *Rajkulo*] Irrigation Management: A Case Study. In Upendra Gautam; and Shrish Rana [Eds.] Challenges to Farmer Managed Irrigation Systems: Proceedings of the International Seminar held on March. Kathmandu, Nepal: Farmer Managed Irrigation Systems Promotion Trust.

Subedi, Rajan; and Gautam, Upendra. [2005]. innovative Mechanism for Effective FMIS Communication. In Prachanda Pradhan, and Upendra Gautam [Eds.] Farmer Managed Irrigation Systems and Governance Alternatives. Proceedings of the third international seminar held on 9-10 September 2004. Kathmandu, Nepal: Farmer Managed Irrigation Systems Promotion Trust.

Tiwari, Sudarshan Raj. [2002]. Lichchhavi Waterworks around the Capital Region. In The Brick and the Bull. Kathmandu, Nepal: Himal Books.

Upadhyay, S. N. [1999]. Legal Regime of Water Resources Use in the Light of Self-governance Act 2055. Annual Report 1999. Kathmandu, Nepal: Water and Energy Commission Secretariat.

Vaidya, Yogesh Nandan. [1999]. Food Security in Nepal. In Ratnakar Adhikari; and Narad Bharadwaj [eds.] Food Security Prospects and Challenges, Report on the National Workshop on Food Security Organized by Forum for Protection of Public Interest [Pro Public], SEWA Nepal and Action Aid, Nepal. Kathmandu, Nepal.

Water and Energy Commission Secretariat. [2005]. National Water Plan, Nepal. Kathmandu, Nepal: Water and Energy Commission Secretariat, His Majesty's Government.

Water and Energy Commission Secretariat. [1992]. Water Resources Act, Nepal. Kathmandu, Nepal: Water and Energy Commission Secretariat, His Majesty's Government.

Wright, Daniel. [2000]. History of Nepal. Delhi, India: Aadarsha Enterprises.

Upadhyay, Surya Nath, 2008. Legal and Policy Aspects of River Basin Management. WWF/Nepal. 2008. Stakeholders' Orientation in River Basin Management: Preliminary Training Manual. Prepared by CMS Nepal for WWF/Nepal and Water and Energy Commission Secretariat, Nepal. Unpublished Report.

In: Nepal in the 21st Century
Editor: Surendra R. Devkota, pp. 241-258
ISBN 978-1-60741-348-6

Chapter 11

WHETHER STRONG SUSTAINABILITY IS OPERATIONAL? AN EXAMPLE FROM NEPAL*

Surendra R. Devkota
Department of Economics, University at Albany, NY, USA

ABSTRACT

This paper explores the ways that local people in different parts of the globe are working at local level toward sustainable development whether knowingly or unknowingly. Community forest management by forming the forest users' group at the local level in Nepal is one of the successful models of sustainability. It exemplifies the ideals of strong sustainability which enhances natural, economic, and social capitals concurrently. The objective of such groups is to try to avoid "the tragedy of commons", and to conserve forests and obtain forest products like fuel wood, fodder, and timber by sustainably managing local forests. In addition, people realize indirect benefits of forest protection such as further control of landslides, and improvement of local watershed and microclimate. Further, user's groups are not only taking the forest products, but they are to increasing the forest stock, which is an act of natural capital enhancement. In addition, local communities are not only satisfying their demand for natural resources, but are also determined to increase their socio-ecological resource potential for future.

Keywords: Sustainable development, Strong and weak sustainability, Natural capital, Forest user's groups, Nepal.

---

*I would like to express my sincere gratitude to Prof. John Gowdy, Rensselaer for his encouragement and comments on the earlier version of this paper. This paper is taken in part from a dissertation submitted in partial fulfillment for the doctoral degree in the Department of Economics at Rensselaer Polytechnic Institute, Troy, New York. Earlier version of this paper was presented at the Second Biennial Conference of the United States Society for Ecological Economics, May 22 - 24, 2003, Saratoga Springs, New York. *Previously published in "Sustainable Development 13:297-310 (2005).*

INTRODUCTION

Sustainable development (SD) is one of today's most highly publicized words after the publication of "Our Common Future" – the Brundtland Report to the World Commission on Environment and Development (WCED) in 1987. The WECD definition, "development that meets the needs of present generation without compromising the ability of future generations to meet their own needs" has attracted many diverse opinions as to the meaning of sustainability. Very recently, Pezzey and Toman (2002), and earlier Pezzey (1992) have comprehensively reviewed the definitions about sustainable development. They have identified three periods of SD:

i. 1974-1986: Response to the limits to growth,
ii. 1987-1996: The emergence of sustainability literature, and
iii. 1997 to 2000: A flourishing but still developing literature on sustainable development.

By analyzing the literature in its empirical, analytical and logical or philosophical context, Pezzey and Toman concluded that there is still a lack of understanding of sustainability constituents and policies. A major reason is the complexity of development, which is non-linear, dynamic, path dependent and multifaceted (Adelman, 2001). Mebratu (1998) summarized the evolution of SD and identified some flaws about it. Some of the flaws are influenced by the fundamental tenets of special interest groups or organizations. In particular, there are a few scholars who question the concept and definition of SD. For example, Beckerman (1994), and Beckerman and Pasek (2001) challenge the definition and usefulness of the term SD. They further argue that the 'concept of sustainable development is morally unacceptable, and is full of logical flaws'. On the other hand, Streeten (1995) progresses forward and views that SD is not limited to maintaining and replacing the natural and physical capitals, but it also should comprise other aspects of society such as politics, institutions, national debt and self sufficiency etc.

A standard goal of development is to raise the living conditions of people, which, obviously, is not a linear objective as mentioned by Adelman (2001). Here, development is viewed from a socioeconomic perspective, which implicitly extends to human welfare vis-à-vis socioeconomic structure, lifestyles, institutions and attitudes. Further, SD involves transdisciplinary interactions among socioeconomic and eco-physical systems, which integrate economic, social, and ecological features, and also maintains a balance among them. The economy aims to maintain or increase per capita utility, ecology focuses on non-declining natural capital, and society seeks to enrich human aspirations (Munasinghe, 2001). All three have their own sustainability characteristics (Goodland and Daly, 1996). Although, some dislike the concept of sustainable development either on moral or physical grounds, it will continue to evolve over time with respect to the ongoing debates on strong versus weak sustainability, optimality versus sustainability, green versus brown, state versus market, first versus third world, north versus south, global versus local, present versus future, close versus open, long term versus short term, nature versus people, conservation versus preservation, durability versus optimality, efficiency versus equity, and dynamic versus static. Key questions are: how to achieve SD, and what to sustain! The operational rules of SD may not be universal and will differ according to bio-geographical and geo-political conditions of the country.

In this paper, one of the great debates, weak versus strong is discussed in the context of forest management in Nepal to support the strong version of SD.

WEAK SUSTAINABILITY

Neoclassical economists use the Cobb – Douglas production function to show a straightforward relationship between non-declining utility and resource use. Solow (1974 and 1986) used the Cobb – Douglas function as;

$$Q = A(t)\, L^{\alpha} K^{\beta} R^{1-\alpha-\beta} \tag{1}$$

where, Q is output, A is factor neutral technological progress as a function of time, L is labor, K is capital, and R is natural resource input. The exponents sum to one so that there will be constant returns to scale. Since Solow (1974 and 1986) defines sustainability as non-declining per capita utility, satisfying equation (1) requires that resources should be available in unlimited amounts and there should be a possibility of substitutability between different types of resources, i.e., human and natural. Solow (1992) further argues, "sustainability does not require that any particular species of owl, or any particular species of fish or any particular tract of forest be preserved."

Solow's formulation is the guiding principle for the supporters of weak sustainability (WS). Pearce and Barbier (2000), Pearce and Atkinson (1993) and Serafy (1996) have defined and justified it as a correct measurement of income, hence sustainability need not bother distinguishing between natural and other forms of capital. The explanations of Pearce and Barbier, and Pearce and Atkinson are simply another conception of the Solow growth model. According to their model, an increase in the rate of savings leads to higher capital stock and a higher standard of living in the future. A low saving rate means a lower capital stock and eventually, a lower national income. In general terms, individuals mostly care about consumption, so policy makers would like to create the state economy in the steady state with the highest level of consumption – the Golden rule level of capital, where investment is also equal to depreciation. Since natural resources, pollution and other environmental considerations are not available in the Solow model, David Pearce and other advocates of the WS justify that saving rate is the key parameter for the sustainable development, alias WS. Eventually, they argue that individual's utility will not decline over time regardless of the availability of natural or man made capital. In other words, WS is simply an optimization consumers' utility subject to the capital or savings. Neumayer (2001) challenged the findings of the genuine saving method proposed by the World Bank, which has accounted forestry, fisheries and mineral resources of some 103 countries. It derived negative saving rates for many Sub-Saharan, Northern African and Middle Eastern countries, therefore failed to pass the test of weak sustainability. Assuming saving rates rather than investment is misleading, if not wrong (Neumayer, 1999). The incompatibility between saving rate and investment in computing the WS is also reported by Hanley et al. (1999) for Scotland.

Further, assumptions of WS correspond with the characters of an economic man (Homo economicus) (Gowdy, 2000). Gowdy has elaborated the WS assumptions as;

i. "Objective of WS and economic man is concurrent – to maximize "utility" whose meaning is reduced to the consumption of goods and services".
ii. "Total utility of the society is nothing more than NNP and money is a substitute for everything. NNP is the interest on total capital stock. WS implies to sustain the economy's capital stock to produce NNP".

For many neoclassical economists the equation (1) is the main mantra for sustainability, despite some flaws on it. One comment of the great mathematical economist, Georgescu – Rogen (1983) is noteworthy who viewed the Cobb – Douglas production function dialectically and concluded that "quantitative ratiocination does not apply". In nutshell, WS is myopic, because when discounting is combined with unlimited substitution it considers only the short run economic gain, and relegates utility to monetary gain. Since it considers environment or natural capital to be substitutable, it is greatly flawed because how long manmade capital will substitute the natural capital is a matter of deep concern. For example, a pacific island country, Nauru, is no longer on the path of sustainability due to exhaustion of one of her natural resources – phosphates and the devastation of its physical environment (Gowdy and McDaniel, 1999). Nauru was ruined owing to following the principles of the WS. Getzner (1999) observed that weak sustainability criteria cannot be applied in order to the protect water resources in Austria.

STRONG SUSTAINABILITY

Reductionists are equating sustainable development with economic growth which could be due to they mixed up between ecological and economic notions of sustainability. Ecological sustainability tries to sustain source and sink functions as material requirements for maintaining the health of humans and ecosystems, whereas economic sustainability objects and values nature's capital inputs into the economy, i.e. production and consumption, either by means of supply of raw materials or waste disposal (Bartelmus, 2003). Although conventional economics still assumes that economic growth may continue indefinitely, this is a misconception, because economic activity is function of throughput – the flow of materials and energy from the sources of the environment. Throughput is also directly correlated with population growth and consumption. Hence, throughput exhausts resources, and adds unwanted byproducts like wastes leading to the un-sustainability of the natural system (Goodland, 1995). Goodland argues that both sources and sinks as the services of environment must be maintained in order to pursue the path of SS. In other words, meeting the basic human needs along with preserving the life support system is the primary gist of SD (Kates et al., 2001). To that end, the stakeholders of sustainable development range from civil societies to politicians and the business community, non-profit organizations to academics. All have a multitude of visions and interests regarding exactly what to sustain. Human needs are not limited to simply consumption and savings. Other objectives of economic growth are;

i. encouraging economic growth,
ii. enhancing equality, and
iii. assuring that natural assets are not degraded (Bromley, 2001).

Yet, there is a commonality in the bottom line of diverse opinions: betterment of human life and the habitat of non-human species. In this sense, SD also embraces the notion of co-evolution of man and nature, because economic systems co-evolve with ecosystems (Norgaard, 1994). Hence, the human race has also a strong tie with nature. Herman Daly (1995), a leading upholder of strong sustainability clarified the many misconceptions about strong sustainability (SS). Daly, for example, explains that "fish catch is not limited by the number of boats but by the remaining fish population. So, natural capital is the limiting factor. We can maximize current welfare subject to the constraint that natural capital be maintained intact over generations". A general delineation between strong and weak sustainability is presented in table 1.

One of the centers of substitutability debates is between the natural and man made capitals. Considering natural capital (comprising renewable natural resources like forest, ecosystem, and non-renewable resources such as fossil fuels and minerals both renewable and non-renewable- Costanza and Daly, 1992) as a limiting factor, environmental functions should not decline over time in order to achieve strong sustainability. For non-renewable resources, it may be difficult to keep intact the resources for long time, whereas for renewable it is possible to maintain the natural capital stock if regenerative capacity is not eliminated. Therefore, resources can be used within the limit of their regenerative capacity ensuring the environmental function will be intact (Hueting and Reijnder, 1998). As economic growth sustains, a clear demarcation evolves between perfect (strong) and poor (weak) substitutions without any intermediate substitutability (Gerlagh and Zwaan, 2002). Gerlagh and Zwaan further argue that it is imperative to hold environmental resources as public property in order to transfer them from one generation to next.

Table 1. Strong and weak sustainability

Strong sustainability	Weak sustainability
(i) Natural and man made capital are complements.	(i) Natural and man made capital are substitutes.
(ii) All natural and other forms of capital such as economical, social made should be independently kept intact over time.	(ii) Total capital stock (i.e., natural + manmade) should be kept intact.
(iii) SS is not only an economic problem, but also a problem of maintaining essential, non-replaceable, and non-substitutable environmental resources.	(iii) Environmental problems as economic problems.
(iv) SS favors precautionary principle, and safe minimum standard.	(iv) WS accepts monetary valuation and cost benefit approach.

Adopted from, Daly (1995), Goodland (1995), Hediger (1997), Gowdy (2000), Pearce and Barbier (2000), Ayres et al., (2001).

If environmental resources are privatized with an assumption of an efficient tool of resource management as advocated by the proponents of weak sustainability that consequently would diminish the natural capital stock in long term because of changes in the economic lifecycle of resources.

Based on the Brazilian Amazon sustainability model Franceschi and Kahn (2003) have concluded that a central focus of sustainable development should be the accumulation of human capital, artificial capital, and natural capital, while protecting the stock of environmental capital. Environmental capital is critical to future economic growth and both the economic and general health of every nation. Their results show that "the inclusion of even the recently delineated strong sustainability criteria falls short in the sustainable development planning and policy process. Simple reinvestment of rents from productive activities into artificial capital is not enough in most cases to support development for the long term. Reinvestment or preservation in the environmental capital stock can be as important for productivity as human or artificial capital".

Forest Management in Nepal: En Route to Strong Sustainability

There is growing evidence that weak sustainability will not sustain the country in terms of socioeconomic development as explained by Gowdy and McDaniel with an example of Nauru. Perpetually, SS is the only path to pursue for the betterment of the present and future. An example set by a so-called Third World country, Nepal, offers an example of the operation of SS.

The primary goal of SS that natural capital should not decline over time has been applied for the forest management at the local community level in different parts of Nepal. Nepal has vast ecological resources ranging from sub/tropical to alpine climatic ranges. A total of 118 forest ecosystems, with 75 vegetation types and 35 forest types have been identified in different physio-graphic zones in three different realms: Palaearctic, Indo-Malayan realm; and Bengalian realm. Of these, 38 types of ecosystems are represented in the protected areas (national parks, wildlife reserves and conservation areas)1. The Department of Forest Research and Survey, a government agency, in 1999 estimated that forest is limited to only 29 percent (4.2 million hectares) of the total country area (147,181sq. km.), compared to the 37 percent (Figure 1) stated in the Master Plan for the Forestry Sector of 1988. Comparing between the recent forest inventory of 1998 with the results of the previous land use study - t he 1978–1979 Land Resource Mapping Project (LRMP), led to the following conclusions.

i. In the Terai plains, the forest area decreased at an annual rate of 1.3% from 1978–1979 to 1990–1991.
ii. In the Hilly Area, the forest area decreased at an annual rate of 2.3% from 1978–1979 to 1994, whereas forest and shrub together decreased at an annual rate of 0.2%.
iii. In the whole country, from 1978–1979 to 1994, the forest area decreased at an annual rate of 1.7%, whereas forest and shrub together decreased at an annual rate of 0.5% (Härkönen, 2002).

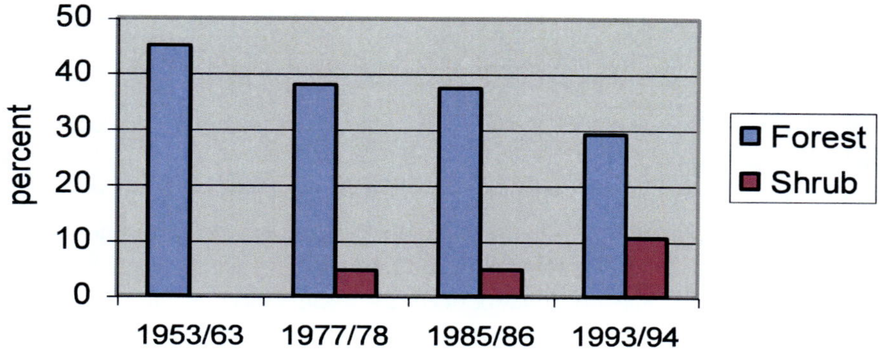

Figure 1 Changes in the forest coverage in Nepal (Unit: Percent of total land area 147181 sq. km).

Table 2. Forest management in Nepal

Years	Tree/ forest protection/management themes
Before 1950	Rulers' private property.
1961-1980s	Tree protection by restricting access to people, state's property and state owned agencies/ companies such as Timber Corporation of Nepal were responsible for cutting and selling timber from forest areas.
Since 1990s	Dual policy: Tree management by government vs. Ecosystem based forest management by local people; Limited access or rights of people but unlimited access of state agency.

About 50 years ago, total natural stocks of trees covered more than two thirds of the country area. Over past fifty years, forests in Nepal underwent several ownership or successors (Table 2). After the forests were nationalized through the Private Forest Nationalization Act - 1956 and a change in the political system in 1961, government of Nepal started a monopoly control over the forest resources. The very simple forest protection policy goal was introduction of the top down approaches such as prohibiting people's access to forests. Meanwhile, roles of indigenous community and their resources needs were simply overlooked. Government adopted two kinds of control policy. Firstly, establishment of the national parks and wild life reserve centers under the protection of the military, and, secondly, forests outside the protected areas were controlled by the public administration such as District Forest Offices. This public office positions in the headquarters of the district. In past, it used to mobilize its semi-skilled forest rangers to monitor forests and to check whether any unwanted forest related activities had happened. Further local political units were also taken into consideration to facilitate the administration for compliance of such control measures. Given the rough and tough nature of hills, governmental institutes were lagging behind to control people's accessibility to forests effectively. On the other hand, local people did not have any other choices for their resources needs such as fuel wood, timber, fodders, grazing etc. Local community can easily deceive such once in a while spot visit of the administration. Public institutes without support of the local people did not herald any substantial change, rather the forests were depleting at a higher rate than their yielding. Both types of forest policies ignored the roles of the local people. The policy mistake of the former one, i.e., army protected national parks, was corrected only in the mid 1990s by introducing the Buffer Zone Rules 1993 so that the conflict between park and people could be minimized. This conflict issues is discussed elsewhere (Wells and Sharma, 1998; Chaudhary, 2000). The other policy mistake of relegation of the role of local people for forest conservation was realized in the Forest Sector Master Plan of 1988, and has been corrected afterwards by empowering the local communities, i.e., by granting some rights to local forest users' group.

After forests in Nepal were nationalized by the government in 1956, and a new political system named 'P*artyless Panchayat'* was introduced in 1961 by the then King, under that new political system, State itself monopolized over the forest resources at several time intervals with different names. For example, the then rulers cleared an undeclared amount of forest area and diverted the money to political gains such as in the general referendum of 1979. Likewise, the government was involved in clearing forest areas and settled people from different parts of the country. During *Panchyat* regime, government itself was engaged in selective felling of forests and supplying the timber and fuel wood demand throughout the country. In spite of the realization of the encroachment of the Terai and inner Terai forests, government bodies were silent in order to get political support (Shretha, 2001). Shretha discussed how the Department of Resettlement encouraged forest encroachment so that it would get political support. A few state owned agencies were established in 1950s such as the Timber Corporation of Nepal (TCN), the Fuel Wood Corporation and the Forest Products Board. For example, 75 percent of the Terai forests of 4.1 million acres were allocated for commercial forestry, and TCN was the sole state agency to execute this job (Nepal Industrial Development Corporation, 1973). TCN was assigned the role of chopping trees to supply timbers and fuel wood at a subsidized rate. As the market price of timber increased, money laundering became an integral part of TCN. Further, resignations of the Ministers of Forestry and his deputy on the same day, March 11 2002, and the Secretary of the same ministry in February 2002 are few examples of institutionalization of forest based corruption in Nepal. Unfortunately, TCN is still functioning in Nepal as an integral part of the state system.

Furthermore, additional causes of forest depletion in Nepal were fuel wood collection from forests, grazing, illegal logging, and marginal expansion of agriculture areas by slash and burn activities. Ives and Messerli (1989) accounted the history and dynamics of deforestation in Nepal. Forests are the main sources of firewood (energy) for majority of people. Out of total 7.91 million tons of oil equivalent (TOE) of energy consumed in 2000/01, fuel wood supplies at 77 percent (Figure 2). Energy consumption at residential sector is significantly high (89 percent). The other sectors' consumption is as industries (5 percent), transportation (4 percent), agriculture (1 percent), and commercial sectors (1 percent). On average, the per capita fuel wood consumption in the mountains is estimated at 640 kg, while it for the Terai is 479 kg/person/year. Despite total state control over forest areas, the government was failing to manage forest areas by the existing political bureaucratic set-up. Massive deforestation began since 1950s with gradual collapse of the feudal forest management system (Gilmour and Fisher, 1991). Further, a couple of donors even predicted the absolute deforestation of the hills by 1993 and of plains by 2000, which should have awakened the politicians and the policy makers. Later on, His Majesty's Government of Nepal came out with a Master Plan for Forestry Sector in 1988, in which the government realized that people's involvement at the local level is necessary in order to save and to manage local forest resources. The Master Plan analyzes forest resources and their potentials, identifies four long term and three medium term objectives.

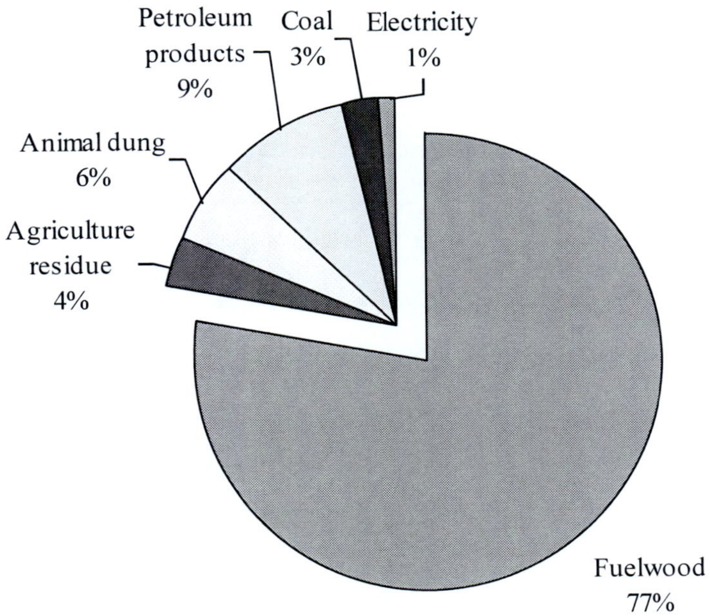

Figure 2. Energy consumption pattern in Nepal.

The long-term objectives is to meet the basic needs of the people, protect the soil and water resources, conserve ecosystems and gene base and consolidating local and national economies. The medium term objectives focus on democratizing the regulation of forests, and making legal, institutional and structural adjustments to that effect. Consequently, the Forest Act and Rules formulated after 1990 try to involve public participation.

Economics of Forests

Forests in the Nepal play a very crucial role in the village economics, where about 90 percent of 23 million people live. Therefore, the forest is a major resource for these people, which provides both economic inputs and environmental services. Some major economic contributions of forests are timber and non-timber forest products like medicinal plants, and fuel wood. Further, forest areas are the major source for forage and grazing cattle, charcoal production and other agricultural activities. Estimation of the total economic value of forests are still sketchy because people take advantage of forests and their products in different forms such as a source of firewood, fodder, timber, medicines, raw materials, foreign exchange, foods, aesthetic value, education, sustaining the watershed, habitat for all types of biological diversity. Nevertheless, the central treasury of the government benefits from revenue generated by both timber and non-timber forest products. Although economic valuation of all types of forests uses and services is still incomplete, the World Bank (1999) has estimated some of them. For example, non-timber forest products like medicinal plants provide up to 50 percent of household income in some areas. Each year, almost 15,000 tons of medicinal plants are harvested and traded in Nepal, with a total value of US $ 8.6 million. This value obviously does not include the smuggled quantity, which is not uncommon. According to previous study of the World Bank in 1991, total exports of forest products from Nepal were estimated to be US$ 12 million in 1988; almost all of it cross-border trade to India. This overwhelmingly consisted of timber exports, estimated at 126,000 m3 in 1988 (Soussan, 1995).

Table 3. Annual financial losses due to deforestation

Physiographic Zones	Annual deforestation (ha)	Deforestation loss (Rs./ha)	Total loss due to deforestation (million Rs.)
Hills and Mountains:			
Deforestation	41,000	125,000	5,125.0
Degradation	54,200	42,000	2,276.4
Terai:			
Deforestation	8,300	500,000	4,150.0
Total			11,551.4

Source: Ministry of Forests and Soil Conservation (2002).

This also does not include the illegal lumbering to India or to the local domestic market. Recently, Ministry of Forests and Soil Conservation (2002) estimated costs due to deforestation in Nepal are about Rs. 11.55 billion per year (Table 3).

The other side of the economic impact of forest is in the village economy. Rural households mostly use the forest and its products for the subsistence of the household economy. For example, Bajracharya (1983) concluded that fuel wood scarcity is problem in Nepali villages, but food deficit lies at the root of the problem. Therefore, deforestation in Nepal is also due to food deficit, because people do trade off between food and fuel wood collection so that they can sell firewood at local market and can purchase the food items. In other words, due to dwindling of forest resources, rural people are compelled to reduce their cattle or goat numbers, which directly affect the household economy. The reduced cattle number will further induce to lessen the agricultural yield because animal manure is still the major sources of the fertilizers. Majority of the agricultural field in Nepal has low content of organic matter and nitrogen (Devkota, 1999).

Community Forestry and Strong Sustainability

Community forestry in Nepal is being a pioneer model of natural resource management to global communities. The World Bank (2001) mentions, " Nepal is a leader in engaging community for protection and management of forest". Recently, Otsuka and Tachibana (2001) discuss the evolution and consequences of community forestry in Nepal. They concluded that scarcity of forest resources encourages the people to form the forest user group (FUG), because to sustain the livelihood and subsistence farming in the hills of Nepal without forests is virtually impossible. As of now, rural conditions are such that both FUG and government should complement each other in order to support livelihood as well as ensure the sustainability of forests. So, community forest management by FUG is the most effective method of resource management for sustainability. Jackson and Ingles (1995) define 'Community forestry refers to the situation where forests are controlled and managed as the common property by groups of rural people who agree to use them to support their farms and households'. Users' rights of the forests in Nepal are ill defined (Karki et al., 1994) and forests were managed as open access property regimes- a situation comparable to the "tragedy of the commons" (Hardin, 1968). Large- scale deforestation in the past was largely due to ever-changing and ill-defined property rights, flawed policies of government, and a lack of proper management compelled the government to seek the cooperation from local people by assigning certain rights. Therefore, community forestry aims to establish the property rights (Acharya, 1998), because property regimes play a key role in development and sustainability (Bromley, 1998).

The Forest Act -1993 and the Forest Regulations–1995 introduced by His Majesty's Government of Nepal are governing the community forestry. In general, the Act defines the policy framework and the Regulation endorses the Act. Some salient features of the above mentioned legislation relating to community forestry are:

1. The land managed under community forestry belongs to the state and the land use rights and forests are owned and managed by the FUG. So, land ownership remains with the state, but the land use rights along with the forest resources except wildlife products, soils, sands, etc. belong to FUGs.
2. FUG is responsible to manage the forest as per its constitution and operation plan, which must be approved by the District Forest Officer (DFO). After approval, FUG will be an autonomous and corporate body with perpetual succession rights. FUGs could initiate plantation of cash crops, such as medicinal herbs, fix prices of forestry products irrespective of the government royalty, establish forest-based industries according to the resources available in their jurisdiction, and use surplus funds in any kind of community development work. But such activities should not hamper main forest stock.
3. Any governmental and non-governmental agencies are allowed to provide any sort of help to FUGs in order to organize and to manage forests.
4. Each member of the FUG is a co-owner and has equal rights over the resources, and outsiders are denied access. FUGs can punish any member who violates the rules of the constitution and/or the operation plan.
5. Benefits should be shared on an equitable basis among the members of FUGs.
6. DFO can take community forests back from FUGs if they violate their constitution. However, the DFO must return the forest as soon as the problem is solved.
7. FUGs will have ecological boundaries rather than political boundaries.
8. State acts as a facilitator by providing technical support and advise to FUG.
9. Any part or amount of national forest forests can be handed over to the communities who are traditional users of the resources, if they are interested as well as are capable of managing the forests.
10. District Forest Officers are authorized to hand over forests to FUGs.

The Community Forestry Division at the Department of Forest aims to hand over about 3.5 million hectares (about 61 percent of total forest area) of forest areas to FUGs. By 2003 there were 12,079 community forestry user groups formed across Nepal, managing 15 percent of Nepal's total forestland area (955,358 hectares out of 6,306,000 hectares of total forestland areas).The total beneficiaries were about 1.34 million people. There are about 556 FUGs are exclusively managed by women.

The ongoing SS working strategy is that a society can sustain itself only by preserving its supply of natural capital (Prugh, Costanza, and Daly, 2000). Further, community forestry schemes, in principle, are enhancing economic, ecological and social capitals (Devkota, 2003). FUGs are trying to reverse a phenomenon of the tragedy of commons based on their social structures, and values. Local people are building up their social capital in order to enhance the natural capital through a game of cooperation. Here social capital implies as a social structure that facilitates cooperation (Routledge and van Amsberg, 2003). Local people living in the hills of Nepal are managing the forests by forming the FUGs. People, living in and around the forest areas, make up a forest user's group, its constitution and management plan by a mutual consultative process. All of these users' group, constitution, and management plan must be approved by the District Forest Office - a government body. Each FUG develops its own forest annual management plan, which also needs to be developed and approved by FUG members and government agency. After approval, FUG will be a legal entity with a social obligation and definitive objective. The objectives are to protect and manage forests and to use the forest products, so that people will receive their basic needs from the forest like fuel wood, fodder and timber. The government does not take any share from it, but FUG has to spend at least 25 percent of revenue generated for enhancing natural capital, i.e., forest stocks enhancement activities like seedling preparation, forest cultivation and allied silviculture practices. FUG also retains some provisions to check free riders such as non-members are not allowed to share benefit. Benefits are shared on equitable basis in general. The harvested products such as green firewood are distributed equally to the members of FUG by applying local standard practices. Economically, FUG members get benefit in terms of fuelwood, fodders, and timber, but magnitude and extent could vary depending up on the member and size of community forestry and resources availability. Empirically, it is matter of further research about the magnitude of all types of capital gain, i.e., economical, social and ecological capitals.

FUG, in standard environmental policy context, follows a subsidiary principle: 'manage local environmental issues locally'. It is also a game of cooperation. For example, users in any FUGs who are obtaining the substantial benefits through collective actions will be much eager to participate in this game of conservation and development compared to the less efficient FUGs. Though there could be differences of interests or opinions among the members in FUGs, mutual trust, transparency, and cooperation are key variables for sustaining such institutes. Laws governing collective actions and cooperation must be fair and reciprocal otherwise maximization of self-interest will ruin the system (Fehr and Fischbahcer, 2002). The longevity of such self-governed systems is also driven by the net benefits (Varughese and Ostrom, 2001).

CONCLUSION

SS is not an oxymoron as claimed by a few scholars, but is a long term vision. WS may provide a short term economic gain, but sustainability of that gain or capital is function of throughput. As evidenced by Gowdy and McDaniel in their Nauru example, over a 100 years period Nauru exhausted its phosphates resources, and now, country is facing the shortage of natural capital and depending on the trust fund for its survival. The trust fund is a built capital based on the mining of phosphates, so is a substitution of the natural capital. How long it will sustain the country is a matter of future study.

Nepal also followed a similar path of weak sustainability in past 50 years. Short term economic gains incurred at the cost of natural capital such as forests and water resources, but people or local communities who are in close contact with resources faced a severe hardship of depleting natural capital. That forced the government to reform the policy measures. Had the FUGs of Nepal, being a successful model of forest management, pursues the ideals of strong sustainability, which comprises an economic, social, and ecological capitals, institution, rights, and game of cooperation. It also embraces many pertinent environmental philosophies from a deep understanding of the value of nature to modern environmental policies such as bargaining power (Coase, 1960), and theories for a sustainable future (Holling et al. 2002). FUG is a user right for people, whereas the state reserves the land ownership right. Therefore, both government and FUG have rights, and bargaining for more power is an ongoing process. Real faith on the fact of forest preservation emerged only after local people got some legitimacy. Now, they could get not only the direct forest products like fuel wood and fodder, but also benefited by the other indirect uses and non-use values of forests like improved local micro-climate, resilience of greenery and bio-diversity. People in different regions are experiencing the resilience of the local ecosystem over a period of one decade. Local people are taking not only the interests from the forest, i.e., fuel wood, food and timber, depending upon the harvest rate, but also are committed to increasing forest stock – a capital enhancement. FUGs in Nepal are flourishing based on the real human behavior, whereby maximization of self-interest as an economic man is replaced by the community interest, since economic man does not represent the true human nature (Tomer, 2001).

Although the history of FUG goes back to the-mid seventies, its expansion started only after restoration of the multiparty system in 1990. During the Panchayat regime, i.e., before 1990, (see Table 2) community forestry was not popular in rural communities because its activities were limited to plantations, and forest users groups (FUGs) were given barren areas or degraded forests with plantations. Community forestry flourished only after changes in the political system in 1990, which led to the formulation and promulgation of the Forest Act and Bylaws of nineties (Dongol, Hughey, and Bigsby, 2002). Hence, politics also played a key role to transfer the rights from the state to the people. FUG is an institution for equity of resources for both rich and poor with an efficient management scheme at a local scale, so it must adhere to the transparency and fairness. There exist some common problems, both at FUG and government levels. Edmonds (2002) discusses the problems and prospectus of FUG, and observes that government initiated such institutions have high potential of community resource management in long term. Intra FUG rights, particularly gender based, are also evolving. Though Aggarwal (2001) observed some pertinent issues related to women and resource management and exclusion of women in decision making process, few other positive aspects can't be overlooked such as there are more than five hundred FUGs exclusively managed by women. It is necessary to have active role of socially weak and economically deprived people in the FUG. Conservation awareness, rights, and responsibility is yet to be assimilated at local level. On the other hand at the top level, the politico-bureaucracy, as usual, does not wish to lose the controlling power. The appropriation lies on bargaining power but with a fair deal of honesty of all parties rather than political foul play.

For instance, national forest management in dense forest areas like in the plain (Terai), is still confusing because, the fulcrum among political bureaucratic set up, donors and non-governmental sectors is not balanced. There is an ongoing debate about the modus operandi of management of the Terai forest (Chakraborty, 2001; Sakurai et al., 2001; Tachibana et al., 2001). Further, in 2001, the government promulgated an Ordinance to collect 40 percent of the income tax from community forest users in the Terai area despite heavy criticisms of the FUG members. Is the political-bureaucracy as always eager to grease their hand from forests, or are so-called non-profit organizations being tempted to profit from lumbering? That announcement of government may discourage to the real spirit of sustainability. Further encouraging results would be expected if government authorities could have tried to bargain on clean development mechanism of the Kyoto Protocol for community forestry that conserves biological diversity as well as sequesters carbon as Klooster and Masera (2000) foresee such potentials in the Mexican community forestry schemes.

Nepal is pioneering sustainable forest management by forming forest users' groups, which exemplify the ideals of strong sustainability. That model needs to be encouraged and could be applied to other socioeconomic development sectors in order to address the poverty. People need rights, which are not just limited to a voting power to elect a vetoing body, but also to socioeconomic as well as environmental rights. Socioeconomic democracy coupled with environmental rights would build up sustainable courses. FUG, which has a successful integration, and cooperation of the society, economy and ecology, also exemplifies both political and economic equity as well as efficiency. In conclusion on the basis of an example analyzed here it can be inferred that SS is not only limited to the debate of natural versus man made capital, but its' jurisdiction is also augmenting to building the institution, game of cooperation, and socioeconomic rights ensuring the sustainability.

NOTES

1 http://www.mope.gov.np/frame.php3

REFERENCES

Acharya, K.P. 2000. *Community Forestry in Nepal: A Model of Common Property Resource Management*, working paper, Division of Forest Research, Ministry of Forest/ Nepal. (http://www.panasia.org.sg/nepalnet/forestry/comm_forestry.htm).

Adelman, I. 2001. Fallacies of Development Theory and Their Implications for Policy, In *Frontiers of Development Economics: The Future Perspective*, Meier, G. M., and Stiglitz, J. E., (eds) New York: Oxford University Press.

Agarwal, B. 2001. Participatory Exclusions, Community Forestry, and Gender: An Analysis for South Asia and a Conceptual Framework, *World Development* 29(10), 1623-1648.

Ayres, R. U., van den Bergh, J.C.J.M., Gowdy, J. M., 2001. Strong versus Weak Sustainability: Economics, Natural Science and Consilience, *Environmental Ethics* 23: 155-168.

Bajracharya, D. 1983. Fuel, Food or Forest? Dilemmas in a Nepali Village, *World Development* 11:1057-1074.

Bartelmus, P., 2003. Dematerialization and Capital Maintenance: Two Sides of Sustainability Coin, *Ecological Economics* 46 (1): 61-81.

Beckerman, W. 1994. Sustainable Development: Is it a Useful Concept? *Environmental Values* 3:191-209.

Beckerman, W., Pasek, J. 2001. *Justice, Posterity and the Environment*. Oxford: Oxford University Press.

Bromley, D. W. 2001. *Institutions, Poverty and Sustainability: Lessons from the Development Experiences* (http://www.aae.wisc.edu/bromley/), Paper Presented at the Lund School of Economics and Management, (Sept. 17 2001), Sweden.

Bromley, D.W. 1998. Property Regimes in Economic Development: Lessons and Policy Implications, In *Agriculture and Environment: Perspectives on De*velopment, Ernst Lutz (ed.), Washington, D.C.: World Bank.

Chakraborty, R. N., 2001. Stability and Outcomes of Common Property Institutions in Forestry: Evidences from the Terai region of Nepal, *Ecological Economics* 36 (2): 341-353.

Chaudhary, R.P. 2000. Forest Conservation and Environmental Management in Nepal: A Review, *Biodiversity and Conservation* 9: 1235-1260.

Coase, R.H. 1960. The Problem of Social Cost, *The Journal of Law and Economics* III: 1-44.

Costanza, R., Daly, H. 1992. Natural Capital and Sustainable Development, *Conservation Biology* 6: 37-46.

Daly, H. 1995. On Wilfred Beckerman's Critique of Sustainable Development, *Environmental Values* 4: 49-55.

Daly, H. 1996. *Beyond Growth: The Economics of Sustainable Development*. Boston: Beacon Press.

Devkota, S.R. 1999. Environment Management in Nepal: Unmanaging the Manageable, *Ecological Economics* 28, 31-40.

Devkota, S.R. 2003. *Strong Sustainability in Nepal: A Structural Economics Approach.* Ph.D. Thesis (unpublished), Department of Economics, Rensselaer Polytechnic Institute, Troy, New York.

Edmonds, E.V. 2002. Government-Initiated Community Resource Management and Local Resource Extraction From Nepal's Forests, *Journal of Development Economics* 68 (1), 89 – 115.

Hughey, M. K. F.D., Bigsby, H.R. 2002. Capital Formation and Sustainable Community Forestry in Nepal, *Mountain Research and Development* 22 (1), 70–77.

Franceschi, D., Kahn, J. R. 2003. Beyond Strong Sustainability, *International Journal of Sustainable Development and World Ecology* 10 (3): 211-220.

Fehr, E., Fischbacher, U. 2002. Why Social Preferences Matter – The Impact of Non-selfish Motives on the Competition, Cooperation and Incentives, *The Economic Journal* 112: C1-C33.

Georgescu- Rogen, N. 1983. Feasible Recipes versus Viable Technologies, *Atlantic Economic Journal* 21-31.

Gerlagh R., van der Zwann, B. C. C. 2002. Long-Term Substitutability between Environmental and Man-Made Goods, *Journal of Environmental Economics and Management* 44(2): 329-345.

Getzner, M. 1999. Weak and Strong Sustainability Indicators and Regional Environmental Resources, *Environment Management and Health* 10 (3): 170 – 176.

Gilmour, D. A., Fisher, R. J. 1991. *Villagers, Forests and Foresters*. Kathmandu: Sahayogi Press.

Goodland, R. 1995. The Concept of Environmental Sustainability, *Annual review of Ecology and Systematics* 26:1-24.

Goodland, R., Daly, H. 1996. Environmental Sustainability: Universal and Non-negotiable, *Ecological Application* 6: 1002-1017.

Gowdy, J., McDaniel, C. 1999. The Physical Destruction of Nauru: An Example of Weak Sustainability. *Land Economics* 75: 333-338.

Gowdy, J. M. 2000. Terms and Concepts in Ecological Economics, *Wildlife Society Bulletin* 28: 26-33.

Hanley, N. et al. 1999. Measuring Sustainability: A time Series Alternative Indicator for Scotland, *Ecological Economics* 28: 55-73.

Hardin, G. 1968. The Tragedy of Commons, *Science* 162: 1243-1248.

Härkönen, E. 2002. 1999 Inventory of Nepal's Forest Resources, *Mountain Research and Development* 22 (1): 85–87.

Hediger, W. 1997. Toward an Ecological Economics of Sustainable Development, *Sustainable Development* 5:101-109.

Holling, C. S., Carpenter, S. R., Brock, W. A., Gunerdson, L.H. 2002. Discoveries for Sustainable Futures in L.H. Gunderson and C.S. Holling (eds) *Panarchy: Understanding Transformations in Human and Natural Systems.* pp.395-417. Washington D.C: Island Press.

Hueting, R., and Reijnders, L. 1998. Sustainability is an Objective Concept, *Ecological Economics* 27: 139-147.

Ives, J. D., Messerli, B. 1989. *The Himalayan Dilemma: Reconciling Development and Conservation* (2001 edition). New York: Routledge.

Jackson, W. J., Ingles, A. W. 1995. Developing Rural Communities and Conserving the Biodiversity of Nepal's Forests through Community Forestry. In *Proceedings of a Seminar on Community Development and Conservation of Forest Biodiversity through Community Forestry.* October 26-28, 1994. RECOFTC Report No. 12, Bangkok.

Karki, M., Karki, J. B. S., Karki, N. 1994. *Sustainable Management of Common Forest Resources: An Evaluation of Selected Forest User Groups in Western Nepal*. Kathmandu: International Center for Integrated Mountain Development.

Kates, R.W. et al., 2001. Sustainability Science, *Science* 292: 641-642.

Klooster, D., Masera, O., 2000. Community Forest Management in Mexico: Carbon Mitigation and Biodiversity Conservation through Rural Development, *Global Environmental Change* 10 (4): 259-272.

Mebratu, D. 1998. Sustainability and Sustainable Development: Historical and Conceptual View, *Environmental Impact Assessment Review* 18: 493-520.

MOPE/UNEP/ICIMOD/SACEP/NORAD, 2001, *State of the Environment – Nepal*, Kathmandu.

Munasinghe, M. 2001. Sustainable Development and Climate Change: Applying the Sustainomics Transdisciplinary Meta-framework, *International Journal of Global Environmental Issues* 1: 13-55.

Neumayer, E. 2001. The Human Development Index and Sustainability – A Constructive Proposal, *Ecological Economics* 39: 101-114.

Neumayer, E. 1999. *Weak versus Strong Sustainability: Exploring the Limits of Two Opposing Paradigms.* Cheltenham: Edward Elgar.

Nepal Industrial Development Corporation (NIDC). 1973. *Prospects of Industrial Investment in Nepal.* Kathmandu: NIDC.

Norgaard, R. 1994. *Development Betrayed: The End of Progress and a Coevolutionary Revisioning of the Future*. New York: Routledge.

Otsuka, K., Tachibana, T. 2001. Evolution and Consequences of Community Forest Management in Nepal, in Aoki, M., and Hayami, Y. (eds) *Communities and market in Economic Development.* New York: Oxford University Press.

Pearce, D. W., Atkinson, G. D. 1993. Capital Theory and the measurement of Sustainable Development: An Indicator of Weak Sustainability, *Ecological Economics* 8: 103-108.

Pearce, D., W., Barbier, E. 2000. *Blueprint for a Sustainable Economy*. London: Earthscan.

Pezzey, J. C., Toman, M. A. 2002. *The Economics of Sustainability: A Review of Literature*, Discussion paper 02-03, Washington D.C. Resource for Future.

Pezzey, J. C. 1992. Sustainability: An Interdisciplinary Guide, *Environmental Values* 1:321-362.

Prugh, T., Costanza, R., Daly, H. 2000. *The Local Politics of Global Sustainability*. Washington, D.C.: Island Press.

Routledge, B. R., van Amsberg, 2003, Social Capital and Growth, *Journal of Monetary Economics* 50 (1), 167 – 193

Sakurai, T. et al., 2001. Timber Forest Management in Nepal and Japan, in Otsuka., K., and Place F., (eds.) *Land Tenure and Natural Resource Management: A Comparative Study of Agrarian Communities in Asia and Africa*. Baltimore: The John Hopkins University Press.

Serafy, S. 1996. In Defense of Weak Sustainability: A Response to Beckerman, *Environmental Values* 5:75-81.

Shrestha, N. R. 2001. *The Political Economy of Land, Landless and Migration in Nepal.* New Delhi: Nirala Publications.

Solow, R. M. 1992. *Sustainability: An Economist's Perspectives* Paper presented at the Woods Hole Oceanographic Institute, Massachusetts on June 14, 1991.

Solow, R. M. 1986. On the Intergenerational Allocation of Resources, *Scandinavian Journal of Economics* 88:141-149.

Solow, R. M. 1974. Intergenerational Equity and Exhaustible Resources, *Review of Economic Studies* 29-46.

Soussan, J., Shrestha, B.K., Uprety, L.P. 1995. *The Social Dynamics of Deforestation: A Case Study from Nepa*l. New York: Parthenon Publishing Group.

Streeten, P. P. 1995. *Thinking about Development.* New York: Cambridge University Press.

Tachibana, T. et al., 2001. Common Property Forest management in the Hills Region of Nepal, in Otsuka., K., and Place F., (eds.) *Land Tenure and Natural Resource Management: A Comparative Study of Agrarian Communities in Asia and Africa.* Baltimore: The John Hopkins University Press.

The World Bank. 1999. *Forest Management in Nepal: Economics and Ecology.* World Bank Technical Paper no. 445, Washington, D.C.

The World Bank. 2001. *Community Forestry in Nepal.* Operation Evaluation Department, No. 217, Washington, D.C.

Tomer, J.F. 2001. Economic Man vs. Heterodox Men – The Concepts of Human Nature in Schools of Economic Thoughts, *The Journal of Socio-Economics* 30: 281-293.

Varughese, G., Ostrom, E. 2001. The Contested Role of Heterogeneity in Collective Action: Some Evidence from Community Forestry in Nepal, *World Development* 29:747-765.

Wells, M.P., Sharma, U.R. 2000. Socioeconomic and Political Aspects of Biodiversity Conservation in Nepal, *International Journal of Social Economics* 25: 226-243.

In: Nepal in the 21st Century
Editor: Surendra R. Devkota, pp. 259-284
ISBN 978-1-60741-348-6

Chapter 12

INCREASED URBAN GROWTH RESULTS IN INCREASED VULNERABILITY: HUMAN/HAZARDS INTERACTIONS IN THE UNCONTROLLED KATHMANDU VALLEY URBAN CONURBATION

Keshav Bhattarai[1] ***and Dennis Conway***[2]
[1]Department of Geography, University of Central Missouri, Warrensburg, MO, USA
[2]Department of Geography, Indiana University, Bloomington, IN, USA

ABSTRACT

This chapter analyzes how rapid urban growth in the Kathmandu Valley has increased urban vulnerabilities. This study uses aerial photos, cartographic maps, satellite images, and aspatial data on GIS platforms to evaluate vulnerabilities associated with the Valley's extremely rapid urban spatial growth from 1955 to the present- 2008.We also analyze urban population growth dynamics and rapid infilling of open spaces, vehicular congestion, and severe problems of accesses for emergency vehicles to provide both general and emergency services. Our spatial analyses using GIS/Remote Sensing(RS) technologies suggest that urban spatial growth has been haphazard within the core area and rural-urban fringes; with unsafe building structures increasing in and around the Valley's many urban cores and along the side of transportation routes. While much of the Valley's agricultural land has been converted to urban uses, the infilling of open spaces has further damaged the regional balance and threatened its overall environmental quality. In addition, a proliferation of poorly constructed housing in spontaneous squatter settlements, which are sited in marginal locations throughout the Valley, has only exacerbated the vulnerability of their populations to seismic disturbances, flooding and landslides. Further analyses of high resolution aerial and World View-1 images reveals that unplanned infrastructure developments, narrow streets and the lack of accessible passages, increasing air and water pollution, and problems of waste disposal have made the Valley- once known for the harmony of its architecture and supporting fertile lands- more vulnerable than ever before. Taken together, these GIS/RS analyses lead us to the conclusion that considerable urban restructuring is desperately needed, under the management, GIS/RS monitoring and guidance of a much better informed and stricter regulatory regime than is presently in place, to ensure the sustainability of this historic city, and reverse, or at least hold up, the current dysfunctional slide into a heightened state of vulnerability and urban crisis.

INTRODUCTION

Urbanization is an irreversible global process, and a dominant phenomenon of many less developed countries due to the concentrated development and population overcrowding in relatively developed geographic areas in their respective national territories. In developing countries such overcrowding and sharing agglomerated facilities has been considered as a forward step to alleviate poverty. In order to analyze positive and negative aspects of population overcrowding in certain geographic locations, several attempts have been made to develop theoretical and mathematical models on urban studies (ADB/ICIMOD, 2006; Jat, Garg, and Khare, 2006; Rahman, 2007; Sudhira, Ramachandra, and Jagadish, 2004; Xian, Crane, and Cory, 2008). As early as in 1826, Von Thünen postulated a concentric rings theory stating that lands located near the urban center are intensively used and probably are converted into dense settlements, whereas lands farther away from the center are used less intensively because of their lower economic values (Perraton and Baxter, 1974). Later urban rent models found similar differential gradients of land uses within cities (Alonso-Villar, 2001; Cavailhès, Frankhauser, Peeters, 2004). However, many urban functional models developed before the mid 1980s were 'non-spatial', making incorporation of the multi-faceted effects of both built-up and biophysical (natural) environments into their matrices difficult to model (Cohen, 2001).

The late 1980s, however, saw the proliferation and adoption of geographic information systems (GIS) and remote sensing technologies in urban studies, which were used to evaluate land use changes as a consequence of various aspects of contemporary urban development-sprawl, de-concentration, decentralization, in-filling, among others.

Subsequent to these advances, urban planners are now using spatial data in GIS platforms to help in the cartographic and visualization representation of all of the urban structural forces because these forces work mutually and in interrelated ways. Government agencies responsible for urban management and physical planning now realize the merits of evaluating the effects of urban infrastructure development and change of, to efficiently manage and encourage particular urban land uses. Almost all the literature on land use and land cover change is in unanimous agreement that the effect of every spatial development needs to be evaluated in a holistic manner. Detail spatial information is needed to analyze urban growth that is usually associated with converting agricultural land for residential, commercial, and business uses, which thereby increases the impervious surface areas (ISA) as well as reduces the local stocks of non-urban land. Rapid urban growth raises concerns about the quality of life due to changes of land cover types from natural to anthropogenic impervious surfaces (Xian *et al*, 2008). Urban expansion increases ISA, which in turn increases nonpoint source pollution or polluted run-off (CWP, 2003). Studies have shown a direct relationship between ISA and population growth; i. e. expansion of urban areas.

Despite these environmental and social problems, worldwide urban population is growing rapidly. For example, the urban population grew from 13% (220 million) of the total population in the 1900s to 29% (732 million) in the 1950s, and it reached 49% (3.2 billion) in 2005 (SWP, 2007). The United Nations projects that by 2030, over 4.9 billion people will live in urban areas, and urban populations will continue to grow rapidly. A review of literature revealed that in the 1950s, there were 78 metropolises with 1 million people each; in 1985, the number of cities with >1 million people increased to 258 of which 42 had over 4 million people, 56 had 2 to 4 million, 158 had between 1 and 2 million, and 300 urban centers had 0.5-1 million people (Dogan and Kasarda, 1988). Today, the number of mega cities with > 10 million people has increased to 19, while other 22 cities have been housing 5 - 10 million people each, and 370 urban areas are accommodating 1-5 million people. Yet, another 433 cities have population from 0.5 to 1.00 million (UN-Habitat, 2006). It is estimated that by the year 2010, there will be over 511 metropolises across the globe with over 1 million people in each. Also, it is estimated that by 2025, over 135 giant urbanized regions will exist with more than five billion, and 90% of the increase will take place in the low and middle-income world (UN-Habitat, 2003) thereby increasing urban vulnerabilities world-wide.

It has been a common practice to use remote sensing images to spatially identify and measure urban vulnerabilities including impervious surface areas (Jat *et al.*, 2006; Rahman, 2007; Sudhira *et al.*, 2004; Xian *et al.*, 2008). Spatial data generated from remote sensing images can then be brought into geographic information systems (GIS) and subjected to statistical analysis, categorical analysis and classificatory modeling. Statistical modeling to identify spatial and structural variables that have significant influences on urban growth has been essential in the context of rapid and irreversible (now global) urbanization processes, but complementary GIS/RS spatial analyses show considerable promise as partners to such methodological inquiries. Urbanization brings a dynamism and urban vibrancy that initiates economic, political, and social innovations (Greene and Pick, 2006), and in so doing, rapid societal, demographic, economic, political, cultural, and technological changes occur. The dynamic development of an urban area is assumed to help alleviate poverty also. The World Bank Reports highlights the reduction of poverty incidence from 42% in 1995-96 to 31% in 2003-04 at the global scale, with greater poverty declines occurring in urban areas than in rural areas. And, since urbanization is widely believed to be a process for vibrant economic growth, it is considered a necessary 'evil,' and thus, even unprecedented rates of urban growth are taken as 'part and parcel' of economic development.

In the developing countries, these urbanization changes are too large and too fast, with an addition of 0.5 million urban dwellers each week in Asian countries (UN-Habitat, 2003) mainly due to governments' limitations to implement equal developments in all geographic sectors. Though mega-cities (>10 million) will undoubtedly continue to grow, most people will be living in cities, the size of Kathmandu (1-3 million people). However, it is difficult to clearly state what criteria qualify an area as urban. The Katmandu Valley's urban centers- with their intriguing parallels to the medieval cities of Europe - have been facing many, or most, of the world's most severe urban problems. Local urban planners and policy makers have been struggling to correct these problems concerning housing standards, the high yet increasing, population density and irregular, small plot sizes, the proliferation of squatter settlements, poor, or absent accessibility for many, the overall increases in impervious surfaces, the scarcity of drinking water, lack of waste disposal places, increasing air pollution and environmental deterioration, and last but by no means least, seismological vulnerabilities.

The rapid and continuous influxes of migrants bring unprecedented changes to urban structures thereby increasing vulnerability. The Kathmandu's urban conurbation's experience has been similar to what Benveniste (1977:28) wrote based on the Utopian philosophy, namely: "a program that is a well known failure is going to solve a social problem, a program that cannot be initiated is going to be initiated or a program that does not even exist is a flourishing enterprise." In other words, the five urban centers of the Valley--Kathmandu, Kirtipur, Lalitpur, Madhyapur Thimi, and Bhaktapur (Figure 1)-- are growing too rapidly without appropriate planning and infrastructure development. Though these cities were developed in a wide range of historical, political, cultural, socioeconomic, and environmental settings, future increments will only exacerbate the problems, not solve any, and vulnerability will be heightened as many peripheral areas are competing to be included within the urban area to utilize city benefits.

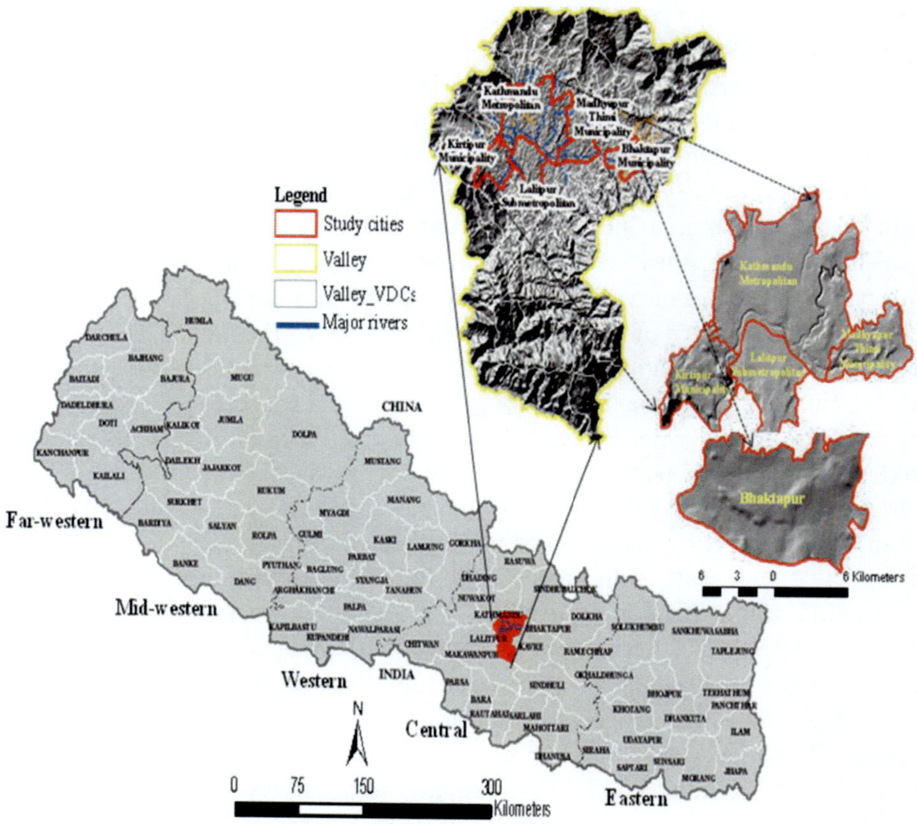

Figure 1. Nepal showing five development regions (black dotted lines) 75 administrative districts (white lines) and Kathmandu Valley (dark red and insets).

This chapter examines the vulnerabilities resulting from the unplanned and rapid urban growth taking place in the Katmandu Valley of Nepal. We intend to demonstrate that this Valley's unplanned and rapid, uneven urbanization is increasing the overall region's vulnerability and exposure to natural hazards, disasters, and crises that could be anthropogenic, biophysical or both in terms of causality. Our study period covers from 1955 to 2008 using aerial photos and cartographic maps (1955-1959/60), CORONA image (1967), Multispectral Scanner image (1975) along with the topographic maps (1977-1979), Thematic Mapper images (1990 and 1997), Enhanced Thematic Mapper images (2000 and 2003), IKONOS image (2000), QuickBird images (2003), and Worldview 1 and Google images (2008). These data are used to visualize and analyze how the Valley's urbanized areas have grown in radial directions around the city centers, or in linear directions along the highways and in the rural-urban fringes of the Kathmandu Valley. Though several urban studies in Nepal have used remote sensing and GIS techniques (Haack and Rafter, 2006; Haack and Khatiwada, 2007; Koirala, 2000; KVTDC, 2002; LRMP, 1986; Thapa *et. al*, 2008), their work does not visualize the details of housing compactness, open spaces, road accessibilities, characteristics and growth dynamics of populations and housing structures at the smallest administrative "ward" level. Spatial analysis of rapid urban development at ward level is essential in the seismologically vulnerable Kathmandu Valley because unprecedented casualties were observed in 1934's earthquakes due to concentrated housing development and the lack of proper accessibilities for evacuation of earthquakes victims at the ward levels. It is our goal to highlight how unplanned urban growth leads to unimaginable losses of lives and properties because past studies have failed to examine urban vulnerabilities and urban sustainability interactions at such smaller units.

In what follows, we first present a brief historical account of the Kathmandu Valley's urbanization experience and its population growth from 1955 to 2008. This exposes the uncontrolled nature of the Valley's urban expansion and the problems created due to sub-standard housing, poor accessibilities and services, drinking water deficiencies; seismic vulnerabilities; waste disposal; and environmental pollution. Then using remote sensing and GIS platforms we analyze the increased vulnerability due to the unprecedented increases of urban growth and sprawl and present a sectoral scenario based on the ward level data of the Kathmandu Metropolitan area, which details the many aspects of environmental and infrastructural deficiencies that the Valley now faces. Finally, in our concluding remarks, we argue that the holistic, visualizing approach used in this chapter will be a useful analytical prototype to assess the inevitable, heightened vulnerabilities that accompany unprecedented, and largely uncontrolled, urban growth in other rapidly growing cities of the South Asian countries.

THE KATHMANDU VALLEY'S URBANIZATION PROCESS

Situated within the 1,200 to 1,500 m elevation ranges and geographic coordinates of 27.36^0 to 27.46^0 N and 85.15^0 to 85.28^0E, the Kathmandu Valley is the Nepal's oldest settlement. This valley was developed by draining a lake between 625 BC and 100 AD during the Kirat rule (Depuis, 1962; Ranjitkar, 1983; Shrestha, Khatry, Sharma, and Ansari, 1986). In the 7th century during the Licchavi rule, it developed into a densely populated grouping of settlements mainly due to its suitable location for trading between Lhasa and India (Thapa *et. al.*, 2008). It was also considered safe from possible aggression by outsiders, due to the presence of mountains all around the Valley. At the same time, the Valley also enjoyed symbolic value as a center of religious significance because of the presence of two holy rivers - Bagmati and Bishnumati (Figure 1). Eventually, the settlements grew and consolidated to form three urban-centered districts--Kathmandu, Lalitpur, and Bhaktapur. These three centers meet the criteria of urban centers which Pradhan (2003) defines as a permanent settlement with over 5,000 people at a density of 386 per square kilometer with over 75% of the adult population engaged in non-agricultural activities.

When the Ranas ruled Nepal from 1846-1950, they built palaces on the main agricultural lands of the Valley core and on peripheral areas close to rivers. These developments encouraged other settlements due to the availabilities of drinking water, electricity, road networks, and employment. After the Rana rule ended in 1950, the country was opened to foreigners and foreign capital, which ushered in business investments and commercial development. Since then, the Valley's agricultural lands were rapidly transformed for urban use, with the ensuing urban development stretching east-west and north-south, and the accelerated growth spurred by rural in-migration into the capital, Kathmandu. The connectivity of highways to India and China (Figure 2) also accelerated the growth of urban settlement in the Valley (Shah, 2003; Thapa *et al.*, 2008; Haack and Rafter, 2006).

The Valley became rich with cultural heritage sites; including palaces, monuments, therapeutic sites such as holy ponds, temples, monasteries, and finely embellished public wells (Sekler, 1979). And today, five UNESCO world heritage sites—Pashupatinath Temple, Bouddhanath, Swayambhunath Monasteries, Durbar Square of Basantapur, and Patan—are located in the Kathmandu Valley.

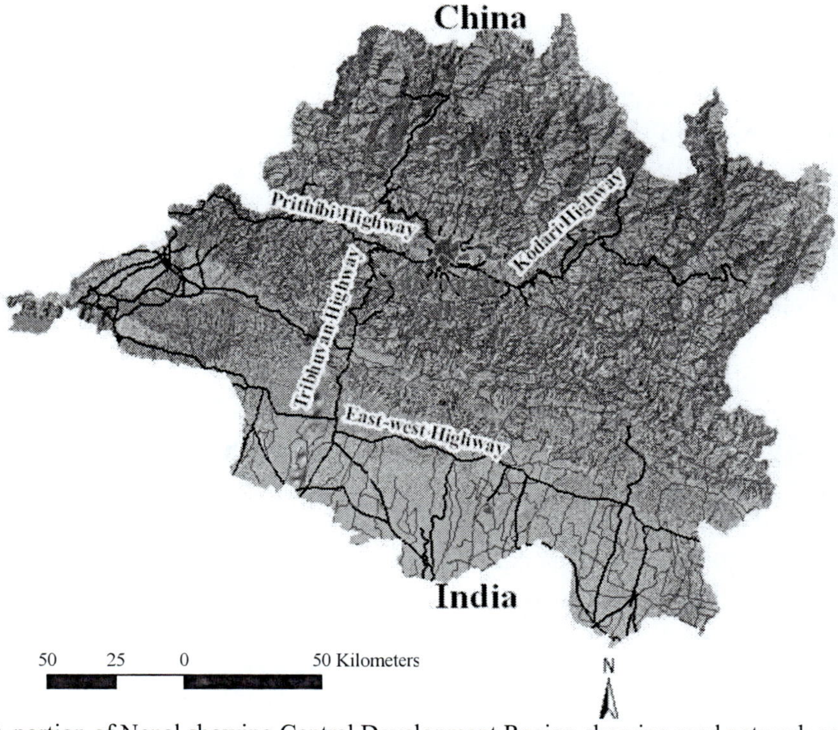

Figure 2. A portion of Nepal showing Central Development Region showing road network connecting the Kathmandu Valley to India and Tibet (China).

The development of ancient civilization and the constructions of historic buildings were also attributed to the amicable climatic conditions with an average temperature of 29.7^0 C in May and 2^0C in (December-January) and average annual rainfall of 1700 mm with maximum rainfall from June to August, and 75% average humidity. During the summer seasons, the easterly monsoon brings rainfalls ranging from 700 to 2100 mm (CBS, 2004).

The Valley has two principal landforms; alluvial and flood plains along the rivers, and slightly more elevated river terraces with loamy and boulder textured soils – with the latter, locally called *tars* with <1% slope surface (Haack and Khatiwada, 2007; Thapa *et al*., 2008). After the unification of Nepal in 1769, the Valley became the country's hub for culture, administration, and academic activities.

A relatively good transportation network and Kathmandu's primacy in the national urban hierarchy also encouraged a lot of in-migrants to the Valley, which initiated the formation of the earliest, unplanned urban developments in fringe areas, at the cost of productive farmlands (Figure 3). Although such rapid urban land development was bound to accompany urban economic growth, the habitual patterns of construction of substandard buildings to meet the subsistence needs of the growing population on one hand and the construction of world class hotels to promote tourism, has always been a major challenge for urban physical planning and to sustain living conditions of the majority population in the Valley, and remains one to this day.

RAPIDLY GROWING POPULATION: A CHALLENGE FOR URBAN PLANNING

Kathmandu was a small town with a little over 5,000 people in the 1910s (Joshi, 1999). Since then, it has experienced phenomenal growth in term of its population growth, physical extent, and regional geopolitical importance. The phenomenal growth of the urban area in size has occurred in a series of uncontrolled, and largely unplanned, growth spurts that have transformed spatially-irregular, peripheral areas into a proliferation of urban nuclei (Figure 3).

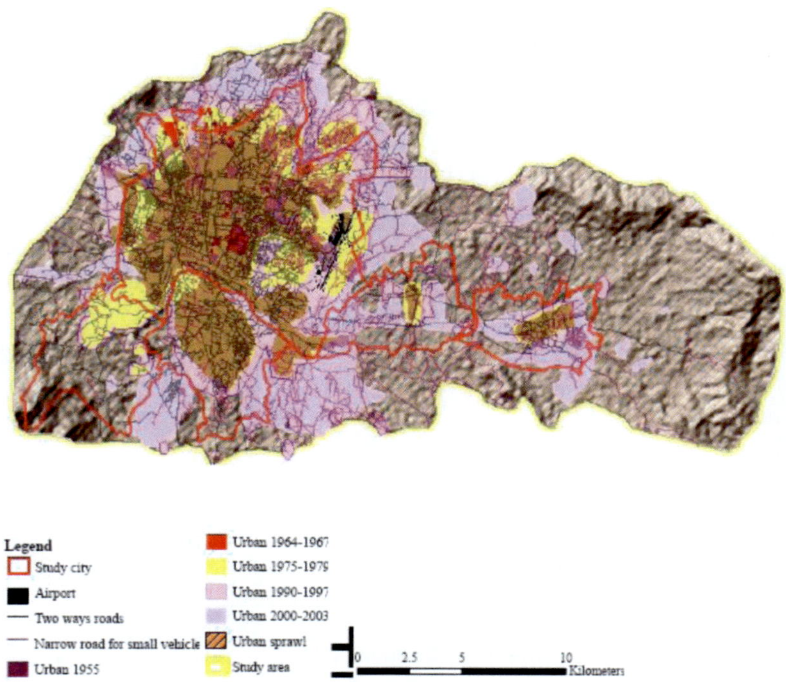

Figure 3. Proliferation of urban nuclei in the Kathmandu Valley (1955-2008). Urban areas are expanding outside the metropolitan, submetropolitan, and municipal boundaries.

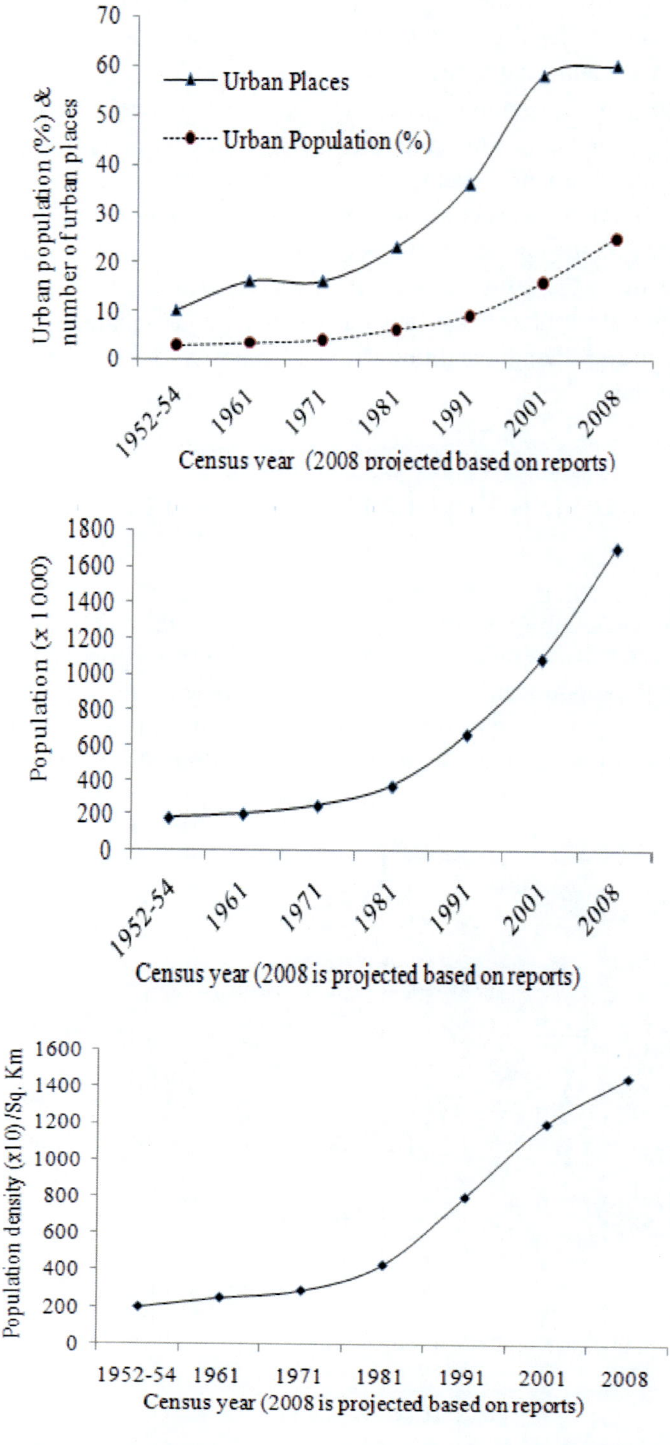

Figure 4. a) Urban population growth from 1952-2008, b) Valley urban population growth, and c) urban population density. Source: Haack and Rafter (2006), Thapa *et al*. (2008); Nepal's Population Report (2007), www.Kantipuronline.com and www.nepalnews.com.

According to the official census (1952/1954), only 10 settlements met the criteria of urban centers in Nepal, which defined as a permanent settlement with over 5,000 people at a density of 386 per square kilometer with over 75% of the adult population engaged in non-agricultural activities (Pradhan, 2003). Five urban centers located in the Kathmandu Valley came within this criterion supported by other facilities. The opening of the Tribhuvan International Airport enabled local airlines – Indian and Nepalese – to provide air-service to some Indian cities in the early 1950s. The construction of the Tribhuvan Rajpath (highway) connecting the Valley to India and of the Arniko Rajmarg (highway) connecting the Valley to China (Figure 2) in the 1960s, all helped fuel the growth and agglomeration of rural settlements in the Valley.

Although only 16% of the total national population lives in urban areas in Nepal, the country's rate of urbanization has been one of the highest in Asia and the Pacific since the 1970s (ADB/ICIMOD, 2006).

The adoption of economic neo-liberalization programs since the late 1980s, has also contributed to this process, with 'privatization' taking away the regulatory authority that physical planning might have imposed, so that the number of Nepal's urban centers has increased from 16 in 1971 to just over 58 (Figure 4a) in 2008 (Thapa *et al.*, 2008). In 1955, Kathmandu Valley accommodated 100% of the total urban population of the country (MDM, 1971), slightly > 50% of the total urban population in 1971 (Hardoy and Satterhwaite, 1981), and >40% in 2008 (CBS, 2008). At the same time, the Valley's urban population has increased by 499% along with the urban population density during the 1954-2008 (Figures 4b –c).

Temporal Analysis of Urban Growth

An analysis of the changes in urban growth using available aerial photos (1955-1958), cartographic information (1955-1968), and CORONA image (1967) reveals that there was a strong sectoral orientation of population concentration until the pre-1970s (Figure 5); however, overtime, the population was dispersed to fill-in open spaces between the transportation routes.

Spatial analysis at the coarser scale (79m x 79m) using MSS (1975) and topographic maps (1977-79) and at finer scale using QuickBird 2003 (0.53 m x 0.53m), and Worldview I and Google Image 2008 (0.5m x 0.5m) shows an overly-crowded urban infrastructure with little proper access- insufficient road- or path-ways - available to a large number of households (Figure 6). MSS images were used to separate urban areas from non-urban areas following unsupervised classification; topographic maps were used to digitize urban features. IKONOS image 2000 (1m x 1m), Quickbird images 2003 (0.53 m x 053 m) were used to identify built-up areas especially the buildings, classified using hybrid classification methods, first, unsupervised classification (identifying objects based on computer groupings of pixels) followed by supervised classification (training computer to organize pixels into user defined classes).

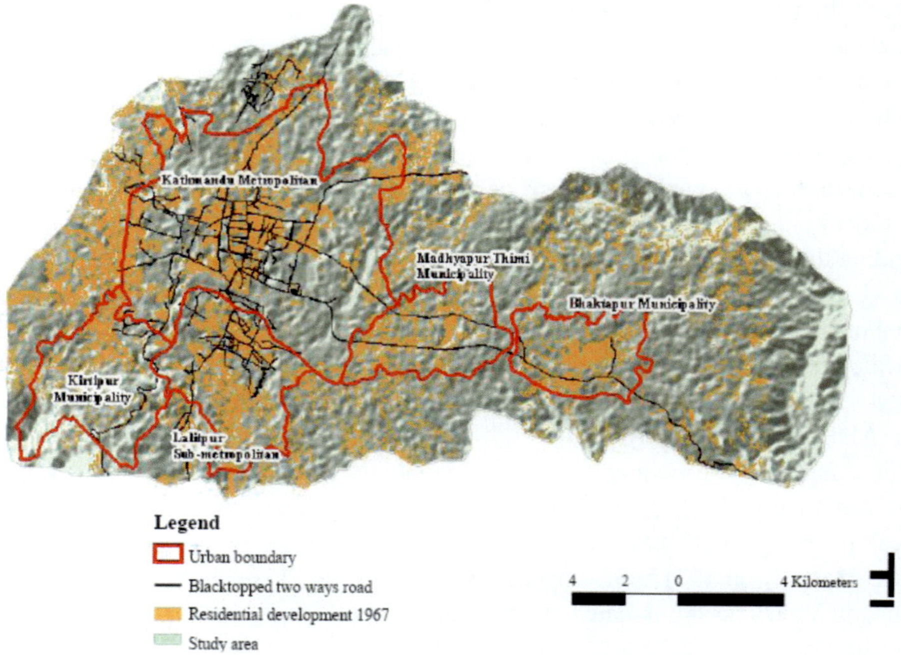

Figure 5. Population distribution along the roads in a sectoral manner (hybrid classification—unsupervised followed by supervised classification of CORONA 1967 image).

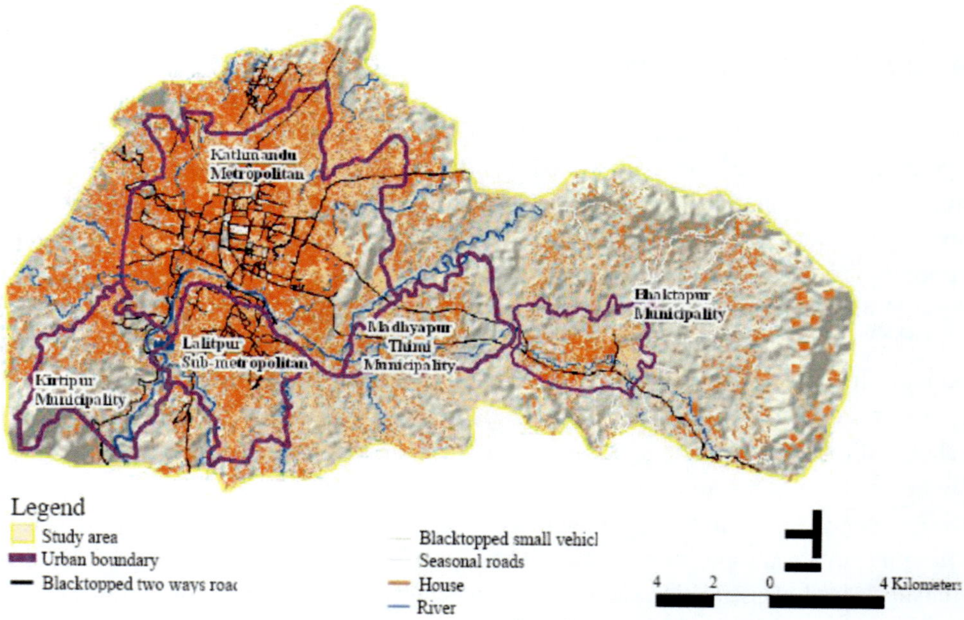

Figure 6. Crowded urban areas without proper accesses including sprawl along the urban fringes as seen on IKONOS 2000, Quickbird 2003, Worldview I and Google images 2008). Google images were **zoomed to maximum on a 24" flat monitor to capture many scenes; these scenes were georeferenced,** subset, and mosaicked to cover the entire study area).

These images were also used for on the fly digitizing to extract built-in features from shaded areas that often appeared black. Feature extracted from classified images were vectorized in Feature Analyst 4.2. These vectorized features were generalized in Feature Analyst 4.2 and cleaned manually where needed. These vectorized features consist of unidentified objects belonging to shaded areas in the images, which were later erased using an erase function in ArcMap with the hand digitized feature used as erase feature. In the IKONOS and Quickbird images, all the buildings were concrete roof display >200 pixel value in the spectral profile in all three bands. Likewise, the buildings with mud mortar and tile roof showed between 150-200 pixel values in the spectral profile in all three bands. For 2008, we had a single band Worldview I image (0.5 m x 05 m), which did not display any spectral characteristics. This Worldview I image of 2008 was merged with the Google Image of 2008 using the wavelet resolution merger (Peng, 2006:257-264 p) in Erdas Imagine 9.1. The wavelet resolution merger between Worldview I and Google Image 2008 was useful to isolate cement concrete (>200 pixel values in bands 1, 2, and 3 and then sharp decrease to 150 pixel value in band 4) from mud mortar and tile roofs (pixel value between 140-190 in all three bands and sharp decrease up to pixel value 90 in band 4).

On the basis of the analyses of the spectral behaviors of electromagnetic radiations, there are over 60% houses with permanent roof materials of mud and tiles and a minority (40%) are made of cement concrete in the study area.. Sampling on IKONOS 2000 and 2003 images revealed that cement concrete surfaces displayed >200 pixel values in all bands (1, 2, and 3), while mud and tiles roofs displayed pixel values between 150 and 200. Blacktopped roads and culverts also show >200 pixel values, while pixel values for dry grasses and water stressed vegetation also showed between 150 and 200 pixel values; thus, making it difficult to separate cement concrete buildings from blacktopped roads and culverts. In order to delineate these features, IKONOS 2000 and Quickbird 2003 images were classified using hybrid classifications (unsupervised classification to remove unidentified features and then supervised classification) following maximum likelihood methods. The classified images were recoded for various classes; especially separating cement concrete buildings from mud mortar and tiled buildings. These recoded images were vectorized and polygons were generalized using Feature Analyst 4.2.

Simultaneously, all the buildings were manually digitized on the IKONOS, Quickbird, and Worldview I images. These digitized buildings were separated into mud mortar and tiles and cement roofed buildings by overlying vectorized features (from classified images) in ArcMap. We used erased functions in ArcMap to remove cement concrete and mud mortar tile roofed buildings (Figure 7a-c) and vice-versa and later these different layers were appended to make a shapefile for the analysis.

Once different buildings were identified, these building layers were used as mask in Feature Analyst 4.2 in ArcMap while auto- vectorizing open spaces (parks, grassland, scattered vegetation, and water bodies). Many narrower roads (1.5-2 meters) which are heavily shadowed and even blocked by buildings were manually digitized. Wider roads (> 4 meters) were extracted from auto vectorization in Feature Analyst 4.2. Later, these auto-vectorized shape-files representing wider roads were generalized and manually cleaned.

Similar methods were followed for 2008; however, the Worldview I image was converted into four bands multispectral image by combining it with the Google Image of 2008 using wavelet resolution merger (Gong, 2006).

(a)

Source:
http://unesdoc.unesco.org/images/0015/001520/152020m.pdf

(b)

http://www.tt.fhkoeln.de/semesterprojects_extern/dmnepal07_08/Final_Report_URM.pdf

(c)

www.kantipuronline.com

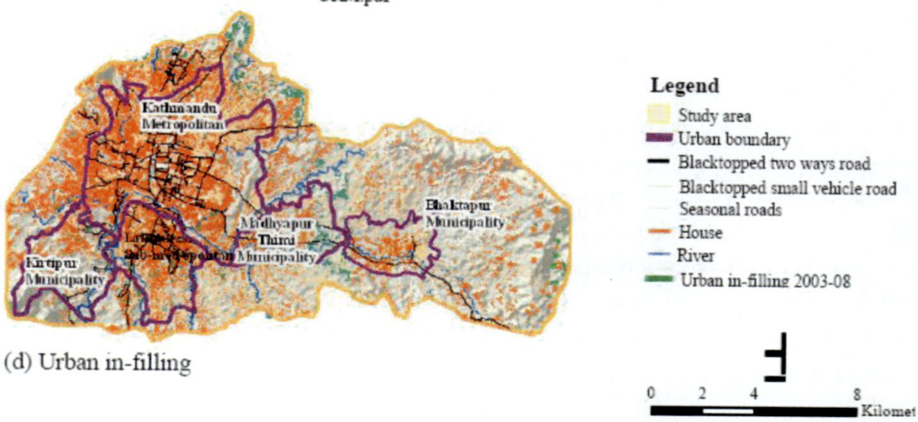

(d) Urban in-filling

Figure 7. a) mud-mortar and tiled roof with less tensile strength to tolerate any types of seismic shaking; b) mixed between mud-mortar and tiled roof and cement concrete that can tolerate some seismic shaking; c) cement concrete building built following strict seismic codes; d) some infilling.

The result revealed relatively clearer pictures of ground features than from the IKONOS and Quickbird images. All built-in structures were clearly separated from the non-built-up features. Once various objects were identified, the concrete and mud and tiles roof buildings were separated using the erase function in ArcMap. However, we faced problems of identifying hybrid buildings, such as in Figure 7b, which had been separated by division, partial demolition, new construction, and addition of floors on existing buildings. Our method failed to isolate such cases where a narrow roof is partitioned with two different roofing materials, cement concrete and mud and tiles.

In addition to partitioning houses, we also observed considerable infilling between houses (Figure 7d). These infillings were noticed by comparing images of two different times. It was observed that there were many infillings along with urban sprawl between 2003 and 2008; probably due to rural migrants coming to Kathmandu for safety and jobs, especially, after the escalation of the People's War in the last decade. Sengupta and Sharma (2006) and Thapa *et al* (2008) estimate the growth of such in-migrants at approximately 20%. This most recent large scale in-migration and accompanying unplanned, and unregulated, rapid urban growth has therefore contributed to infrastructure bottlenecks, even higher residential densities, and overall environmental degradation due to the decline in open 'green-spaces' within the urbanized areas and the wholesale reduction of agricultural lands in the Valley at large.

Today, in 2008, the Valley's residential density is >1,000 persons/ha with three-four storied building typologies (Adhikari, 1998:41). Though this residential density in

Kathmandu is lower than in Hong Kong (>4,800 persons/ha) and Thailand (≈ 2,950 persons/ha), it is much higher than in the US suburbs (<10 persons/ha), but is close to Malaysia (1,100 persons/ha). Urban planners (Adhikari, (1998) suggests that the Valley population has to be reduced to at least 300 persons per hectare (ppha) population density with optimal 500 ppha, but instead, the Valley's population is still increasing and open 'green-spaces' are shrinking.

Lack of Open Spaces and Environmental Deterioration

Rapid population growth and infilling in the Valley puts a great strain on the urban green environment. Households need some open spaces for a healthy environment. An open space is defined as the ratio of circulation area divided by total area that is specific to cultures and places. Parks and playgrounds, schools and colleges, hospitals, public transportation, telephone lines, sewers and discharge pipes are considered open spaces (Figures 8 a-f). Figure 8f presents scenarios of open space and built-up areas for the Kathmandu Valley from 1955 to 2008.

These open spaces were first auto-digitized from 1955-1958 aerial photos using Feature Analyst 4.2, generalized, and then cleaned manually. Same shapefile was overlaid on the topographic maps, IKONOS, Quickbird and Worldview I and Google images to estimate open-space and built-up areas for the subsequent years. Polygons covered by buildings in the subsequent years were deleted from the original shapefile. Areas inside the building compounds were captured using digitizing options in ArcMap. Our estimation revealed that the open space area in Kathmandu is decreasing in the subsequent years (Figure 8).

Caminos and Goehert (1978 *cited in Ojima*) recommended an open area of 150 m^2 per 10,000 m^2 of built-up area while the World Bank housing project recommends 20 to 25% open space for a built-up area. For the safety of an individual, a 2 m^2 space is needed per person. In general, 5-10% open space is needed for housing purposes; however, the unplanned housing schemes leave not much open spaces in the Kathmandu Metropolitan area (Figures 8a-f), which is well below any Western standards. Even in Manhattan, New York US, with skyscraper buildings, an average of 19.2 m^2 natural area is available for each average building; in London, it is 30.4 m^2 for each building while accounting for the city's surrounding Green-belt spaces; in Paris, it is 12.2 m^2; and in Tokyo, it is 2.1 m^2 (Ojima, 1996).

The above numerical values of 'open space' may not be the best measures when assessing 'accessibility' and its efficiency and cost-effectiveness as it pertains to a metropolitan area's housing growth and development. For example, only 12-16% open spaces are maintained in Singapore, but all houses are accessible by emergency vehicles. Nonetheless, for cities like Kathmandu to serve 2-3 storied spontaneous and institutional housing styles, sufficient open spaces are needed to rescue people from possible seismic vulnerabilities. Contemporary planners in the Valley suggest a 40:60 ratio, for built-up and non-built-up land, by 2021, which will be higher than the 32:68 ratio that they envisioned in 2001.

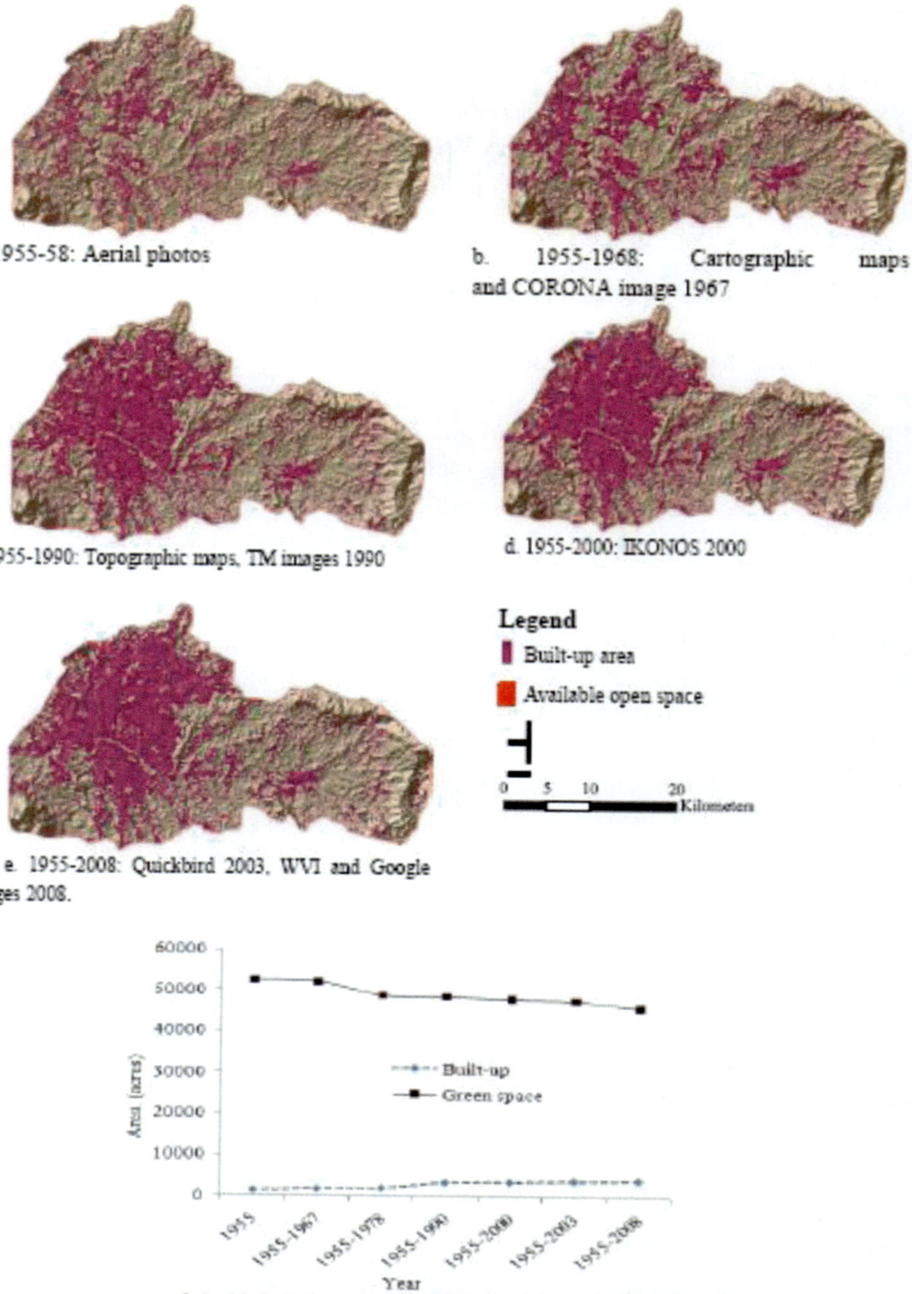

Figure 8. Open areas vs. built-up areas (1955-2008).

A detailed analysis of the Kathmandu Metropolitan area at its smallest administrative level—the Ward--based on the Worldview I and Google image 2008 (Figure 9 a-b) revealed that it is almost impossible to meet this goal given the diminishing sizes of open spaces in all the sectors in general and in Core and Central sector (Figure 9 a- b) in particular, as a result of the infilling of housing in open spaces throughout the Valley (Figure 7d).

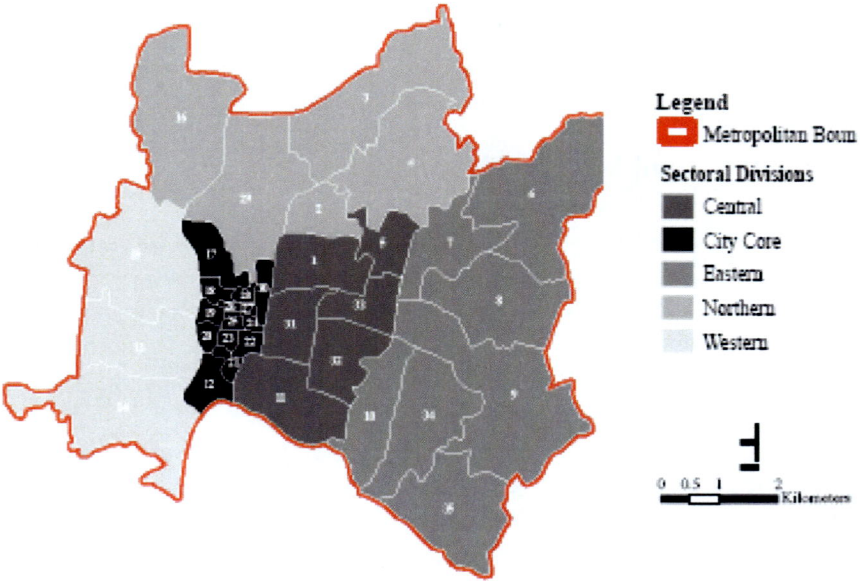

(a)

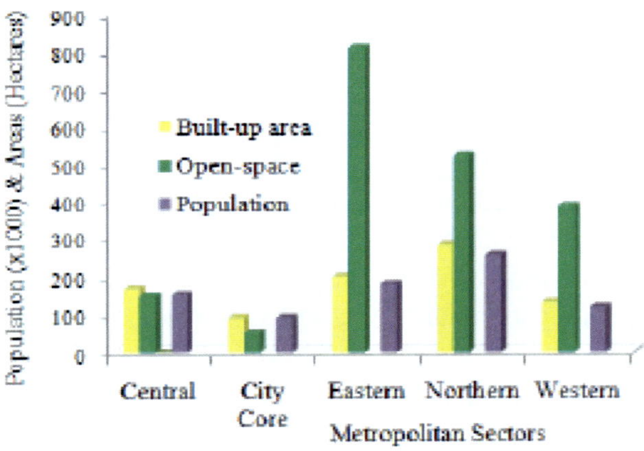

(b)

Figure 9. a) Kathmandu Metropolitan area showing ward divisions, and b) built-up, open space, and population in five sectoral divisions of the Kathmandu Metropolitan area. The population for each ward level was **estimated following Lo's (2006) "Dwelling Unit-related Demographic Models" (p. 351).**

The losses of agriculturally productive areas, increasing incidences of infilling and reduction of open space has exacerbated urban vulnerabilities with the possibilities of losses of lives and properties in events of natural disasters. For example, the City Core of the Kathmandu Metropolitan (Figure 9 a) area was heavily damaged during the 1934 major **earthquake that rocked the capital city with >7.8 magnitude** "M_w" earthquake. Likewise, the Central Sector of the metropolitan (Figure 9 a) had also suffered heavy losses during that earthquake. The loss of open spaces in these sectors (Figure 9 b) has increased further urban vulnerabilities. Not to mention the higher slope and low land face vulnerabilities from heavy rains and mud sliding. Additionally, the loss of open spaces and vegetation due to their fast conversions into substandard buildings has made the bowl-like geography and generally low wind speed Valley as a sink for pollutants during the winter seasons (Haack and Rafter, 2006).

Housing Standards and Varying Types

The UN has long defined a housing standard as a "measure of accessibility, at a given time and place and in a given set of cultural and economic conditions" (1968: 9), while Mood defined it as "necessary to safeguard the health and welfare of the occupants of the dwelling and the persons residing in the vicinity of the dwelling" (1969:4). Furthermore, APHA defined housing standard as a "safe dwelling unit with sanitary facilities fit for human habitation by governing the condition and maintenance (1971)."

In the Kathmandu Valley, spontaneous and institutional types of houses are built, but many of them do not meet "the required health, safety, seismic scales and external environment" (Adhikari, 1998: 29). These 'spontaneous' types consist of individual houses built with local materials including thatch roofs, bricks, mud, reinforced concrete (rod and concrete cement- RCC), and RCC pillars. These buildings were built without following regulations, such as building codes and municipal regulatory controls. As observed from the Worldview I (0.5 m^2) and Google 2008 images, some of the buildings constructed under this spontaneous typology are built on 750-900 m^2 plots with at least 4 m in the front, 6 m in the back, and 4 m in the sides. Others within this category include residential buildings constructed on 400 m^2 land, occupying up to 51% of the plot with <4 m from the front and back of the plot and 3 m from the sides of the plot boundary, while others are constructed on plots of 200 m^2 with a maximum permitted built-up area of 55% leaving at least 3 m in the back and 2.5 m in the front. Also, within this spontaneous typology are government institutional buildings constructed on plots >900 m^2 area with at least 5 m distance between the house and the boundary of the property at the front, 7 m at the back, and 5 m from either side.

Modern expensive building with hyperbolic parabolic roofs, large concrete cantilevered beams and slabs and concrete steel structures designed with modern engineering methods are very common in smaller plots (Adhikari, 1998). To avoid high expenses, many houses are constructed with an intermediate technology as suggested by Schumacher (1979) for Third World countries including India, Pakistan, Sri Lanka, the Philippines, Thailand, Ghana, and Egypt.

These buildings constitute a sloping roof with brackets, net windows, carved doors, and exposed brick walls (Adhikari, 1998). Most of the houses are built very compact (Figure 10 a) on small sized irregular plots to overcome the shortage of land, irrespective of the increasing cost after certain limit of increasing housing density per hectare (Figure 10 b); even some buildings are constructed close of national heritages (Figure 10 c) to overcome the cost of land.

Overtime, though the building materials have been changed from mud mortar, adobe, stone built to rod cement concrete to bear high stresses, overcrowding and decreasing plot sizes have been the biggest problems in the Kathmandu's urbanization.

(a)

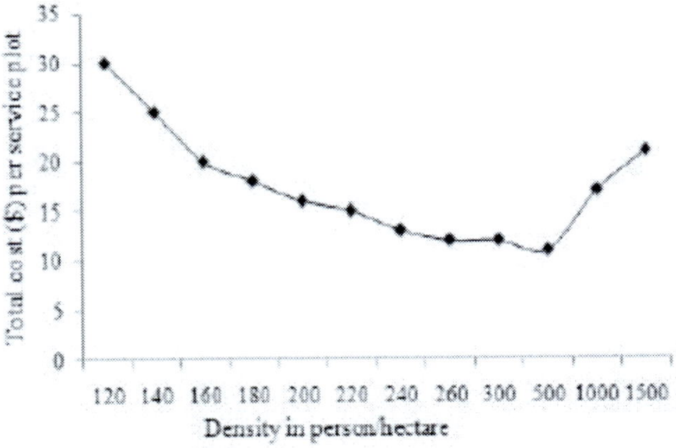

(b)

(c)

Figure 10. a) compact building; b) graph showing decreasing cost of compact buildings per hectare until the density per hectare reaches 600 person, and then increasing cost of compactness or population density per hectare; and c) some of the private buildings are constructed near the national heritages (Figure 10 b was adopted from Adhikari, 1998 with some modifications with the inclusion of new information).

Plot Sizes

The recommended official plot sizes in the Kathmandu Valley are similar to those in Latin American Cities which also have their spontaneous settlements, such as *favelas, barrios*, and *colonias miserias* (plot size ≈100 m^2); however, our Worldview I image reveals that houses are built on plots as small as 15 to 45 m^2. Adhikari (1998) also observed similar conditions from his extensive field studies. An analysis of the housing density *vs* housing cost equation revealed that high housing density in Kathmandu decreases the cost of unit housing up to 600 persons/ha (Figure 10 b), but increases afterwards (Adhikari, 1998). This analysis was done with the integration of information from Adhikari (1998), a price list of unit acreage of land obtained from the Land Reform Office, Kathmandu, and the housing compactness from our Worldview I 2008 image.

Despite these significant relationships between housing densities and housing costs, smaller plots are sold by private land brokers to meet individual buyer's economic (use-value) interests, but the resultant housing is lacking needed open spaces, proper drainage systems, supplies of water and electricity (Poudel, 2007a). Some houses are even constructed with reinforced concrete (RCC) on smaller plots, between 2- 4 *anas* $\approx$ 63 to 127 m^2:1 *ropani* $\approx$ 16 *anas* $\approx$ 509 m^2; often without proper sewage outlets (Adhikari, 1998:39). These densely packed houses developments have hindered accessibility services.

Problems of Accessibility

Effective transportation network provides good connectivity and movement of people, traffic, and goods both within urban areas and between urban and hinterlands. However, inefficient transportation especially narrower streets and cul-de-sacs limit the accessibility of emergency vehicle services. A classic example of the "Tragedy of the Commons" is evident in Kathmandu, due to individual households' thoughtless efforts to maximize the private use of every square inch of their land, at the expense of the common good (Adhikari, 1998). In inner areas of the Valley's city centers, the narrower streets ($\leq$ 2.5 meters) and sturdy wall fences for security reasons are not only posing problems of accessibility, but they have also created 'housing compounds' which serve as garbage sites and dust bowls in the dry season and filthy-water ponds during the rainy seasons. In the absence of effective rules and/or their lack of implementations, inner-city land plots have been subdivided to maximize profits, with the result that road widths have been further narrowed.

The western-style suburbs with larger open spaces are unaffordable due to high population to land ratios and low income conditions. In the western countries, roads are categorized by their widths and services they provide; for example, collectors (8 m width, serving over 150 houses with 10.5 right-of-way), secondary (6 m width, serving at least 15 houses with 10.5 right-of-way), and local (4 m width, serving 25 houses with 5 m right of way). Many countries such as UK, USA, India, Russia, Norway, Finland, the former Yugoslavia, and Holland have used geo-space (underground space) to increase open space areas. In Kathmandu, underground/subway transportation is non-existent because of economic reasons and possible seismic vulnerabilities. And, also because of the generally very low incomes at the household level, the purchase of a private automobile is totally out of the question for many households.

Many narrower roads without right-of-ways are taken as the normal way of living due to the lack of vehicles by the majority of the households. Not withstanding that these right-of-ways would have worked as the forerunners for future vehicular roads (Adhikari, 1998:46) if, or when, living standards rose, but such long-term planning is missing in Kathmandu, making services difficult at present and impossible for the future. A bicyclist and pedestrian needs at least 2 m wide road, a pedestrian, bicyclist and motorbike rider together need at least 3 m wide roads, and emergency vehicles need at least 4, 5, and 7.5 m wide roads with adequate turning radii. Though 7.5 m wide roads would best serve the purpose, given the high people to land ratio, it could be compromised with 4 m wider road. Unfortunately, housing units are so crowded in Kathmandu that many of the houses are not accessible by vehicular roads (Figure 11) making the Valley vulnerable to plans for evacuation in response to severe and disastrous seismic activities.

An analysis conducted by converting types of houses as points (centroids but areas attached to each points in an attribute table) and major roads as lines and computing distances from each section of road to individual housing unit revealed accessibilities problems (Figure 11) for rescuing people in case of emergencies and also for other service areas, such as drainage.

Lack of drainage facilities is further aggravated by the solid residential compound walls that interface the narrow roads. Seepage from individual septic tanks in the tiny residential plots severely contaminates ground water (Adhikari, 1998). Additionally, drinking water pipes often follow the narrow serpentine streets and run parallel to sewage pipes making services difficult. As sprawl has spread to the far limits of the Valley, the metropolitan government is unable to provide essential utilities and services to the increasing number of houses in narrow spaces at such lengthy distances (Poudel, 2007a).

A house with 30 m^2 floor-space needs at least 40 m^2 plot to accommodate a family of six. However, the majorities of the houses are built without meeting these requirements, and in average, four people share a small room of 12-15 m^2. **Following Lo (2006) "Dwelling Unit-related Demographic Models" (p. 351), an integration of information of building areas and** actual population of Central and Core Sectors (Figures 10 a –b) revealed that in average, 4 people share 9 m^2 built-up area.

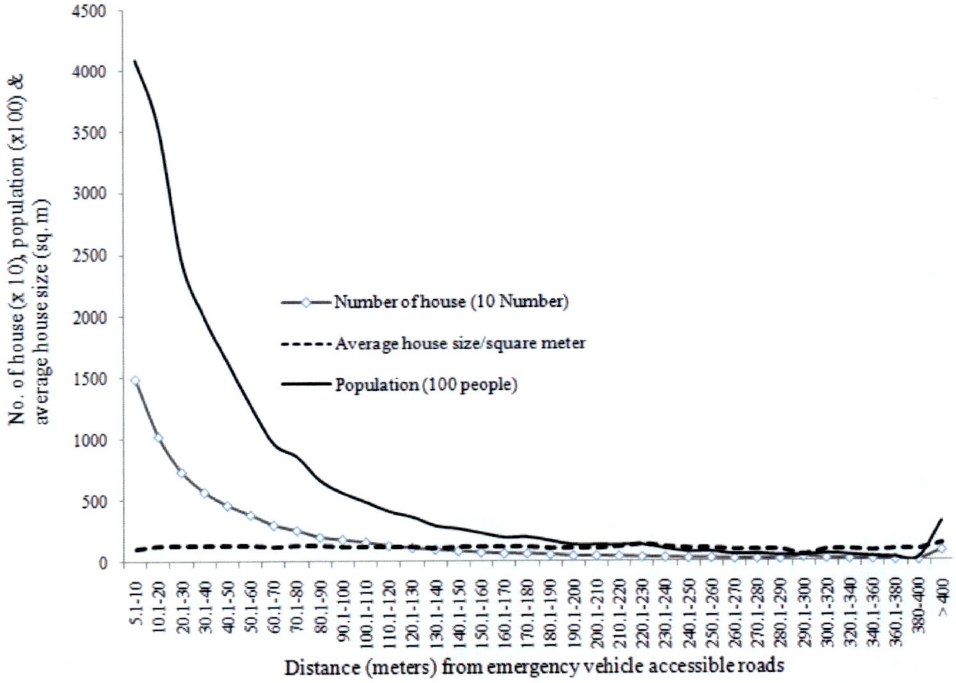

Figure 11. Distances to individual housing units from serviceable roads. Average plinth areas of houses were estimated from Worldview I and Google 2008 images, population for each housing dwelling unit **was estimated following Lo (2006) " Dwelling Unit-related Demographic Models" (p. 351).**

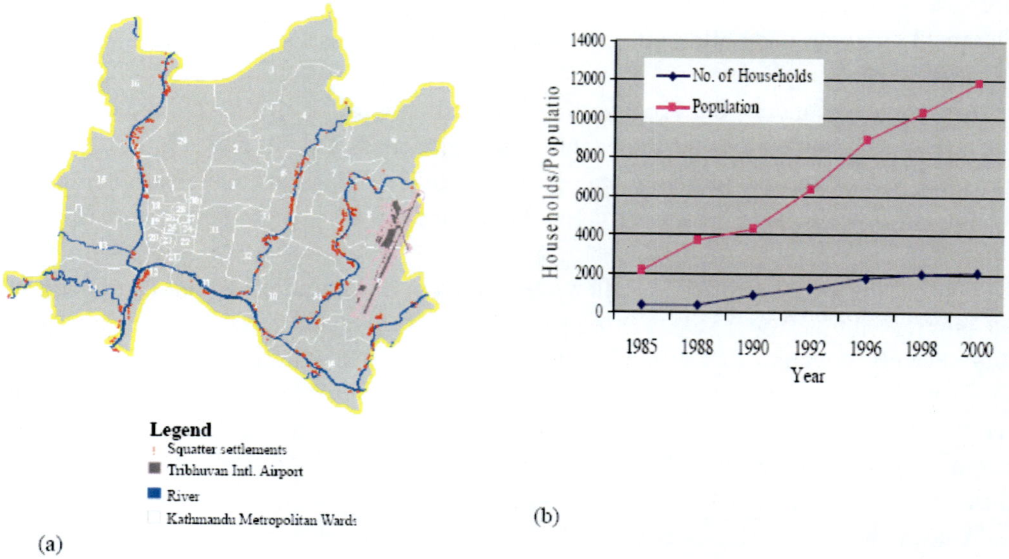

Figure 12. a) Locations of squatter settlements along the low level river banks; and b) findings from Pradhan and Perera (2005); and http://emi.pdc.org/cities/CP-Kathmandu-08-05.pdf.

These substandard, yet often exorbitantly-priced housing, have increased land prices also making many people unable to afford for housing but to squat on open lands. A comparative look of the IKONOS 2000, Quickbird 2003 and Worldview I and Google 2008 images revealed the mushrooming of spontaneous slum settlements along the river banks and open spaces (Figure 12 a). Pradhan and Perera (2005) also observed similar situations (Figure 12 b). A survey of literature revealed that 1/3rd of the Kathmandu's residents live in slum dwellings and over 18,000 people are squatting lands without land rights (Pradhan and Perera, 2005). The occupations of ecologically sensitive and marginal areas such as riverbeds and lowlands along dangerous or untenable flooding areas without proper access to clean water and sanitation further increases urban vulnerabilities. Furthermore, squatting areas of national heritages (Kathmandu Post, 2003; Sengupti and Sharma, 2006) further aggravates the urban vulnerabilities in seismic sensitive city.

Seismic Vulnerabilities

The Kathmandu Valley is located in the Himalayan arc, which in the last decade, has experienced three major earthquakes (>7.8 magnitude "M_w") causing huge losses of lives and properties. Each year, the Himalayan arc experiences earthquakes and earth's crust upheavals of about 3 cm average elevations, due to the regular push of the Tibetan plate on the Indian plate. In the 20th century alone, over 11,000 people have lost their lives in Nepal due to the earthquakes, and geologists expect the possibility of such dangers anytime in the future (Andreas, 1995; DRMP, 2005). The Valley is very susceptible to seismic-related and caused damages due to the presence of huge structures, such as temples and monasteries carved with heavy rocks, bricks, mud-mortar, masonry, and timber (Figure 10 c). Past studies have suggested that brick and stone masonry structures used in the construction of the majority of houses built by intermediate technology have suffered the most damage, because of their low tensile and shear strengths when largely amplified short-period waves shake the ground (Jaishi, We-Xin, Zong, and Maskey, 2003). These temples and monasteries were built close to water, and in tranquil and contemplative environments, which were suited for mediation and spiritual inspirations. Until the 1980s, these heritage structures were distant from densely populated areas. Recently, however, the combination of rapid population growth and declining land availability has lead to the siting of a large number of settlements near to these temples and monasteries (Figure 10 c), making such settlements more vulnerable to any ground tremors and seismic shocks.

Similar to many developing countries of the global South, where "86% of the households face more than one threat" (Degg 1992: 203-304), contemporary urban dwellers in the Kathmandu Valley face many risks due to structural construction practices, inadequate planning for road access, high population density, and weak institutional capacities (DoR, 2004).

PROBLEMS OF DRINKING WATER

One in three people do not have regular access to drinking water in the Valley at present. According to a 2001 estimation of the Nepal Water Supply Corporation (NWSC), >146 million liters (@78 liters/person/day, excluding 11% non-domestic consumption) of water is needed each day (mlpd) for the Valley with an expected increase to 346 mlpd (@92 liters/person/day) by 2016 (Poudel, 2007b). In 2007, WaterAid estimated that one third of all households lack safe drinking water in all the Valley municipalities (Thapa *et al.*, 2008). Yet, over the last two decades, successive governments have been promising people they would be provided with enough fresh water from the Melamchi River, 40 miles to the north-east of Kathmandu, but it has been delayed due to several technical, political and financial reasons (Poudel, 2007 c). In addition to the aforementioned water scarcity, poor management and maintenance of the delivery system has resulted in >54% of the water leakage ("unaccounted for") that enters the city's distribution system (Pandey, 2007).

Although the majority of households are connected to the Valley's water supply network, since the 1980s, water supply to individual households has been rationed due to the relative scarcity of water and the deplorable, physical state of the distribution network. Sometimes water is supplied on just one or two days of a week. According to the Urban Program Operation Framework 2005-2010, published by WaterAid Nepal, on an average, 78% population receive water in each alternate day that is contaminated with coliform bacteria (Pandey, 2007). WaterAid believes this might be due to the parallel setup of drinking water and sewer pipes along the existing serpentine roads in between jammed houses.

Private entrepreneurs have made huge investments in water tankers, underground storage tanks (cisterns), and roof tanks ($\approx 2\ m^3$) and in the production of mineral waters using the reverse osmosis process to supply water in the Valley. Then, the additional costs to purchase store tanks, pipe work and purification processes for individuals' homes are also making water supply a difficult and increasingly costly task in the Valley. A family spends US$27.00 a month to buy water from private tankers for domestic uses and pays US$5.00 per month for mineral waters (Poudel, 2007b). To overcome increasing water prices, underground water is extracted at twice the sustainable recharge rate leading to the depletion of the water table. In many places, arsenic contamination has also been reported from the deep ground water (Amatya and Fowler, 2005). In some places, the depleted ground water table has led to the sinking of land, especially in previous waste disposal "landfill" areas, causing damage to valuable properties.

Waste Disposal

In the Valley, current municipal waste generation is estimated at 0.61 kg per capita per day. This infectious biodegradable waste is now 2-3 times larger than it was in 1960. Garbage is often dumped in vacant lots and open areas and such exposure of garbage often attracts vermin, mice, or birds creating hygiene problems. Ideally, the best way to solve various garbage problems the Valley faces would be to decrease the amount of trash generated, but it scarcely feasible to expect a return to the life style of ancient times, where people's lives and material support systems were more suited to a natural, low-impact cycle of use, reuse and organic disposal. Garbage such as paper can be recycled and many kitchen refuses can be reused as a fertilizer by composting them, while incinerated garbage can generate >1900 kcal/kg heat. Research is needed for the development of different types of garbage disposal systems. A similar garbage disposal problem in Tokyo, Japan, has been solved by creating 130 meters wide, 30 meters deep, and 60 meters underground disposal plants (Ojima, 1996), but in the Valley such waste disposal would only contribute to higher pollution levels and lower air quality.

Conclusion

Our analyses from remote sensing and GIS techniques reveal that the Kathmandu urban vulnerabilities are increasing due to unplanned urban structures, lack of access for emergency vehicles, loss of agricultural lands, and loss of open spaces due to overcrowding of people and residential buildings. The current urban growth patterns are haphazard, and generally unregulated in the new infilling and rural-urban fringe areas. This haphazard growth pattern in transitional rural-urban areas, along with the dense population of the urban core, has been a great concern to urban administrators and planners, in their rather futile efforts to try to enforce and maintain adequate housing standards in this seismologically-sensitive Valley. Though the towns of the Valley evolved under strict religious restrictions with idyllic and picturesque serenity, the Valley's increasing congestion due to its increasing high population to land ratio has led to the formation and growth of slums with water-logged situations during the monsoon season and dust bowls during the dry seasons. Our analyses of images reveal that unplanned infrastructure developments, narrow streets and the lack of accessible passages, increasing air and water pollution, and problems of waste disposal have made the Valley- once known for the harmony of its architecture and supporting fertile lands- more vulnerable than ever before.

In theory, the urban population should enjoy better access to services, facilities, but the Valley's residents suffer from serious deficiencies of almost all of the more promising urban advantages. The continued existence of the Valley's rich cultural heritages is under threat. In recent times, shortages of fully-serviced land for housing have pushed up land prices so high that much of the residential property has become unaffordable to medium and low income people. It is essential to discourage rapid urban growth, and if possible, reverse migration to reduce spontaneous slum settlement growth and expansion. Strict regulations are needed to regulate residential densities, land subdivisions, to retain open spaces, and to layout roads and create provision for drainages. A sectoral analysis of the Kathmandu metropolitan area exemplifies that current urban structure without open spaces and jammed building will lead to several urban vulnerabilities in this seismological sensitive overcrowded city.

Judicious urban planning and sustainable urban growth management are critical for human, economics, and environmental well-being during periods of high growth, such as currently being experienced in the Valley. Introduction of a rural-urban boundary to improve roads, water, power, phones and sewages in already developed areas and restricting development in the agricultural zones by not providing infrastructure might help regulate urban growth and alleviate vulnerabilities.

Our analyses lead us to the conclusion that urban restructuring with strict regulations are needed to ensure the sustainability of this historic city, and reverse, or at least hold up, the current dysfunctional slide into a heightened state of vulnerability and urban crisis. Projecting these analyses, conclusions and policy implications beyond Kathmandu and whole of Nepal, we believe this chapter's holistic, visualizing approach might very well serve as a useful analytical remote sensing/GIS-based prototype to assess the inevitable, heightened vulnerabilities that accompany unprecedented, and largely uncontrolled, urban growth in other rapidly growing cities of the global South.

REFERENCES

ADB/ICIMOD (2006). Asian Development Bank/International Center for Integrated Mountain Development, *Environment Assessment of Nepal: Emerging Issues and Challenges*, Kathmandu.

Adhikari, Ambika Prasad (1998). *Urban and Environmental Planning in Nepal: Analysis, Policies and Proposals*. IUCN-The World Conservation Union: pp. 132.

Alonso-Villar, O. (2001). Large Metropolises in the Third World: An Explanation. *Urban Studies* 38(8), 1359–1371.

Amatya, P. and G. Fowler (2005). ENPHO magazine cited in Poudel (2007).

APHA (1971). Housing: Basic health principles and recommended ordinance. Washington DC. American Public Health Association.

Andreas, P. (1995). Images of century, the changing townscapes of the Kathmandu Valley. GTZ/UNDP.

Baton, M. R. and R. I. Mayes (1993). Out-of-plane seismic response of reinforced masonry walls. *J. Struct. Eng.* ASCF: 11899): 2495.

Benveniste, Guy (1977). The politics of expertise, 2nd ed. San Francisco: Boyd and Fraser.

Bourne, L. S. (1982). *Internal Structure of the City*, Oxford, England: Oxford University Press.

Cavailhès, J., P. Frankhauser, D. Peeters (2004). Where Alonso meets Sierpinski: An urban economic model of a fractal metropolitan area. *Environment and Planning A*, vol. 36 (8):1471-1498.

CBS (2008). Centre Bureau of Statistics, Government of Nepal.

CBS (2004). *Nepal Living standard Survey 2003/04, Statistical Report*, Volume II. His Majesty's Government of Nepal, Kathmandu.

Cohen, N. (2001). *Urban Planning Conservation and Preservation*, McGraw-Hill.

CWP (2003). *Impacts of Impervious Cover on Aquatic Systems*. Center for Watershed Protection, Ellicott City, Maryland, 368p.

Degg, M. (1992) Natural disasters: Recent trends and future prospects. *Geography*: 198-209.

DoR (2004). *Department of Road: List of important roads and status*. Road Statistics, Government of Nepal.

Depuis, J. (1962). Les basins interieurs du Kashmir et du Nepal. *Annals de Geographie*, 71 (384):156-166, cited in Pradhan (2003).

Dogan, M. and J. Kasarda (1988). *The Metropolis Era: Mega-Cities.* Newbury Park: Sage.

DRMP (2005). Kathmandu Valley, Nepal, Disaster Risk Management Profile: Last Review, August 2005. http://emi.pdc.org/cities/CP-Kathmandu-08-05.pdf#search=% 22Squatter% 20settlements% 20in%20Kathmandu%20Valley%22

Gong, P. (2006) Image processing methods. In Ridd, M. K, and J. D. Hipple (eds). Remote Sensing of Human Settlements: Manual of Remote Sensing, Third Edition, Vol. 5. ASPRS, The Image and Geospatial Information Society. p. 208-271.

Greene, R. P. and J. B. Pick (2006). *Exploring the urban community: A GIS Approach*. In Clarke, Keith C. (ed.). Prentice Hall Series in Geographic Information Science.

Haack, B. N., and G. Rafter (2006). Urban growth analysis and modeling in the Katmandu Valley, Nepal. *Habitat International*, 30: 1056-1065.

Haack, Barry N. and G. Khatiwada (2007). Rice and bricks: Environmental issues and mapping of the unusual crop rotation pattern in the Kathmandu Valley, Nepal.

Hardoy, J. and D. Satterthwaite (1981). *Shelter Need and Response: Housing, Land and Settlement Policy in Seventh Third World Countries*, Chichester, John Wiley.

IUCN, The World Conservation Union (1999). *Environmental Planning and Management of the Kathmandu Valley*. His Majesty's Government of Nepal, Ministry of Population and Environment.

Jat, M. K., P. K. Garg, and P. K. Khare (2006). Assessment of urban growth pattern using spatial analysis techniques. *In Proceedings of Indo-australian conference on Information Technology in civil engineering* (IAC-ITCE), 20-21, February, pp 70.

Jaishi, B., R. We –Xin R., Zong, Zhou-Hong, and Maskey, P. N. (2003). Dynamic and seismic performance of old multi-tiered temples in Nepal. *Engineering Structure*, 25: 1827-1839.

Joshi, J. (1999). *Housing and urban development in Nepal: An analysis and design of participatory development process*. Revised edition. Naveen Press, Kathmandu, Nepal.

Joshi, P. S. (2004). Road to nowhere: The proposed Outer Ring Road completely ignores past plans for Kathmandu Valley's organic growth. *Spotlight*, Issue #223 (26), November 04 - 02 December).

Kathmandu Post (2003). UN Park Stalled due to squatters, November 17.

Koirala, H. (2000). RS and GIS in assessing urban environment: A case study of the Kathmandu Metropolitan city. http://www.pages.hotbot.com/edu.geoinformatics/f118.html.

KVTDC (2002). Kathmandu Valley town Development Committee, *Long-term Development Concept of Kathmandu Valley Urban Development Committee, Kathmandu.*

Lave, J., D. Yule, S. Sapkota, K. Basnat, C. Madden, M. Attal, and R. Pandey (2005). Evidence for a Great Medieval Earthquake (~1100 A.D.) in the Central Himalayas, Nepal. *Science* 307 (1302-1305), 25 February, 2005.

Lewis, D. and Jaana, M. (2005) Urban vulnerability and good governance. *Journal of contingences and crisis management*, Vol. 13(2): 50-53.

Lo, C. P. (2006).Estimating population and census data. In Ridd, M. K, and J. D. Hipple (eds). Remote Sensing of Human Settlements: Manual of Remote Sensing, Third Edition, Vol. 5. ASPRS, The Image and Geospatial Information Society, p. 337-399.

LRMP (1986). Land Resource Mapping Project, HMG published maps for Nepal at 1:50,000 scale.

Mayer, H. M. and C. F. Kohn (1959). *Readings in Urban Geography*. Chicago: University of Chicago Press.

MDM (1971). *Mechidekhi Mahakalisamma, Madhyamanchal Bikaschhetra.*

Mood, E. (1969). *Housing code standards: Three critical studies*. The National Commission of Urban Problems, Washington DC. http://www.asian-forum.net/conference/paper/ 11-2002PaperNepalThapa-2.pdf. Retrieved on May 11, 2008.

Nepal Population Report (2007). Ministry of Population and Environment, Government of Nepal.

Ojima, T. (1996). Japanese Geo-space infrastructural system. In *Geo-space Urban Design*, Golany, Gideon S. and Toshio Ojima (eds). John Wiley and Sons, Inc. pp. 257-310.

Pandey, U. (2007). Director of Nepal Water for Health (NEWAH).

Perraton, J.; Baxter, R. (1974). *Models, Evaluations and Information Systems for Planners*. Lancaster: MTP Construction.

Poudel, K. (2007a). Power Crisis, *Spotlight*, April.

Poudel, K. (2007b). World Water Day. *Spotlight*, March 30, 2007.

Poudel, K. (2007c) Melamchi. *Spotlight*, May 18, 2007.

Poudel, K. (2007d). Opening Up Opportunities, *Spotlight*, August 03, 2007.

Pradhan, P. K. (2003). *Manual for urban rural linkage and rural development analysis*. New Hira Books Enterprises, Kirtipur, Kathmandu, Nepal.

Pradhan, P. and R. Perera (2005). *Urban Growth and its Impact on the Livelihoods of Kathmandu Valley, Nepal*. UMP-Asia Occasional Paper No. 63.

Rahman, A. (2007). Applications of remote sensing and GIS technique for urban environmental management and sustainable development of Delhi, India. In *Applied Remote Sensing for Urban Planning, Governance and Sustainability* Netzband, M, W. L. Stefanov, and C. Redman (eds). Springer. pp. 165-193.

Ranjitkar, N. G. (1983). *Changes in Agricultural Land Use and Land Value in Urban Fringe of Kathmandu City*, Ph. D. Dissertation, Institute of Humanities and Social Sciences, Tribhuvan University, Kathmandu, Nepal.

Schumacher, E. (1973). *Small is beautiful*. Harper and Row.

Sekler, E. (1979). Use of collective spaces in Patan and other historic towns of the Kathmandu Valley, Nepal. *Monumentum*, Vol. xviii-xiv.

Sengupta, U. and S. Sharma (2006). The challenge of squatter settlements in Kathmandu: Addressing a policy vacuum. *International Development Planning Review*, 28(1): 105-126.

Serageldin, I. and A. Steer (1994) (eds) *Making development sustainable*. The World Bank, Washington D.C.

Shah, B. (2003). Heritage conservation and planning new development in Bhaktapur, Nepal. In 6th US/ICOMOS International symposium on Managing Conflict and Conservation in Historic Cities, Annapolis, MD, April 24-27.

Shrestha, C. B., P. K. Khatry, B. Sharma, and H. Ansari (1986). *The Historic Cities of Asia—Kathmandu Center for Nepal and Asian Studies (CNAS)*, Tribhuvan University, Kathmandu.

Sudhira, H. S., T. V. Ramachandra, and K.S. Jagadish (2004). Urban sprawl: Metrics, dynamics and modeling using GIS. *International Journal of Applied Earth Observation and Geoinformation*, 5: 29-39.

SWP (2007). *The State of World Population 2007.* http://esa.un.org/unpp/p2k0data.asp

Thapa, R. B., Y. Murayama, and S. Ale (2008). City profile Kathmandu. *Cities* 25: 45-57.

Thapa, A. B. (2007). Himalaya and Eartquake. *Spotlight*, VOL. 27, NO. 16, December 28, 2007 (Paush 13 2064 B.S.)

UNFP (2007). United Nations Population Fund. Speed, scale of urban growth will require 'revolution in thinking', warns UNFPA: *Asian, African Cities to Swell by Equivalent of one China, One U.S. Combined. The State of World Population 2007: Unleashing the Potential of Urban Growth.* United Nations, New York, 27, June 2007.

UN-Habitat (2003). *The Challenges of Slums: Global Reports on Human Settlements,* London and Sterling, VA: Earthscan.

UN-Habitat (2006-07). *The State of the World's Cities Report 2006/7 Urban and Slum Trends in the 21st Century* (contributors: Eduardo Lopez Moreno and Rasna Warah)

UN (1968). *Methods for Establishing Targets and Standards for Housing and Environmental Development*, United Nations, New York.

World Bank (1995-96). *Resilience Amidst Conflict: An assessment of Poverty in Nepal 1995-96 and 2003-04.*

Xian, G., M. Crane, and C. McMahon (2008). Quantifying multi-temporal urban development characteristics in Las Vegas from Land sat and ASTER data. *Photogrammetric Engineering and Remote Sensing*, Vol. 74(4): 473-481.

In: Nepal in the 21st Century
Editor: Surendra R. Devkota, pp. 285-302

ISBN 978-1-60741-348-6

Chapter 13

THE POLITICAL ECONOMY OF FEDERALISM IN NEPAL: ECOLOGICAL FOOTPRINT APPROACH

Surendra R. Devkota
Department of Economics, University at Albany, NY, USA

"The establishment of a Civil Constitution in society is one of the most important facts in human history." Kant

ABSTRACT

After the election of Constitution Assembly in 2008, Nepal entered into a republican set up. Writing a new constitution with principles of federalism is the major mandate for the Assembly. As 21st progresses, it is expected that Nepal will go along with democracy and federalism to pave the way for sustainability by advancing social, economic and ecological capitals and minimizing the either types of injustices and inequalities.

INTRODUCTION

The Stanford Encyclopedia of Philosophy[1] assumes Johannes Althusius (1557-1630) is the father of modern federalist thought. But it was David Hume who in his Essay XVI "*Idea of a Perfect Commonwealth - 1752*"described a federal structure of Great Britain. A comprehensive structure and function of a federal system in the United States of America written by James Madison (1751-1836), Alexander Hamilton (1755-1804) and John Jay (1745-1829) published in *The Federalist Papers*[2] accounts different aspect of federalism in the US.

From the early pioneer federal constitutions in the United States of America (1776), Switzerland (1848), and Canada (1867) to recently federated system of governance in

---

1 http://plato.stanford.edu/entries/federalism/
2 http://thomas.loc.gov/home/histdox/fedpapers.html

Belgium (1993) and Ethiopia (1995) nearly forty percent of people in more than two dozens of countries[3] constitute the federal political systems. The stylized model of federal system in these countries ranges from a centralized governance like India to highly divided federalism such as Canada and Spain that comprises of a wide variation of federal institutions, politico-economic prospects and practices, and devolution of authority from center to sub-national governments. Nepal, after the abolition of the monarchy in May 2008 by the 601 members the Constitutional Assembly, may join the federal club of the nations, only if she adopts the federal system of distribution of powers and responsibilities in the forthcoming constitution.

"Federalism refers to a means of governing a polity that grants partial autonomy to geographically defined subdivisions of the polity" Feeley and Rubin (2008, p.21). It implies the devolution of authority by geographical divisions that will also embrace the socio-political capital and resources including individual identity to build up a political regime. Federalism will address the sources of political identity and restore as well as modulate emotive feelings of people and community in particular areas. But federalism and decentralization are not mutually exclusive. Feeley and Rubin say, "while federalism generally results in a fairly high level of decentralization, decentralization does not necessarily lead to federalism." Federalism grants sub-national governments a final authority in some areas of governance, while decentralization is simply a 'managerial strategy'.

In order to build up a federal character at least two levels of government is required. Anderson (2008) outlines it as, "One at national level and other at sub-national level with genuine authority and primarily accountable to their electorate and a written constitution that has delegated legislative and fiscal authority as to subsidiary government(s) and requires their consent to amend the constitution."

One of the noted 20th century philosophers of federalism, Daniel Elazar (1987) explicitly explored about federalism. Elazar explains (p. 5) that federal principles are rooted in combing both "self-rule" and "shared rule" that links individuals, communities, and polities and maintain both unity and diversity with appropriate "structure" and "process". It involves both creation and sustainability of unity and the devolution of power in the name of diversity like in Switzerland. But one has to be aware of the fact that it may lead to disunity like in Iraq. So Elazar further explains that federalism streamlines both organization of power and pursuit of justice (p.84). It may fail if federalism is imposed upon on societies if they feel as subordinate of the central government. Ackerman (1981) concludes "strong local governments will be attractive if people are grouped geographically by their taste for public services and if it is difficult to impose costs on other jurisdictions."

The conventional wisdom of a federal government is as a question of constitutional law that balances between the national government and the sub-national governments is cast in terms of rights, powers, and judicial determinations. The basic assumptions of federalism involve the requirement that a federal government needs a constitution so that the sharing of authority essential to the federal principle can be laid down and maintained. Tarlton (1965) examined the elements of federalism under two different lenses - symmetry and asymmetry. Tarlton's symmetrical model:

---

[3] Argentina, Australia, Austria, Belgium, Bosnia-Herzegovina, Brazil, Canada, Comoros, Ethiopia, Germany, India, Malaysia, Mexico, Micronesia, Nigeria, Pakistan, Russia, St. Kitts and Nevis, South Africa, Spain, Switzerland, United Arab Emirates, United Sates of America and Venezuela.

"An ideal symmetrical federal system would be one composed of political units comprised of equal territory and population, similar economic features, climatic conditions, cultural patterns, social groupings, and political institutions. In the model symmetrical system each of the separate political units would in effect be miniature reflections of the important aspects of the whole federal system."

"There would be no significant differences from one state to another in terms of the major issues about which the political organization of a state might be concerned. Nor would there be significant differences in terms of the political machinery and resources with which the state would approach those major issues. In the model symmetrical federal system each state would maintain essentially the same relationship to the central authority. The division of power between central and state governments would be nearly the same in every case. Representation in the central government would be equal for each component polity, and support of the activities of that central government would also be equally distributed. In the symmetrical model no significant social, economic, or political peculiarities would exist which might demand special forms of representation or protection."

The asymmetrical model:

"The ideal asymmetrical federal system would be one composed of political units corresponding to differences of interest, character, and makeup that exist within the whole society. The asymmetrical federal system would be one in which, as Livingston says of federal systems generally, the diversities in the larger society find political expression through local governments possessed of varying degrees of autonomy and power."

"In the model asymmetrical federal system each component unit would have about it a unique feature or set of features which would separate in important ways, its interests from those of any other state or the system considered as a whole. Clear lines of division would be necessary and jealously guarded insofar as these unique interests were concerned. In the asymmetrical system it would be difficult (if not impossible) to discern interests that could be clearly considered mutual or national in scope (short of those pertaining to national existence per se)."

Earlier, a set of common political principle of federalism was published by Rogers (1935) and which are:

i. the principle of territorial integrity of member states,
ii. the principle of political integrity,
iii. the principle of equal status of each community,
iv. the principle of equal treatment or non-discrimination, and
v. the principle of adaptation.

Since federalism is to create national and sub-national regimes with explicit devolution of power to pave for a better socio-political, economic and environmental development, economics of federal structure is very crucial to sustain the spirit of federalism. To which, both political and economic federalism need to be considered (Wibbels, 2000).

Fiscal decentralization in general reduces the role of the central government and increase that of the sub-national governments such as regional or state and local. Economists such as Charles Tiebout's theory of local expenditure and Richard Musgrave's theory of public finance were pioneers in the field of public finance. Tiebout's model (1956) assumes that consumers-voters are mobile and fully aware of prices, taxes, and public goods in each region and choose to live in that region where they can enjoy the highest level of utility. This theory is about consumers –voters' 'vote with their feet' and this 'voting' creates an approximate 'market - type equilibrium'. Tiebout then suggested that the competitive forces which tend to make local governments allocate resources in a Pareto optimal fashion. It is a theory of consumers-voters who are rational and utility maximizing, but Bewley (1981) claimed that Tiebout theory may not lead to Pareto optimal so could not be a satisfactory theory of local public goods.

Gordon Clark, an upholder of the theory of local autonomy, believes that Tiebout's model is not a theory of local state or government (Clark, 1984). In his 'Theory of Local Autonomy', Clark explicitly discusses two sorts of power: power of initiation and power of immunity. The former is about local government's actions, duties, and responsibilities – power of local government to legislate and regulate, and the latter is power of local dwellers to oversight the local authority as well as immunity of local government from the authority of higher ties. In other words, both responsibility and accountability will justify the socio-political theory of local autonomy.

Federation could be compromise between unitary government and extreme decentralization Oates (1972). He elaborated the difference between the unitary and federal forms of government in terms of allocation of resources, distribution of income, and stability of government (Table1). But, Feeley and Rubin dispute that fiscal federalism is simply a managerial strategy. Take a look at India's political economy since 1990s a Nehruvian centralized command is substituting by the federal market economy. The nature of competition after 1991 has been transformed from a vertical to a horizontal one. Singha (2004) discusses the center –states dynamics in India, where states have always been competing with each other. In the pre-liberalization period, i.e. before 1991, the primary form of regional competition was vertical through the national state, but after 1991 the primary mode is horizontal competition between and among the regional states. Subsequently, as of now India's regional states now enjoy considerable political and economic autonomy.

Table 1. Salient feature of unitary and federal forms of government

Unitary	Federalism
Stability:	
A centralized form of government could maintain a high level of price stability and employment that also controls money supply.	Sub-national government depends upon the fiscal policy to stabilize its economy. But it will enhance economic efficiency due to local competition and innovation.
Redistribution:	
A unitary government may be more effective in achieving the redistributional objectives.	Free rider behavior would prosper unless strictly regulated.
Allocation:	
A highly centralized government would be effective to provide a certain class of goods and services.	Federalism will promote public decision making process and institutional strengthening.

Source: Oates (1972).

"The principle of economic federalism prefers the most decentralized structure of government capable of internalizing all economic externalities, subject to the constitutional constraint that all central government policies be decided by an elected or appointed central planner" Inman and Rubinfeld (1997). They postulated three principles of federalism:

- "it encourages an efficient allocation of national resources;
- it fosters political participation and a sense of the democratic community; and
- it helps to protect basic liberties and freedoms."

Inman and Rubinfield outlined the role and scope of national and sub-national governments. For example, the central government can provide public goods and correct spillovers in either of two ways: provide the goods directly or mandate outcomes or subsidize or tax the local governments to provide the efficient levels of the activity on their own. In many cases, central governments use both approaches. For instance, in the United States, national defense, social security, and environmental protection are directly provided or mandated by the federal government, while low income assistance, interstate highways, and basic research are largely managed through central government price subsidies or matching grants to state and local agencies or nonprofit organizations.

Fiscal federalism lead to an increase in human capital – a key indicator for economic growth (Brueckner, 2006) but there must be a good cooperation in between Center – Sate relation. Conflicts of interest may emerge between or among the national and sub-national governments and political parties. In a federal state, obviously, there could be a tug of war between the central and sub-national governments on taxation and revenue sharing. In general federal model public borrowing could be open to all types of government. Federal government will have major tax base in these areas such as customs and excise, corporate income tax, personal income tax, while sub-national governments will share taxes on consumption and sales tax and partially in personal income. The sub-national governments may have to rely on some further sources of revenue such as property tax that may alone be a heavy burden for local residents to sustain the sub-national governments. Further, distribution of income in order to create an egalitarian society will be a perennial mantra of political parties. A politico-economic debate about the efficacy of horizontal versus vertical equity will continue. It should be noted that inter-state production and consumption of goods with distorting taxing policy may lead to the fiscal war. Consequently, spirit of regional equilibrium and competition may be difficult to achieve and that may spur the income inequalities across the states. One should be clear that fiscal federalism or complete decentralization does not mean to weaken the central government but to make the local government much more responsible to the needs of people (Bardhan, 2002). Therefore, it would be sensible move to allocate revenue powers and expenditure responsibilities in the constitution.

Why Federalism in Nepal

Although more than 50 years of experimentation of different pieces of modernization theory under unitary government system, Nepal's economy is still dependent up on the donors' kindness, income inequality has spurred, cities are inhabitable; social capital is eroding, ecology is deteriorating, and majority of people are still struggling to satisfy their basic needs. Over the period of five decades of central planning system, socioeconomic and ecological injustices were so rampant that instead of trying to minimize these lots of rent seekers had emerged who benefited from such policies. A recent structural analysis of Nepal's economy is available in Devkota (2008, 2007), and Mahat (2005). Socioeconomic injustices are not the new agenda for Nepal, since the country inherited a very feudal and oligarchic society. Historically, for example, in 1953 political leaders like B P Koirala, D R Regmi, and T P Acharya had signed a minimum common program for the principle of "nationalism, democracy, and social justices". In the words of B P Koirala:

> "What is being done today is that experts trained at Havard and at London universities economics departments prepare a very good plan at the top. Then the plan is sent to the districts. The district authorities issue some kind of flat for the implementation. And the people are asked to work on that plan No local leadership is created. It is through bureaucratic machinery, with a psychological antagonism between the bureaucracy and the people. And the people start thinking that the job of development is the responsibility of the government, with participation by the people unwelcome. That is why, despite all the aid that has been received, there has been no development."

The local needs and center's contribution is in opposite direction. The situation is like juxtaposing two pyramids of flows of problems and resources (box 1), which is also analogous to the power pyramid concept of Elazar (1987, p.35). Norberg-Hodge observed a similar centralized development experience in the nearby region of Ladakh, which also became of victim the modernization paradigm that led to the disruption and degradation of self – reliant local economies. Earlier Haq (1976) also discussed the sins of a centralized developing planning in Pakistan that failed to address the poor community in the country; a situation is similar to Nepal. Haq also concluded that both mixed economy and the generous assistance of developed countries to upgrade the living standard and growth were inappropriate models of development.

As Nepal entered into a republican state in 2008 (please also see Chapters Two and Three), she now needs a new development strategy to alleviate poverty and to ensure sustainability. Socioeconomic development philosophy and policies including institutional reforms are necessary to alleviate rural poverty. Villages have been relegated to the bottom in terms of availability of socioeconomic development institutions as well as resources where the crux of problems exists (Box 1). This needs to be reversed in order to sustain the village economy and to reduce the level of poverty. Therefore in order to break the vicious cycle of poverty vis-à-vis under-development, each village unit should be assigned as a socioeconomic development unit. To complement the village economy, a district unit can play a developmental planning and monitoring role. The village and district are politico-administrative units, which have to deal with lots of socioeconomic problems, but have an insignificant resources and rights. Institutional reforms to strengthen the local government units are essential so that they will be complemented by economic and development planning, and implementation facilities.

Box 1.

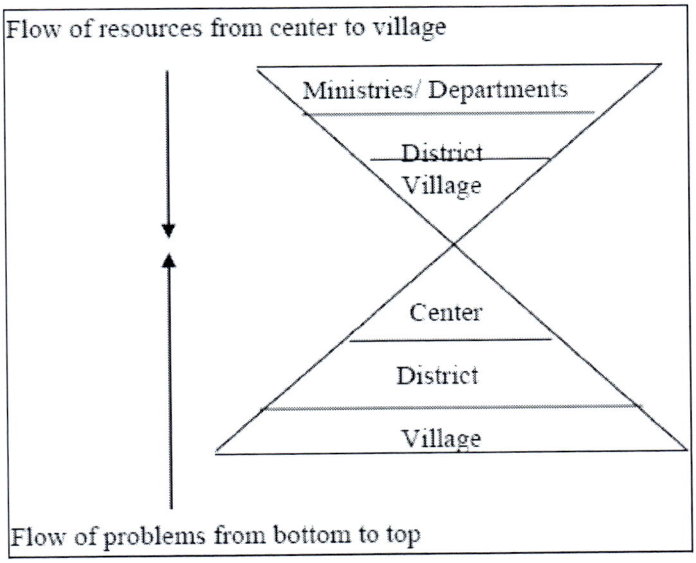

Once local units are ensured through basic socioeconomic developmental structures like health clinics, basic education, technical assistance to farmers, local community infrastructure, and conservation programs, local communities would become sustainable with reduced income disparity. Institutional arrangements are the necessary foundations for vibrant economic systems, poverty alleviation and sustainable development cannot take place without them. To this end, philosophy of federalism is gaining momentum in Nepal.

In a traditional society like in Nepal, particularly the roles of elites, middle class and ordinary citizen and political interplay amongst themselves is very crucial to sustain both democracy and federalism. For example, how elites could manipulate the political power in their favor and enjoy today at the cost of future generations. In general, elite does not like democratic process that empowers citizens (Acemoglu and Robinson, 2006) also witnessed in Nepal. Middle class, a buffer between elites and citizens, has a potential to change from non-democracy to democracy or vice versa. If a so-called upper section of the middle class colluded with elites like Nepal's new millionaires emerged after 1990 due to political business and profiteering of rent seeking policies, ordinary citizens' needs and demands could be undermined. Consequently, transitory democracy becomes uncertain due to citizens' threat of revolution, and the country floats amidst the waves of democracy and non-democracy. But the ultimate destination, according to Moore's (1966) term could be at the bourgeois revolution so that a political space will be available for all. For instance, emergence of new authoritarian rulers like in Latin America could be parallel in Nepal. Within a span of one decade Latin America turned from the democratic governance into the centrist technocratic governments. A wave of the Leftist governments has surfaced in the South American continent from Venezuela to Brazil, Argentine, Bolivia, Uruguay, Peru, Chile, Ecuador, and almost in Mexico. Whether it is only dissatisfaction with the quality of the democratic representation or could there be other factors? Paradoxically, in Central and Eastern Europe various explanations such as economic deprivation and huge inequality, criticism of civic society and intellectuals, popular demonstration, and divisions within the communist party leadership may have contributed to the collapse of the communism. Although the Communist Party of Nepal-Maoists' so-called proletariat ethno-federalist democracy has not explicitly been defined, it seems that could be *de facto* political mantra to grab the power. Federalism should herald a *de jure* political at national and sub-national governments to establish socio-political sustainability.

Federalism to be scripted in the forthcoming constitution should correct all the misdeeds of the past by overhauling the old top-down socio-political structures and devising a new vision to drive economic development, minimize either types of injustices and inequalities, and institutionalize democratic values. While restructuring, sub-national and/or local governments should get a primary focus because rural economy needs to be self-sustaining so that people will enjoy their politico-economic rights, utilize the resources, and build-up a system of accountability.

POLITICS ON FEDERAL STRUCTURE

Nepal has entered in to a new dilemma of creating an optimal politico-economic jurisdiction that includes optimal size, structure and scope of each sub-national government in the constitution. It may turn an opportunity for establishing a socio-political just society as well integration of regional resources for economic development, or may push the nation into a cycle of conflict over ownership of resources and /or further continue of political identity struggle.

Major political parties in Nepal such as the Nepali Congress, and the left ideologue like the Nepal Communist Party (United Marxist Leninist) and the Nepal Communist Party (Maoist) have shown their commitment in the interim constitution of 2008 to create a federal structure. But the federal model is yet to be worked out. One version of federal structure proposed by the left parties such as the Maoist is ethnicity based federal model, and Nepali Congress has yet to publish its model (as of December 2008), but the Nepali Congress has already decided to restructure the country in its central committee meeting of Ashad 8 and 9 2060. Furthermore one of its ideologues Mr. Narahari Acharya strongly upholds the federalism for creating equitable society (Acharya, 2007).

Ethnicity based federalism in Nepal could be very complex. The Census of 2001 by the Central Bureau of Statistics of Nepal records 103 castes and ethnic groups (Chhetri 15.8 %, Brahmin 12.7%, Magar 7.1%, Tharu 6.7%, Tamang 5.6%, Newar 5.5%, Muslim 4.3%, Kami 3.9%, Yadav 3.9%, Rai 2.8%, Gurung 2.4%, Damai 1.7%, Limbu 1.6%, Thakuri 1.5%, Sarki 1.4%, Teli 1.3%, Harijan 1.2%, Koire 1.1% and nearly seven dozen ethnic castes of less than one percent) and 106 languages and dialects, of which the Indo-Aryan language family constituted 79.1% (48.6% Nepali, 12.3% Maithili, 7.5% Bhojpuri, and 5.9% Tharu), and Tibeto-Burman 18.4% (5.2% Tamang, 3.6% Newari, 3.4% Magar, 2.2% Rai-Kiranti, 1.5% Gurung, and 1.4% Limbu). Many languages or dialects are spoken by a small number of people; for instance, 58 languages are spoken by less than 10,000 speakers, and 28 by less than 1,000. Likewise, out of 23 million people, the 2001 census also reveals 80.6% of the population as Hindu, 10.7% Buddhist, 4.2% Muslim, 3.6% Kiranti, and the rest as belonging to other religions (Christian, Jain, and Sikh). The distribution of different ethnic communities and their socio-cultural diversity is unique in Nepal. The heterogeneous mixture of all ethnic population in one society makes it impossible to have an absolute majority of one particular ethnic group in existing political set up such as village development committee. Based on such realities it would be very difficult, if not impossible, to delineate ethnicity based federal structure for a multiethnic, multicultural, multilingual, and multi-religious nation like in Nepal. A critical discussion about ethnic dimension of Nepali politics is available in Hangen (2007). Further detail about demography and ethnicity is discussed in Chapter One.

If federal lines are drawn to create sub-national governments on majority rule of ethnicities, minor ethnic population or communities may always be a subject of repression (Brennan and Hamlin, 2000). Breton (1964) had examined the economics of nationalism and discussed ethnicity or nationalism is a public capital good that can be enhanced through investment, which ultimately yields monetary flow of rewards primarily to the middle class. Breton categorically defines ethnicity or nationality as "an individual or a group is the fraction of the total stock of wealth in a given territory owned by person of the same ethnic or national origin as the person or group under consideration" and argues that "investment in nationality investment in nationality implies a transfer of resources from the working class to the middle class." Subsequently, as Breton views, a new conflict of interest may emerge between the 'new' and the 'old' middle classes that may end up antagonism in the community. But Watkins (1978) challenged Breton's theory on methodological ground.

Whether federalism is the only division of population and territory? Roeder (2007) argues that federalism is not division of population according to the communal membership. Territorial division based on the community is segmentation (Box 2) which "divides the population into separate communities or people and allocates members of these community different decision rights that will create a 'segment –state'." Segment –state is nothing but ethno-federalism – Lenin's doctrine of early 20th century employed in the formation of Soviet national republics. The communist ideologue parties in Nepal like Maoist and to some degree the UML are also advocating the ethno-federalism which seems a parallel policy of Vladimir Lenin's step.

Roeder advances his discussion in both making and breaking of the Russian Federation (p.188) and tug-of-war between nation-state and segment-state. The conflict between the nation-sate and segment-states ended up by claiming a sovereign state by segment-states in late eighties and early nineties. Federalism in modern Russia has been contractual after the introduction of the Federation of Treaties in 1992 and in 1994 which has consolidated the power of the president at the center and limited the segment-state's decision making authority as well as excluded the ownership of natural resources under their jurisdiction. The combination of territorial federal and traditional ethno-federal principle causes conflict since the latter promotes the disintegrative forces. As of now, Russian federalism is endangered by Putin's centralization of presidential power since 2000 (Gruder, 2002). As of now Russia has *de facto* federalism (Mitin, 2008).

Box 2.

No Communal partitioning	No territorial partitioning	Territorial partitioning
	Unitary	Federal
Communal partitioning	Corporate	Segmental

Source: Roeder (2007)/

Nepal could draw a very recent and real life experience from Ethiopia. While creating an ethno-federalism in 1995, the ruling Ethiopian People's Revolutionary Democratic Front has imposed an ethno-linguistic "holding together" federal. All languages are equally recognized. Every national group has the right to develop and promote its own culture and preserve its own history and they are entitled to a full measure of self-government including their own institutions within their territories and representation in regional and federal governments. The Ethiopian experiment is unique in that it allows for the possibility of self-determination. Subsequently, many groups are making claims for self-determination, language, and cultural recognition as well as for their own territory in the construction of a novel form of federalism based largely upon ethnic identities. In fact, Ethiopian ethnic federalism seems pursuing the Soviet-style version of multinational or ethnic federalism that suits only in non-democratic system, and democracy and federalism may not go together at all in Ethiopia (Turton, 2006). AAlen (2006) concludes that "Ethiopia today lacks two basic pre-conditions for mitigating ethnic conflicts in federal states: a democratic system of governance and an inclusive and sustainable pan-national identity."

Ethnic fragmentation coupled with the segregation may lead to low supply of public goods such as education that it may perpetuate the vicious cycle of poverty (Alesina, Bagir, Easterly, 1999). They observed that the shares of spending on productive public goods such as education, roads, sewers and trash pickup in the U. S. cities (metro areas/urban counties) are inversely related to the city's ethnic fragmentation and concludes "ethnic conflict is an important determinant of local public finances." They further argue that in cities where ethnic groups are polarized, and where politicians have ethnic constituencies, the share of spending that goes to public goods is low.

Since Nepal has both social and geographical diversities, exclusive consideration of social diversity in the federalism may be incomplete. Differences of socio-political attributes such as economic interest, religion, race, nationality, language, historical background, dissimilarities of political institutions produce a demand for federal system of diversities, which could be counter-demanded by unitary state. Henceforth, the federal system is a compromise between these two demands, and the federal constitution draws the lines of this compromise (Livingston, 1952). But Dikshit (1971) explains that federalism is a compromise between centripetal and centrifugal forces. Based on Livingston's concept of federalism that is a polity of regionally grouped diversities to solve the problems of human organizations that comprises spatial difference and similarities, Dikshit explains that federalism should embrace the structural- functional characters. Structure in a federal system is geographical patterns of regional diversities and constitutional instrumentalities to preserve them, whereas functionality is the process of national and sub-national governmental progress to maturity. In this sense the notion of geographical federalism is parallel to Elazar's structure – process of socio-political federal model. Earlier, Elazar (1987 p. 68) pointed out that the fundamentals of federalism must combine both 'structure' and 'process' of government to streamline the federal character of any polity. For instance, in Switzerland, Canada, and USA both structure and process are far better than in Italy and Austria. India lies in the middle of these.

After analyzing the political and federal structure in East African countries like Kenya, Tanzania, Uganda, and Zanzibar by Frank (1968), Rhodesia and Nyasaland (Spiro, 1968), the West Indies (Flanz, 1968) , and Malaysia (Trager, 1968) Frank concluded that the only primary factor of federation is supremacy of the political federal value and political commitment for ideological federalism that aims to manifest destiny and national greatness will success. He argued that certain secondary and tertiary factors such as language and ethnic balance may be superficially be favorable for federalism but are not sufficient to ensure success.

ECOLOGICAL FOOTPRINT FOR CREATING FEDERAL STATES

Based on above discussion of different aspects of federalism and that of its need in Nepal, the purpose of creating federal structure is to divide the nation for the benefits of certain section of political masses. Therefore any federal restructuring model needs to be examined by:

- its scientific basis,
- economic feasibility, and
- social acceptance in order to ensure the model's applicability and sustainability.

To which, spatial information of country that includes geophysical and natural resources profiles could be utilized to employ for both scientific and economical analyses. Meanwhile, society needs to be fully aware of both rights and resources available at their disposal so that they could crave a path of sustainable development. As mentioned earlier, the need of federalism in Nepal is for a balanced socioeconomic development and justified use of resources as well as to reduce the increasing gap of income inequality and to complement such desires every federal state must have access to resources under their jurisdiction. For example, natural resources such as forest and rivers have been the victims of rent seeking policies at the center level because "a greater amount of natural resources increases the number of entrepreneurs engaged in rent seeking and reduces the number of entrepreneurs running productive firms" (Torvik, 2002). If that trend continues, Nepal may end up as one of the recent countries that exemplify the so-called 'curse of natural resources'. Curse of natural resources implies that countries with huge natural resource endowments tend to grow more slowly than resource poor countries (Sachs and Warner 2001). Hence, to sustain politico-economic federalism in Nepal country's spatial information could serve a strong foundation. To this end, ecological footprint analysis may be useful criteria for creating the federal states.

The notion of ecological footprint (EF) is to measure biophysical resource requirements in order to sustain a given regional population in terms of land areas (Wackernagel and Rees, 1996). The EF is not to determine the maximum human population that an area can support, but to examine the productive territory actually used by resident. Since all economic and individual activities have impacts on the earth by means of use of resources and services of nature as well as generations of wastes, and these impacts are converted to biologically productive land area. So EF calculates the need of natural capital to maintain the current material throughput of economies. The EF calculation is based on resources flows, resources consumed, and waste flows, and such flow and consumption patterns can be converted into the biologically productive land areas. Rees (2000) further correlates EF with I= PAT formula of Ehrlich- Holdren (1971), where I is environmental impact, P is population, A is affluence (GDP per capita), and T is technology. The population ecological footprint (Fp) corresponds to Impact (I), so EF accounts for both population size and resource consumption. It gives a utilitarian view of nature, since economy is part of society, which is part of the biosphere (Chamber, Simmons, and Wackernagle 2000).

EF methodology has continuously been advanced and a 'Global Footprint Atlas-2008'is also available on www. Footprintnetwrok.org. The World Wide Fund for Nature is also popularizing the EF output by its publication of 'Living Planet Reports'. Despite its usefulness and popularity at the global scale, EF is not out of criticism. Two issues of journal "*Ecological Economics*" Volume 29 (1) and Volume 32 (3) discusses both sides of the EF. Grazi, Van den Bergh, Rietveld, P. (2007) concludes that EF analysis could mislead the spatial sustainability analysis but Bagliani et al. (2008) has employed EF at three spatial scales: province, district and commune in Siena, Italy. Even household level EF has been carried out in the United Kingdom by Craid and Roy (2006) and they found that energy and transportation are the two prime contributors of the footprint.

The use EF in Nepal would be at least to design a sustainable structure of sub-national regions. This article may not be able to develop a ready to use EF model for that purpose due to limitation of data, but available secondary information indicates that EF of Nepal scale is already at too high. For example, York, Rosa and Dietz (2005) placed Nepal at 103 out of 139 countries with an impact intensity of 7.18. Their basis of the ecological footprint intensity is = EF/GDP and a low number is assumed to be of good indicator. The Living Planet Report of 2008[4] developed by the World Wildlife Fund records total footprint of Nepal as 0.8 global hectares per person and water footprint is 849 cubic meter per person per year. The footprint value is derived from the cropland, grazing and forest lands, and at present, 1.8 hectares per person is the accepted ecological benchmark for global sustainability. In both cases, land is the critical factor. In Nepal it is one of the most political commodities since the creation of Nepal.

Land Resources in Nepal

Both physiographic and land use profiles of the country are tabulated in Tables 2 and 3, which show that the country has 20 percent of land suitable for agricultural purposes. Historically trend of cultivated land-use change in Nepal is alarming. For example, in 1965/66 the total cultivated land area was about 1.84 million hectares and that has been increased at 2.9 million hectares in 2000. The source of any kind of new lands is the forest areas.

Table 2. Physiographic regions and population distribution

Ecological regions with altitude range (meters)	Land area (% of 1, 47, 181 sq. km)	Population (% of total population 23,151 423 in 2001)
Mountains (4877 to 8848)	35	7.3
Middle Hills (610 to 4877)	42	44.3
Terai (up to 610)	48.4	23

Sources: Central Bureau of Statistics (2001) www.cbs.gov.np.

[4] http://assets.panda.org/downloads/living_planet_report_2008.pdf (As of December 1 2008)

Table 3. Land use Types

Land Use	Areas (x 1000 hectares)	Percent
Cultivated land	2968	20
Non-cultivated land	998	7
Grassland	1745	12
Forest land	4269	29
Shrub land/degraded forest land	1559	11
Other land uses	3179	22
Total	14,718	100

Source: ICIMOD (2001).

Historically government of Nepal assumes that land belongs to state, and people's property right on land is at the hand of government. Figure 1 shows a historical land tenancy situation in Nepal.

According to the 1961 Census, 97.1 percent of people living in the rural areas were entirely dependent upon agriculture. The same Census also revealed a very unequal farmland distribution pattern among the Nepalese households. For instance, about 75 percent of households had one or less than one hectare of land and eight percent of households owns 39 percent of cultivated land. The latest Nepal Living Standard Survey of 2003/04 estimates that about 78 percent households are still dependent upon agriculture that contributes at least one thirds of total gross domestic product.

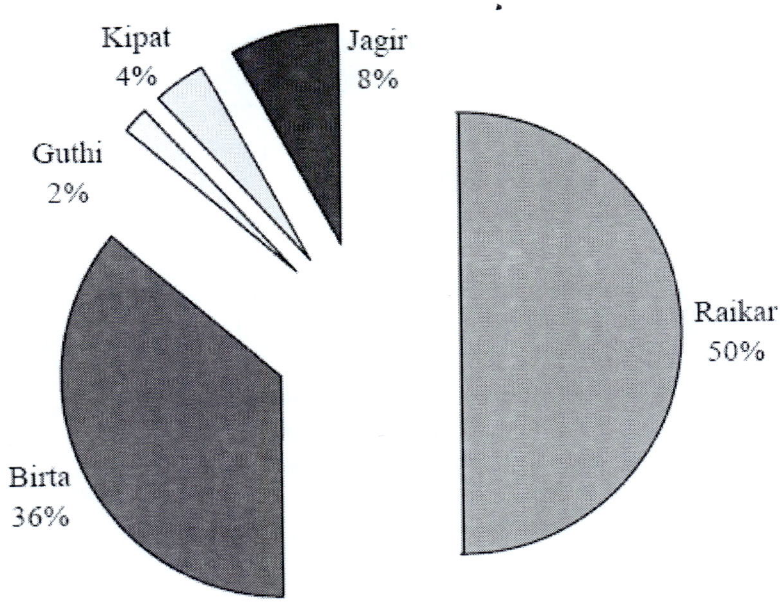

Source: Regmi (1977).

N.B.:

Birta – Privileged land ownership; *Guthi* – Land owned by the charitable institute

Jagir - Land assigned to government employee; *Kipat* - Communal land ownership

Raikar – State land.

Figure 1. Land tenure in Nepal in 1952.

In past fifty years, there had been many attempts to appropriate the large land holdings and to distribute land to landless people, as well as to secure tenancy rights, but almost all efforts failed. After the Royal coup in 1960, the then king Mahendra introduced a comprehensive land reform program in 1964 with a new Land Act-1964. The land reform program had acute social and psychological consequences, but had little impact on agrarian structure. Land reform was one of the early prescriptions of the donors for Asian countries, because the hidden objective was to check further growth of communism (Ladejinsky, 1977). A new provision of land ceiling was enforced (Table 4). This land ceiling excludes land for residential occupancy. The objective of this measure was to appropriate the large land holdings and to distribute land to landless people, as well as to secure tenancy rights. Regmi (1977) discussed both objectives and impacts of this policy along with land tenure system in Nepal. The land reform program had extreme social and psychological consequences, but had little impact on agrarian structure.

The outcome of the 1964 Land Reform effort was insignificant. For example, in 1971, six percent of the farmers with average holdings of 16 hectares still owned 44 percent of land, while 56 percent of the farmers with average holdings of 0.21 hectares had only 12 percent of the land. The government was able to confiscate only 66, 000 hectares of land above the ceiling, though the expectation was for nearly 600,000 hectares. Out of that land, only 34,000 hectares were redistributed (K.C, 1986), which is about one percent in terms of output.

The 2001 summer parliamentary session of Nepal passed another so-called revolutionary Land Bill that further downsized the previous land ceilings (Table 4). But there was no systematic procedure to redistribute land and at the end political labor forces grease their hand rather than the real land-less people. A political decision was made without any calculation of socioeconomic implications. The new ceilings are based essentially on perceived differences in regional population density and subjective judgment (Thapa, 2001).

The country has yet to investigate the outcome of the 2001 land appropriation measures. Consequently, land allocation to the so-called landless people has become a never-ending process since the 1960s without any significant positive outcome (Shrestha, 2001). To justify this politics on land appropriation, the Maoist lead government has also formed a high level commission of land appropriateness in November 2008.

Land distribution is further fragmented because of the land inheritance system in a typical Nepali family structure. Land is the basic form of family wealth and income generating sources. Children do have the heredity rights to parental property including the land. As a family grows; children as they mature would like to be independent, either parent will give their parts of land to their offspring or they will ask to their parents for some land so that s/he will be able to take care of him/herself by land-based agricultural activities.

Table 4. Agriculture and holding ceilings between 1964 and 2001

Region	Unit	1964	2001
Terai	Bigha	25	11
Hill	Ropani	80	75
Kathmandu valley	Ropani	50	30

Sources: K.C. (1986), and Regmi (1977).

Offspring may switch to other businesses by selling the part or all of the land obtained from their parents. This system of land inheritance and allocation between or among offspring and parents reduces the land ownership size per family, which depends on the stock of land owned by parents, and family size. Eventually, in each successive generation, available land will be further fragmented. This kind of land inheritance system primarily hampers the poor families who have less land. The poor will further become destitute due to the lack of sufficient land to feed them. For example, if one family has two offspring and three hectares of land, and if the parents wish to distribute their land equally among themselves, each will end up with one hectare. This family may survive at the subsistence level, but what will happen to the next generation? The dynamics of family multiplication and land fragmentation is ongoing. The Nepal Living Standard Survey 2003/04 estimates that average size of agricultural land is 0.8 hectares (1.1 hectares in 1995/96) and nearly 45 percent (40 percent in 1995/96) of households hold less than 0.5 hectares. Both of these indicators reveal a very unsustainable household economy in Nepal. It is estimated that nearly 1.2 million out of total 4.2 million families do not have any lands (CBS, 2001).

On the other side, concern on land productivity can't be simply ignored. For example, between 1961/62 to 1980/81 there was an increase in the amount of cropland by 1.7 percent annually, but productivity decreased by 0.58 percent annually (Yadav, 1987). The stagnation of grain production in the plain (Terai) triggered an economic crisis in Nepal, which led to a huge gap between production and supply of total food grains (Seddon, 1994), because, during 1980s, agriculture was still one of the significant contributors of the GDP. As of now, farming sector contributes nearly 33 percent of GDP. National Planning Commission in 2007 reveals that the average annual growth rate of agriculture sector during the 10th Plan (2002-2007) was merely 2.7 percent. The World Bank (1991) viewed that the agricultural land-base is approaching the saturation point, but the scope for increasing productivity still exists.

It is highly imperative if both government and political parties could abandon their populist slogan of land reform because the dynamics between land and population has changed significantly. Different regimes never bothered to reckon the cost and benefits of that particular policy. Imposition of politics and polices of subjective judgment from the top needs to end. Therefore further politics on land by state may not revolutionize Nepal.

CONCLUSION

Creation of federal states with respect to the dynamics of both natural resources endowment and demography could pave the way for sustainable development. The mission of federalism is not only to exercise certain socio-political rights by political parties and their entities but it also should allocate economic rights to sub-national governments. Political gerrymandering in the name of ethno-federalism could end up a situation where federalism and democracy may not be compatible like in Ethiopia or even in contemporary Russian Federation. Repetition of a failed dogma of ethno-federal models as in Ethiopia and Russia could be a futile exercise.

Ethnic diversity in Nepal is one of the salient social capitals that must be enhanced for advancing socioeconomic development. Equating ethnic diversity with a piece of federal land may not deliver a sustainable society. Therefore creation of new federal states should not only be on scientific basis but also be economically viable and socially acceptable in order to minimize social, economic and ecological injustices and build up an equitable society.

Henceforth, ecological footprint approach may serve a compatible formula for creating federal states with socio-political, ecological and economic rights at sub-national governments, which will provide an ample opportunity to enhance social, economic, and ecological capitals at different scales across the country. It may also complement to solve the multiple problems as raised in the theory of Himalayan degradation (Ives and Messerli, 2001). To this end, optimal basis for creation of federal states could be based on the major river basins like Koshi, Gandakai, Rapti, Karnali and Mahakali river watersheds. Nepal in 21st century must avoid the 20th century mistakes such as 'curses of natural resources' and 'tragedy of commons' and pursue a path of prosperity and sustainability.

REFERENCES

AAlen, L. 2006, Ethnic Federalism and Self-Determination for Nationalities in a Semi-Authoritarian State: the Case of Ethiopia, *International Journal on Minority and Group Rights* 13: 243–261.

Acemoglu, D., Robinson, J.A. 2006, Economic Origins of Dictatorship and Democracy, Cambridge: Cambridge University Press.

Acharya, N.H. 2007, Democratization of State, Kathmandu: Sambatsar Publication.

Ackerman-Rose S. 1981, Does Federalism Matter? Political Choice in a Federal Republic, *Journal of Political Economy*, 89(1): 152.165.

Alesina, A., Baqir, R., Easterly W. 1999, Public Goods and Ethnic Divisions, *The Quarterly Journal of Economics*, 114 (4):1243-1284.

Anderson, G. 2008, Federalism: An introduction, Ontario: Oxford University Press.

Bagliani, M. et al. 2008, Ecological Footprint Analysis applied to a sub-national area: The case of the Province of Siena, Italy, *Journal of Environment Management*, 86:354-364.

Bardhan, P. 2002. Decentralization of Governance and Development, *Journal of Economic Perspectives,* 16(4):185-205.

Bewley, T. F. 1981, Critique of Tiebout's Theory of Local Public Expenditures, *Econometrica*, 49 (3): 713-740.

Brennan. G., and Hamlin, A. 2000, Nationalism and Federalism: The Political Constitution of Peace. In Galeotti, G., Salmon, P., Wintrobe, R. (ED) Competition and Structure: The Political Economy of Collective Decisions – Essays in Honor of Albert Breton, New York: Cambridge University Press, pp. 259-283.

Breton, A. 1964, The Economics of Nationalism, *Journal of Political Economy*, 72(4): 376-386.

Brueckner , J.K. 2006, Fiscal Federalism and Economic Growth, *Journal of Public Economics*, 20: 2107-2120.

Central Bureau of Statistics, *Population Census 2001*, (Kathmandu:CBS, 2001).

Chambers, N., Simmons, C., Wackernagel, M. 2000, Sharing Nature's Interest: Ecological Footprints as an Indicator of Sustainability. London: Earthscan.

Clark, G. L. 1984, A Theory of Local Autonomy. *Annals of the Association of American Geographers,* 74 (2):195-208.

Craid, S. Roy, R. 2006, Household Ecological Footprints — Demographics and Sustainability, *Journal of Environmental Assessment Policy and Management*, 8(4): 407–429

Diskshit, R. D. 1971, Geography and Federalism, *Annals of the Association of American Geographers,* 61 (1): 97 -115.

Ehrlich, P., Holdren, J. 1971, Impacts of Population Growth, *Science,* 171: 1212- 1217.

Elazar, D. 1987, Exploring federalism, Tuscaloosa: The University of Alabama Press.

Feeley, M M. and Rubin E. 2008, Federalism: Political Identity and Tragic Compromise, Ann Arbor: The University of Michigan Press.

Flanz, G. H. 1968, The West Indies, In Why Federalism Fails (Thomas M Frank Editor), New York: New York University Press.

Frank T.M. 1968, East African Federation, In Why Federalism Fails (Thomas M Frank Editor), New York: New York University Press.

Frank, T.M. 1968, Why Federation Fails, In Why Federalism Fails (Thomas M Frank Editor), New York: New York University Press.

Grazi, F., Van den Bergh, J. C.J.M.·, Rietveld, P. 2007, Spatial welfare economics versus ecological footprint: modeling agglomeration, externalities and trade, *Environment, Resources Economics* 38:135–153.

Gruder, A. H., 2002 Is Russian Federalism Sustainable? *Perspective on European Politics and Society,* 3(1): 67-91.

Hangen, S. 2007. Creating a New Nepal: The Ethnic Dimension, Washington: East West Center.

Haq, M. Ul. 1976, The poverty curtain: choices for the Third World, New York: Columbia University Press.

ICIMOD. 2001, State of Environment – Nepal, Kathmandu: GON/ MOPE/ SACEP /NORAD/ UNEP.

Inman R. P., and Rubinfield, D.L. 1997, Rethinking Federalism, The Journal of Economic Perspectives, 11, (4): 43-64.

Ives, J.D., Messerli, B. 2001, The Himalayan Dilemma: Reconciling Development and Conservation, New York: Routledge and The United Nations University.

K.C, Ram B. 1986, *Land reform progress and prospectus in Nepal*, Research Report Series No. 2, HMG/ USAID /GTZ / Winrock Project, (Kathmandu, 1986).

Ladejinsky, W. 1977, Too late to save Asia, In L. J. Walinsky, (Editor) *The selected papers of Wolf Ladejinsky agrarian reform as unfinished business*, (New York: Oxford University Press, 1977).

Livingston, W.S. 1952, A Note on the Nature of Federalism, Political Science Quarterly, 67 (1): 81-95.

Moore, B. 1966. Social Origins of Dictatorship and Democracy: Lord and Peasant in the Making of the Modern World. Beacon Press (1993 Edition).

Mitin, D. 2008, From Rebellion to Submission: The Evolution of Russian Federalism Under Putin, Problems of Post-Communism, 55(5):49-61.

National Planning Commission. 2007, Three Year Interim Plan (2007/08-2009/10), Singha Durbar:NPC.

Norberg–Hodge, H. 1992, *Ancient futures: learning from Ladakh*, San Francisco: Sierra Club Books.

Oates, W. 1972, Fiscal Federalism. New York: Harcourt, Brace, Jovanovich.

Regmi, M.C. 1977, *Land ownership in Nepal*, Delhi: Adroit Publishers.

Rees, W.E. 2000, Eco-footprint Analysis: Merits and Brickbats, *Ecological Economics*, 32(3):371-374.

Rogers, Mc L. N. 1935, The Political Principles of Federalism, *The Canadian Journal of Economics and Political Science*, 1(3): 337-347.

Sachs, J.D., Warner, A.M., 2001, Natural Resources and Economic Development: The Curse of Natural Resources, *European Economic Review*, 45: 827-838.

Seddon, D. 1994, Democracy and Development in Nepal, In Michael Hutt (Editor), *Nepal in the nineties: versions* of *the past, visions of the future*, (Bombay: Oxford University Press, 1994).

Shrestha, N. R.2001, *The political economy of land, landless and migration in Nepal*, New Delhi: Nirala Publications.

Singha, A. 2004, The Changing Political Economy of Federalism in India: A Historical Institutionalist Approach. India Review, 3(1): 25–63.

Spiro, H. J. 1968, Federation of Rhodesia and Nyasaland, In Why Federalism Fails (Thomas M Frank Editor), New York: New York University Press.

Tarlton, C.D. 1965, Symmetry and Asymmetry as Elements of Federalism: A Theoretical Speculation, *Journal of Politics*, 27 (4) 861-874.

Thapa, P.J., 2001, The cost benefit of land reform, *Himal South Asia,* October, 2001.

The World Bank. 1991, Nepal: Poverty and Income, *World Bank country case study*, Washington, D.C., 1991).

Tiebout, C. M. 1956, A Pure Theory of Local Expenditures, *The Journal of Political Economy,* 64 (5):416-424.

Torvik, R. 2002, Natural Resources, Rent Seeking and Welfare, *Journal of Development Economics,* 67: 455–470.

Trager, F.N.1968, The Federation of Malaysia, In Why Federalism Fails (Thomas M Frank Editor), New York: New York University Press.

Turton, David, ed. 2006. Ethnic Federalism: The Ethiopian Experience in a Comparative Perspective. Oxford: James Curry.

Wackernagel, M., Rees, W. 1996, Our Ecological Footprint: Reducing Human Impact on The Earth, British Columbia: New Society.

Watkins, M. 1978, The Economics of Nationalism and the Nationality of Economics: A Critique of Neoclassical Theorizing, *The Canadian Journal of Economics*, Vol. 11, supplement: The Harry G. Johnson Memorial Symposium, pp. S87-S120.

Wibbels, E. 2000, Federalism and the Politics of Macroeconomic Policy and Performance, *American Journal of Political Science*, 44(4): 687-702.

Yadav, R. P. 1987, Comments on economic policies and performances in Nepal, In Leo E. Rose (Editor) *Nepal: perspectives on development issues*, Occasional Paper no 12, Center for South and Southeast Asia Studies, (Berkeley: University of California, 1987).

York, R., Rosa, E.A. Diet, T. 2005, The Ecological Footprint Intensity of National Economies, *Journal of Industrial Ecology*, 8(4) 139-154.

List of Contributors

ASHOK REGMI, PH. D. is a faculty at the Arizona State University, Arizona, USA.

BISWO POUDEL is a PhD candidate at the University of California at Berkeley, USA.

DENNIS CONWAY, PH.D., is Professor of Geography at the Indiana University, Bloomington, IN, USA 47405.

GANESH B. SINGH is Lecturer at Tribhuwan University and teaches to graduate and under graduate students, and also a Ph.D. candidate at Lucknow University, Lucknow, India.

GANESH KHANIYA is a free lance researcher. He was program officer of Farmer Managed Irrigation System Promotion Trust (FMIS Promotion Trust), Nepal for several years (2001-2008). He holds a bachelor degree in civil engineering from Bangladesh University of Engineering and Technology (1996). He has his master's degree in anthropology from Tribhuvan Uniiversity, Nepal (2005) and bachelor degree in English literature in 2000. He teaches part time in the post-graduate program of interdisciplinary water resources management of Nepal Engineering College, Bhaktapur, Nepal. In later times, he has been intensively engaged in the water supply and sanitation studies in the villages and emerging cities of Nepal. There are several community irrigation and water supply case studies to his credit.

HARI BANSHA DULAL, PH.D. is a consultant at the Social Development Department at the World Bank. He is the author of several publications on climate change, natural resource management, social capital, gender, and poverty alleviation.

PROF. KARL-HEINZ KRÄMER is affiliated to the Department of Political Science at the South Asia Institute, University of Heidelberg (Germany) and is Nepal tutor for InWEnt - Internationale Weiterbildung und Entwicklung (Capacity Building International), Germany. Since 1973 he has been engaged in research on modern history, politics, and society of Nepal. His books include *Das Königtum in der modernen nepalischen Geschichte* (Sankt Augustin: VGH, 1981), *Nepal – der lange Weg zur Demokratie* (Bad Honnef: Horlemann, 1991), and *Ethnizität und nationale Integration in Nepal* (Stuttgart: Steiner 1996). Besides, he has coauthored several books on Sherpa society and language together with his wife Lhakpa

Doma Sherpa.

KESHAB BHATTARAI, PH.D. is Professor of Geography at the University of Central Missouri, Warrensburg, MO, USA 64093.

ROBERTO FOA is a doctoral researcher at the Department of Government at Harvard University. He was previously appointed Peter Martin Fellow at the Financial Times, and since 2006 has helped to design the Social Development Indicators Project, an international study of social institutions, at the World Bank in Washington DC, USA.

SHALIGRAM POKHAREL, PH. D. is currently an Associate Professor at the School of Mechanical and Aerospace Engineering, Nanyang Technological University, Singapore. Dr. Pokharel has research in energy planning and management and supply chain systems. Prior to joining the University, Dr. Pokharel worked as an Energy Planner with the Water and Energy Commission Secretariat of the Government of Nepal for about 14 years. He has obtained Mechanical Engineering from the University of Kashmir in 1986. He obtained M. Sc and Ph. D. in Systems Design Engineering from the University of Waterloo, Canada in 1992 and 1997. He research in Masters, PhD and Post Doctoral Fellowship at the University Waterloo was related to energy planning and policy making.

UPENDRA GAUTAM, PH.D. had served as Associate Professor at the Public Administration Campus, Tribhuvan University, Nepal and a consultant to USAID, DFID, the World Bank, ADB, IFAD, and UNDP. He has provided planning and implementation assistance to water and agricultural development projects in Nepal, India, Guyana and China. Between 1995 and 2005, he was engaged in several consulting assignments to promote water user associations in China, which is one of the measures to reform water management in rural area. Currently he is President of CMS (1992-), a private sector consulting firm, founder Chairman of FMIS Promotion Trust (1997-), Research Professor (institutional development) and Chairman of Nepal Engineering College (1994-), Secretary General of China Study Center, Nepal (1999-), Founding member/Treasurer Jalsrot Bikas Sanstha (JVS-Nepal Water Resources Development Association, 2001-). He has edited books including *Challenges to Farmer Managed Irrigation System*, 2001; *Farmer Managed Irrigation Systems in the Changed Context*, 2002; *South Asia and China*, 2003; *Hydropower Pricing in Nepal Developing a Perspective*, 2004; *China the United States and Nepal*, 2004; *Farmer Managed Irrigation Systems and Governance Alternatives 2005*; *Irrigation in Transition, 2007.*

INDEX

A

B

C

F

G

J

K

L

M

N

Q

S

T

U

V

W

Z